THE ADAPTABLE CITY / 2
Europan 13 results

The EUROPAN 13 results catalogue presents at the European scale the 154 prize-winning projects in 49 cities from 15 participating countries.

The projects of the 44 winners, 49 runners-up and 61 special mentions are classified into 4 thematic sites families:

How to integrate vacant sites in urban development?
How to transform physical obstacles into new connections?
How to use new inputs to change urban space?
How to create positive dynamics from a difficult situation?

Each sites family is introduced by a point of view of experts
putting into perspective a selection of projects
in relation to the corresponding topic.
Each site is presented by an interview of the representative.
Each project is presented through images,
a text of the team and the point of view of the jury
(for the winners and runners-up).

Contents

MAP OF SITES 4

INTRODUCTION:
THE PROJECT THROUGH THE PRISM
OF THE ADAPTABLE CITY 6
Didier Rebois, architect, teacher,
Secretary General of Europan

WINNING PROJECTS
154 projects: 44 winners, 49 runners-up
and 61 special mentions

How to integrate vacant sites in urban development?

POINT OF VIEW:
REDISCOVERIES - OF MODERN MYTHS
AND ANCIENT MEMORIES 18
Jens Metz, architect, urbanist, teacher (DE)

BARREIRO (PT) 26
Winner - Between the Lines
Runner-up - Insert Coina
Special mention - Sewing Spaces in-Between

BERGEN (NO) 30
Winner - Our City, Our Collective
Runner-up - Møllendal West - From Pilot Project
to Regional Implementation
Special mention - Her har eg mitt hjerte,
her har eg mitt ly

BORDEAUX (FR) 34
Runner-up - L'Agora moderne,
incubatrice d'initiatives locales
Runner-up - Les grandes manœuvres
Special mention - Regarde-moi, je te vois

FELDAFING (DE) 38
Winner - Forest for Rest
Runner-up - The Magic Park of Feldafing

GENÈVE (CH) 42
Winner - La ville intermédiaire
Runner-up - Open Space Fabric
Special mention - Emphuteusis
Special mention - Un-City

LEEUWARDEN (NL) 46
Winner - Te Huur
Runner-up - Urban Prescriptions
Special mention - Iepen House
Special mention - Leeuwarden 2.0

METZ (FR) 50
Winner - BA128 Résonances Économes
Runner-up - B.A.S.E.
Runner-up - Cycles-Sol-Air

NACKA (SE) 54
Winner - Lucker
Runner-up - The Ends of the City
Special mention - ABC-X
Special mention - Decks and String
Special mention - New Cityfront Closer to Nature
Special mention - The Hanging Gardens City of Bergs

ZAGREB (HR) 60
Winner - Swap on the River
Runner-up - Hey! There is a River Beyond

How to transform physical obstacles into new connections?

POINT OF VIEW:
PHYSICAL AND STRATEGIC OBSTACLES
TO REVITALISATION 66
Aglaée Degros, architect, teacher (BE/NL)
and Mathias Rollot, Doctor in Architecture, teacher (FR)

A CORUÑA (ES) 74
Winner - Nice to 'Sea' You
Runner-up - Embroidering the Edge
Runner-up - Walk along Burgo's Estuary

BAMBERG (DE) 78
Winner - Tradition : Adaption : Verknuepfung
Runner-up - CT*Bamberg

GJAKOVA (KO) 82
Winner - SEAMbiosis
Runner-up - Caravanserais
Special mention - Strip(e) the Common

GRAZ (AT) 86
Winner - Walzer

INGOLSTADT (DE) 88
Winner - Waldstrasse
Runner-up - Re-Connect

IRÚN (ES) 92
Runner-up - Ura Eta Natura
Special mention - Mugaz Gaindiko - Over the Border
Special mention - United Uses of Irún

LIBRAMONT (BE) 96
Special mention - 50 Shades of Green

MARNE-LA-VALLÉE (FR) 98
Winner - Ville N(M)ature
Runner-up - La déprise
Special mention - Relational Landscape

MOULINS (FR) 102
Winner - The Theory of Evolution
Runner-up - When the Allier Becomes City
Special mention - Les Alliés de Moulins

OS (NO) 106
Winner - Osurbia - Redefining Suburbia
Runner-up - Preparing Density
Special mention - Limelight

PALMA (ES) 110
Winner - Salvemos el horizonte
Special mention - Grace, Let's Go Swimming
Special mention - Seambiosis

SAINT-BRIEUC (FR) 114
Winner - Landscape Focus
Winner - Seaside Boulevard
Runner-up - Versants Versatiles

SEINÄJOKI (FI) 118
Winner - Notch
Runner-up - Semaphore
Special mention - Intermezzo
Special mention - I Went Down to the Crossroads
Special mention - Somewhere over the Railway

How to use new inputs to change urban space?

POINT OF VIEW:
"NEGOTIATE AS YOU GO ALONG":
INFRASTRUCTURES FOR SHARED
"HYBRID" TERRITORIES 126
Socrates Stratis, Doctor in Architecture,
urbanist, associate professor (CY)

POINT OF VIEW:
NEW INPUTS, NEW PUBLIC SPACES 130
Carlos Arroyo, linguist, architect, urbanist,
teacher (ES)

BONDY (FR) 134
Winner - Bondy's Count
Special mention - BoNDy Nouvelles Dynamiques
Special mention - Re_Bondying

ESPOO (FI) — 138
Winner - Wild Synapse
Runner-up - Pärske
Special mention - Piilokoju
Special mention - Tumbling Dice
Special mention - Weaving the Woods

LANDSBERG (DE) — 144
Winner - Living With(in) Nature
Runner-up - Forest First

LUND (SE) — 148
Winner - Culture Symbiotic
Runner-up - Monster Planning
Special mention - Frontside
Special mention - Playful Path!

MOLFETTA (IT) — 152
Winner - Hold the Line
Runner-up - Molfetta, Terra e Mare
Special mention - A Walk to Re(New-Imagine-Activate)
Special mention - SeaSide

MONTREUIL (FR) — 156
Runner-up - Serendipity of Fields
Special mention - From Punctual to Usual
Special mention - OuLiPo

SANTO TIRSO (PT) — 160
Winner - FOODlab Santo Tirso
Runner-up - 3tirsolines
Special mention - Play Time

SCHWÄBISCH GMÜND (DE) — 164
Runner-up - Creative City
Runner-up - Nodes
Runner-up - Un-Break my Hardt
Special mention - Playful Hardt

ST PÖLTEN (AT) — 170
Winner - Ju(MP) in the Water - Kiss that Frog
Runner-up - The Elastic City
Special mention - A(US)trium
Special mention - Osmose

STAVANGER (NO) — 174
Winner - Forus LABing
Runner-up - Rise of Nature
Special mention - Indigo

TRONDHEIM (NO) — 178
Winner - The False Mirror
Runner-up - More Trondheim!
Special mention - The Rim

VERNON (FR) — 182
Winner - Insécable distance
Runner-up - Navigable Collections
Special mention - Vernon sur Seine

WIEN (AT) — 186
Winner - Publicquartier

How to create positive dynamics from a difficult situation?

POINT OF VIEW:
REGENERATIVE METAMORPHOSES
OF INHABITED MILIEUX
AND PROJECT CULTURE — 190
Chris Younès, anthro-philosopher, teacher (FR)
and Julio de la Fuente, architect, urbanist, teacher (ES)

AZENHA DO MAR (PT) — 198
Winner - Limenochora
Runner-up - Second Lines
Special mention - Amphibia
Special mention - Resonance(s) as Chan(c)ge

BARCELONA (ES) — 202
Winner - In Motion
Runner-up - Domestic Infrastructure
Runner-up - Sustainable Interface
Special mention - Computers Aren't Food
Special mention - Gent del barri
Special mention - Urban Species Evolution

BRUCK/MUR (AT) — 208
Runner-up - Together

CHARLEROI (BE) — 210
Runner-up - Making Room for Gilly
Runner-up - The Heterotopia Pool
Special mention - Gilly "Made It Yourself"
Special mention - Sur les pavés, la place !

GERA (DE) — 214
Winner - Colonization of the City Centre
Runner-up - Connected_Urbis
Special mention - Das Ist Gera
Special mention - Gera's Golden Centre

GOUSSAINVILLE (FR) — 218
Winner - Base Vie
Runner-up - Des racines et des ailes
Special mention - Vieux Pays - Stepping Forward

JYVÄSKYLÄ (FI) — 222
Winner - The Nolli Gardens
Runner-up - New Kids on the Blocks
Special mention - Exchange City
Special mention - Fog
Special mention - Tree Village

LA CORRÈZE (FR) — 228
Winner - Clubhouses
Winner - Sharing Islands
Special mention - New Nomads

LINZ (AT) — 232
Winner - All Tomorrow's Parties
Special mention - LinkingLinz

MARL (DE) — 236
Winner - WEEE Marl!
Runner-up - GReen-GRay Factor
Special mention - The Spine

ØRSTA (NO) — 240
Winner - Connecting Ørsta
Runner-up - Urban by Nature
Special mention - Utmark

SELB (DE) — 244
Winner - Urban Toolkit
Runner-up - Round the Corner
Special mention - Identity + Intensity

STREEFKERK (NL) — 248
Winner - In-Between
Runner-up - Protodike
Special mention - Opínaanvan

WARSZAWA (PL) — 252
Winner - River Gate
Runner-up - Apport Plus Support
Special mention - I Am a Treasure

ANNEXES — 257
JURIES — 258
EUROPAN SECRETARIATS — 263
CREDITS — 264

MAP OF SITES
Europan 13

HOW TO INTEGRATE VACANT SITES IN URBAN DEVELOPMENT?

HOW TO TRANSFORM PHYSICAL OBSTACLES INTO NEW CONNECTIONS?

HOW TO USE NEW INPUTS TO CHANGE URBAN SPACE?

HOW TO CREATE POSITIVE DYNAMICS FROM A DIFFICULT SITUATION?

BELGIQUE/BELGIË/BELGIEN
CHARLEROI P. 210
LIBRAMONT P. 96

DEUTSCHLAND
BAMBERG P. 78
FELDAFING P. 38
GERA P. 214
INGOLSTADT P. 88
LANDSBERG P. 144
MARL P. 236
SCHWÄBISCH GMÜND P. 164
SELB P. 244

ESPAÑA
A CORUÑA P. 74
BARCELONA P. 202
IRÚN P. 92
PALMA P. 110

FRANCE
BONDY P. 134
BORDEAUX P. 34
GOUSSAINVILLE P. 218
LA CORRÈZE P. 228
MARNE-LA-VALLÉE P. 98
METZ P. 50
MONTREUIL P. 156
MOULINS P. 102
SAINT-BRIEUC P. 114
VERNON P. 182

HRVATSKA
ZAGREB P. 60

ITALIA
MOLFETTA P. 152

KOSOVO
GJAKOVA P. 82

NEDERLAND
LEEUWARDEN P. 46
STREEFKERK P. 248

NORGE
BERGEN P. 30
OS P. 106
ØRSTA P. 240
STAVANGER P. 174
TRONDHEIM P. 178

ÖSTERREICH
BRUCK/MUR P. 208
GRAZ P. 86
LINZ P. 232
ST PÖLTEN P. 170
WIEN P. 186

POLSKA
WARSZAWA P. 252

PORTUGAL
AZENHA DO MAR P. 198
BARREIRO P. 26
SANTO TIRSO P. 160

SCHWEIZ/SUISSE/SVIZZERA/SVIZRA
GENÈVE P. 42

SUOMI-FINLAND
ESPOO P. 138
JYVÄSKYLÄ P. 222
SEINÄJOKI P. 118

SVERIGE
LUND P. 148
NACKA P. 54

DIDIER REBOIS, architect, teacher at the Paris-la-Villette School of Architecture (FR). General Secretary of Europan and coordinator of the Scientific Council.

Introduction
The Project through the Prism of the Adaptable City

The purpose of the European catalogue of results is to reflect the outcome of the Europan 13th session.

Strategies for defining the 21st-century city? A theme and three sub-themes

This session continued the theme of the Europan 12 competition, *The Adaptable City*, applying it in new variations. For Europan, it is important that the processes arising from the competition should do more to involve the actors as protagonists of the project, but in different forms. Urban projects need to be able to evolve over time, so the challenge is to conceive them differently. The trick is to be able to combine the long term – a vision for the future that is necessary for the transformation of a context – with a flexible project that proposes spatial solutions and modes of production that can adapt to a city that is moving, changing, dynamic.

How can we escape from the still prevalent rigid functionalism to produce Europe's cities, while adapting to changes in ways of life and the environment?

Europan uses this thematic as a background to emphasise three sub-themes as questions to the actors and competitors: first, how can the project develop around value as sharing and solidarity?; second, at a time of economic crisis and also of private sector dominance in the production of cities and architecture, how can we devise new ways of organising urban commissions and the actors, that give a greater role to a bottom-up approach? And finally, how can the project concentrate more on the production processes over time than on ready-to-build objects?

Sites and people that are motivated, but looking for pragmatic solutions

49 sites located in cities in 15 European countries were selected around this theme. It is noteworthy that despite a severe crisis in the public finances, Europan found active partners with interesting sites. For the urban players, the notion of adaptability is about the compatibility of spaces to urban practices, but also about integrating unpredictable timeframes into the production of urban projects.

While the objective of the municipal players is still to obtain a vision for the future of their sites, which can form the basis for political choices and will appeal to their constituents, there is also a realistic need for these projects/visions to be embodied in highly practical implementation proposals.

The aim may be to change the image of a site for a transitional period, until conditions are more favourable to fulfilling the full ambitions of the project. Or it may be to find "triggers" that will usher in a first phase of change, with no short-term obligation to implement the full project. And when a more long-term perspective is possible, it is still expected that the projects should, over time, be able to attract potential investors.

In the catalogue, these sites are presented alongside an interview with a local representative who explains the municipality's goals.

Experimental projects proposing a mix of realism and innovation

For the competitors, therefore, the task was to carry out the complex exercise of conceiving projects that combine a vision for the future, innovation in the project design process and pragmatism in implementation. Naturally, different interpretations emerge in the responses, but the juries were keen to choose winning teams that were proposing innovative project practices around one main question: how to reconcile the need to define spaces able to adapt to perpetually changing uses and practices?

The winning proposals that this article wishes to explore are those that propose changes in professional practices and challenge the traditional role of the architect. It will draw on the projects themselves, but will also cite the post-competition interviews conducted by

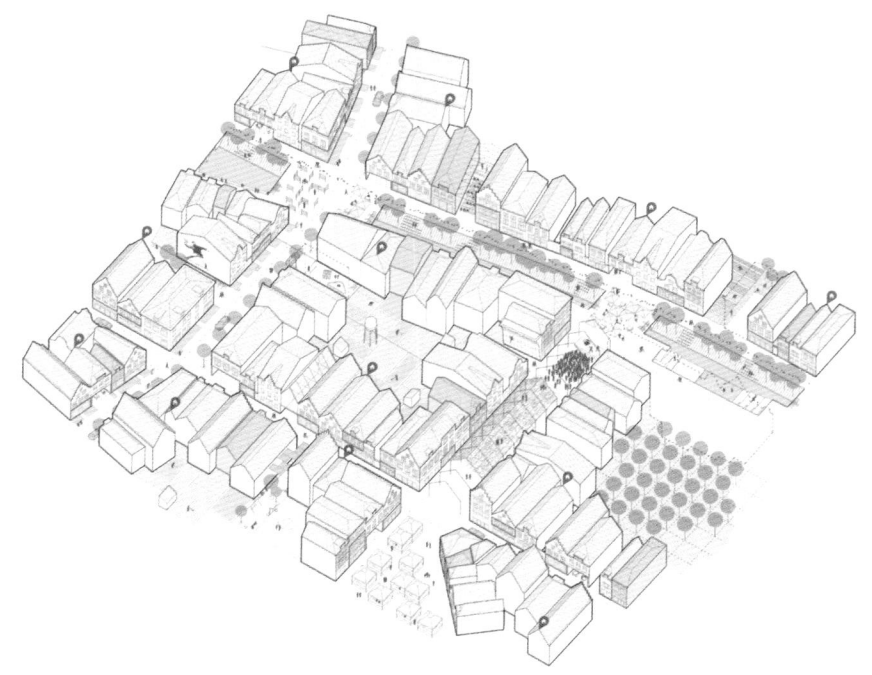

1 - LEEUWARDEN (NL), RUNNER-UP - URBAN PRESCRIPTIONS > SEE MORE P.48

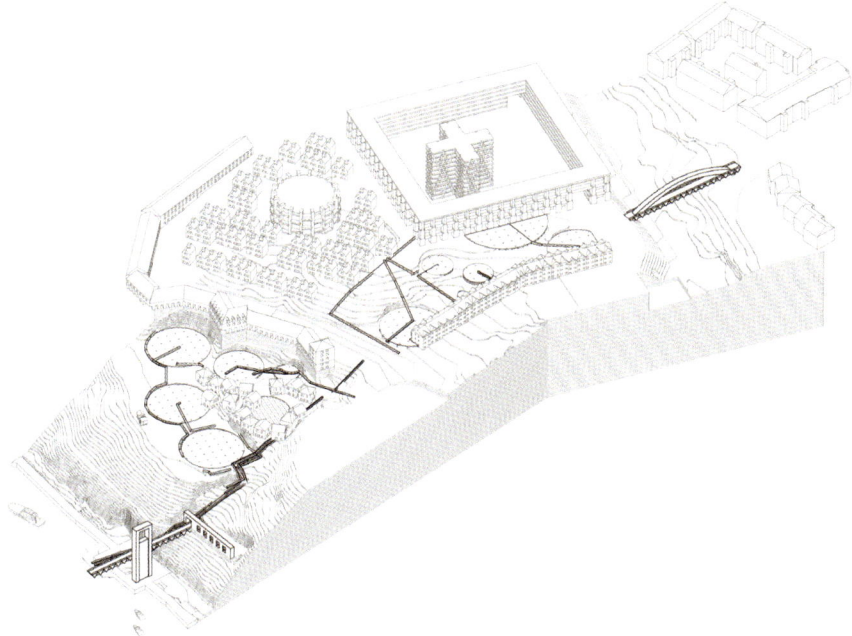

2 - NACKA (SE), RUNNER-UP - THE ENDS OF THE CITY > SEE MORE P.56

Europan Europe with the winning teams about their positions on the question of adaptability and the way it is tackled in their projects.

The project as a lasting urban form that accommodates changing uses

Some of the winning teams argue that urban form and architecture are enduring factors. For them, the challenge is to reuse stable typologies that can adapt to new uses. In some cases, this means harmonising with the existing refurbished urban fabric; in others it means creating new building forms designed to last. Only the uses change with time and the city has a permanent dimension capable of absorbing these changes without its structure and its spaces being affected.

The title of the runner-up project in Leeuwarden (NL), Urban Prescriptions (fig.1), puts its cards on the table. The challenges are to reclaim built-up plots in a historical fabric and to introduce a new program into a former museum site. For the team, this means reconciling respect for the existing qualities and adaptability, i.e. a change in program. The team proposes to reinforce the public spaces in the block through small-scale micro-interventions that will render it adaptable without fundamental alteration. "We believe that the city of the future will not significantly change, it will just be used differently." In this restored urban structure, the team proposes to convert courtyards into eco-productive areas: water will be returned to the abandoned channels, temporary uses will be proposed for vacant areas and convertible public spaces will be created. However, this intervention leaves open the integration –in the long term– of future uses, which will need to be agreed with residents.

This same standpoint is found in teams that are not working on an existing fabric, but on a future new neighbourhood, linked with a perception of the nearby fabric. "The contemporary city is not one but several places. It is a complex structure, multilayered, varied, made up of complementary and interconnected ideas, concepts and systems," according to the runner-up team on the Nacka site (SE),The Ends of the City (fig.2). "It is time to rethink urban form as a factor of resilience, rather than something futile that demands constant rehabilitation." On a riverside industrial storage site, the team proposes to build a new urban form, sharply defined by large buildings that form juxtaposed urban signals. However, these big architectures are designed to be flexible and to accommodate to changing uses. For example, the floors can host different functions and the programs can be converted from housing to workplaces. The lasting object-project cannot be separated from the process whereby it is reused.

In Barreiro (PT), with Between the Lines (fig.3), the winning team adopts exactly the same attitude in another architectural style. It compacts lines of buildings that resonate with the landscape as large structural units onsite. These lines are nevertheless "sufficiently flexible to accommodate the needs and desires of the potential users and self-organized initiatives".

3 - BARREIRO (PT), WINNER - BETWEEN THE LINES > SEE MORE P.27

4 - GRAZ (AT), WINNER - WALZER > SEE MORE P.87

The winning team in Graz (AT), *Walzer* (fig.4), also starts with the idea that "buildings generally live longer than the programs for which they were designed. That is why we propose an adaptable structure that can accommodate the current program, but also possible future adaptations." Their design for the station site is a structure that is massive and unitary but, for protection from railway noise, is built around large interior squares. And this assumes certain specific spatial arrangements to allow changes of use.

This position is a renewed version of a fairly traditional attitude in the culture of the European city: it had been revived in the 1980s with the return of the city as a matrix around the same slogan – "The city doesn't change, only uses change."

The public space project as a framework for construction over time

Other winning teams are also looking for a potentially unifying structure, but exclusively through public space rather than buildings which, in their view, do not follow the same timeframes. For them, the public dimension of the city is what can be defined and controlled over time, whereas buildings – which relate more to the private sphere – are less easy to program and are more arbitrarily embedded in time.

The winning team in Ingolstadt (DE), *Waldstrasse* (fig.5), clearly states it: the first priority is public space, with the aim of maximising the character of the Northern half of the town. Their idea is that public policies and structures should implement and manage such a program. To this end, the team proposes a series of 5 strategies and 25 initiatives to form the framework for a clearly planned decision-making timetable. From urban-scale parks to interior courtyards, this is a global strategy on public space entailing a non-linear implementation process. It is this strategy that will decide how the construction programs will be realised.

5 - INGOLSTADT (DE), WINNER - WALDSTRASSE > SEE MORE P.89

6 - SCHWÄBISCH GMÜND (DE), RUNNER-UP - CREATIVE CITY > SEE MORE P.165

In Schwäbisch Gmünd (DE), the runner-up team with its *Creative City* (fig.6) project also largely concentrates on public space, noting the lack of pedestrian streets and space that the inhabitants can share in this modern part of the city. The team conducts a close analysis of possible programs to develop new ways of life through specific building interventions (housing, boarding houses, social centres, cultural foundations). However, all these programs will be linked by a participatory public space with citizen involvement, which allows implementation to be spread across different sites and over the long term.

In Molfetta (IT), a city seeking to rehabilitate its seafront, the runner-up team, *Molfetta, terra e mare* (fig.7), proposes "activity points that can be realised over time..." and it is the outcome of the first operations "that will make it possible to build a promenade as a link". It will be this public space –an urban promenade reconnecting city and sea– that will act as a backbone to ensure the coherence of an urban space that is at present highly fragmented. It is interesting to see, in these young teams, such confidence in the existence of an urban public service and political officials capable of sustaining a long-term development project in their use public space as a fairly rapid way to provide urban coherence. This raises the question, jokingly asked by the winning team in Ingolstadt whether: "Wouldn't this be too much work for the politicians?…"

7 - MOLFETTA (IT), RUNNER-UP - MOLFETTA, TERRA E MARE > SEE MORE P.154

The ecological project associating the long term of the territory and the short term of the development

The winning project in Moulins (FR), *The Theory of Evolution* (fig.8), conceptualises this double temporality as they gather reflections from Natural Sciences, through which concepts of Adaptability, Transformation, Evolution, etc. are developed, around one question: "How do living species evolve and guarantee their survival facing modifications of their environments?" If Darwin and Lamarck answer the question in an opposite way, the team

8 - MOULINS (FR), WINNER - THE THEORY OF EVOLUTION > SEE MORE P.103

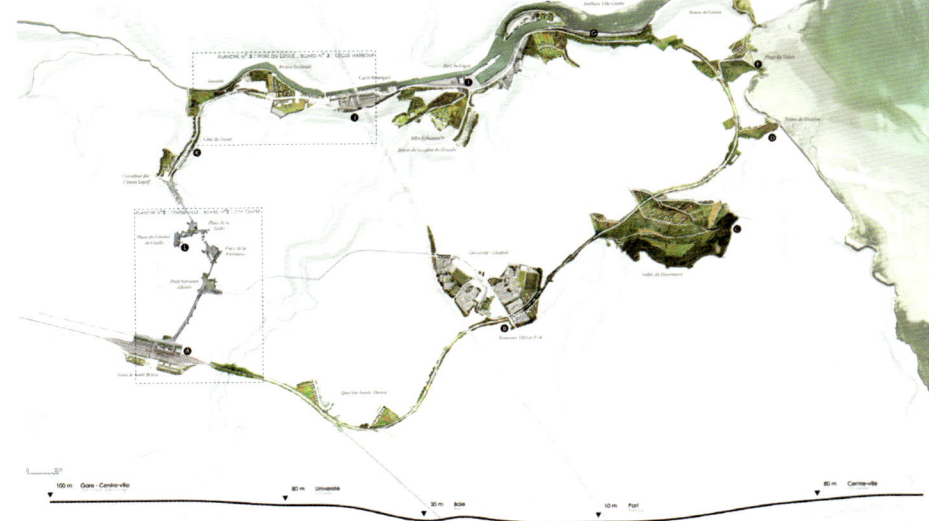

9 - SAINT-BRIEUC (FR), WINNER - SEASIDE BOULEVARD > SEE MORE P.116

nevertheless argues that both doctrines prove to be complementary for the urban project on sites with a higher natural value. The team considers that the reflection on such a site – located around a river with contrasting banks, one urban and the other mainly landscaped– should include the long term of the territory: the slow evolution of the Allier River, bridge lines, floods, dikes and floodplains act as a network of elements structuring the project. Still, faster development linked to "urban economy as well as the values of the parcels and the rents" should not be forgotten. This reflection creates a double temporality implying the association of expertises in terms of project: the one of the landscaper, working on the long-term, topography, hydrography, geology and ground characteristics, and the faster evolution of the city. One of both runner-up teams in Saint-Brieuc (FR), Seaside Boulevard (fig.9), is also confronted to a territory of natural valleys around which the city developed and the topography of which allowed the preservation of the urban development. Just like in Moulins, the team proposes a double scale: the long-term, creating a natural boulevard as a matrix following the abandoned railway; and the short-term, implementing projects to open up potential sites for development and "the installation of new programs as innovative initiatives."

The runner-up project in St Pölten (AT), Ju(MP) in the Water - Kiss That Frog (fig.10), lies as well on the creation of an environmental system through a structure that is defined by water, as a large-scale grid capable of integrating different architectures and programs. It is "a new urban model that develops in time phases and is structured on water lines and basins", as well as "a new vision of public space that puts everyday life into direct contact with nature".

Masterplan/project versus acupuncture/project?

Among the teams which believe that public intervention is essential to maintain the long-term coherence of the urban project, a few accept the idea of a masterplan. Nothing reprehensible in that! But the question is how to maintain adherence to a plan that will prescribe urban form and guarantee its implementation piece by piece over time?

In any case, this is the wager of the runner-up team in Selb (DE), Round the Corner (fig.11), which proposes "a systematic approach based on a strong new masterplan…" Working in a town that has shrunk as a result of industrial decline and is looking to regenerate its central nucleus, the team wants to stabilise the form of a town-centre district through a "process of urban consolidation, by eliminating infrastructural barriers and creating urban places". However, since the project cannot be implemented in one go, the team proposes that it should start with a regulatory structure and "seek to adapt to opportunities through flexible phasing". Can the town's urban planning department stick to this proposal and guarantee to take the project forward over time? In any case, after Europan 9 it had already introduced with the winning team Gutiérrez-delaFuente Arquitectos an acupunctural approach to amenities and housing in the town.

At the opposite extreme from the creation of a masterplan is the Colonization of the City Centre (fig.12) winning project in Gera, another municipality experiencing downgrowth. The team proposes reinforcing a large marginal space in the heart of the town centre, by a process of colonisation based not on a plan, but on an acupunctural approach that revitalises an existing area by injecting new uses. "As the town has a limited budget to invest in urban development, our project's concept is based on the idea of developing this district sector by sector, in constant

10 - ST PÖLTEN (AT), WINNER - JU(MP) IN THE WATER - KISS THAT FROG > SEE MORE P.171

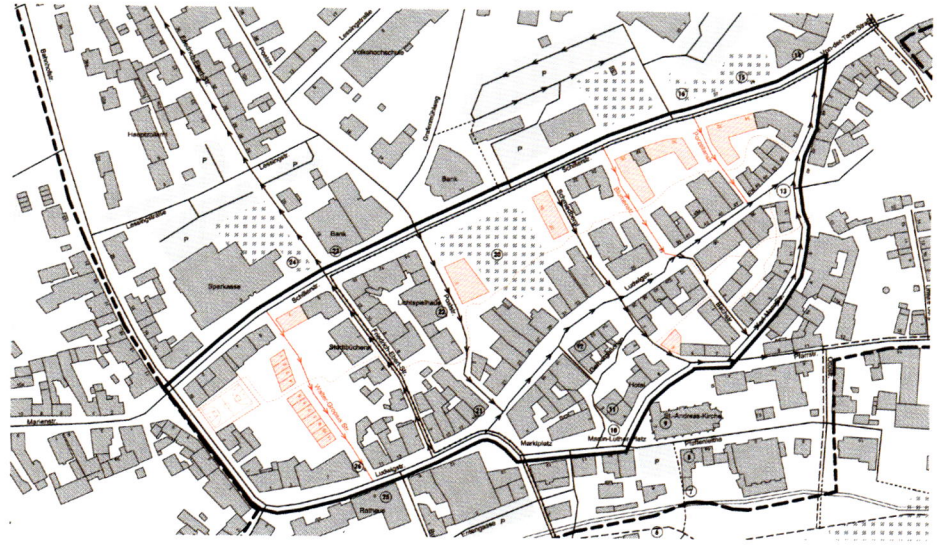

11 - SELB (DE), RUNNER-UP - ROUND THE CORNER > SEE MORE P.246

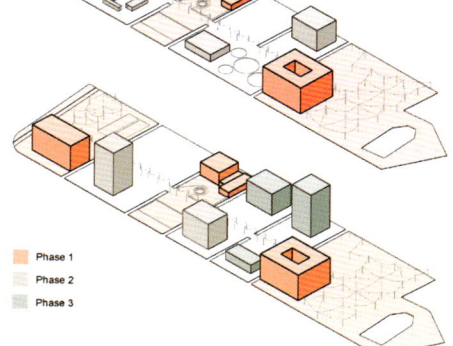

12 - GERA (DE), WINNER - COLONIZATION OF THE CITY CENTRE > SEE MORE P.215

13 - GJAKOVA (KO), RUNNER-UP - CARAVANSERAIS > SEE MORE P.84

collaboration with its residents." The team proposes beginning with the construction of three buildings, followed by the injection of temporary uses such as container garages, private gardens, play areas, and open-air cinema and a Biergarten (open-air bar), which will occupy the space until more substantial programs can be implemented. It is a tribute to slowness which, around a "starter" urban project, proposes that the next steps should be explored in collaboration with citizens.

Between two project strategies that operate in similar contexts and in the vacancy of the urban fabric, it is interesting to consider which approach to adopt: long-term control through a masterplan or a more open system in which the eventual outcome is not known in advance. This difference in method is a good example of the diversity of ways in which the winning teams seek to manage adaptability.

The project that emerges from the existing physical and human fabric

Many teams reject the idea of arbitrarily planning new structures or objects on the sites. They consider that these sites have a history, both in physical space, but also in practices. And they think that the attempt to revitalise these often peripheral areas requires respect for what is already there. For some, therefore, the outline of the project emerges from a meticulous analysis of this existing state.

The runner-up team in Gjakova (KO), *Caravanserais* (fig.13), is radical in this respect. The diagnosis of a changing urban situation –the riverside areas– accounts for 95% of the conceptual work. This diagnosis, which brings familiarity with the minute details of both spaces and practices, forms the basis of micro-interventions intended to reinforce the urban structure and the identity of the place as a social value.

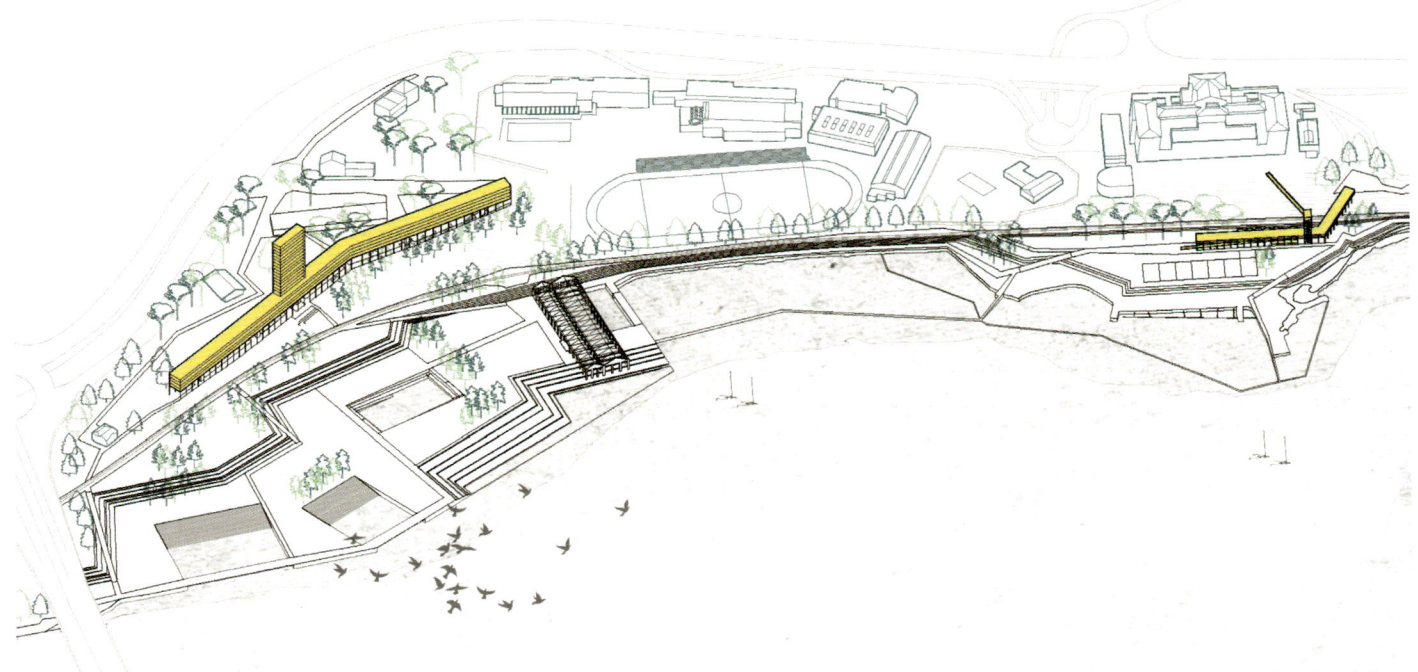

14 - A CORUÑA (ES), RUNNER-UP - EMBROIDERING THE EDGE > SEE MORE P.76

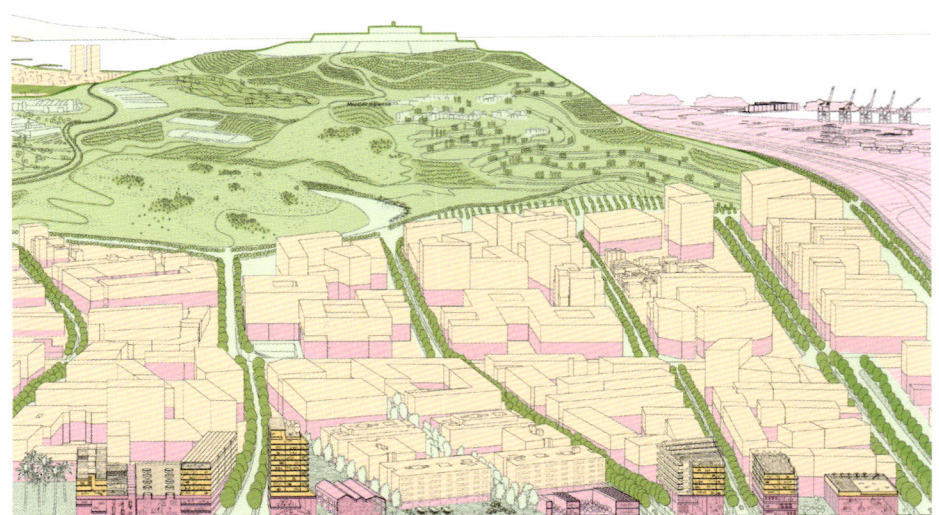

15 - BARCELONA (ES), RUNNER-UP - SUSTAINABLE INTERFACE > SEE MORE P.205

16 - CHARLEROI (BE), RUNNER-UP - MAKING ROOM FOR GILLY > SEE MORE P.211

The runner-up project in A Coruña (ES), *Embroidering the Edge* (fig.14), proposes a remodelling of the seafront. For the team, the principles of adaptability and self-organization relate to the idea of revealing the values of the place and drawing on them to define a new future. To achieve this, it emphasises the importance of the place, of morphology, of perception and evolution, involving human beings as both inhabitants and makers of their environment. The goal, as Cedric Price called for in architecture, is prevention rather than cure.

In Barcelona (ES), the runner-up project, *Sustainable Interface* (fig.15), as a follow-on from the same team's earlier Europan 12 winning project, begins with a meticulous study of the site with the aim of detecting the possibilities of introducing flexibility of uses over time and maintaining a reversibility that will allow the site to return to its original state. Their goal is to introduce into the existing fabric production spaces and activities that are compatible with housing. They devise typologies capable of accommodating such a mix: "active plinths" (productive and commercial spaces) that sustain "lively emergences" (housing, offices, hotels).

Finally, the runner-up project in Charleroi (BE), *Making Room for Gilly* (fig.16), starts with the layered urban structure of this slightly obsolete district as an opportunity to develop flexible buildings capable of defining public space. With this gradual process, anchored in the existing fabric, the project aims to transform the site over time, in keeping with its users' needs.

17 - BARCELONA (ES), WINNER - IN MOTION > SEE MORE P.203

The project as a flexible strategy, adaptable to varying uses

Some winning teams refuse to predefine a global physical structure capable of accommodating flexible uses, because they think that these forms can no longer accommodate to changes in the city. They prefer to propose a flexible strategy, as a system that would itself be able to adapt to changing uses.

Typical of this attitude is the winning team in Barcelona (ES), *In Motion* (fig.17), which takes the view that the adaptable city requires strategies for constructions where "the built fabric is no longer a fixed element, but a group of heterogeneous elements with different degrees of change". On an industrial site slated for conversion, they see the priority as being able to accommodate to movement by introducing new strategies that combine adaptability, self-sufficient systems, an ecosystemic perspective and a social approach to housing. The architecture itself must be able to adjust rapidly to keep pace with changing uses.

In Santo Tirso (PT), the runner-up team, *3tirsolines* (fig.18), proposes a project that is able to adapt to the needs of the local population by creating a flexible strategy around 3 lines: a connective green axis; a renovated market that becomes public space; increased building density to encourage the influx of new inhabitants and activities. Their project is not a finished form, but a strategy based around principles and that must be capable of adapting to real needs at any time. It is conceived more as a "system of working that involves several urban agents choosing between different activities and actions".

18 - SANTO TIRSO (PT), RUNNER-UP - 3TIRSOLINES > SEE MORE P.162

In Zagreb (HR), the winning team, *Swap on the River* (fig.19), proposes a flexible strategy that activates the site "by injecting temporary programs and creating ephemeral realities". The aim is to activate the riverbanks as an area for leisure and events. Their approach is to implement a project mechanism that allows changes and adaptations.

19 - ZAGREB (HR), WINNER - SWAP ON THE RIVER > SEE MORE P.61

The process-project: negotiated uses and actor interactions

Some teams, adopting a similar attitude also based on flexible strategies, assume the role of tacticians, making the project a nexus of actor interactions and negotiated uses.
The project is less formalised, the vision of the future no doubt less defined, but the project is permanently negotiated around responses to change and precise urban goals, without the precise outcome of the process necessarily being known in advance.
For example, *Bondy's Count* (fig.20), the winning project in Bondy (FR), is conceived around actions that invite the local economic actors and users to play a role in the site's transformation. This site, well positioned along the Canal de l'Ourcq on the way out of Paris, is at present essentially an area of commercial activities and the brief is to make it compatible with business and residential activities. To achieve this, partial rearrangements of the plot structures have to be negotiated with the economic players, so that new uses can be introduced while still improving the commercial dynamic. "We consider the process-project as a set of negotiations in which, in the long term, investors, city dwellers and residents are the future protagonists."
In Metz (FR), on the site of an abandoned former airport, the goal is to attract activities that will replace the old function with new dynamism. The runner-up project, *Cycles-Sol-Air* (fig.21), tries to incorporate each part of the program into "a redevelopment strategy for the former airport based on a balanced and inclusive process-project, which will benefit everyone while integrating the existing activities and neighbourhoods". It proposes testing functions with the participation of the users and conceiving a process that adapts over time. "Adaptability is inherent to an approach

20 - BONDY (FR), WINNER - BONDY'S COUNT > SEE MORE P.135

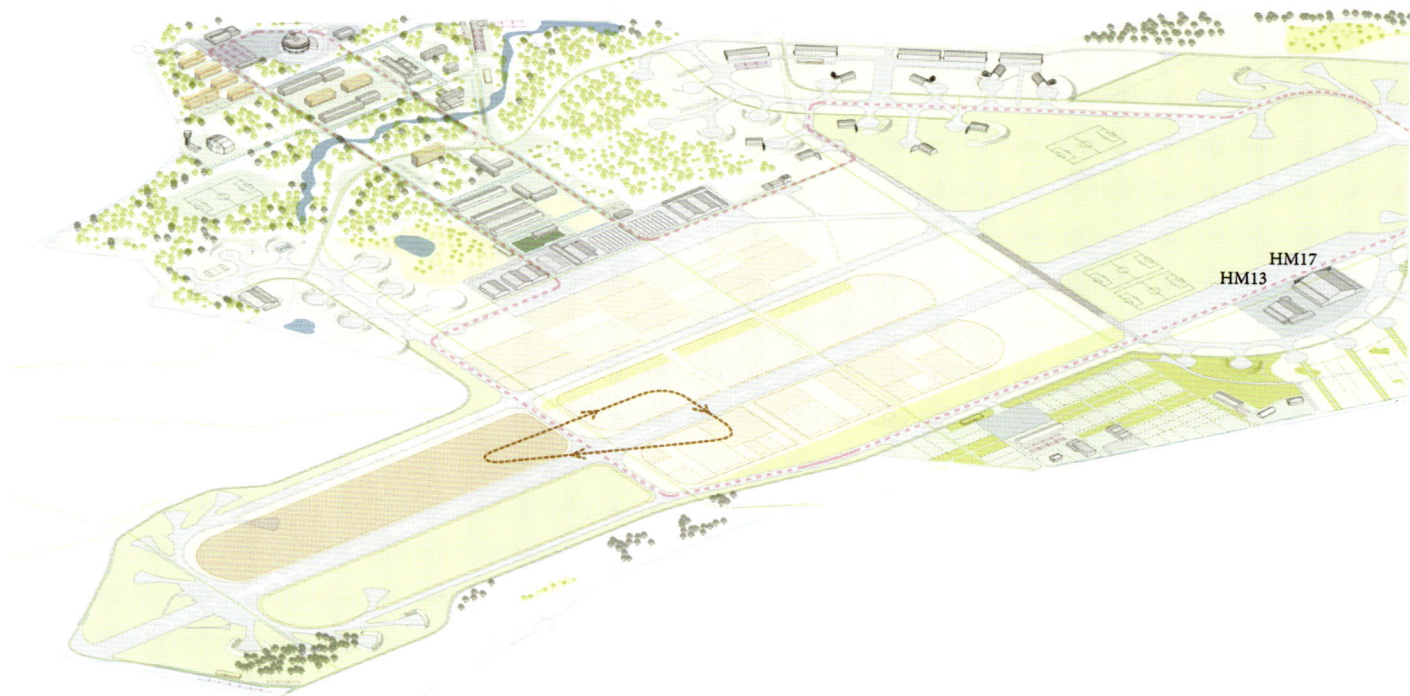

21 - METZ (FR), RUNNER-UP - CYCLES-SOL-AIR > SEE MORE P.53

of this kind: self-organization, sharing and participatory projects are an integral part of the strategy" and should drive a bottom-up process.

Finally, the runner-up project in Trondheim (NO), *More Trondheim!* (fig.22), takes the same approach in its plan to revitalise a still functioning brewery by adding other programs based around public activities and leisure. For them, the theme of adaptability reflects the needs of the site: "Working with strategies that are both programmatic and spatial and can develop over time, rather than proposing a finished masterplan." And it is these well-defined strategies which "form a solid framework that will enable different things to take shape, depending on increases in prices and mortgage rates, demographic segregation and economic groups".

This catalogue recording the results of the Europan 13 session provides a way for readers to find their way through the multiplicity of sites and winning projects, based on a presentation around the session's four big themes, each introduced by an article by one or two experts which seeks to offer an interpretative framework.

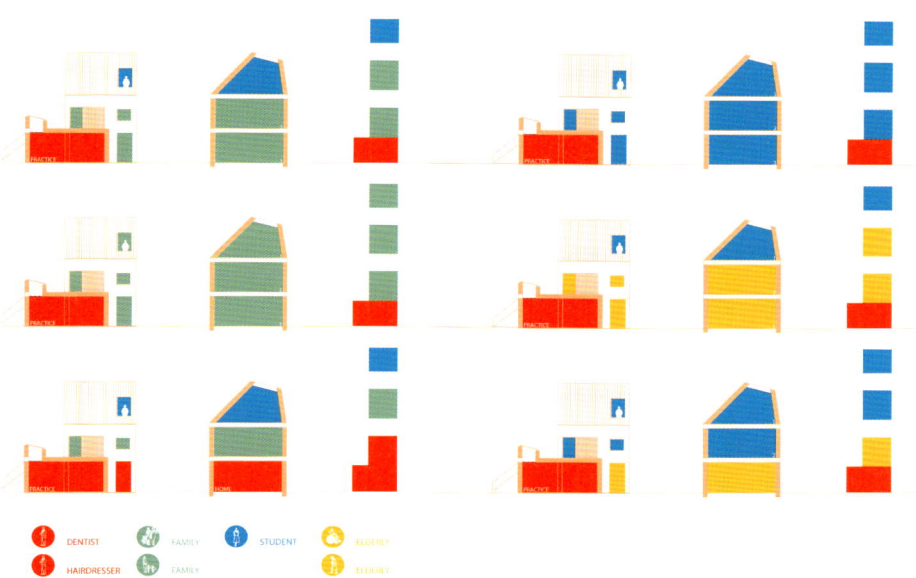

22 - TRONDHEIM (NO), RUNNER-UP - MORE TRONDHEIM! > SEE MORE P.180

HOW TO INTEGRATE VACANT SITES IN URBAN DEVELOPMENT?

**Point of view: Rediscoveries -
Of Modern Myths and Ancient Memories** p. 18
by Jens Metz

Barreiro (PT)	p. 26
Bergen (NO)	p. 30
Bordeaux (FR)	p. 34
Feldafing (DE)	p. 38
Genève (CH)	p. 42
Leeuwarden (NL)	p. 46
Metz (FR)	p. 50
Nacka (SE)	p. 54
Zagreb (HR)	p. 60

Changes in economy, governance or society can give rise to overwhelming vacant spaces in the urban landscape: entire building complexes waiting for new users, former military zones, leftover green areas… These spaces cannot be taken up in normal/organic urban development as they are far too large and in need of full adaptation. Where should we therefore search for elements to fill the emptiness up and when can we consider it as a value? How can we give sense to vacancy and integrate it in new ways of making the city?

JENS METZ, architect and urbanist. Founder of plattformberlin office (DE). Guest professor at the Frankfurt UAS. Member of Europan's Technical Committee
www.plattformberlin.com

Point of view
Rediscoveries - Of Modern Myths and Ancient Memories

"As to your Newton, I confess I do not understand his void and his gravity; I admit he has demonstrated the movement of the heavenly bodies with more exactitude than his forerunners; but you will admit it is an absurdity to maintain the existence of Nothing."

FREDERICK THE GREAT, KING IN PRUSSIA,
IN A LETTER TO VOLTAIRE, NOV. 25, 1777

Berlin. Thinking of vacancy in an urban context, it is my city that first comes to my mind. Berlin has been the capital of voids, at least for the last fifty years, if we consider them as missing parts in a city's fabric, clearly identifiable "other" spaces, open, free, full of generosity and unexplored possibilities (fig.1). Here, in the mythic home of space pioneers and temporary activations, a role model for almost all sorts of voids could be found, smaller or larger, voluntary or by inadvertence, poetic or violent. Berlin, mon amour.

Historically, the larger urban unbuilt areas in Berlin are, due to its polycentric structure, forming gaps or areas reserved for particular purposes between them. World War II changed the face of the city, causing multiple scratches and broken teeth, wounds and missing links. From the numerous open plots that have not been rebuild after the evacuation of the debris of war to the large voids visible in its centre until recently, the sensation of openness and unfinished characterise the city as a "Stadtlandschaft", a city-landscape, made of discontinuities, sudden shifts of spatial perception and large interior perspectives.

Looking at these urban voids, retracing their history, their appearance and later fill up –or not–, the debates and controversies around them, there are three recent case-studies as archetypes of voids. Their nature has been transformed in the last 25 years, due to changes in economy, governance or society. None of these reasons have been unique, it has always been a juxtaposition of different influences that made these voids change their affectation, also according to unexpected occasions, change of moods or political upheavals. Their fate could also be seen as a coming-of-age story, where the previously young and rude city becomes mature, covering the scars of an excessive and exhausting youth by the unified cardboard-like scenery, turning an uncertain yet identifiable smile into a hollow grin, or, as an opposite posture, exposing the cracks and wrinkles in a fragile wink. *Nostalgia burns in the hearts of the strongest.*

Potsdamer Platz, the former economic centre and going-out venue in the heart of the city, was demolished in the war and abandoned during the Cold War due to the construction of the wall in its centre (fig.2-3). The decision to recover the place was driven by economic interests; it was rebuilt very soon after the fall of the Berlin Wall "as if nothing had happened", according to the urban dogma of the "critical reconstruction", with the notable exception of some moderate towers. There was no public debate, the pressure was too high. The result is well known, the former void has disappeared, replaced by the globally accepted mix of fashion brands, coffee shops and urban entertainment, masked by what Charles Jencks qualified as "trophy buildings of the worst kind", the botoxed face of global capitalist architecture. *Someone shot nostalgia in the back.*

The park Gleisdreieck (fig.4.) is a younger example of the transformation of a vacant site inside the city. A former railyard right in the South of Potsdamer Platz, it was abandoned for many years, pioneer plants took over the site making it almost inaccessible. The shift of the ownership from the railway company to the city of Berlin and the development of Potsdamer Platz made it possible to realise a new park on the site. The constructions needed an ecological compensation in terms of unsealed surfaces, and there was a large public demand for green spaces. The discussions between the developers and the inhabitants were tough, finally a compromise was found and it was decided to redefine the borders by new constructions, also meant to balance the costs for the park.

The third, most recent and probably trend-setting vacant site is the former airport Tempelhof (fig.5), a huge open space in the middle of densely populated housing areas. Constructed in the National Socialist era as "central airport", it was used by the American army during the Berlin airlift shortly after the war, and then again it served as civil airport until 2008. Over the years, the discussion about

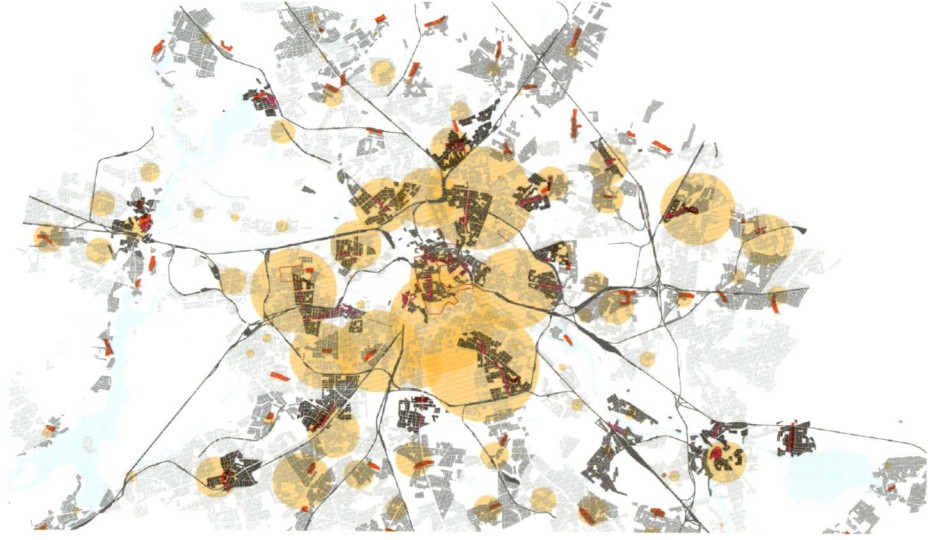

1 - BERLIN (DE)

2 - 3 - BERLIN - POSTDAMERPLATZ CROSSED BY THE WALL AND REBUILT

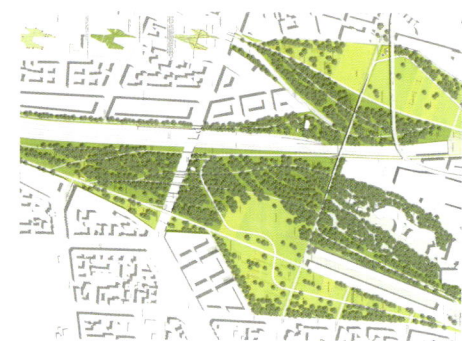

4 - BERLIN - NEW PARK GLEISDREIECK

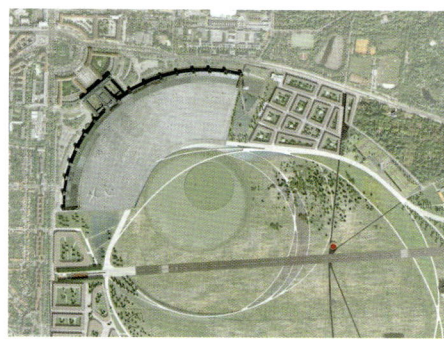

5 - BERLIN - AIRPORT TEMPELHOF TRANSFORMED INTO A PARK

its future never stopped, different scenarios were developed, but the city and the architects never managed to convince the public opinion. A referendum was held, opposing the official plan to build at the margins, and a citizens' initiative to not build anything. After the never-ending story of the construction of the new Berlin airport, the posters with the bored face of the mayor and the question: "Would you confide another airport to this man?" put the final nail in the coffin of both the plans for urbanisation and the political career of the city's commander-in-chief. Now, the situation is blocked, in times when there is a need for both housing and qualified public space, the field has neither equipment nor any services, as no construction at all is allowed. A disaster in communication, a Waterloo for urban planning and a cautionary tale for the power of BANANA – Built Absolutely Nothing Near Anything Nor Anyone.

Filled, framed or faded. Three examples, in the course of a few years, which show an altered position regarding urban voids and the decision-making processes, but also reflecting profound changes in economy, the modalities of governance or societal conventions. In having a close look at the sites, although very different in scale and location, they are unified by the search for a new destiny in urban development. Blind spots, wastelands, no man's lands, leftover spaces... they are in need of full adaptation. These spaces are far too large to be simply weaved with the surrounding fabric or filled up with known structures. With reference to authorship, Michel Foucault has shown which conclusions can be drawn from methods, narrative structures and representations of plans regarding forms of authority and decision-making processes. Interpreted in this way, the panorama of sites reveals itself as a mirror of current debates on urbanity.

Reconnections

Some of the vacant sites basically need a reconnection with their surroundings, tightening the loose fabric and redefining a closer relationship with natural elements. This is especially the case of the sites connected to water, whether lake or river, as the city offers a façade with transversal, visual or physical connections.

In Nacka (SE), the site right on the shoreline was inaccessible for more than 50 years, due to its occupation with oil cisterns (fig.6). Today, it is waiting to be rediscovered, offering a dramatic setting and immediate access to a natural reserve. An infrastructural hub at the river Tagus in Barreiro (PT) will be obsolete in the near future due to the construction of a new bridge (fig.7). This gives the city the unique occasion to promote a new centrality, combining elements of the built heritage and landscape features with additional activities. The site in Bergen (NO) has a beautiful natural setting close to a lake and a river at the edge of the city centre (fig.8). The brief did not only ask for a diverse urban neighbourhood and innovative models of collective housing as pilot projects, but interestingly also for new forms of property and the appropriate governance. The city of Zagreb (HR) proposes a reflection area of several kilometres along the banks of the river Sava, with four specific sites for possible scenarios inside this large perimeter (fig.9). A very contemporary situation familiar to many European cities, a sort of waiting time until further decisions, filled with temporary public occupations.

Reinterpretations

Other sites do not simply need to be reconnected, but rather reinterpreted, as the former programs have been removed while the structures –buildings or urban fabric– are still in place, forming different kinds of heritage. Here, the task was to attract new users, intensify urbanity and find out what kind of infill could give sense to these current urban voids. Additionally, the question of governance

6 - NACKA (SE)

7 - BARREIRO (PT)

8 - BERGEN (NO)

9 - ZAGREB (HR)

10 - BORDEAUX (FR)

11 - LEEUWARDEN (NL)

12 - GENÈVE (CH)

13 - FELDAFING (DE)

14 - METZ (FR)

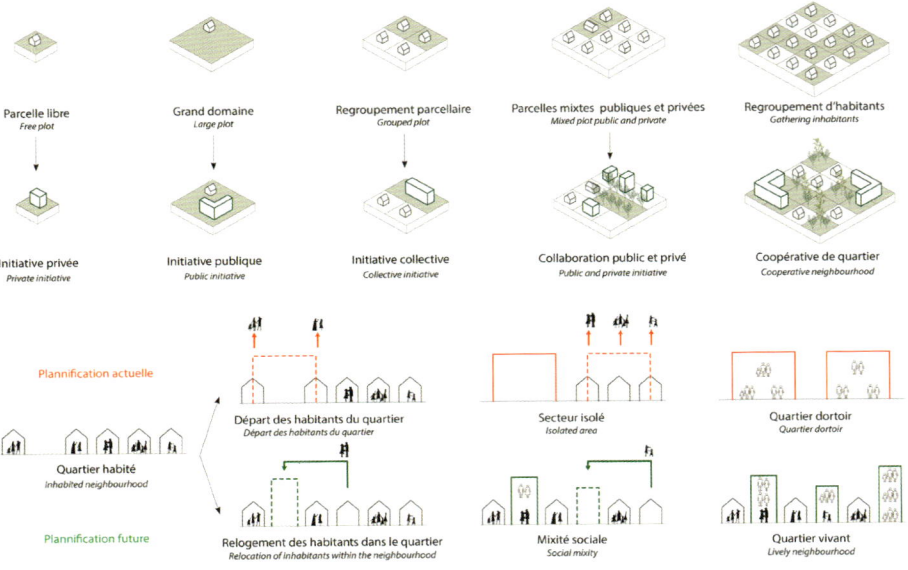

15 - GENÈVE (CH), WINNER - LA VILLE INTERMÉDIAIRE > SEE MORE P.43

was raised, in how far the changes in economy and society could give way to new forms of management, implying both private and public actors.

The site in Bordeaux (FR) comprises a listed historical fire station built at the beginning of the 1950's (fig.10). Its future is part of the mutation of the whole Garonne Eiffel sector, and the challenge is to deal with the tension between the heritage and additional new programs and to organise the subsequent realisation process. As in many other European towns and cities, the city centre of Leeuwarden (NL) has undergone a transformation, both in terms of use and infrastructure (fig.11). More and more retail outlets are going out of business, leading to vacancies and deterioration. The city needs a strategic solution to the decline of the threshold areas leading to the main locations in the centre, intervening both in public space and inside the buildings. In Genève (CH), the proposed site is part of a suburban fabric made of small plots owned by a multitude of private landowners (fig.12). Recent densification processes led to a patchwork of small development projects, without any overall urban project or coordinated land-use strategy. Therefore, the brief asked for a method to structure the future urban design, a flexible pattern that allows adaptation to different situations.

Reinventions

A third group of sites comprises former military areas liberated by the Europe-wide reorganisation of military forces and their concentration on fewer and smaller sites, finally a movement of economy. These "olive fields" offer interesting development perspectives for the cities, as the former enclaves are part of the urban agglomerations from now on; nevertheless these out-of-scale territories have to be reinvented in almost all possible fields, from program to structure.

The military training campus right in the South of the village of Feldafing (DE) was originally built as an elite school for the National Socialists in an idyllic location next to a lake (fig.13). Today, several identical buildings in alpine style still remain on the site as testimonials of the sinister past, and the main task was to propose a reorganisation of the site in different zones, allowing for a flexible and differentiated development. BA128 in Metz (FR), a former military airbase, has a mind-blowing scale; it needs to be gradually converted by a long-term process, incorporating multiple uses (fig.14). A remarkable demand in the brief was the conception of new ways of constructing and managing projects, which aimed to foster the emergence of local initiatives, including a wide variety of potential partners.

Toolkits and catalogues

The proposals discuss contemporary questions of urban forms –light city Vs. condensed city, village Vs.suburbia–; in short, the question of urbanity and how to achieve it. Finally, it is about "human beings creating volumes", as stated Swedish jury member Rolo Fütterer during the debates at the Europan 13 Forum of Cities and Juries in Bratislava (SK). By deconstructing the projects, their proposed methodology and their visual presentation, a number of comparable approaches appears, in terms of strategy, expression and proposed programmatic keys, always in search for concepts that overcome the specific problematic on-site and give a more general, conceptual vision.

A number of winning entries proposes collections of possibilities, prototypes for the occupation of spaces, as models that could subsequently be adapted to the specific situation. The design itself is often random, a square or a circle with people gathering around, occasionally named forum, agora, stage or plaza. Some of them appear as pure demonstrations of ill-conceived lists of possible interventions, while others try not only to establish toolkits and catalogues, but also aim to create an intelligent overlapping of ubiquitous spatial arrangements and the local context.

16 - METZ (FR), WINNER - BA128 RÉSONANCES ÉCONOMES > SEE MORE P.51

In Genève, winning project *La ville intermédiaire* (fig.15) proposes a charter to densify the largely underused area, developing a series of tools to resolve the resulting conflicts. This rule-based concept is completed by a toolkit with proposals to upgrade and adapt the existing villas. The winner in Metz, *BA128 Résonances Économes* (fig.16), sets up a large ecological park on the former airbase. The existing landscape typologies in the region are identified and set up as models for the structuration of the vast space, using archetypes as the prairie, the orchard or the agricultural greenhouse. In Leeuwarden, runner-up *Urban Prescriptions* (fig.17) proposes a catalogue of situations, treatments and small interventions to upgrade the public spaces in the centre. A clever and well-targeted adaptation of the omnipresent toolbox, applied at all scale levels, from the city in its entirety to the profile of a street, not without reminding Camillo Sitte or Christopher Alexander around the corner.

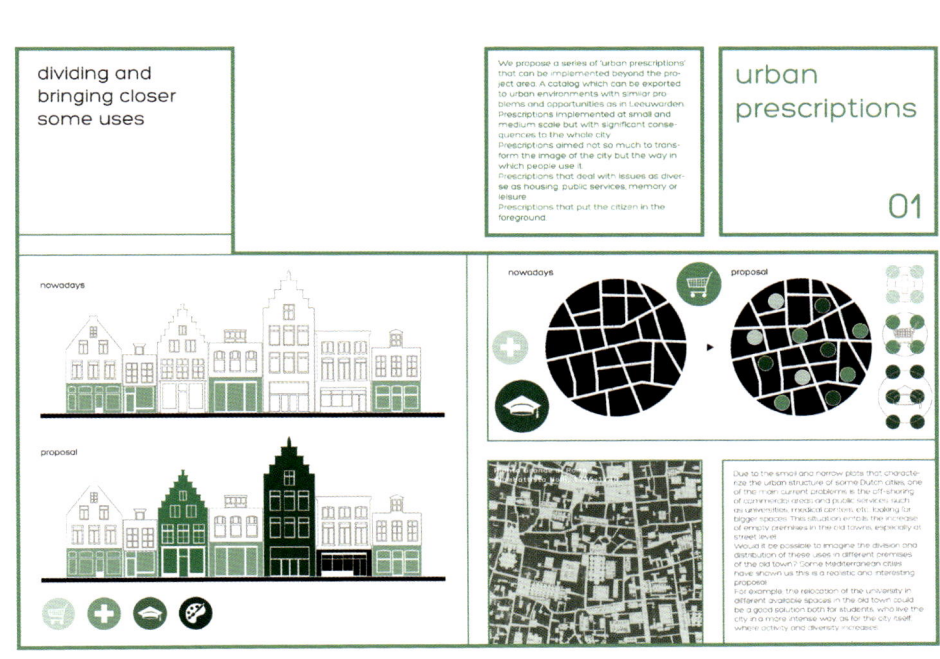

17 - LEEUWARDEN (NL), RUNNER-UP - URBAN PRESCRIPTIONS > SEE MORE P.48

18 - METZ (FR), RUNNER-UP - CYCLES-SOL-AIR > SEE MORE P.53

Imbrications of scales

It is noticeable that since the shift of the competitions topic from housing to more urban issues sometimes around the turn of the millennium, the range of scales has considerably augmented. The participants seek to reflect from the dwelling to the house, the city block, the quarter to the entire city, and even further in the region. An imbrication of scales, from macro to micro and vice versa, that reflects the attention given to the individual plot within an urban system and the question about how far an individual lot can contribute to the development of the city as a whole.

Again, winning project BA128 Résonances Économes in Metz gives an example of a territorial approach by trying to reconnect the formerly inaccessible airfield to its surroundings through the revival of the margins, connecting the already present transportation interfaces to the central void and densifying the peripheral cores. It intensifies the existing by extension, using the newly gained space. The runner-up on same site, *Cycles-Sol-Air* (fig.18), goes further beyond in history, discovering the traces of a roman aqueduct and a baroque castle that used to be on the site. They are trying to not only anchor their project on the present territory, but also in the past, considering that a territory has a kind of inscribed memory to take into consideration. In Bergen, the winner *Our City, Our Collective* (fig.19), starts the reflection on the scale of the entire agglomeration. The lake close to the site is interpreted as a sort of central park instead of a barrier; it becomes a meeting point with the proposal of a promenade around it, which links all the currently isolated areas. The project thus creates a walkable shared space along the shoreline that connects the new city quarter and its neighbourhoods.

Romantic heroism

Some of the projects could be seen as reminders of an era when architecture was a cultural discipline, and not only a marketing tool to produce exchangeable boxes. They are triggering the imaginary by a narrative, often based on archetypes, presenting a new romanticism, collages of situational poetry, tales and traces that are interwoven in an ongoing

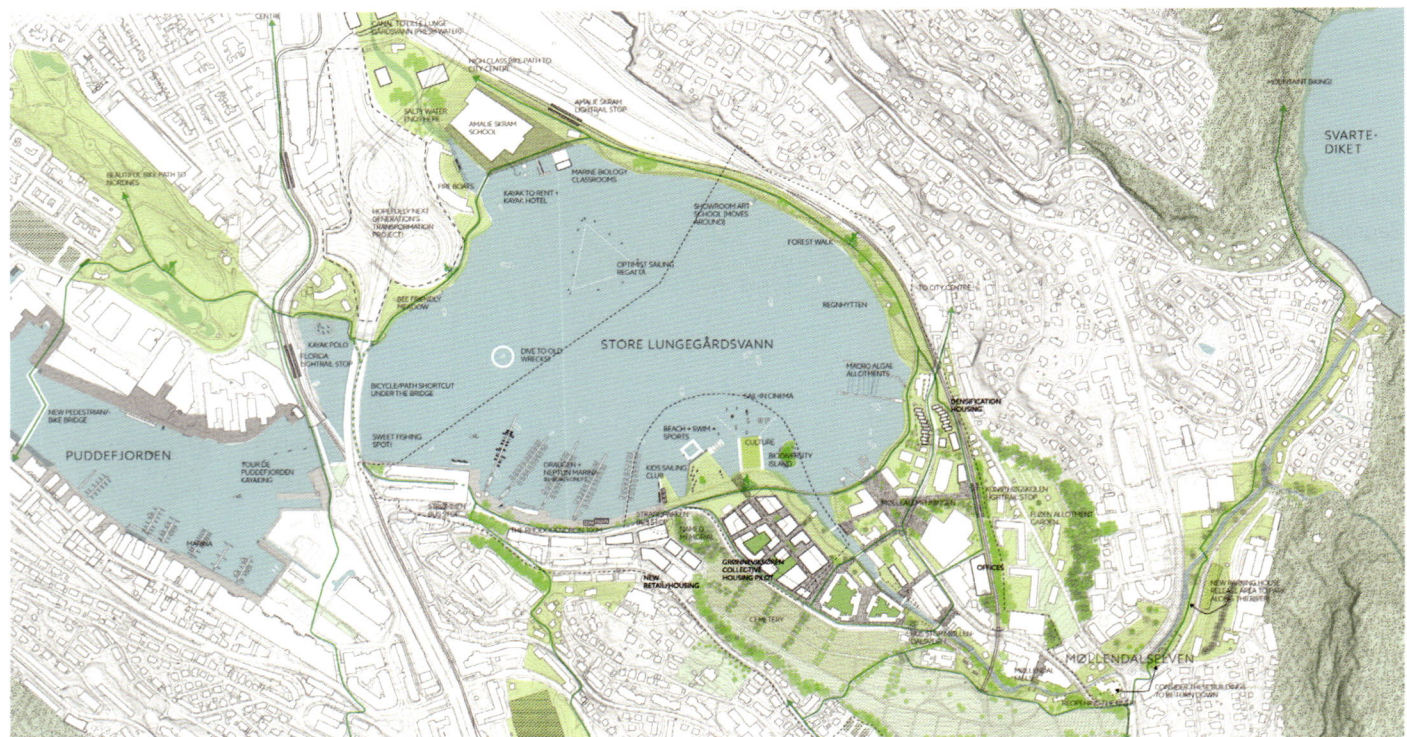

19 - BERGEN (NO), WINNER - OUR CITY, OUR COLLECTIVE > SEE MORE P.31

20 - FELDAFING (DE), RUNNER-UP - THE MAGIC PARK OF FELDAFING > SEE MORE P.40

story. Piranesis drawings of the Campo Marzio seem to filter through as a background picture. Rossi is back, at several levels, a return both to his nostalgic drawings and his vision of the city, always more solid figure than fabric, closer to Athens than Rome.

The runner-up in Feldafing *The Magic Park of Feldafing* (fig.20), has a romantic subtheme; it sets up a network of associations, imaginary connections and allusions, therefore creating cultural interferences in time and space. But the proposal is not only romantic – it is also very intelligent in terms of strategy, reinterpreting the site as the spatial continuity of the experience of the landscape, punctuated by follies that could be easily adapted to different programs. The winning team in Bergen *Our City, Our Collective*, uses a peaceful imagery to pass its political statement –a manifesto on social housing in Norway today. The large porous block breaks with the current production of dwellings, creating a critical mass that allows a large ground floor with shared facilities and common services. The runner-up in Zagreb *Hey! There is a River Beyond* (fig.21), disguises its highly analytical approach with colourful, almost naïve visualisations that very well illustrate the playful intentions and the imagined participative process.

Other projects are more heroic in their expression. The winner in Barreiro *Between the Lines* (fig.22), designs a framework as "limits for an open future", a local mega-structure as

21 - ZAGREB (HR), RUNNER-UP - HEY! THERE IS A RIVER BEYOND > SEE MORE P.62

22 - BARREIRO (PT), WINNER - BETWEEN THE LINES > SEE MORE P.27

23 - NACKA (SE), RUNNER-UP - THE ENDS OF THE CITY > SEE MORE P.56

elevated walkable grid, that allows another view of landscape. It creates new public spaces, both mineral and landscaped, which set up a dialogue with the heritage buildings on-site. The runner-up in Nacka *The Ends of the City* (fig.23), suggests an assemblage of typologies on an artificially created topography of ten plateaus on the sloped site. Its key statement is the "resilience of urban form in time", a statement that tries to reinterpret past typologies in a new assemblage, mingling both intimacy and monumentality.

Beyond mixity

Besides the questions of strategy and form, there is the art of dynamic programming, or what could be called the design of the process. Uses, actors, temporality, all these often maverick parameters have to be taken in consideration to create a projects' alchemy. As the commonly used and until now proved standard operation procedures tend not to work correctly anymore, there is a need for new solutions. The most interesting proposals tackle the question on both edges. On the one hand, the perpetuation of ephemeral events to activate a site, a kind of a permanent revolution; on the other hand, the creation of collective structures and new forms of governance, neighbourhood-building as a laboratory experiment of intermediate democracy.

One of the runner-up projects in Bordeaux *Les grandes manœuvres* (fig.24), uses already tested methods to activate the site and transform it into a mixed-used core for the quarter. The concept could be characterised as a festivalisation, linking intelligently strategy and tactics by a series of manoeuvres in time and space. They consist in the creation of an autonomous administration for the site, a minimum restoration and minor extensions for the listed buildings, and the installation of a theatre company that plays the site with its huge co-constructed machines. The winner in Leeuwarden *Te Huur* (fig.25), proposes a focalised bottom-up strategy to reactivate the city against the backdrop of the European cultural capital in 2018. By countering the shortage of hotel rooms for this event with

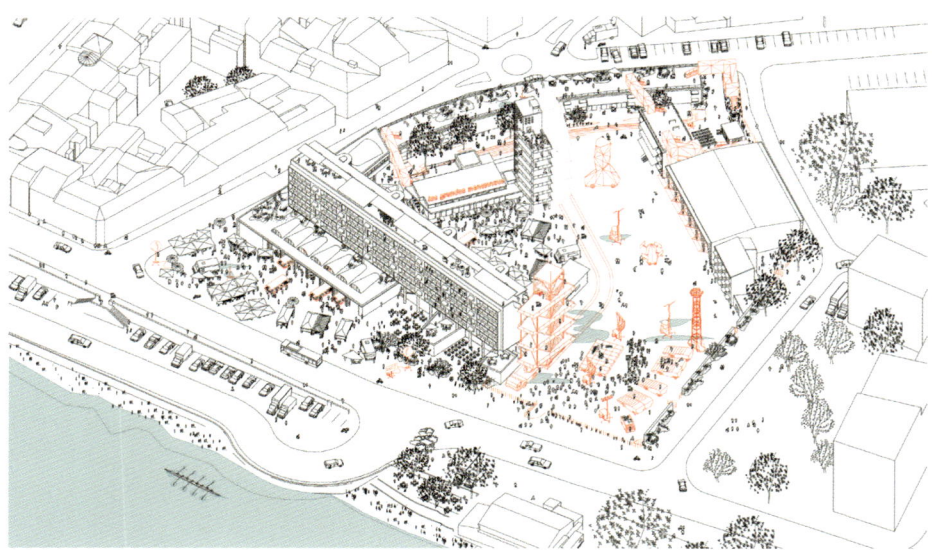

24 - BORDEAUX (FR), RUNNER-UP - LES GRANDES MANŒUVRES > SEE MORE P.36

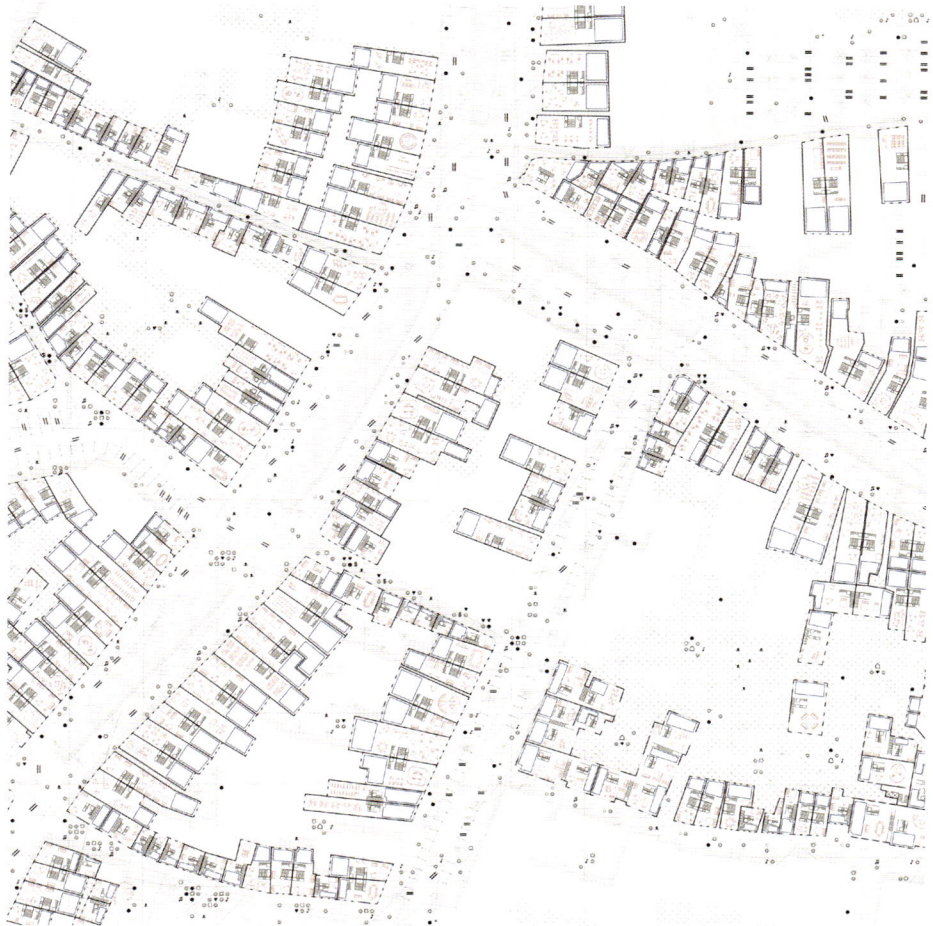

25 - LEEUWARDEN (NL), WINNER - TE HUUR > SEE MORE P.47

Adapting adaptability

The prize-winning projects as a whole propose, independently of the individual site, a range of options on how to deal with voids, less determined by the character, the situation or the size of the individual situation than by the authors' conceptual approach. Their points of view determine the creation of a specific arrangement, a new story or a flexible framework to start a future development. It is also interesting –to better understand the choice of the winning entries– to read the jury reports. They clearly state whether they search, in some cases, for radical innovation, or, on other sites, for pragmatic realism.

And then, listening to the cities' representatives and their motivations helps understand a lot about current trends in the debate about urban planning procedures. It leads to a crucial question: How to use Europan? In some cities, the specific format helps gain time, cool down a hectic and premature debate, think carefully and consciously about the future of a site, without the pressure of a classic competition. Other cities, on the contrary, understand Europan as a tool to speed up interminable and fruitless arguments, as a Jack-in-the-box-like game changer to suddenly put a site on the map and create a buzz to break up a blocked situation. This is probably the most incredible quality of Europan, the possibility to adjust the format according to the specific conditions on the site.

Adaptability also can be adaptable.

the current vacancies in the area, a synergy is created that re-dynamises the centre. Locals and trans-locals are mixed, the new inhabitants bring new activities, an ambitious plan whose directness is both intriguing and striking. The runner-up in Metz *Cycles-Sol-Air*, builds its program on priorities, necessary measures to activate the site, so-called permanences as lasting programs and a proposal of not less than 128 alternances, temporary events largely inspired by what happens on Tempelhof.

As an example of the attempts to conceive new models of living together, the runner-up in Bergen *Møllendal West* (fig.26), proposes a non-profit housing strategy that challenges the traditional property development in Norway. The project proposes an intermediate density between the centre and the areas of detached homes, thus aiming to create an urban neighbourhood both in terms of space and of a careful reflection on communities and their necessary diversity. Even if the expression is rather modest, the proposal tries to raise a relevant political discussion on the modalities of production of subsidised housing. The search for alternative governance is also tackled in the winning project in Genève *La ville intermédiaire*, with the imagination of a legal-organisational interface that is neither public nor private, but takes the form of a collective charter. The authors imagine this structure as an intermediate body in-between the municipal authorities and the individual private stakeholders to federate them and integrate them in a common process, providing a framework for future negotiations in order to initiate the necessary development.

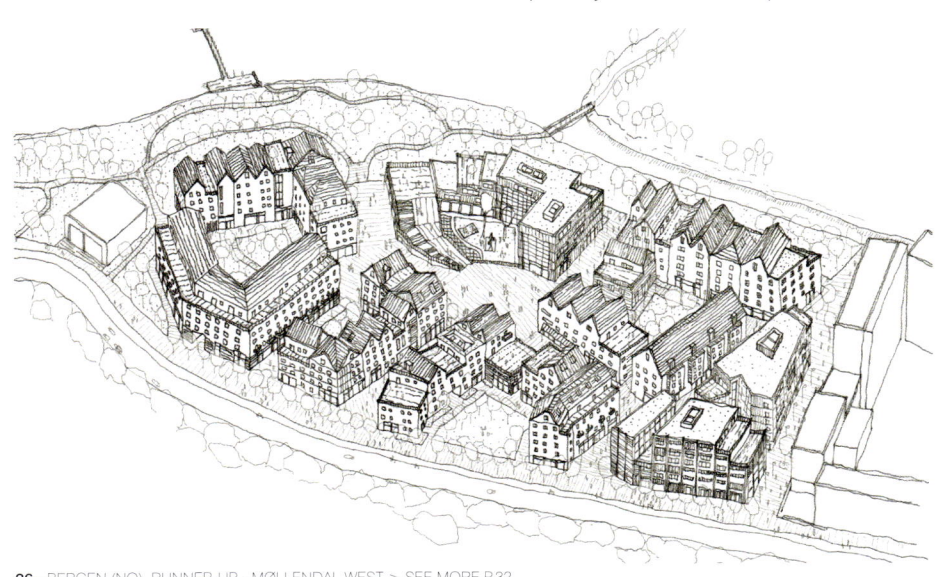

26 - BERGEN (NO), RUNNER-UP - MØLLENDAL WEST > SEE MORE P.32

BARREIRO
PORTUGAL (PT)

CATEGORY: **LANDSCAPE – ARCHITECTURAL**
LOCATION: **BARREIRO MUNICIPALITY**
POPULATION: **78,764 INHAB.**
STRATEGIC SITE: **27.71 HA**
PROJECT SITE: **3.35 HA**
SITE PROPOSED BY: **BARREIRO MUNICIPALITY**

OWNER(S) OF THE SITE: **TRANSPORT COMPANIES AND MUNICIPALITY**
COMMISION AFTER COMPETITION: **PARTIAL URBAN STUDY, SUBJECT TO SCENARIO AND ACTORS DEFINITION**

Interview of the site's representative
Rui Lopo, Councilman, Municipality of Barreiro

PRESENTATION OF THE SITE WITH REGARDS TO STRATEGY

The gradual disengagement of structures linked to rail and river heritage has led to an increase of empty spaces, which –being a part of the history and identity of Barreiro– should be kept. Furthermore, the location and landscape feature framed by the Tagus estuary and the river Coina feature a "light" of its own in almost a cinematic sense, as gazebo and pier, stage and scenery. The intended objective is a strong attractiveness of this space, enhancing different experiences and integrating uses and activities with strong value gains, becoming a destination, an attraction point for a new centrality in Barreiro.

HOW IS THE SITE CONNECTED TO THE SESSION TOPIC - THE ADAPTABLE CITY?

With the landscape potential of this territory, it is essential to find common objectives among various actors in an area marked by multiple urban, economic and social conditions.
It is also essential to have flexibility and creativity in urban interventions, favouring local resources and values, allowing several actions that can be implemented autonomously, depending on the availability of agents to act on this space, and the feasibility and adaptation to future interventions.

DID YOU DEFINE A SPECIFIC PROCESS FOR THE URBAN DEVELOPMENT OF THE SITE AFTER EUROPAN COMPETITION?

A strategic and fundamental objective of Barreiro has been the urban regeneration of riverside areas. From the continuity of work in progress, rehabilitation and attractiveness shall be promoted, in functional, economical, environmental and heritage conservation points of view.

LUCIE WEBER (FR)
REMY GIRARDIN (FR)
ARNAUD CASEMAJOR-LOUSTAU (FR)
ARCHITECTS

JOACHIM BOLANOS (FR)
FRANCESCO LOCONTE (IT)
ARCHITECTS

1 RUE DES JUIFS
67000 STRASBOURG, FR
T. +33 683364548
LUCIE.WEBER@LIVE.FR

WINNER - BARREIRO (PT)

Between the Lines

TEAM POINT OF VIEW The site has always been the transport hub linking the land to the Coina River, which beyond its industrial character has many green areas to valorise. Our proposal aims at enhancing these features and giving it a new meaning. We are seeking to improve the experience of the site by extending the waterfront promenade through the entire site and implementing soft mobility links within the city of Barreiro and the Lisbon metropolis, creating green spaces on land and encouraging water related activities. We propose an incremental project development first by acting on the boundaries of the site to transform it progressively to its core. The aim is to act on its boundaries to redefine the site. On the East side, the link to Seixal serves as a backbone to reinforce the fishing and marina activities through reorganizing the movements and parking of both boats and cars. On the West side, the former interchange area is to become a park. Acknowledging the rail heritage, the existing structures will be refurbished.

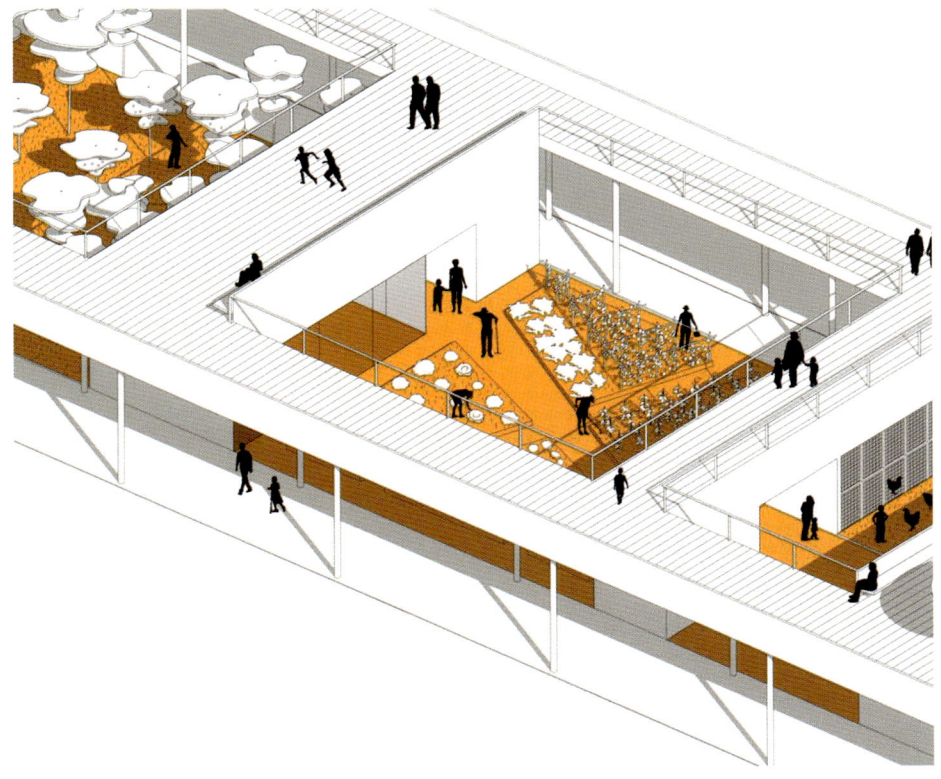

The limit between the park and the interchange terminal is a permeable filter, a flexible and versatile structure that can accommodate a wide range of activities allowing local resident's participation. The future is now opening between those two lines.

JURY POINT OF VIEW The project proposes a focus on program and feasibility of the several parts through strong design concepts characterizing the project area as an independent and coherent unity. The parking area, once the transport interface is removed, may adopt a landscaping soft leisure role.

MASSIMO DICECCA (IT)
ELISA AVELLINI (IT)
MARCELLA CLAPS (IT)
ANDREA DE SANCTIS (IT)
DARIO MARCOBELLI (IT)
ARCHITECTS

VIA MONTECALVARIO 51/B
70022 ALTAMURA (BA), IT
T. +39 3336598807
MASSIMODICECCA@HOTMAIL.IT

RUNNER-UP - BARREIRO (PT)
Insert Coina

TEAM POINT OF VIEW The site has become a clear example of enclave inside the urban territory of Barreiro. It is a grey zone, with memories kept by the inhabitants yet slowly fading away. The edges barely communicate with the city and the river. What affects Barreiro is a common "disease" to many other disused European areas, traceable to an uneven urban growing process strictly linked to unsustainable wasting-producing urban choices.

We have tried to conceive our project in a different way, investigating the perspectives Europan 13 proposed: self-organization, sharing and process. Since the beginning, our main goal has been to consider the city as a process rather than a static object. We had the need to clarify the future transformations of Barreiro and the possible key-forces linked to that transformation. Consequently, we intend to involve social and economical actors, together with architectural and natural ones, in order to coordinate both horizontal and vertical strategies. We are not pursuing any sort of populist urbanism. Instead we propose a series of design actions and reactions that could make this site an "adaptable", coherent and open-structure part of the city. Barreiro has to go back to speak again with its territory and people. To this extent, a first fundamental operation has to be the re-appropriation of its borders. We worked on a gradual, step by step process to define identities and places and to finally re-know them.

JURY POINT OF VIEW This project is an interesting proposal on implementation phasing methodology and activities mix integration. There is scarce information supporting parking dimension and rational use evolution.

DAVID CASTANHEIRA (PT)
FRANCISCO CARRASCO (PT)
JOÃO PEDRO GOMES (PT)
LUÍSA FRANÇA (PT)
ARCHITECTS

ANA GASPAR (PT)
PEDRO GOMES (PT)
ARCHITECTS

RUA DE CERCA Nº19 - 2ºESQ.
2800-050 ALMADA, PT
T. +351 964937194
INFO@ALLXCOLLECTIVE.COM
WWW.ALLXCOLLECTIVE.COM

SPECIAL MENTION - BARREIRO (PT)

Sewing Spaces In-Between

TEAM POINT OF VIEW Rehabilitating and reconnecting, structuring and sprawling, densifying and consolidating. Rehabilitating spaces and buildings of interest, reconnecting them through an urban platform that structures and sprawls the intervention to an urban structure communicating between levels, layers and spaces, densifying and consolidating. Sewing, adapting and shaping architecture, nature and people that indwell them athwart a spatial, social and ecological convergence, never forgetting Barreiro's memory and heritage –natural and industrial–, allying a transport network and infrastructures. Sewing spaces in-between.

 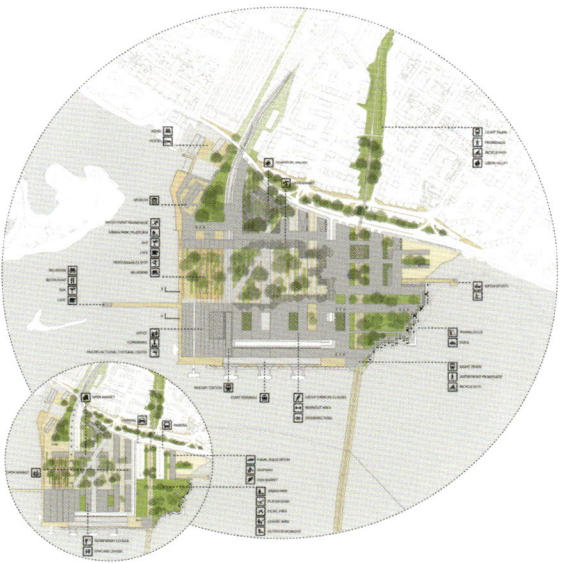

BERGEN
NORGE (NO)

CATEGORY: **URBAN – ARCHITECTURAL**
LOCATION: **GRØNNEVIKSØREN, BERGEN**
POPULATION: **268,000 INHAB.**
STRATEGIC SITE: **64 HA**
PROJECT SITE: **7.7 HA**

SITE PROPOSED BY: **BERGEN MUNICIPALITY**
(IN COLLABORATION WITH HORDALAND COUNTY)
OWNER(S) OF THE SITE:
BERGEN MUNICIPALITY AND BIR AS
COMMISION AFTER COMPETITION:
BUILDING COMMISSION

Interview of the site's representative
Gyda Strømme, Urbanist,
City planning office
Europan Norway

PRESENTATION OF THE SITE WITH REGARDS TO STRATEGY
The Bergen Region is currently undergoing a rapid growth with an expected rise of 100,000 citizens in the coming 15 years. In order to sustainably accommodate this growth, a coordinated area- and transport plan was devised based on a new light-rail system. The Europan site is located close to a planned light-rail stop and the plan's aim is that the new and planned light-rail lines will be the start for a significant densification of the existing urban fabric. The site's location and quality makes it suitable for showcasing progressive solutions in urban design and architecture.

HOW IS THE SITE CONNECTED TO THE SESSION TOPIC - THE ADAPTABLE CITY?
Much of the Møllendal area has for decades been inaccessible and unsuited for public use. Now, however, a transformation is on its way. The municipality of Bergen has asked for a new housing project that can introduce new ideas of sharing and co-residing. The Europan site at Grønneviksøren is to be a pilot for active mixing of different demographics, different concepts for sharing and for sustainable lifestyles.

DID YOU DEFINE A SPECIFIC PROCESS FOR THE URBAN DEVELOPMENT OF THE SITE AFTER EUROPAN COMPETITION?
Meeting with the winning team in December 2015 was a positive experience for the municipality who serves as owner, planning authority and developer of the valuable site. The Bergen municipality will invite the winners to a local workshop in February 2016 and arrange for meetings discussing strategic, urban and architectural solutions for the site based on the winning project. The aim is to develop a series of options to achieve the municipality's goal: a housing pilot at Grønneviksøren. The municipality of Bergen intends to commission the winners for developing the preliminary project for this pilot.

PERNILLE HEILMANN LIEN (NO)
TOMAS AASSVED HJORTH (NO)
ARCHITECTS
IWAN THOMSON (NO)
LANDSCAPE ARCHITECT

KARI TØNSETH (NO)
STUDENT IN LANDSCAPE ARCHITECTURE

URTEGATA 32A
0187 OSLO, NO
T. +47 95204945
PERNILLE@LALA.NO
WWW.LALA.NO
WWW.KAMMAN.NO

WINNER - BERGEN (NO)
Our City, Our Collective

TEAM POINT OF VIEW A VERY BASIC MANIFESTO

-1- Housing projects of the future are more diverse! We want the wishes and needs of the inhabitants to direct our building typologies, not the market driven developers.

-2- Our streets are also a space we share! In a dense city, they should be looked at as an extension of our living rooms. Hierarchy puts pedestrians and bicyclists first, public transport second and motorized vehicles last.

-3- The future city citizens ride bikes! Not cars, within the city. Not only to transport themselves, but also to transport lighter goods.

-4- Densification with quality! The main quality of the city is social interaction. Good cities have high social interaction at a low cost.

-5- Sustainability is not an add-on! It is a part of how we plan, build and live. The most climate-friendly square meter is perhaps the one that we do not build so we have to consider carefully.

-6- Diversity = a thriving city life! By offering a wide variety of housing units and typologies we can attract a wide variety of people, old, young, families, singles, students – with different daily routines, needs and economies

-7- Sharing is caring! We can share on different levels and for different reasons: inside a housing unit, among several units in a cluster, in the neighbourhood, in the district, in Bergen as a city. For economic, sustainable, social reasons, for our personal gains and the common good.

JURY POINT OF VIEW The project shows a clear idea and strategy on all scales. It recognizes the water promenade and the water body of Store Lungegårdsvann as a garden for the city –a central park– with an importance for Bergen as a whole. Through continuing and reinterpreting the neighbouring urban fabric of the student housing, the project proposes two hybrid city blocks consisting of a common porous ground floor that responds to urban connections in its surroundings, while the upper floors resemble two larger perimeter blocks. The proposal shows a richness in ideas and guidelines for a cooperative housing pilot and how to active the use of the waterfront.

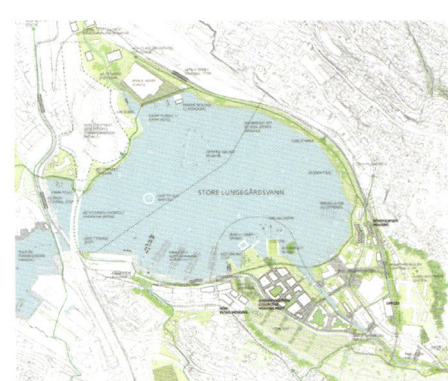

PAUL MOTLEY (GB)
ARCHITECT

ROBIN SØNDERGAARD (NO)
CHRIS SCAPLEHORN (GB)
ARNE BASSØE-ERIKSEN (NO)
STUDENTS IN ARCHITECTURE

ROBINCHS@OUTLOOK.COM

RUNNER-UP - BERGEN (NO)
Møllendal West –
From Pilot Project to Regional Implementation

TEAM POINT OF VIEW The premise of this proposal is the conviction that the current housing shortage and concomitant rise in house prices is in part caused by a lack of innovation within the housing sector in Norway. The municipality, commercial developers and local co-operative housing associations are unable to meet the actual housing demand. We would like to investigate the potential of a societal housing model, which would to some extent relive the pressure on these actors whilst at the same time be present as a non-profit alternative in a competitive and commercial housing market.

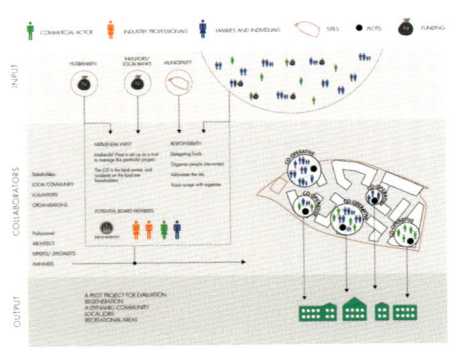

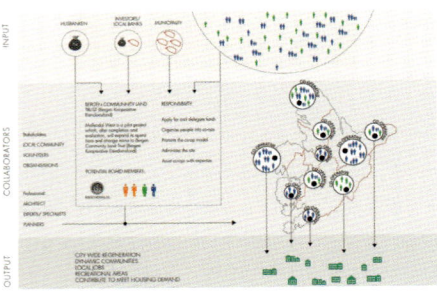

JURY POINT OF VIEW The project gains distinction with its proposal on developing a non-profit housing strategy in Bergen that challenges the traditional property development in Norway. The urban scheme suggests a density somewhere between the city and suburbia by mixing two typologies. While neither the typology nor the urban plan is remarkable, the project is seen as a strong comment on how to build a neighbourhood in a fast growing city. In this sense, the proposal is complimentary to the winning project that pinpoints important aspects to consider for the city when developing Grønneviksøren as a pilot project.

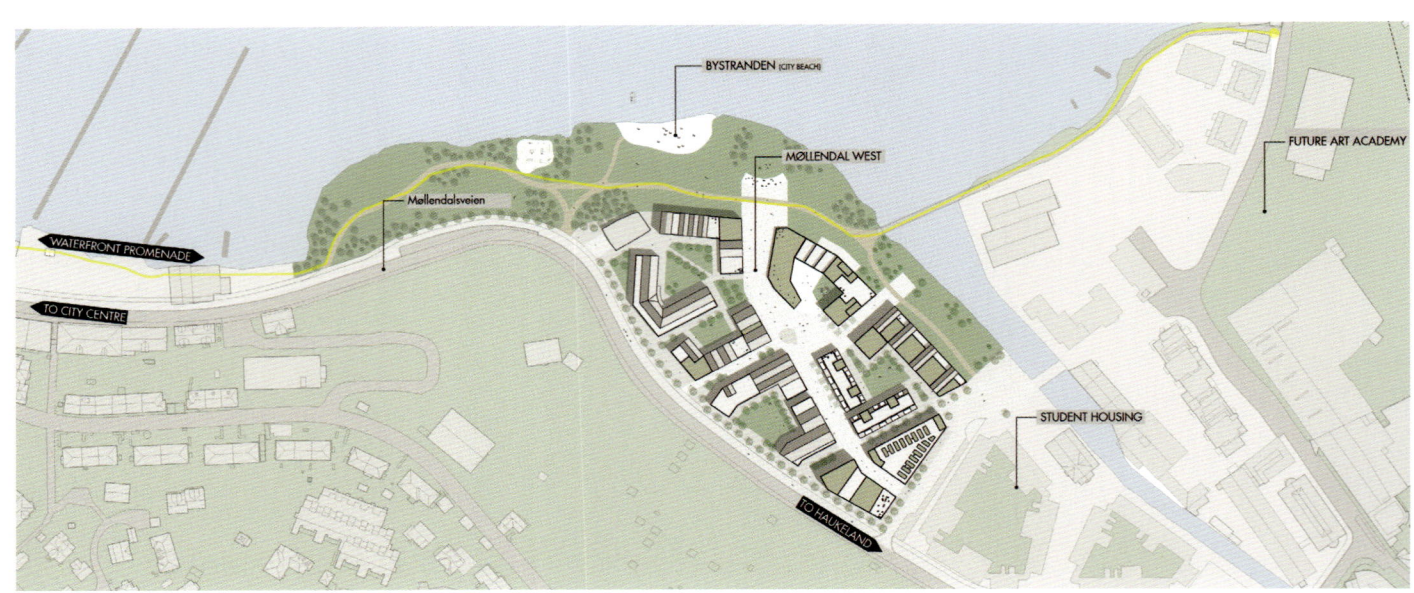

SIGNE HELLAND NYBERG (NO)
ARCHITECT

ANDERS OLIVARIUS BJØRNESETH (NO)
KENNETH LARSSEN LØNNING (NO)
ELINE MOE EIDVIN (NO)
CHRISTOPHER WILKENS (NO)
ARCHITECTS

BJØRNESETH+LØNNING
OFFICE@BJO-LO.COM
WWW.BJO-LO.COM

SPECIAL MENTION - BERGEN (NO)

Her har eg mitt hjerte, her har eg mitt ly

TEAM POINT OF VIEW The project challenges the usual construction methods related to affordability and typology. It emphasises the concept of do-it-yourself and develops a construction system illustrated in a housing catalogue with a set of basic rules on how to put your own housing modules together. The raw housing module, easily transported to the site, allows "creativity with predictability" and the inhabitants develop a sense of community and a set of shared functions through the process.

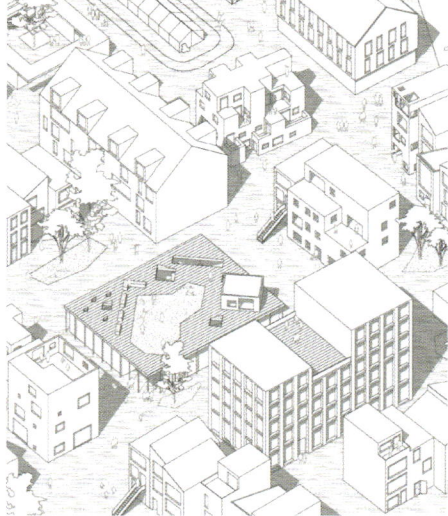
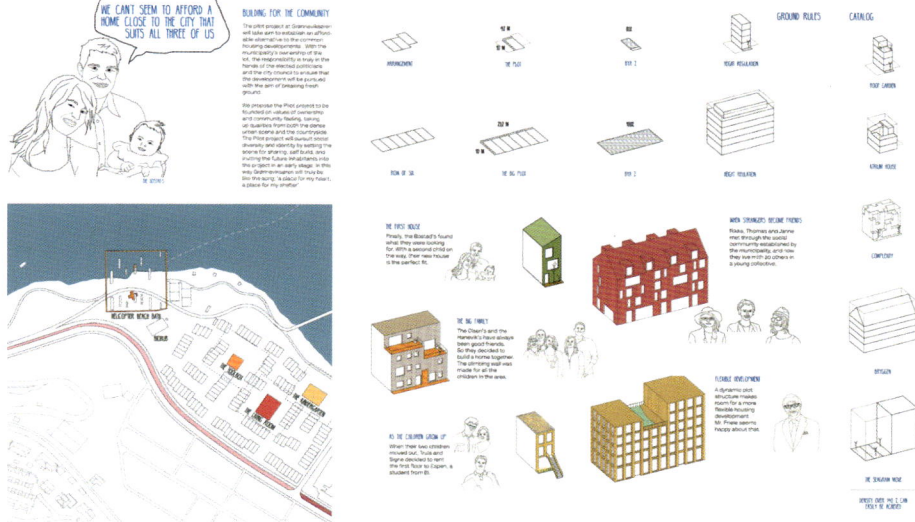

BORDEAUX
FRANCE (FR)

CATEGORY: **URBAN – ARCHITECTURAL**
LOCATION: **BORDEAUX, BASTIDE DISTRICT**
POPULATION: **239,399 INHAB.**
STRATEGIC SITE: **5 HA**
PROJECT SITE: **1.3 HA**

SITE PROPOSED BY: **EPA EURATLANTIQUE, METROPOLITAN BORDEAUX, THE CITY OF BORDEAUX**
OWNER(S) OF THE SITE: **EPA EURATLANTIQUE**
COMMISION AFTER COMPETITION: **DETAILED STUDY OF THE CONVERSION OF THE BENAUGE FIRE STATION. FOLLOW-UP OPERATIONS CAN BE INITIATED WITH PRIVATE PARTNERS**

Interview of the site's representative

PRESENTATION OF THE SITE WITH REGARDS TO STRATEGY

The Benauge Fire Station stands on the right bank of the Garonne facing the 18th century river front of the left bank, the historic centre of Bordeaux. The fire station is a provocative, emblematic landmark in the urban landscape. With the planned departure of the fire brigade, concerns for the future of an architectural complex of 1.3 ha in the heart of the city arise. The future of the fire station is part of the transformation of the whole sector: development along the banks of the Garonne and renovation of the Bastide district. There is a desire to open the site to the rest of the city and to maintain a degree of public space.

HOW IS THE SITE CONNECTED TO THE SESSION TOPIC - THE ADAPTABLE CITY?

What to do with an old concrete fire station and a block of housing on pilotis in the heart of the city? A diversity of functions, uses and temporalities need to be coordinated. The site has the potential to become a laboratory for another way to construct the city with new actors.

The fire station is a place for a project process along the theme of the adaptable city. The issues of opening up a heterotopic complex to the rest of the city, redevelopment strategies for 20th century architectural heritage, transformation programmes, approaches to co-construction and participatory processes become topics to be re-invented.

JULES EYMARD (FR)
PAUL JAQUET (FR)
MAXIME ROUSSEAU (FR)
ARCHITECTS

34 RUE MANON CORMIER
33000 BORDEAUX, FR
AGORAMODERNE@GMAIL.COM

RUNNER-UP - BORDEAUX (FR)

L'Agora moderne, incubatrice d'initiatives locales

TEAM POINT OF VIEW Within a weakened welfare state, who can guarantee the common interest? In addition to its powerful investment potential, we believe the civil society is coming with a territorial consciousness. Alongside the client –who decides– and the construction manager – who executes–, we should include a sharing manager. For this, creating synergies between private investments and local concerns is fundamental. The fire station renovation is an opportunity to think about an incubator for local initiatives, based on a territorialized multiplying effect, by which each invested euro is amplified for the common interest.

Nowadays, the Garonne stands up as the metropolitan Agora for Bordeaux and takes up the challenge to reunite both banks. In this ecosystem, the Caserne de la Benauge has all the necessary potential to become a new district Agora. Thus the project will become a spot for exchanges and inter-district cooperation.

These are the basis for the station renovation, as a specific heritage, a district agora and an incubator for local initiatives. They define a framework to instigate future investors to innovate and initiate new ways in synergy with the district. Beyond answering the district's priority needs, all these intentions will favour meetings and other random chances to connect, from which we hope new motivations for the system to reinvent itself will emerge.

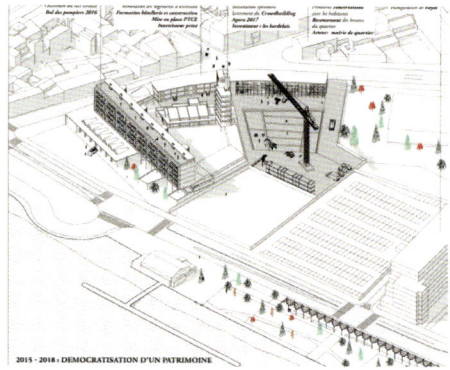 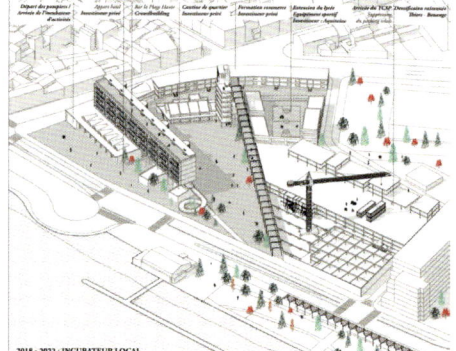 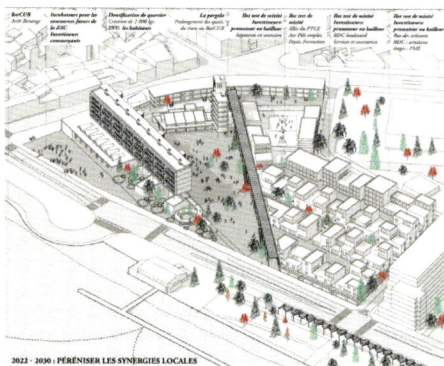

JURY POINT OF VIEW Without being utopian, the project proposes arrangements that do not exist and would multiply the effects of the existing local programmes: a residential hotel allows the inhabitants to remain as tenants while their homes are renovated, and counters the inevitable gentrification of the Benauge district; A business incubator gives very small companies an opportunity to test their businesses with the advantage of the showcase effect; A Territorial Renovation Competitiveness Hub provides a way for local voluntary sector and private neighbourhood renovation initiatives to pool their efforts; etc.

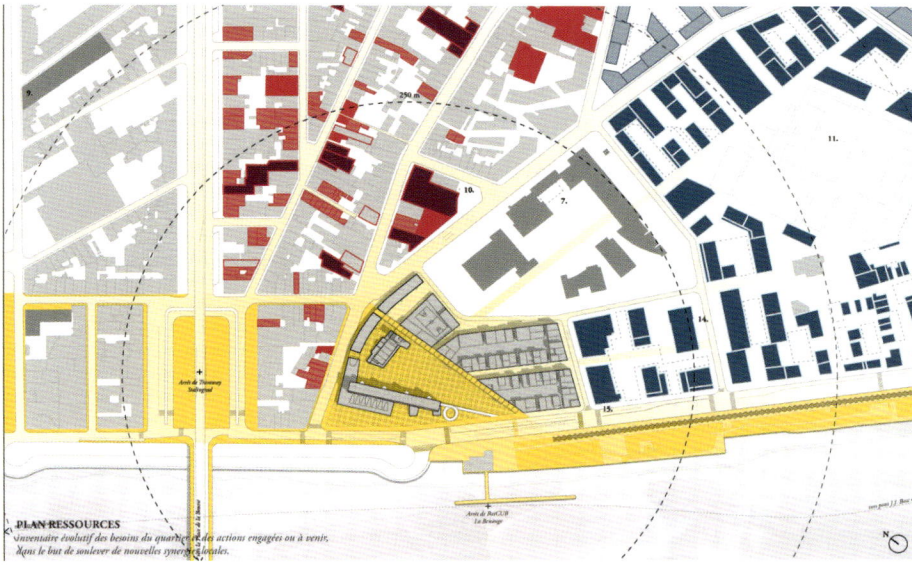

FRANÇOIS DANTART (FR)
MARCEL MALHÈRE (FR)
DELPHINE COURROYE (FR)
SILVIA PIANESE (IT)
AURÉLIEN LE ROUX (FR)
EVA JANUEL (FR)
ARCHITECTS
ROMAIN MARTEN (FR)
ENGINEER-ARCHITECT

43 RUE GRANDE BIESSE
44200 NANTES, FR
T. +33 601809475
FRANCOISDANTART.ARCHI@GMAIL.COM

RUNNER-UP - BORDEAUX (FR)
Les grandes manœuvres

TEAM POINT OF VIEW The project instantaneously begins with the creation of a worksite huts area providing the whole urban development zone and financing the transformation of the fire station. The Grandes Manœuvres association coordinates all stakeholders (public, private, inhabitants) and leads every step of the process, from funding to implementation. The project spreads out from the courtyard. In the pioneer phase, public space appropriation through field-based produced urban furniture reveals the site potential and its community vocation. According to an incremental strategy, buildings are gradually colonized and refurbished at a minimum level with an economical view, so that they respect the monument authenticity. The new functions slip into the existing buildings, taking advantage of their architectural qualities and bring the site to life in tune with the spirit of the place.

The participatory dynamic strengthens the site attractiveness and reinstalls the fire station in its quarter even before the firemen departure, which enables the installation of the activities making the site radiating in the city.

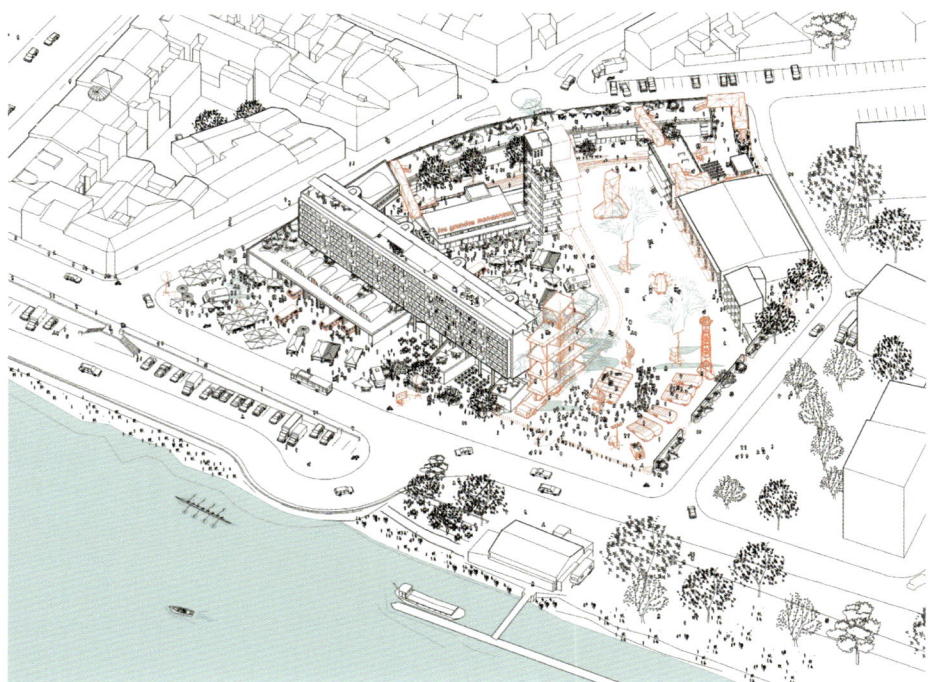

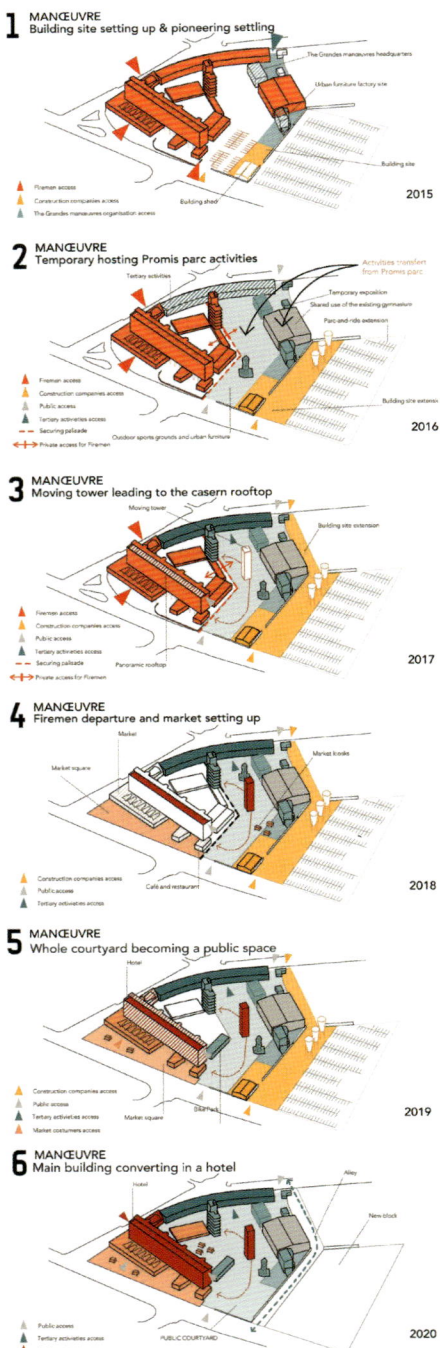

JURY POINT OF VIEW The quality of this project lies in its implementation of a tried and tested method of recapturing and enhancing vacant urban fabric. The festivalisation of the development through the implementation of co-constructed street furniture creates an address and value. The project clearly identifies the partners. And the arrangement and phasing process proposed illustrates the implementation of an ultimate programme that is respectful of the existing heritage and its specific characteristics.

NICOLA SCARAMUZZI (IT)
FABIO BIAGIO SALERNO (IT)
ELIANA MARTINELLI (IT)
DAVID RAVEGGI (IT)
FRANCESCO SABBATINI (IT)
LUCA SAMMARTINO (IT)
ARCHITECTS

EUGENIA CECCHETTI (IT)
FABIO SEMERARO (IT)
ARCHITECTS
NICOLA BONDI (IT)
STUDENT IN ARCHITECTURE

QAYIN ARCHITETTURA
T. +39 3474072890
QAYINARCHITETTURA@GMAIL.COM
WWW.FACEBOOK.COM/QAYINARCHITETTURA/

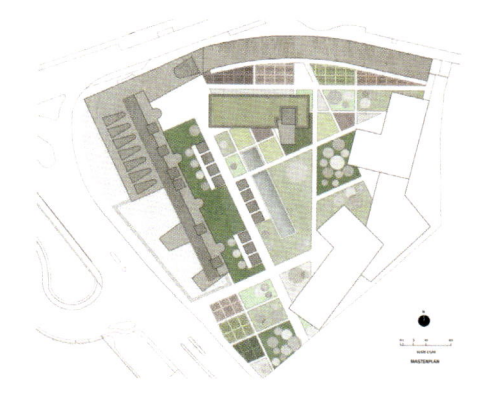

SPECIAL MENTION - BORDEAUX (FR)

Regarde-moi, je te vois

TEAM POINT OF VIEW The city is an architecture growing on itself and developing on the physical signs of the past. The barracks –like the cathedral– represent one of the signs for Bordeaux through which the community measures spaces. They will for the first time reveal themselves to the city and become a creative hub. We will not take action on the outer shape with its essential features; we will rather empty the map aligned with the theory of modern movement, placing modular inner spaces easily convertible over time and suitable for artistic events to attract all the citizens of Bordeaux.

FELDAFING
DEUTSCHLAND (DE)

CATEGORY: **URBAN - LANDSCAPE - ARCHITECTURAL**
LOCATION: **FELDAFING, TELECOMMUNICATIONS SCHOOL**
POPULATION: **4,100 INHAB.**
STRATEGIC SITE: **10 SQKM**
PROJECT SITE: **31 HA**
SITE PROPOSED BY: **FELDAFING MUNICIPALITY**

OWNER(S) OF THE SITE: **BIMA (INSTITUTE FOR FEDERAL REAL ESTATE)**
COMMISION AFTER COMPETITION: **THE COMPETITION RESULTS WILL BE INTRODUCED AS IMPULSES INTO AN EXTENSIVE CITIZEN PARTICIPATION PROCESS FOR FURTHER DEVELOPMENT**

Interview of the site's representative
Bernhard Sontheim, Mayor, Municipality of Feldafing

PRESENTATION OF THE SITE WITH REGARDS TO STRATEGY

The municipality would like to establish new uses on the Bundeswehr site –expected to become free in 2019– mainly in the fields of research and development, teaching and residential use. The goal is to realize long-term solutions over a period of about 20 years and therefore structure the development in a way that is as socially compatible as possible for the small municipality of Feldafing –with its approx. 4,200 residents– and to provide expansion possibilities for the already existing facilities.

HOW IS THE SITE CONNECTED TO THE SESSION TOPIC - THE ADAPTABLE CITY?

Since the area to be freed up amounts to approx. 1/7th of the area of Feldafing that has already been built, this site's conversion for civilian uses will change the face of Feldafing with respect to social structure, infrastructure and so forth. Integration in terms of urban planning or links to the existing part of the municipality should be kept in mind. The implementation of missing facilities –such as a larger event space or a generally accessible open space to be used for municipal purposes– should be considered in the planning, creating additional benefit for the public.

DID YOU DEFINE A SPECIFIC PROCESS FOR THE URBAN DEVELOPMENT OF THE SITE AFTER EUROPAN COMPETITION?

The designs rewarded by the jury will be presented to the Municipal Council at the beginning of 2016; then to the citizens in February or March 2016. We hope that the high quality proposals also convinces a broad public, so that we can begin the urban planning work – on this basis and involving the architects– and develop a layout plan for implementation prior to the withdrawal of the Bundeswehr.

PABLO ALLEN-VIZÁN (ES)
ELISABETH GARCÍA-ASENSIO (ES)
ARCHITECTS

ALSENSTRASSE 23-A
50679 KÖLN, DE
WWW.PABLOALLEN.COM

WINNER - FELDAFING (DE)
Forest for Rest

TEAM POINT OF VIEW The project is based on Citizens, Health and Leisure with a focus on free outside spaces as Biergarten, fairs, markets and sports –activities that we should see as part of the landscape outside a low-density architecture.
Our proposal takes care of the forest, which should be almost another type of forest. The connection to the city could include an exhibition or concert hall, a museum or a multi-use pavilion. It is connected to a square where all kinds of markets can take place. Leisure and the existing uses have to be improved and connect the lake and the forest in the South of the site. The typologies in this location provide us with a chance to interpret it. We propose small echoes of the landscape. We must activate the site with a bit of architecture and a lot of landscape. The roofs –presented as folds– become part of the forest and the program hides under them. The city and the citizens decide on when and what to build and they can even choose the future program of the fold.

JURY POINT OF VIEW The project proposes an easily comprehensible strip concept. The strips facilitate a flexibly usable organization system that, in the course of development in which broad aspects are unforeseeable, seems reprogrammable and hence "adaptable". This project formulates a unique and unconventional contribution to the future development of the site that continues the existing park landscape in a clever way and creates new, open fields of possibility.

FRANCISCO JAVIER CASTELLANO PULIDO (ES)
TOMÁS GARCÍA PÍRIZ (ES)
JUAN ANTONIO SERRANO GARCÍA (ES)
PALOMA BAQUERO MASATS (ES)
SERGIO ÁLVAREZ GARCÍA (ES)
ARCHITECTS

CUAC ARQUITECTURA (F. J. CASTELLANO, T. GARCÍA)
INFO@CUACARQUITECTURA.COM
WWW.CUACARQUITECTURA.COM
SERRANO+BAQUERO (J. A. SERRANO, P. BAQUERO)
ESTUDIO@SERRANOYBAQUERO.COM
WWW.SERRANOYBAQUERO.COM

RUNNER-UP - FELDAFING (DE)

The Magic Park of Feldafing

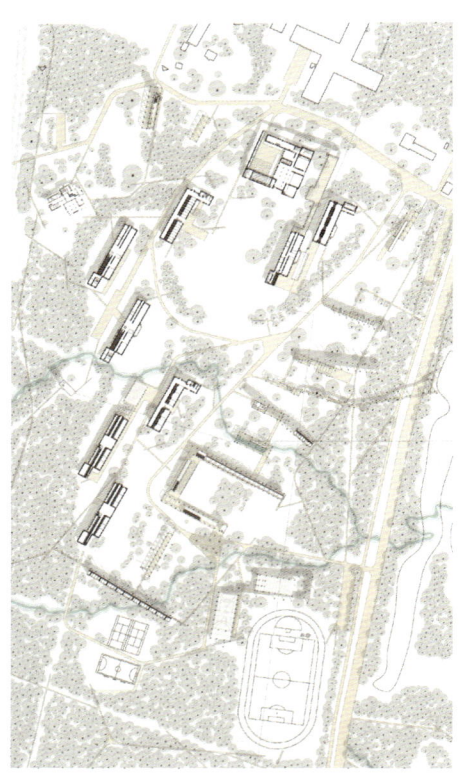

TEAM POINT OF VIEW Reconnecting landscapes. Infrastructural picturesque. The term picturesque comes to deep in the past of the Telecommunications School as a "ville colonie", traditionally marked by the harmonic relationship between building and garden. The old and modern villas of Feldafing are characterized by large cared green surfaces. This is why "The Magic Park" is presented as a great colony without fences and where the green field is made public – a park in which the old roads are substituted by paths and pedestrian roads. This net of paths is structured by sequences and visual cores around the trees revealing the presences of the streams and at some strategic points lake Starnberg. The scenery is discovered along the walk. The architecture inside the park is submitted to the nature – it is left as nature, as fallen trees after a storm. The Strumblockhaus, the Casino or the current Canteen remain untouched (at least apparently). The rest of the buildings are alternatively dismantled to preserve the essence of the park, transformed into modern ruins in new and exciting architectures emerging from the remains of the old ones. Still, as an infrastructure, the ruins also allow the recycling of valued elements such as the structure (as a sustain of the new and lighter architectures) and the nets of sanity and supplying of services.

JURY POINT OF VIEW The work sets itself the challenge to reinterpret the site. It focuses on the atmospheric effect of a staged landscape space. It is based on insights from intensive research on traces and stories of development and the conceptual building blocks directly derive from this. The project offers to ascribe a new and unique character to the location and overwrites the historical coding in a respectful manner.

GENÈVE
SCHWEIZ/SUISSE/SVIZZERA/SVIZRA (CH)

CATEGORY: **URBAN - ARCHITECTURAL**
LOCATION: **ONEX - BERNEX - CONFIGNON**
POPULATION: **1,240 INHAB.**
STRATEGIC SITE: **TERRITORY OF THE ONEX, BERNEX AND CONFIGNON MUNICIPALITIES**
PROJECT SITE: **54.8 HA**
SITE PROPOSED BY: **REPUBLIC AND CANTON OF GENEVA**
OWNER(S) OF THE SITE: **PRIVATE OWNERS AND STATE OF GENEVA**
COMMISION AFTER COMPETITION: **MANDATE TO STUDY AND ASSIST THE TRANSFORMATION PROCESS OF THE SUBURBAN SINGLE DWELLING AREA**

Interview of the site's representative

PRESENTATION OF THE SITE WITH REGARDS TO STRATEGY

On this site, the State of Geneva wants to test a less centralised and constraining form of planning in order to improve the efficiency of the planning and housing production chain. As a guide for a progressive urban transformation the conceptual approach should therefore be the support for the definition of new operating modes, renewing the logics of actors or the modes of validation by the authorities, therefore avoiding blockages. Regarding the density of urbanisation and public access to open spaces, similar results to the ones made with the existing tools should anyway be achieved.

HOW IS THE SITE CONNECTED TO THE SESSION TOPIC - THE ADAPTABLE CITY?

Morphological as well as social diversity is the base for the mutation process to consider, the issue of which also consisting in reconciling densification with social and land realities.

DID YOU DEFINE A SPECIFIC PROCESS FOR THE URBAN DEVELOPMENT OF THE SITE AFTER EUROPAN COMPETITION?

The four conceptual proposals rewarded by the jury introduce non-rigid approaches and allow quite a large spectrum for evolution.
The Planning Office could give a mission to the 4 teams to create a sort of think tank on the preconditions (charter, local animation, legal instruments, etc.) to then make them work in teams on a site, or potentially give a site to each of the teams.

YONY SANTOS (ES)
MOUNIR AYOUB (FR)
ARCHITECTS

NURIA FERNÁNDEZ (ES)
VANESSA LACAILLE (FR)
ARCHITECTS

1 RUE JOSEPH-PASQUIER
1203 GENÈVE, CH
T. +41 789172010
MAIL@YONYSANTOS.CH

WINNER - GENÈVE (CH)
La ville intermédiaire

TEAM POINT OF VIEW The densification of detached houses neighbourhood in the Geneva metropolitan area is a possible way to reduce the cruel shortage of housing. The neighbourhood of Onex, Confignon and Bernex has the human, territorial and urban potential of its own mutation into a new city model that enjoys the benefits of urban and qualities of rural:
This is the intermediary city.

JURY POINT OF VIEW The project proposes the implementation of a legal-organisational interface that is neither public nor private but takes the form of a collective charter. The content takes the particular needs of stakeholders into account so that dialogue becomes possible. The charter is accompanied by a series of tools that allow a specific response to situations of conflict that may arise. These tools also propose a series of planning strategies that address the densification needs of a particular territory, these strategies integrating the notions of upgradeability and adaptation over time.

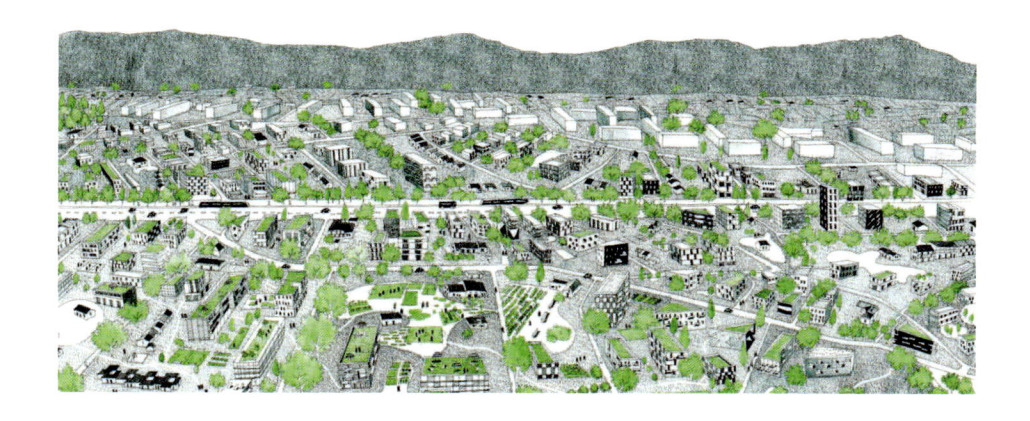

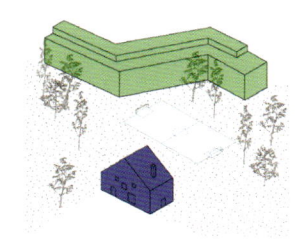

Logm. collectifs + Logm. individuels / Aire de jeux
Housing complex + individual houses / Playground

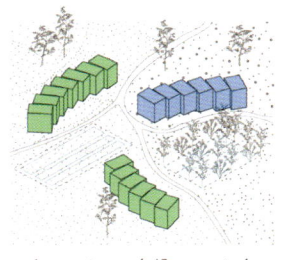

Logements groupés / Espace partagé
Collectif housing / Shared space

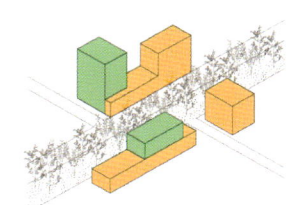

Logements + Bureaux / Esplanade urbaine
Housing + Office / urban Esplanade

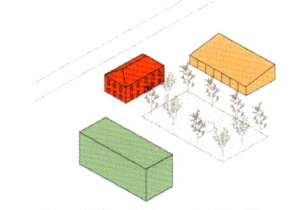

Logement + activités + équipement public / Place publique
Housing + activities + public facilities / Public square

LAURA MARTÍNEZ ALONSO (ES)
MARTA DE LAS HERAS MARTÍNEZ (ES)
MIGUEL GONZÁLEZ CASTRO (ES)
MARÍA NUÑEZ RODRÍGUEZ (ES)
ARCHITECTS
ANÍBAL HERNÁNDEZ SÁNCHEZ (ES)
ANTHROPOLOGIST

CALLE PINAR DE SOMOSAGUAS 112
28223 POZUELO DE ALARCÓN, MADRID, ES
T. +34 640518383
PATATAFRITAPUBLICA@GMAIL.COM
WWW.OPENSPACEFABRIC.TUMBLR.COM

RUNNER-UP - GENÈVE (CH)

Open Space Fabric

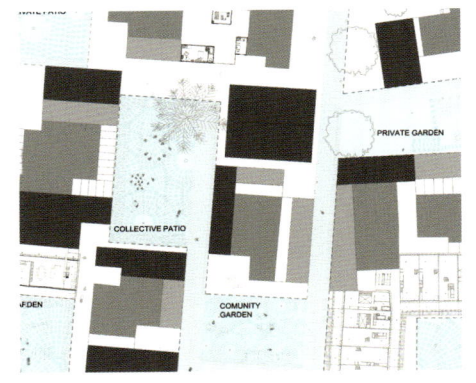

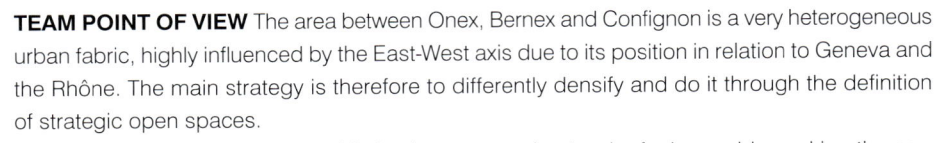

TEAM POINT OF VIEW The area between Onex, Bernex and Confignon is a very heterogeneous urban fabric, highly influenced by the East-West axis due to its position in relation to Geneva and the Rhône. The main strategy is therefore to differently densify and do it through the definition of strategic open spaces.

The existing plot pattern is the guide for the proposed network of urban voids, making the new development compatible with the current urban fabric and with property rights. These open spaces are reserved to become squares, patios or orchards, always according to the needs and desires of the community. The landscape progressively changes, an additional layer of public and collective spaces allows all actors to intervene in the process at different moments. We propose a process rather than a closed project that will emerge from the application of technical rules, the participation of the stakeholders and its interaction with the urban, social and ecological context.

A representative stripe of land, with a North-South orientation to get all this diversity without losing the East-West perspective, is used as an example. Through this abstraction we can better analyse the urban fabrics to propose different densification strategies. The stripe is a very useful tool out of which we can more easily establish a coherent set of rules to apply to other territories with similar characteristics.

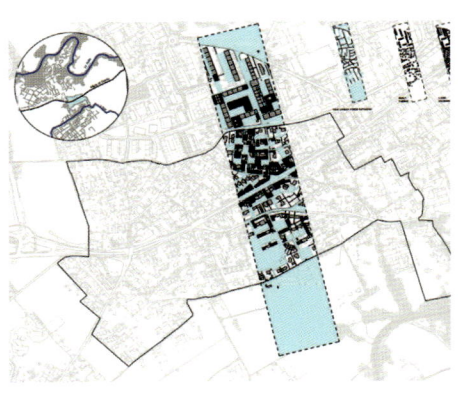

JURY POINT OF VIEW The proposition revolves around three main objectives:
- Articulation of a will to conserve elements on the site and a need for resilience;
- Work on the potential of the site and not on the basis of a tabula rasa;
- Search for urban forms that stimulate the birth of new community forms.

A North-South 'slice' illustrates the process reflecting the consistency of the proposition. The preview explicitly conveys the main ideas of the proposition and opens up the fields of application to be developed in more detail.

NICOLAS LOMBARDI (FR)
JÉRÔME HERVE (FR)
LAURA ROS MARTINEZ (ES)
CRISTINA ROS BALLESTER (ES)
MATTHIAS SCHWEISSHELM (DE)
ARCHITECTS

MAGALI GARIN (FR)
LAWYER

20 RUE DE L'OURCQ
75019 PARIS, FR
T. +33 688771202
NCLSLOMBARDI@GMAIL.COM

SPECIAL MENTION - GENÈVE (CH)
Emphutheusis

TEAM POINT OF VIEW The project "Emphutheusis" presents various densification scenarios rather than an applied result. Literally meaning "the action of planting" in ancient Greek, 3 strategies of intervention characterize the project:
- The improvement of the existing network of green spaces to unify both sides of the site;
- The densification of the villa territory to open up this area to the Avenue de Chancy with a large range of public spaces;
- The identification of underused land for implementation of public services and future development according to the urban densification planned for 2050.

CLARA RODRÍGUEZ LORENZO (ES)
NATALIA VERA VIGARAY (ES)
ARCHITECTS

GRUBBEVÄGEN 50
90354 UMEÅ, SE
T. +34 659567913
NVERAVIGARAY@GMAIL.COM
WWW.FRSQR.COM

SPECIAL MENTION - GENÈVE (CH)
Un-City

TEAM POINT OF VIEW We propose a progressive transformation of the low-density villa area into a socially diverse city that adapts to the society needs over time. We generate a spatial software or protocol based on the maintenance of a maximum footprint ratio of 30% to keep the countryside lifestyle identity of the site. The system allows the owners to sell part of their land, the whole property or build until fulfilling this occupancy. The available land situation is then something open that can generate multiple uncertain scenarios that allow the new developments to coexist with the current villas.

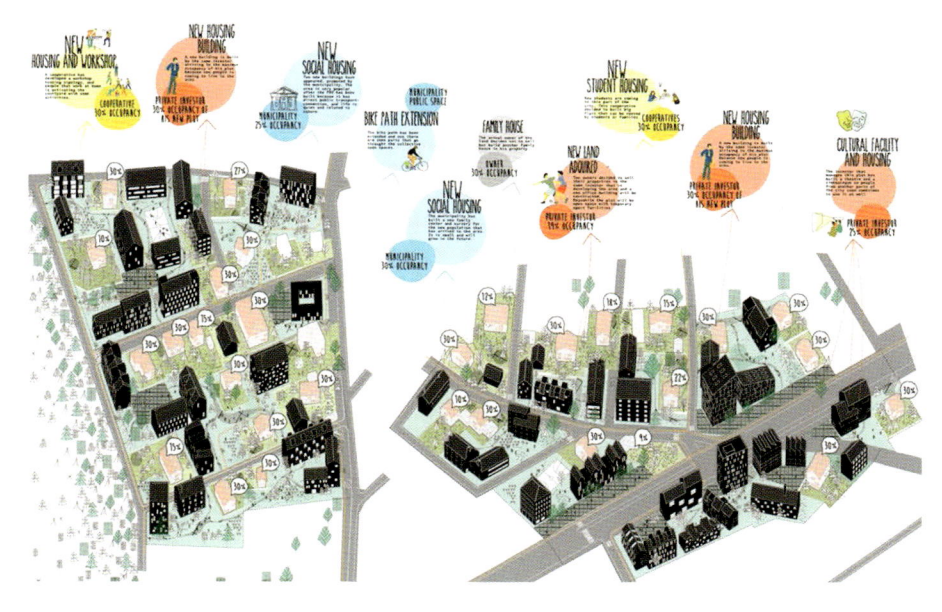

LEEUWARDEN
NEDERLAND (NL)

CATEGORY: **STRATEGIC - URBAN – ARCHITECTURAL**
LOCATION: **LEEUWARDEN, SOUTH-EAST CITY CENTRE**
POPULATION: **108,000 INHAB.**
STRATEGIC SITE: **19.3 HA**
PROJECT SITE: **0.43 HA**
SITE PROPOSED BY: **IR. ABE BONNEMASTICHTING**
OWNER(S) OF THE SITE: **PUBLIC AND PRIVATE OWNERS**
COMMISION AFTER COMPETITION: **INVOLVEMENT IN LOCAL DESIGN ASSIGNMENT**

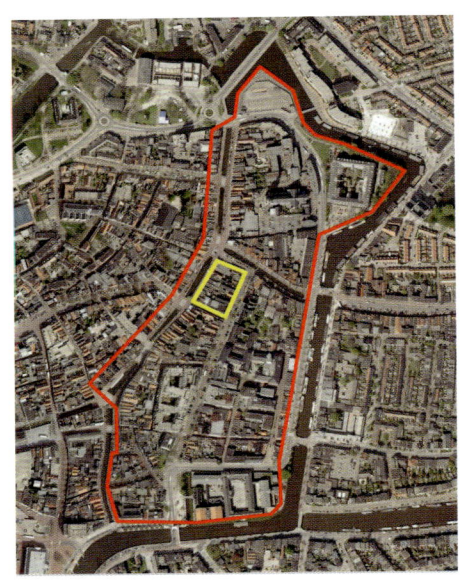

Interview of the site's representative

PRESENTATION OF THE SITE WITH REGARDS TO STRATEGY

The Southeast part of the city of Leeuwarden has many historical, striking buildings. But many residential properties and shop premises are vacant and/or struggling with overdue maintenance. The area deserves upgrading whereby new sustainable uses for vacant shop premises are devised. The study site covers the entire Eastern part of the historical city centre. Within this area the "building block" (project site) —bordered by Voorstreek, Tuinen, Turfmarkt and Koningsstraat– is exemplary. The objective is the preservation and restoration of the historical, visual quality and the residential function, complementary to the other city centre functions. The city council is constantly alert to ideas for an innovative approach to housing and new forms of accommodation such as communal housing for the elderly or mixed-generation housing.

HOW IS THE SITE CONNECTED TO THE SESSION TOPIC - THE ADAPTABLE CITY?

As in many other European towns and cities the city centre of Leeuwarden has undergone a transformation, both in terms of use and infrastructure. Both during daytime and in the evening the lively atmosphere has declined: more and more retail outlets are going out of business, leading to vacancies and deterioration. Leeuwarden aspires to a dynamic development of the city centre, one that anticipates the opportunities that a changing society offers. It envisages a return to a combined residential-work function with smaller shops, studios and offices among the housing in a way that reflects the needs of the inhabitants as well as autonomous developments.

CLAUDIA MAINARDI (IT)
GIACOMO ARDESIO (IT)
ALESSANDRO BONIZZONI (IT)
VERONICA CAPRINO (IT)
ANTONIO BUONSANTE (IT)
ARCHITECTS

FOSBURY ARCHITECTURE
VIA PINTURICCHIO 21
20133 MILAN, IT
T. +31 644360461
FOSBURYARCHITECTURE@GMAIL.COM
WWW.FOSBURYARCHITECTURE.COM

WINNER - LEEUWARDEN (NL)
Te Huur

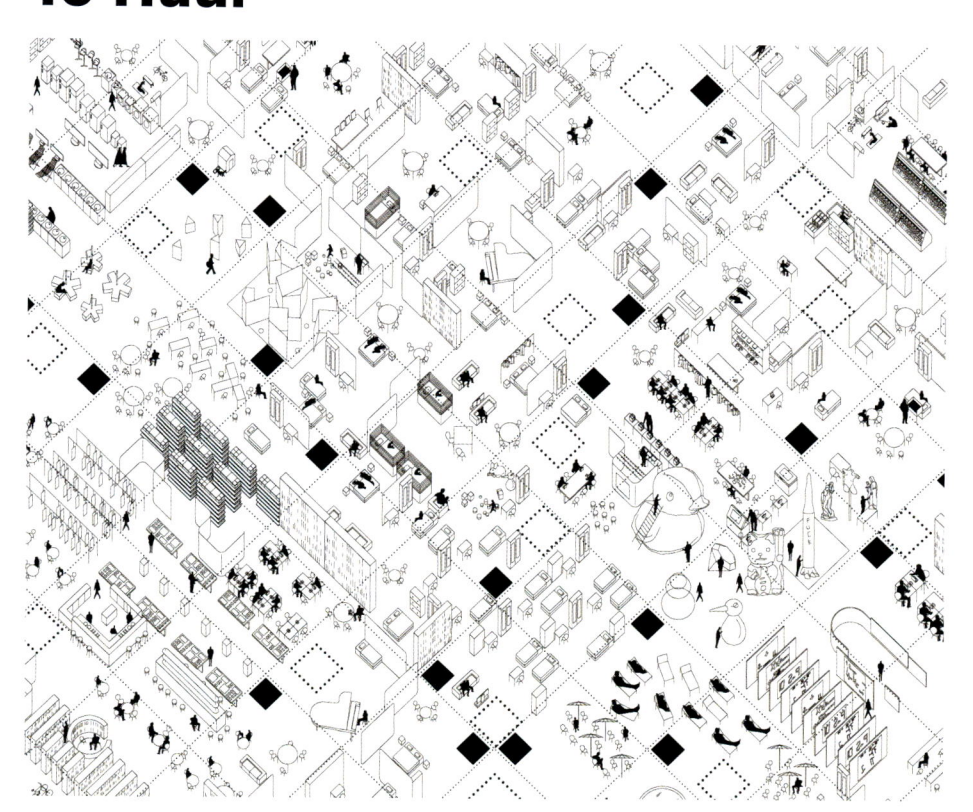

TEAM POINT OF VIEW Leeuwarden is a beautiful city that does not need anything else than the definition of an approach able to combine the promotion of the city centre and the involvement of the citizens in this process. Through a careful investigation of the current living condition, the project proposes a bottom-up strategy that, starting from the problems related to the depopulation process of the centre, will be able to reactivate the urban core. Only reviving the centre, the shops will have a market; the services will have users; the tourists a context to visit. In a shrinking city there is definitely no need to built new dwellings. The vacancies are a resource to define new ways to inhabit and work. The models offered by the sharing economy clearly define an alternative and more resilient pattern for the requalification of the areas. The sharing of the space is a useful tool to create the condition for start-ups, co-workings, and other programs.

The peer-to-peer economies represent as well an instrument to tackle the need of new accommodation for tourists, during the year when Leeuwarden is the European Capital of Culture and the following ones.

What we expect is the occupation in the short term of the vacant spaces through a wide catalogue of possible activities and the stabilization in the long term of this weak system trough the energies of the inhabitants, who have decided to invest in this city.

JURY POINT OF VIEW This unique project tackles with a clever approach the problems Leeuwarden is facing. The plan visualises the city's ambition of being progressive and it is very –perhaps excessively– concentrated. The proposal's strength is its intelligent understanding of the assignment on different levels: the age group that Leeuwarden needs to support a dynamic environment, a novel interpretation of the Existenzminimum (subsistence level) for that group, and the potential economic value of the vacant spaces in the area.

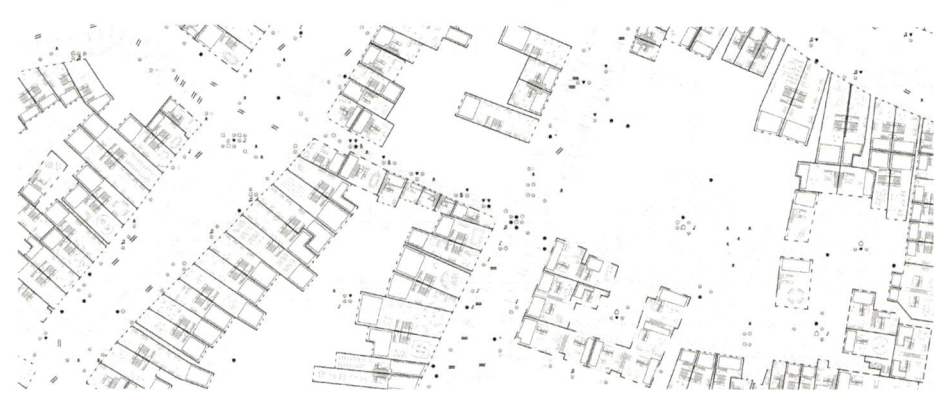

ADRIÀ GUARDIET (ES)
SANDRA TORRES (ES)
ARCHITECTS

10 CALLAO STREET
08014 BARCELONA, ES
T. +34 609167770
ESTUDI@ESTUDI08014.COM
WWW.ESTUDI08014.COM

RUNNER-UP - LEEUWARDEN (NL)
Urban Prescriptions

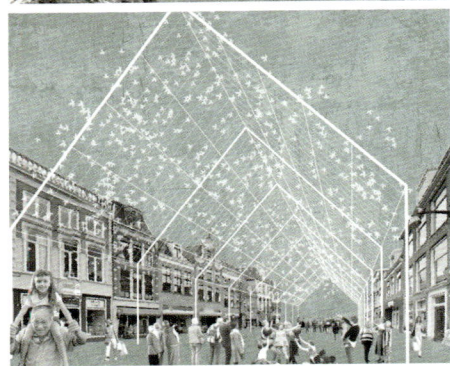

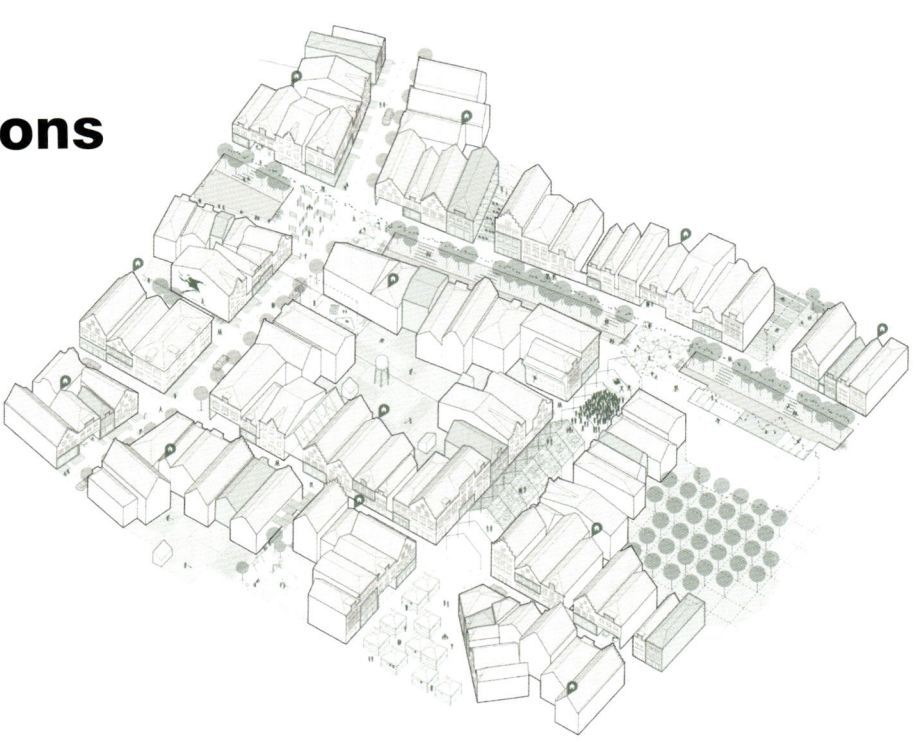

TEAM POINT OF VIEW We propose a series of 'urban prescriptions' to implement beyond the project area. A catalogue that can be exported to urban environments with similar problems and opportunities as in Leeuwarden. Prescriptions implemented at small and medium scale but with significant consequences to the whole city. Prescriptions that put the citizen in the foreground. Our prescriptions are as follows:
- Strengthening links between water and citizenship by recovering former canals, creating 'water nodes' or placing water tanks into the inner courtyards;
- Placing strategic uses in currently empty premises of the old town to change the current trend of off-shoring of public and commercial uses;
- Restoring the inner courtyards as open areas to develop different community activities (urban gardens, tree plantations, leisure activities, etc.);
- Filling the empty plots and vacant premises with different strategies: from fast and cheap occupations to more structural and long-term actions;
- Transforming the canal banks as a transmission vehicle of greenery and culture to bring them closer to the citizenship;
- Progressive transformation of housing by promoting typological diversity, social renting, temporary housing, etc. or improving their energetic behaviour;
- Temporary and flexible public spaces allowing a diversity of uses and atmospheres with only some minor changes.

JURY POINT OF VIEW The proposal's departure point is the creation of a traffic-free city. The plan is very different from other toolbox plans: it does not lead to an ill-conceived list of possible interventions but applies the toolbox at all scales, from the city in its entirety to the diverse street profiles and courtyards. The tools are realistic and sensitive to the present situation in Leeuwarden: they address spatial, social and programmatic subjects. However, the plan puts forward a number of not really innovative opportunities for dialogue.

DANIELE PASIN (IT)
MARCO MANUNTA (IT)
LIDIA SAVIOLI (IT)
CHIARA VIOLI (IT)
ARCHITECTS

121 BOULEVARD DAVOUT
75020 PARIS, FR
T. +33 781788141
MPSV.ARCHITECTS@GMAIL.COM
WWW.IEPENHOUSE.COM

SPECIAL MENTION - LEEUWARDEN (NL)

Iepen House

JURY POINT OF VIEW Take some empty vacant square meters. Add a few kilos of furniture. Mix them with a spirit of sharing and open-mindedness and make it leaven with an efficient organisation: you get the Iepen House. Thought as a system of spaces to share spread across the city, Iepen House aim to help the regeneration of Leeuwarden city centre as well as any other vacant city centre in the Netherlands and beyond. When you put the four ingredients together, you create a system of spaces, people and activities that connect and bring a new appeal to the area. You will have an "additional Chez moi".

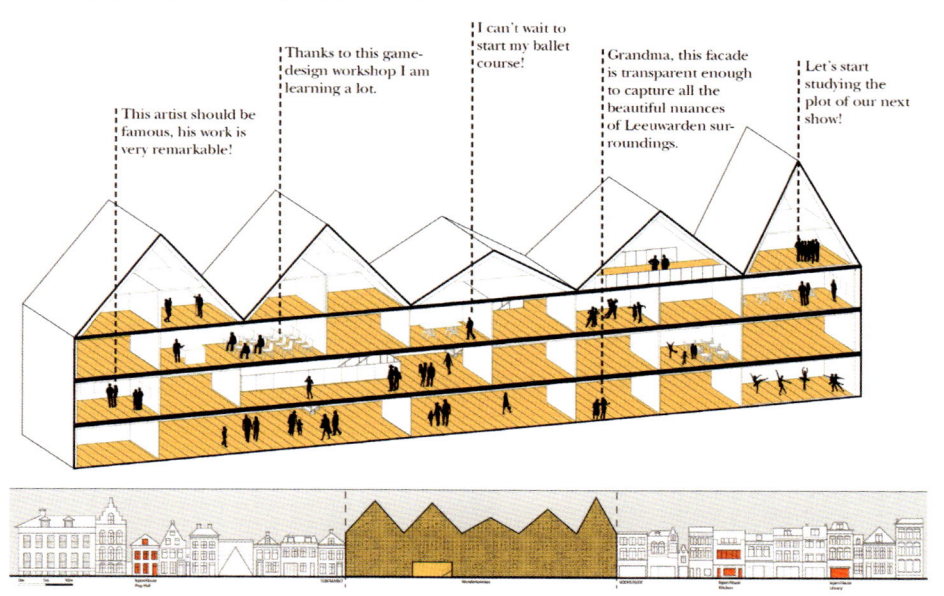

ANDREY HODKEVICH (BG)
NEDKO NEDEV (BG)
ARCHITECTS

T. +359 887886169 / AHODKEVICH@GMAIL.COM
T. +359 888219063 / NEDEV.MAIL@GMAIL.COM

SPECIAL MENTION - LEEUWARDEN (NL)

Leeuwarden 2.0

JURY POINT OF VIEW "Leeuwarden 2.0" is a possible conceptual interpretation of the consequences of the Information Revolution. This is an architectural experiment that proposes a different typology of architectural space – a "Process Structure". A concept inspired by the key factor in the digital age –the computer–, which shifts the attention from tangible to non-tangible space. Designed to be located at the historical heart of Leeuwarden, it investigates the possibility to become a Global Capital of Culture for 2018. It reveals a new concept of architectural space, a new layer on top of the existing architectural fabric of the city.

METZ
FRANCE (FR)

CATEGORY: **URBAN**
LOCATION: **METZ MÉTROPOLE – AUGNY, MARLY, MOULINS-LÈS-METZ**
POPULATION: **120,000 INHAB.**
STRATEGIC SITE: **600 HA**
PROJECT SITE: **350 HA**
SITE PROPOSED BY: **METZ MÉTROPOLE, ÉTABLISSEMENT PUBLIC FONCIER LORRAINE**
OWNER(S) OF THE SITE: **MINISTÈRE DE LA DÉFENSE. FUTURE OWNERS: ÉTABLISSEMENT PUBLIC FONCTION LORRAINE AND METZ MÉTROPOLE**
COMMISSION AFTER COMPETITION: **ORGANISATION OF A WORKSHOP WITH THE CHOSEN TEAMS – FURTHER IN-DEPTH URBAN STUDY – PROJECT MANAGEMENT ASSIGNMENTS FOR PUBLIC SPACES – PARTICIPATION PROCESS. FOLLOW-UP OPERATIONS CAN BE INITIATED WITH PRIVATE PARTNERS**

Interview of the site's representative

PRESENTATION OF THE SITE WITH REGARDS TO STRATEGY

After developing to the North and then to the South-East, the conurbation is beginning balanced development to the South-West, triggered by the military's release of Airbase 128 at the heart of a strategic area. The aspiration for the conversion of the site depends on three prerequisites: to develop job and wealth creating activities, in particular targeting sectors that offer a potential for growth and innovation; to capitalise on the model of the Centre Pompidou-Metz in expanding the city's influence; to bring the population closer to jobs and services in order to improve their quality of life. The conversion of military and industrial brownfield sites –to be undertaken by Metz Métropole– offers a real potential for renewal and large-scale support for the aspiration.

HOW IS THE SITE CONNECTED TO THE SESSION TOPIC - THE ADAPTABLE CITY?

Formerly a 400-ha monofunctional site, closed to the public, BA128 needs to be gradually converted into a jointly managed shared space, open to everyone, incorporating multiple uses, and thereby to be gradually integrated into its immediate urban and natural environment.
To achieve this, 4 primary uses have been chosen: sports and leisure, renewable energy, peri-urban agriculture and small business activities.
This deep transformation is based on the following principles: introduction of a long-term process including the recycling and reversibility of uses and spaces; rational use of space by pooling public and private spaces and amenities; focus on the relation between city and nature, which entails protection of natural areas and the provision of high-quality services; new way of constructing and managing projects, which aims at fostering the emergence of local initiatives and including a wide variety of potential stakeholders.

LAETITIA LAFONT (FR)
ARCHITECT-URBANIST
THOMAS VERGES (FR)
LANDSCAPE ARCHITECT

MATHILDE CATALAN (FR)
ARCHITECT

ATELIER LAETITIA LAFONT
42 RUE D'AVRON
75020 PARIS, FR
T. +33 675814551
ATELIERLAETITIALAFONT@GMAIL.COM
WWW.ATELIERLAETITIALAFONT.COM

WINNER - METZ (FR)
BA128 Résonances Économes

JURY POINT OF VIEW The project proposes occupying the edges as a way of reconnecting the site to its territory. By extending the existing intermodalities and the links with the city centre, the team seeks to reconnect the existing urban entities on the outskirts of the site by densification, diversification and the enhancement of private land. All this takes place in a landscape infrastructure organise like an ecological park in which the "Nature" present is enhanced and completed.

TEAM POINT OF VIEW Between public impetus and citizen initiatives.
The adaptable city is thrifty. We do not believe that a "sustainable" project is compatible with the liberal logic of the "always more". The right balance between spending, produced effort and the achieved effect must be conceptualised differently. Living in Frescaty means living in a strategic and privileged quality district near Metz. Made of certain rusticity the project synthesizes both the city and the countryside.
This transversal and prospective approach aims to synergize urban and landscape dynamics to identify metropolitan issues. To affirm the economical, social and environmental vocations of the BA 128 Frescaty site, considering its development and diversity of uses and programs implies finding a right measure: to be both ambitious and adapted to contexts and environments. Each pattern engages in an overall ecological but also productive logic, drawing the outlines of the living spaces of tomorrow. This attitude requires finding resonances and solidarity both locally and on a wider scale, in order to promote the expertise and resources offered by the territory.
The project recognizes what exists, and make it the starting point of a collective story narrative mutation. The project is born of hybridization between pre-existing elements and future development. It becomes a vector of links and brings of new uses in a rich and varied environment.

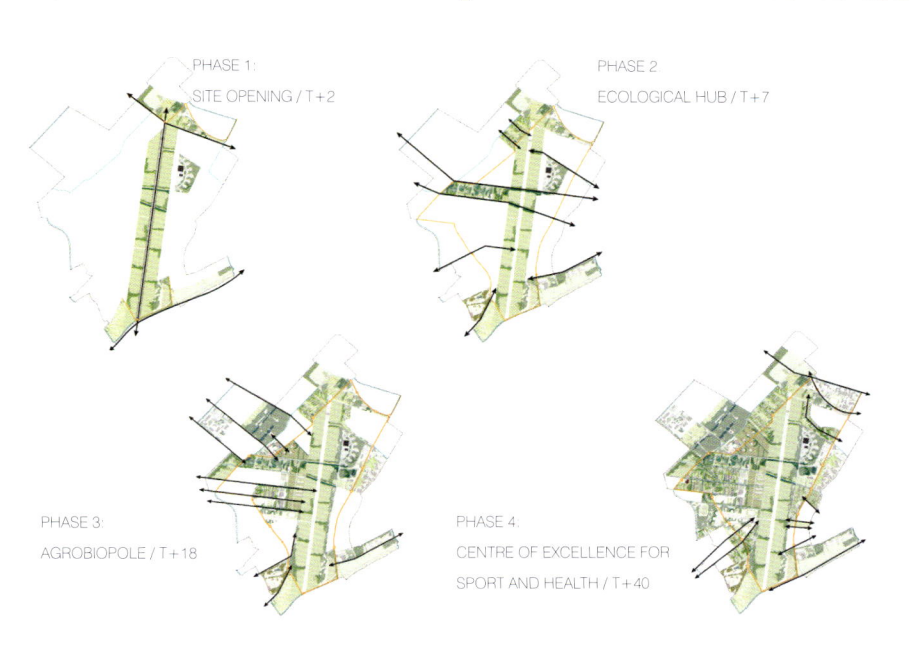

PHASE 1:
SITE OPENING / T+2

PHASE 2:
ECOLOGICAL HUB / T+7

PHASE 3:
AGROBIOPOLE / T+18

PHASE 4:
CENTRE OF EXCELLENCE FOR
SPORT AND HEALTH / T+40

OCÉANE FOLLADOR (FR)
ARCHITECT-URBANIST
THIBAUT NGUYEN (FR)
SOCIOLOGIST-URBANIST

THOMAS REZÉ (FR)
URBANIST
JÉRÉMY LAUNAY (FR)
FARMER

6 RUE DU MARAIS
44000 NANTES, FR
T. +33 626515804
FOLLADOR.OCEANE@GMAIL.COM

RUNNER-UP - METZ (FR)
B.A.S.E.

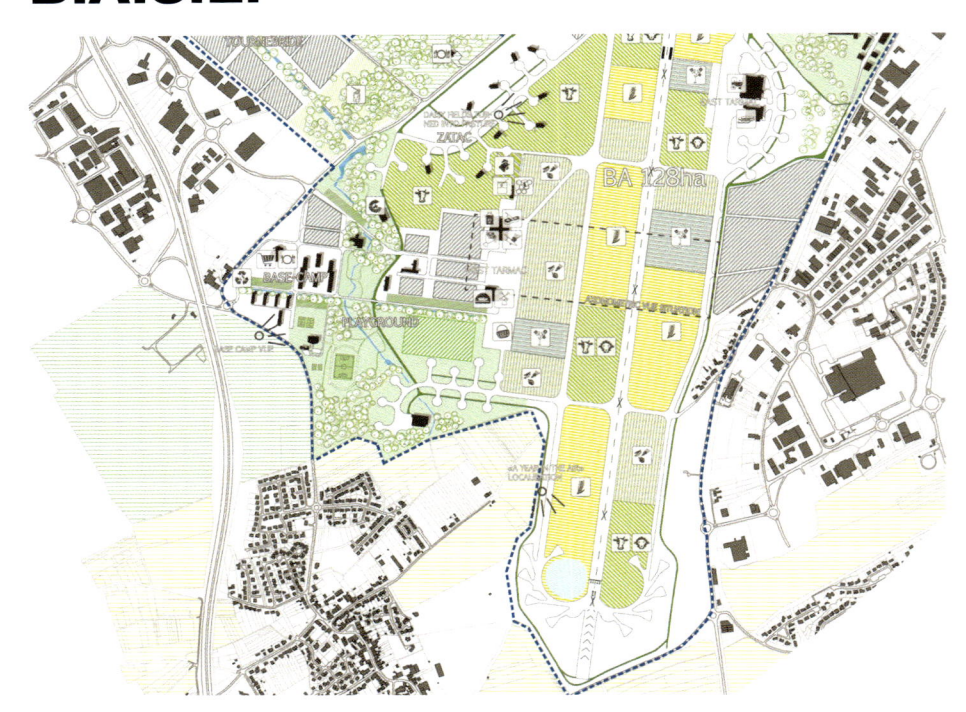

JURY POINT OF VIEW The project is founded in a participatory and community-based approach. The team proposes to organise public events in order to foster the emergence of projects and community choices. A coordinating body dedicated to the programming process will have the role of fostering the emergence of emblematic projects through debate. The aim is to establish a dialogue and cooperation between citizens and professional. Programmatic zoning is proposed in 5 places as a basis for development. The rest of the site is densified by "block potentials", spaces left to particular initiatives, available for diverse and experimental programming.

TEAM POINT OF VIEW Once a secret area kept away from the city, Metz Frescaty BA128 opens up to the Metz population. Through the long fences, we used to see the embankment and the runway. Now that it is open, the extraordinary territory might paradoxically intimidate. Beyond the fences the visitors might feel overwhelmed in this 400ha land, shaped by a history of conflicts. The BA128 indeed needs to be domesticated. Its location between urban and rural encouraged us to design it as a hyphen bringing city and countryside together.
The B.A.S.E. (Balance / Agility / Serendipity / Experimentation) approach cares about both these major issues. Sociability and appropriation shape the project and provide a fertile ground, where creativity and local initiatives can flourish.
Propositions from the B.A.S.E. approach are set in this framework. The main part of the project –named "Base Agricole 128ha"– embodies all the principles of our perspective. It involves the re-use of 128 hectares of land for local farming. All the citizens will be invited to take part to the project conception and build the foundations for a local, social and solidarity-based economy.

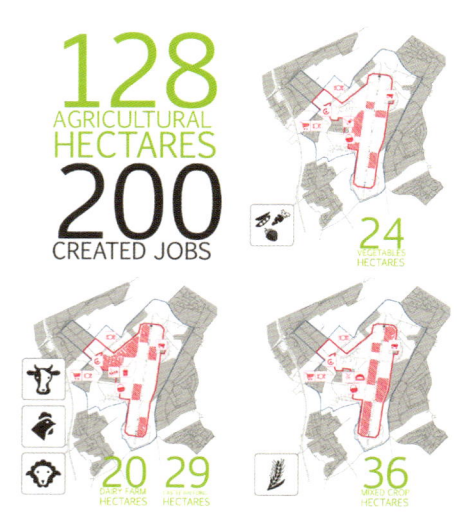

128 AGRICULTURAL HECTARES
200 CREATED JOBS
24 VEGETABLES HECTARES
20 HECTARES **29** HECTARES
36 HECTARES

ANTOINE ALLORENT (FR)
FANNY CHENU (FR)
ARCHITECTS

GUILLAUME NICOLAS (FR)
ARCHITECT-ENGINEER

16 BIS AVENUE BOSQUET
75007 PARIS, FR
T. +33 666551586
ALLORENTOINE@HOTMAIL.FR

RUNNER-UP - METZ (FR)

Cycles–Sol–Air

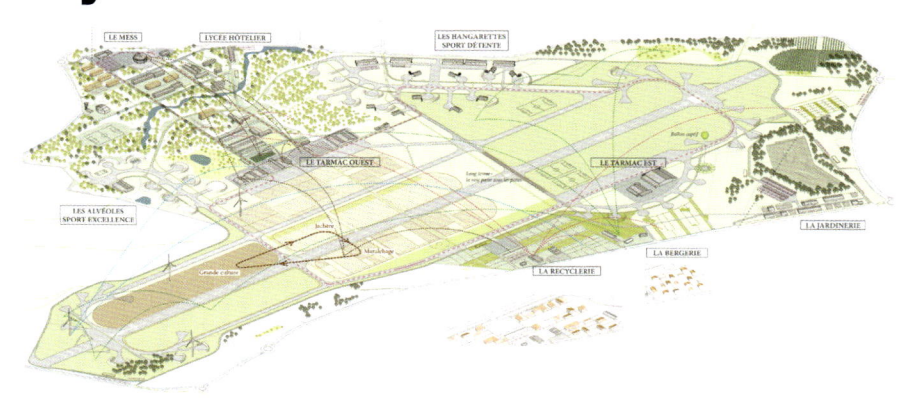

TEAM POINT OF VIEW In the course of history Frescaty has been a place for gatherings, farming and more recently a disputed military ground. Now that the military is gone, how can this huge territory open up onto its surroundings again, between town, country and commercial area? Drawing on the context, the project recreates continuity by connecting the forest dots where the buildings once lay. It preserves the empty space of the airfield, making future gatherings possible while reaffirming its agricultural purposes. Besides, recycling materials and previous uses offers new opportunities and serves purposes likely to meet today's needs as well as tomorrow's.

The synergies created both internally and with the surrounding environment allow restoring exchanges between the various hubs and their outlying activities, i.e. catering school, farm produce processing, agronomic research, allotments, garden centre, wood workshop, recycling facility, self-construction workshops, recreation and sport areas.

The project's management differs from the commercial aspect of the activities around by promoting a socially responsible economy, with co-operative and non-profit businesses, community associations and an emphasis on rehabilitation. This results in a gradual stage process giving priority to the setting up of young farmers, the recycling facility and partially opening the grounds to the public. In the long term the ensuing dynamics should benefit the entire area.

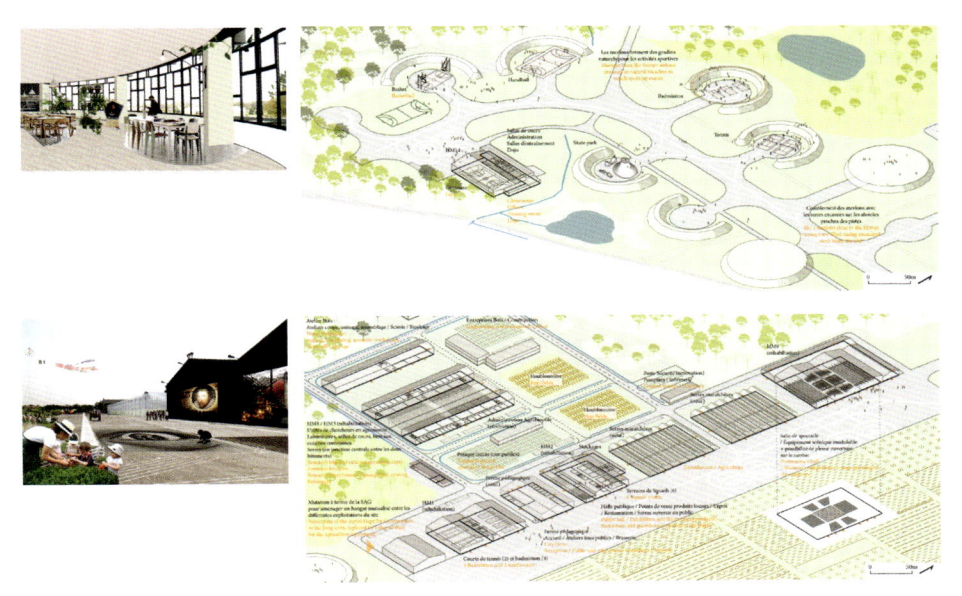

JURY POINT OF VIEW On the basis of the historical context and a very thorough analysis, the team proposes to reoccupy the existing buildings for the development of a varied set of programs. The project is introduced in a reasoned and precise way. All the activities are described in detail, installed and connected by the definition of the internal networks and connections. In addition to the programming, the project develops a nonexhaustive list of 128 possible activities. The project stands out for its very precise and detailed installation on the basis of a reoccupation of the existing buildings.

NACKA
SVERIGE (SE)

CATEGORY: **URBAN – LANDSCAPE – ARCHITECTURAL**
LOCATION: **NACKA**
POPULATION: **CITY 95,000 INHAB.**
STRATEGIC SITE: **40 HA**
PROJECT SITE: **17 HA**
SITE PROPOSED BY: **NACKA MUNICIPALITY**

OWNER(S) OF THE SITE: **NACKA MUNICIPALITY**
COMMISION AFTER COMPETITION: **URBAN AND LANDSCAPE STRATEGIC STUDY DEVELOPMENT OF PLAN PROGRAM AND MASTERPLAN IN COLLABORATION WITH MUNICIPALITY AND OTHER PARTNERS**

Interview of the site's representative

PRESENTATION OF THE SITE WITH REGARDS TO STRATEGY

The strategic site area is characterised by a dramatic topography; as a consequence the settlements are broken up into islands, separated by forest-covered hills. The existing housing areas are mainly suburban areas that politicians in general want to turn more urban and city-like.

The project site is an existing area of oil storage built in the '50s and is today run by Statoil. The current site-leasehold right runs out in 2019, which opens up for other uses. There are no collective memories of the site from inside the area; yet from the outside, Bergs has been a significant landmark for more than half a century. Within a decade it will be opened up to constructions. The whole process of planning, opening up and colonising the site will be central to the task. Nacka's Northern coast is connected to Stockholm city centre with a ferry for commuters. The site has an outstanding location.

HOW IS THE SITE CONNECTED TO THE SESSION TOPIC - THE ADAPTABLE CITY?

One of the most spectacular sites in the Stockholm region will soon be accessible and subject to planning. The project site area has been closed to the public for more than 60 years. The main target is to transform the existing area of oil storage tanks to housing, workspace, public and recreational space; in other words to transform it to a new part of Nacka with its own identity.

The market would obviously like to develop this area to an attractive seaside housing enclave; one of the challenges is to make Bergs accessible to a greater public and to connect it to the rest of Nacka.

KARL ZETTERHOLM (SE)
ARCHITECT

NYBOHOVSGRÄND 10
11763 STOCKHOLM, SE
T. +46 739703265
KARLZETTERHOLM@GMAIL.COM

WINNER - NACKA (SE)
Lucker

TEAM POINT OF VIEW Berg is centrally located in the Stockholm region but by urban standards it is fairly peripheral both in relation to central Stockholm and central Nacka and the coming subway, which is set to become the spine of future development in Nacka.

"Lucker" seeks an urbanity that does not overlook its regional position but also that can create new centralities and that has distinct urban qualities not based on formal mimicking of inner city urban patterns. Its character comes from its closeness and openness to the landscape. It is generous to those who want to participate in building it looking to create a true diversity. "Lucker" aims to:
- create a physical structure to foster a vital peripheral urbanity.
- develop a planning model that can handle unpredictability and change while creating a clear visual urban character.
- encourage integration and affordability.

JURY POINT OF VIEW The "Lucker" proposal offers a masterplan grid that can be of beneficial use for the municipality of Nacka, without major adjustments. The proposal permits to build in stages and suggests a planning strategy that encourages integration. The concept addresses the two most demanding issues of this location – how to integrate a peripheral site in an existing urban fabric and how to generate a structure close to an exposed waterfront, on the edge of nature.

ADRIAN PHIFFER (RO)
ARCHITECT

DIMITRIOS KAROPOULOS (CA)
LIUSAIDH MACDONALD (GB)
STUDENTS IN ARCHITECTURE

192 SPADINA AVENUE, UNIT 308
TORONTO, ONTARIO M5T 2C2, CA
T. +1 6478387991
OFFICE@ADRIANPHIFFER.COM
WWW.ADRIANPHIFFER.COM

RUNNER-UP - NACKA (SE)
The Ends of the City

TEAM POINT OF VIEW Whilst many contemporary urban themes converge on the Nacka site, how to build the post-oil city? How to build the edge of the city? How to re-adapt industrial sites into domesticated urban areas? How to plan a highly adaptable city? Our proposal brings into light an almost forgotten aspect of urban planning: the resilience of urban form in time. We refuse to accept the dichotomy of Object Vs. Process put forward in the competition brief and prefer to intertwine both concepts as a strategy to plan the Adaptable City.

Despite the magnificent industrial presence on the Nacka site, we have decided not to fall in love with it. Nacka seems to be the type of site where any existing condition can be a solid point of departure in the design process. More than anything, the white tanks are extremely tempting. They are beautiful, yet useless when one has to imagine a city. We prefer to start our project from the most basic condition of the site – the ground. Stripped of any built form, the site presents itself in a "naked" position revealing a complex collection of plateaus where different urban realities can be imagined. The proposed plan accepts the fragmented nature of the ground and takes it as a theme. Each plateau seems to dictate what it should hold above it. This understanding of the site forms the basis for a design made up of solitary urban moments that vary in type.

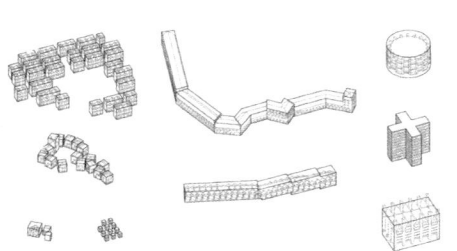

JURY POINT OF VIEW "The resilience of urban form in time" is the key phrase of this proposal, suggesting a dramatic assemblage of typologies. The landscape formation is the starting point of the design. Ten plateaus are identified and given different characters. The proposal offers programmed spaces as well as shelters for informal and temporary use. The buildings are organised to support everyday activities as well as sublime and ceremonial events. The building types are chosen to hold public institutions and shared spaces in cosy enclosures and monumental voids.

THEO STORESUND (SE)
OSKAR GRUNDSTRÖM (SE)
LINDA HÖGBERG ANDERSSON (SE)
ARCHITECTS

BJURHOLMSGATAN 32
11663 STOCKHOLM, SE
T. +46 704883312
OSGRUND@GMAIL.COM
LINDA.HOGAND@GMAIL.COM
THEOSTORESUND@GMAIL.COM

SPECIAL MENTION - NACKA (SE)

ABC–X

TEAM POINT OF VIEW ABC-X is a proposal for the area of Bergs with mainly three urban rules applied. They make the area accessible in three ways; horizontal streets to make it accessible for transport, vistas going up the hill to give a clear order of the area, and reserved round footprints from the demolished oil cisterns to create focal points of different sizes. Low-rise housing/workspace cover the rest of the area. The proposal enhances what we call the X-factor –the ability to communicate both internally and externally– and tries to take the idea of the communal ABC-cities from the 60's further.

NATALIE ADELHOEFER (SE)
RUBEN STUIJK (BE)
ARCHITECTS

RUDOLFSTRAAT 55
2018 ANTWERPEN, BE
T. +49 1637097601
T. +32 474835931
NATALIE.ADELHOEFER@GMX.DE
RUBEN.STUIJK@GMAIL.COM
WWW.NATALIE-ADELHOEFER.BLOGSPOT.SE

SPECIAL MENTION - NACKA (SE)

Decks and String

TEAM POINT OF VIEW Reconnecting Bergs to Nacka municipality
The project reuses the site's defined features as the three existing platforms, footprints and links by transforming them with the help of two decks (new built structure, two platforms) and a string (light structure, walk- and bicycle ways) into new housing and recreational spaces. Both decks overlap in a central part creating a dense urban atmosphere while leaving the rest of the site as open un-built spaces. The buildings on top of the decks offer cross-connections and views of each building with both natural green spaces and fantastic views over the waterfront and the city of Stockholm.

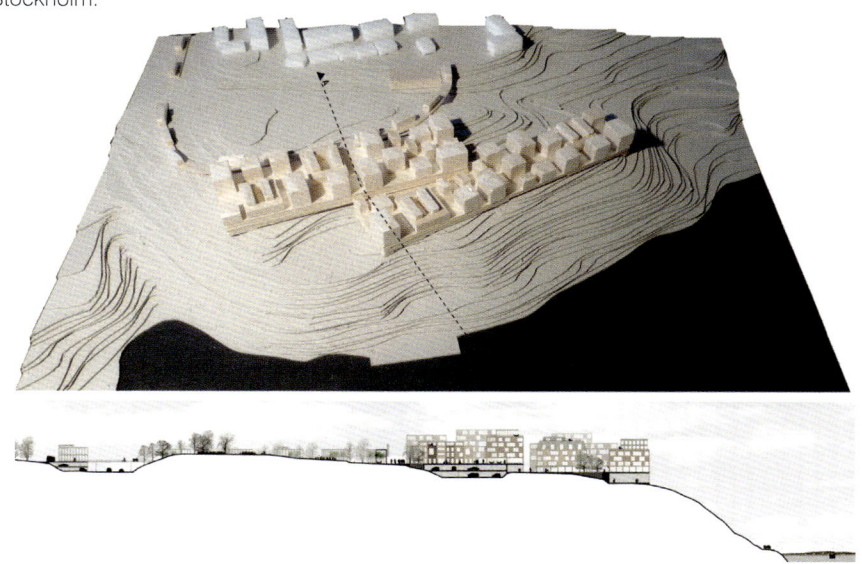

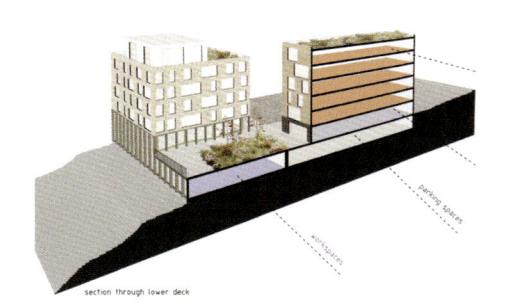

JOHAN ALTENIUS (SE)
KAROLINA ÖRNEBLAD (SE)
ARCHITECTS-URBANISTS
JENNY OLAUSSON (SE)
ARCHITECT

ESPERANTOPLATSEN 7-9
41119 GÖTEBORG, SE
T +46 709955251
INFO@ALSTUDIO.SE

DAVID BONSIB (SE)
DANIEL LARSSON (SE)
JOHANNA LJUNGDAHL LUNDBERG (SE)
ARCHITECTS-URBANISTS
EIRINI FARANTATOU (GR)
ARCHITECT

URBAN MINDS
TRIEWALDSGRÄND 1
11129 STOCKHOLM, SE
T. +46 735844981
DAVID@URBANMINDS.SE
WWW.URBANMINDS.SE

SPECIAL MENTION - NACKA (SE)

New Cityfront Closer to Nature

TEAM POINT OF VIEW Bergs unique location by the water on the boundary between the city and nature makes it a place with great potential to develop new attractive and sustainable housing and businesses and become a meeting place for outdoor recreation in close proximity to the city. A mixed building structure with a varied and small-scale property division is proposed in the area with respect to landscape and views over the sea. The expansion is proposed to stages and accommodates dwellings of approximately 170,000 sqm, services and commercial, space for activities, ecosystem services and outdoor recreation.

SPECIAL MENTION - NACKA (SE)

The Hanging Gardens City of Bergs

TEAM POINT OF VIEW The proposal focuses on topics as the connection between private and public, nature and the city. How could a new structure ensure vibrant life or diversity in an outpost location by exploiting the direct link between the city and the sea? The development is set out to be an on-going process and the project creates a structure of negotiation through a role-play. The approach of battling to reach land subdivision agreements is stimulating and points toward new participatory planning tools with a result that gives back more to the city than it takes.

ZAGREB
HRVATSKA (HR)

CATEGORY: **URBAN - ARCHITECTURAL**
LOCATION: **ZAGREB**
POPULATION: **790,000 INHAB.**
STRATEGIC SITE / PROJECT SITES:
1.5 HA +4.5 HA +5.8 HA +16 HA
SITE PROPOSED BY: **CITY OF ZAGREB**

OWNER(S) OF THE SITE: **CITY OF ZAGREB, PRIVATE OWNERS**
COMMISION AFTER COMPETITION: **THE SITES ARE PROPOSED FOR TEMPORARY PUBLIC USE, ORGANIZED BY THE CITY IN COOPERATION WITH NGOS, CITIZENS' ORGANIZATIONS AND SIMILAR STAKEHOLDERS**

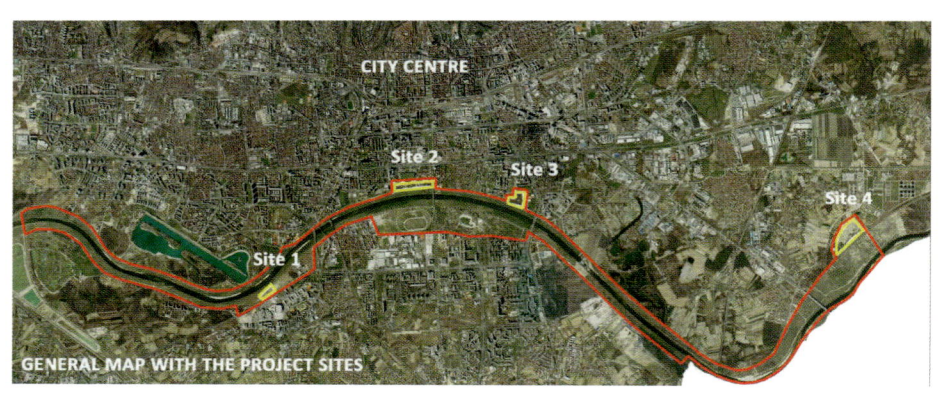

Interview of the site's representative

Ana Magdic, Architect, City Office of Strategic Planning and Development, City of Zagreb

PRESENTATION OF THE SITE WITH REGARDS TO STRATEGY

The city of Zagreb proposed four sites positioned along the Sava river, derelict and unused at the moment, yet with a potential to provide good and dynamic public space. The aim of the project is to propose experimental uses on sites of high attractive potential, on which renewal and development has stopped due to various circumstances, transition processes or economic situation. While waiting for the final use of the proposed sites, the City proposes to launch a reflection for new temporary uses. The expected result is a representation of possible public use scenarios for derelict spaces through the implementation of new activities, accessible to the public, while avoiding aggressive and permanent interventions in space.

HOW IS THE SITE CONNECTED TO THE SESSION TOPIC - THE ADAPTABLE CITY?

The program can be associated to each of the three subthemes of adaptable city: self-organization; inclusion of the inhabitants into the decision-making process is considerable through NGOs and citizens' organizations; sites can be shared both in terms of purpose and in terms of time.

DID YOU DEFINE A SPECIFIC PROCESS FOR THE URBAN DEVELOPMENT OF THE SITE AFTER EUROPAN COMPETITION?

There is a recommendation that after the competition the City of Zagreb and Europan should organize a seminar and invite the authors of both prize-winners to elaborate on the entries and bring light onto the social context – and where presentation to all stakeholders and interested public would be first step in process to follow.

GENERAL MAP WITH THE PROJECT SITES

CARLOS ZARCO SANZ (ES)
SARA PALOMAR PEREZ (ES)
ZUHAL KOL (TR)
JOSE LUIS HIDALGO (ES)
ARCHITECTS

JOAQUIN COSTA 4, 3B
28200 (S. L. DE EL ESCORIAL) MADRID, ES
T. +34 626197758
INFO@OPENACT.EU
WWW.OPENACT.EU

WINNER - ZAGREB (HR)
Swap on the River

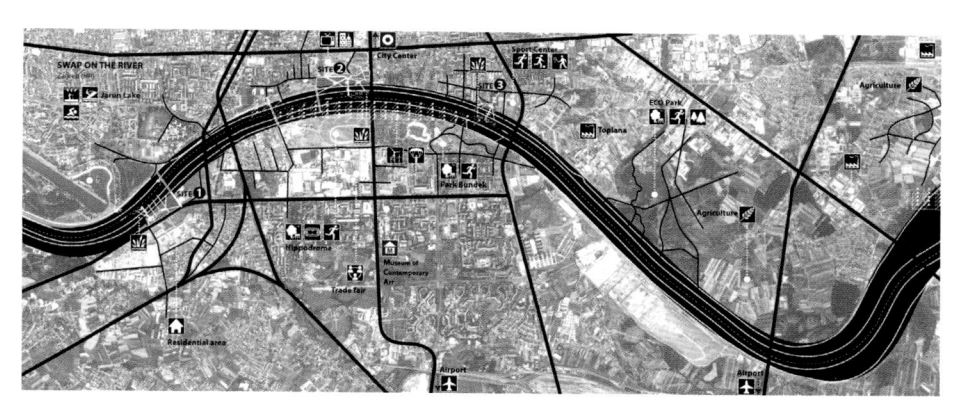

TEAM POINT OF VIEW As the river runs through approximately 20 km adjacent to the city, the question raises as how intervention on four separate sites can have holistic effect to change movements and relationships of the entire river with the city. Therefore, the proposal introduces a framework of negotiation in which a constant conversation of the sites/their surroundings/programs is promoted through movement and exchange on/around the water. Since this framework strategy requires tactics to be supported and operated in different levels, the project functions on three scales of interventions: XL – river and city; L – four sites and their surroundings; S,M – activator pavilions and their combinations. This multi-scalar approach develops a design mechanism allowing for change and adaptation but still enabling the uniformity of the design as long as it serves within the main envelope of negotiation. The common concerns of each scale tactics are allowing flexible development; anticipating active participation of the user and ecology; conceiving continuous and legible spatial organization for more interaction; while considering the significance of open spaces as public spaces and addressing these issues in multiple program scenarios in the process of new culture.

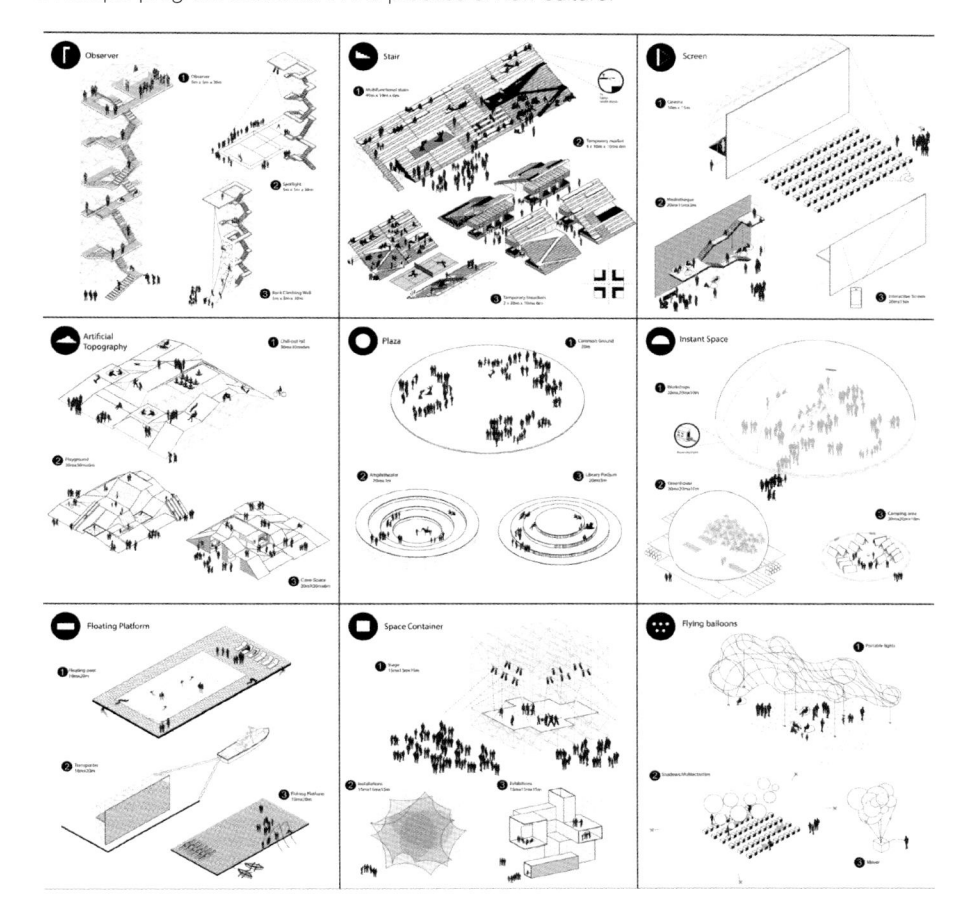

JURY POINT OF VIEW The project offers a good connection between the four sites and the different uses proposed are well built in. It has a very clear graphic outline and a very reasonable intellectual viewpoint. The proposal creates visual links in order to attract people who would normally settle in areas of the old centre of Zagreb. With the appropriate tools, this work regenerates the totality of the four sites and gives their exiting character a new physical and social identity without forgetting an adequate structural and ecological approach.

EMANUELE ROMANI (IT)
FRANCESCA CODEN (IT)
FILIPPO PASINI (IT)
MARGHERITA LOCATELLI (IT)
ARCHITECTS
ALESSANDRO BENETTI (IT)
LORENZO SANTOSUOSSO (IT)
ARCHITECTS-URBANISTS

127 AVENUE PHILIPPE AUGUSTE
75011 PARIS, FR
T. +33 662211285
OFFICINA.OBLO@GMAIL.COM
WWW.OBLO.CC

RUNNER-UP - ZAGREB (HR)
Hey! There is a River Beyond

TEAM POINT OF VIEW How to reintroduce a permanent strategic value to Sava River through its temporary re-design?
This fundamental question involves a series of challenges that the project has to deal with: some areas would probably undergo a permanent development in the next years, while an overall metropolitan strategy should be outlined, undisclosing the potential of the Sava River beyond its actual situation. These premises suggest the definition of a set of rules, parameters and models that would possibly be developed to rebuild a long lost relationship between the city and the River. The answers look for a more polarized layout of the riverfront: the specific features of each site are enhanced and integrated to the Sava network. A sensible and delicate approach is developed, one that has more to deal with participatory and architectural acupuncture than with traditional pervasive urban planning. Inhabitants regain awareness of the landscape by being directly involved in an open source strategy, while architects act as mediators and coordinators converging all the actors involved and supporting the municipality during the whole process.
In search of a physical and social adaptability the project responds to the current economic circumstances, getting maximum results at the lower costs. By all these means, the project would possibly generate a flywheel effect on the city and the region.

JURY POINT OF VIEW The project reads the four sites as four different conditions of how the urban fabric interacts with the River Sava. It adopts a two-lane strategy: to increase the continuity of soft traffic circulation along Sava; and to develop a strategy of diversification of the four sites to a broad range from urban activation. Intelligent tools of urban acupuncture and process of participation envision the change of the sites. But the proposed elements do not seem strong enough to really trigger the change towards more urban activity as stated in the project.

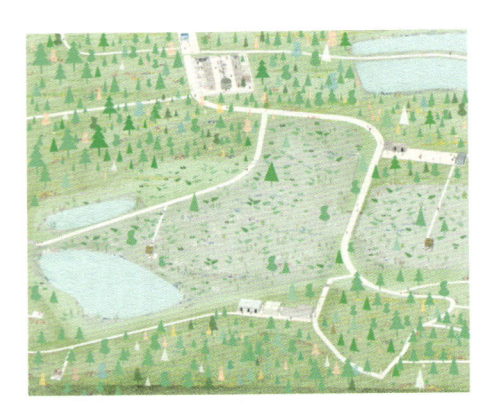

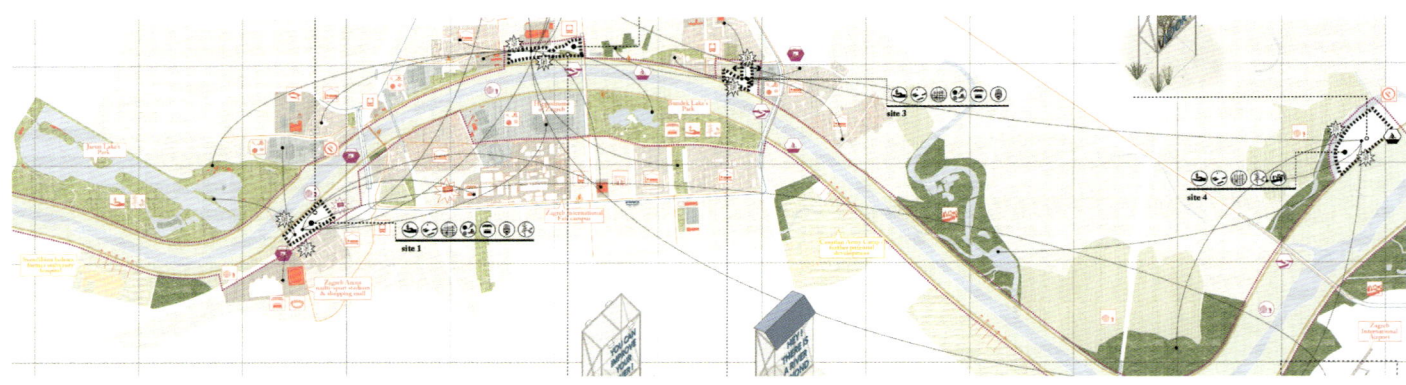

HOW TO TRANSFORM PHYSICAL OBSTACLES INTO NEW CONNECTIONS?

Point of view: Physical and Strategic Obstacles to Revitalisation   p. 66
by Aglaée Degros and Mathias Rollot

A Coruña (ES)	p. 74
Bamberg (DE)	p. 78
Gjakova (KO)	p. 82
Graz (AT)	p. 86
Ingolstadt (DE)	p. 88
Irún (ES)	p. 92
Libramont (BE)	p. 96
Marne-la-Vallée (FR)	p. 98
Moulins (FR)	p. 102
Os (NO)	p. 106
Palma (ES)	p. 110
Saint-Brieuc (FR)	p. 114
Seinäjoki (FI)	p. 118

We understand "bridges" as linear connections between different contexts spanning over a barrier, which may be a river, a railway track or other physical obstacles. But we can sometimes transform the obstacle so that it allows movement in different senses and directions, becoming a connecting element rather than separating barrier. The obstacle may be inhabited, cut or criss-crossed; it can become an opportunity to increase density, change the functions on either side or bring a new perspective to a familiar context.

AGLAÉE DEGROS, co-founder of Artgineering, an urban design agency in Rotterdam (NL) and Brussels (BE). Cosmopolis guest professor in the department of Geography at Vrije Universiteit Brussels. Member of Europan's Scientific Council.
www.artgineering.nl

MATHIAS ROLLOT, Doctor in Architecture, investigating-commissioner and co-founder of LAMAA (L'atelier pour le Maintien d'une Architecture Artisanale), Paris (FR). Member of Europan's Technical Committee.
www.lamaa.org

Point of view
Physical and Strategic Obstacles to Revitalisation

'France embodies everything religious zealots everywhere hate: enjoyment of life here on earth in a myriad little ways: a fragrant cup of coffee and a buttery croissant in the morning, beautiful women in short dresses smiling freely on the street, the smell of warm bread, a bottle of wine shared with friends, a dab of perfume, children playing in the Luxembourg Gardens, the right not to believe in any god, not to worry about calories, to flirt and smoke and enjoy sex outside marriage, to take vacations, to read any book you like, to go to school for free, to play, to laugh, to argue, to make fun of prelates and politicians alike, to leave worrying about the afterlife to the dead…"

This fine passage published in the *New York Times* following the attacks of November 13 is about France, but it also sums up the very essence of European urban life. It touches us as urban designers and architects because it is a reminder of how in Europe we have created a spatial environment suited to a free and open way of life: streets lined with café terraces, squares where events are staged, parks where children play…

For this free and open way of life to be able to develop, the city is constantly adapted, regenerated, reinvented. And there is no doubt that the challenges it faces today – demographic, economic, sociological, ecological – entail enormous changes; it has to tackle its weaknesses and failures while retaining the territorial strengths that give free rein to urban life.

While these weaknesses are primarily social, we should not forget that many cities are, at this time, places in crisis[1], with extreme social and economic divisions, where wealthy and luxurious neighbourhoods sit alongside dingy areas with very high levels of poverty and unemployment, with the emergence of unprecedented urban violence, like the assaults committed on the concourse of Cologne station during the 2016 New Year festivities. Many cities need to deal with their own spatial weaknesses, whether arising from growth, decline, or simply geographical location. These difficulties take a number of forms. First, there is the position of the railway, which divides the city into different entities: from the part "in front of" the station to the more neglected part "behind", from the part that is too close and therefore affected by noise, to the part that is too far away to benefit… Then there are river crossings, which can cause segregation between left and right bank, like the Allier in Moulins (FR) which creates a sharp division between centre and periphery (fig.1). Or there are the roads, which produce such environmental problems that they damage local quality of life and are unhealthy to live near…

Today's city is, more than ever, a fragmented territory marked by numerous physical and nonphysical fractures.

Some of the fractures mentioned above are clearly obstacles inherited from the European city's industrial past: rail infrastructure, large-scale road infrastructure and river structures. For its part, modern urban design has treated them as boundaries that define areas. Canarias Avenue in Palma (ES), a six-lane barrier, separates the beach area from the residential fabric (fig.2). In this approach to urbanism, spatial distribution is based on the setting of surfaces and boundaries. It is not well suited to our contemporary, post-industrial era, in which it is connection that is considered to be fundamental.

This is an issue that the French philosopher Edgar Morin covers extensively in his work. Explaining in *La Méthode* that "knowing is first about being able to distinguish, and then linking what has been distinguished", he emphasises the value of the link and the fact that complexity, which characterises our modern world and the kind of thinking it needs, comes from the Latin word "complexus" which means binding. There is no doubt that this is the biggest current challenge facing our profession, to create links between the fragments of the city so that life can freely unfold in it.

In the category of projects submitted for the Europan 13 competition "How to transform physical obstacles into new connections?" the entrants and winners all clearly identified the fragments of cities to be linked, caused by the physical obstacles. Most of these fragments were in fact clearly indicated in the site descriptions. Most of the entrants also subscribed to the post-industrial urbanistic vision of creating links between the fragments. It was in the implementation of the strategy that they differed, choosing between three categories of approach: Using construction to reconnect and regenerate; Drawing on local dynamics to create links; Revealing and modelling the specific potential of boundaries.

1 - MOULINS (FR)

2 - PALMA (ES)

Using construction to reconnect and regenerate (fig.3)

Among these winning projects, a first group of responses chose as their solution the design of a large-scale architectural or urban ensemble. Their response to the multiple risks of segregation is to commit to a city of sharing. Our examples for this group are the winning projects on the St-Brieuc (FR), Os (NO), Irún (ES), Bamberg (DE) and Graz (AT) sites. To begin with St-Brieuc, the winning project here looked at the possibility of establishing new connections between the large-scale mobility networks, the territory and the coastal landscape. The quest here is to establish a new dialogue between city and nature and to examine the territorial identity that may arise from this exchange. It was in this effort to redirect the city towards the sea and to reassemble the "landscape-puzzle" that the team conceived *Seaside Boulevard* (fig.4), Forming a circular shape that is both a matrix connected with the existing fabric and at the same time a "promotional space" for potential future developments, this boulevard acts as a tool that helps to span the difficult geography that characterises the town. A structuring narrative that forms the basis for multiple potential openings, it is also a symbolic proposal, which seeks to transform not only practices but also the imaginative experience of the place.

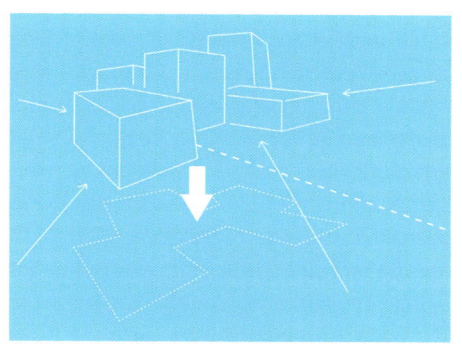

3 - USING CONSTRUCTION

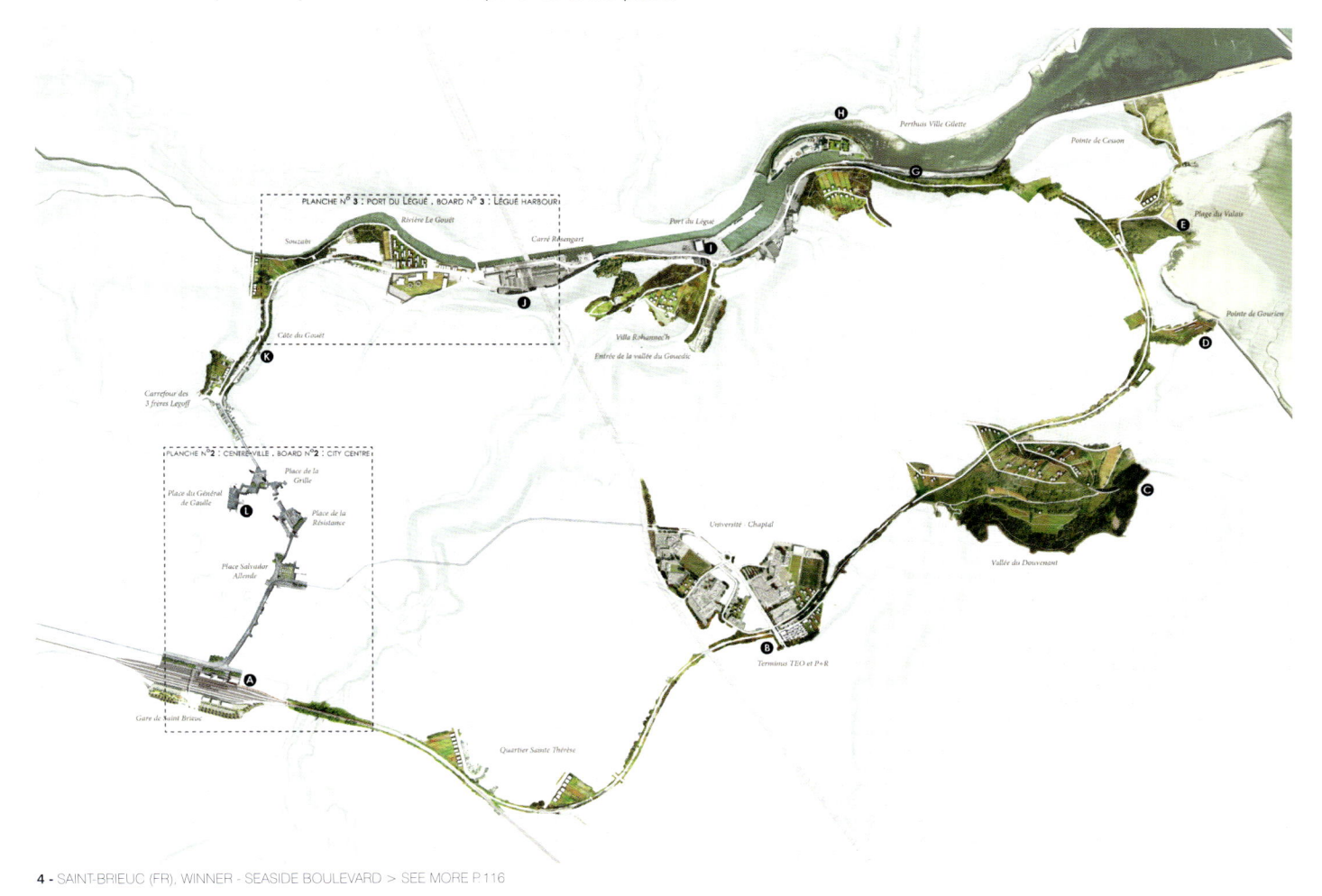

4 - SAINT-BRIEUC (FR), WINNER - SEASIDE BOULEVARD > SEE MORE P.116

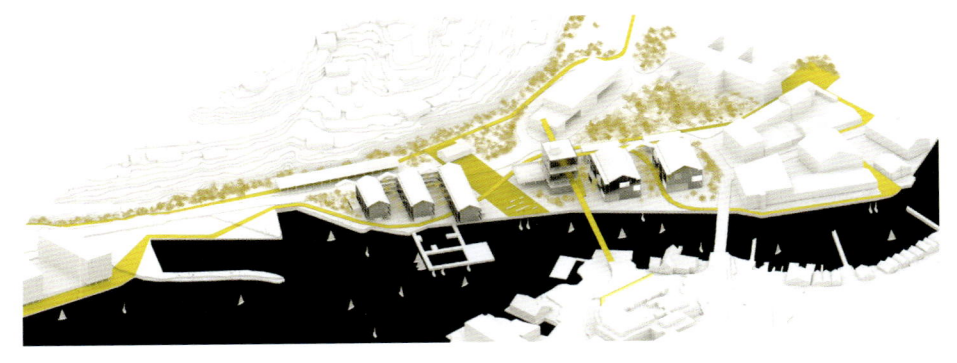

5 - OS (NO), WINNER - OSURBIA - REDEFINING SUBURBIA > SEE MORE P.107

In a somewhat similar way, in Os, the winning project also proposes working between mobility structures and built fabric. On this site, the task was to transform a small, disparate fabric that was blocking a dialogue between the town centre and the seafront: how could this place become a new area capable of reconnecting a fabric and disconnected banks? In an exploration of the meaning of "suburban", the team identifies and proposes to reinterpret 6 specific icons: the individual dwelling, the car park, the shopping centre, the gas station, cultural identity and the structural axis. This is how *Osurbia - Redefining Suburbia* (fig.5) seeks to respond to future demographic change in Os, while at the same time preserving its identity in a possible move towards an "osurbia" capable of physically crossing the existing obstacles and forming an attractive new urban polarity.

For Irún, the task was to work on the relation between the city and its large rail centre. The runner-up project *Ura Eta Natura* (fig.6), stresses the importance of thinking about urban transformation in terms of natural ecosystems and a productive inhabited landscape. It therefore incorporates the station site into reflections and studies relating to a larger geographical area, approaching the need to cross the rails as only part of a necessary set of reconnection projects situated at different places and different scales. In this way, it demonstrates that there is no incompatibility

6 - IRÚN (ES), RUNNER-UP - URA ETA NATURA > SEE MORE P.93

7 - BAMBERG (DE), WINNER - TRADITION . ADAPTION : VERKNUEPFUNG > SEE MORE P. 79

between the need for physical connection, a dense urban fabric, and landscape quality and the presence of nature.

In Bamberg, the goal was to work out new dynamics between the town centre, the station and the fast developing Bamberg East district. The question was how to fit in with the changes already underway, and pursue and reinforce the processes of revitalising this large, disparate urban fabric. To answer this question, the winning team focused its efforts on highlighting an urban project capable of improving the structure of the built fabric, establishing new public spaces, offering a wider choice in terms of mobility and programme, while at the same time unifying the neighbourhood within a new, more legible structure. In all this, the claim made by *Tradition: Adaptation: Verknuepfung* (fig.7) is that it is by focusing on the development of the district itself that the problems of disconnection caused by the rails can be resolved.

Libramont too faces problems in matching rail infrastructure to urban fabric. The special mention project *50 Shades of green* (fig.8), proposes densifying the competition site through further construction. Grasping the possibility of building on either side of the rail front, it proposes the creation of a new, relatively dense district, with an emphasis on urban agriculture. In this, it too seems to wish to show how the issue is not just one of rail crossings and station access, but also of giving meaning to the whole urban area around.

8 - LIBRAMONT (BE), SPECIAL MENTION - 50 SHADES OF GREEN > SEE MORE P. 97

9 - GRAZ (AT), WINNER - WALZER > SEE MORE P.87

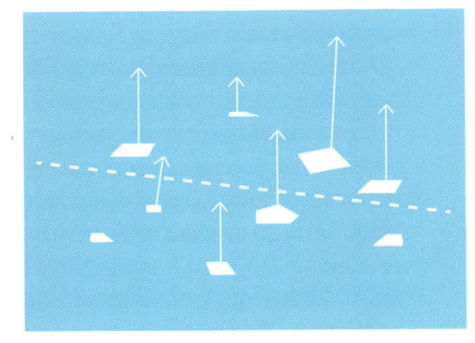

10 - DRAWING ON DYNAMICS

In Graz, finally, the municipality was looking for a proposal for the conversion of a site situated in front of the railway line and the station. Here, the physical fracture caused by the railway line was minimised by the winning project *Walzer* (fig.9), by means of a very thorough multi-functional programme. Simultaneously hybrid and unitary, durable and adaptable, assertive and discreet, the formal proposition ignores paradoxes to offer a high quality architectural ensemble. It is "by giving a new reason" for crossing the railway line, it might be said, that the project spots the possibility for a more successful connection with the town centre, and convinces in its design of a structuring element for the metamorphosis of the district.

Drawing on local dynamics to create links (fig.10)

Every one of these submissions shows the capacity of the teams to propose a high-quality urban-architectural solution, capable of creating links beyond the obstacle in question, but also more broadly to regenerate not only the urban sites presented for the competition but also their surrounding areas. In quite a different way, a second set of proposals chose to tackle the obstacles by focusing instead on the local and micro scale, networking and bottom-up processes. Innumerable responses took this approach. Here, we will look at the winning projects on the sites in Gjakova (KO), Moulins (FR) and Ingolstadt (DE), and show how all these winning projects, whether rhizomatic, thematic or conceptual, are strategies that focus on stimulating citizen involvement in order to link and revitalise the sites.

In the case of Gjakova, the objective is to grasp the potential offered by the watersides. Currently unused despite their advantageous urban location – right in the heart of the town – can these docks be redeveloped at limited cost? To prove it, the winning team (fig.11) highlights the capacity of cultural activities and events to promote temporary uses of the place, with little need for initial facilities or physical transformations. By identifying areas capable of accommodating concerts, summer film screenings or seasonal markets, *SEAMbiosis* makes a persuasive case: from small elements inserted here and there (wooden decking, built-in benches, "treasure hunts", etc.), substantial urban dynamics could emerge.

The riverbanks at Moulins were also one of the sites in this session's competition. Larger in scale, and creating a much greater discontinuity between the two sides of the river, these banks undoubtedly constitute a missed opportunity. Drawing on a theoretical alignment between Lamarck's "transformism" and Darwin's "evolutionism", the project conceives and presents its proposals within a unified perspective. Through this distinctive interpretative framework, the winning team proposes in *The Theory of Evolution* (fig.12) nine different initiatives ranging from the architectural conversion of sheds to the planting of trees, from the invention of a "viewpoint-slide" to the installation of an "amphibious neighbourhood" or houses on stilts. In each case, the idea is the same: with a renewed dialogue between the wider landscape and human habitat, they propose a set of interventions to revitalise local activity and enhance the relationship with the "obstacle" of the River Allier.

While it is not the river that is the issue in Ingolstadt, but rather the problem of urban devitalisation and the need to introduce new force into the relationship between mobility and urban quality, once again it is a unificatory approach that characterises the winning *Waldstrasse project*. Suggesting 25 different, localised actions (setting aside a space for events, adding new bus stops, redrawing the profile of the streets, etc.) on a unified ground space, the proposal seeks to turn the main street into a more attractive linear park, where pedestrian mobility can become more than an environmentally desirable way of moving around by generating new urban practices.

11 - GJAKOVA (KO), WINNER - SEAMBIOSIS > SEE MORE P.83

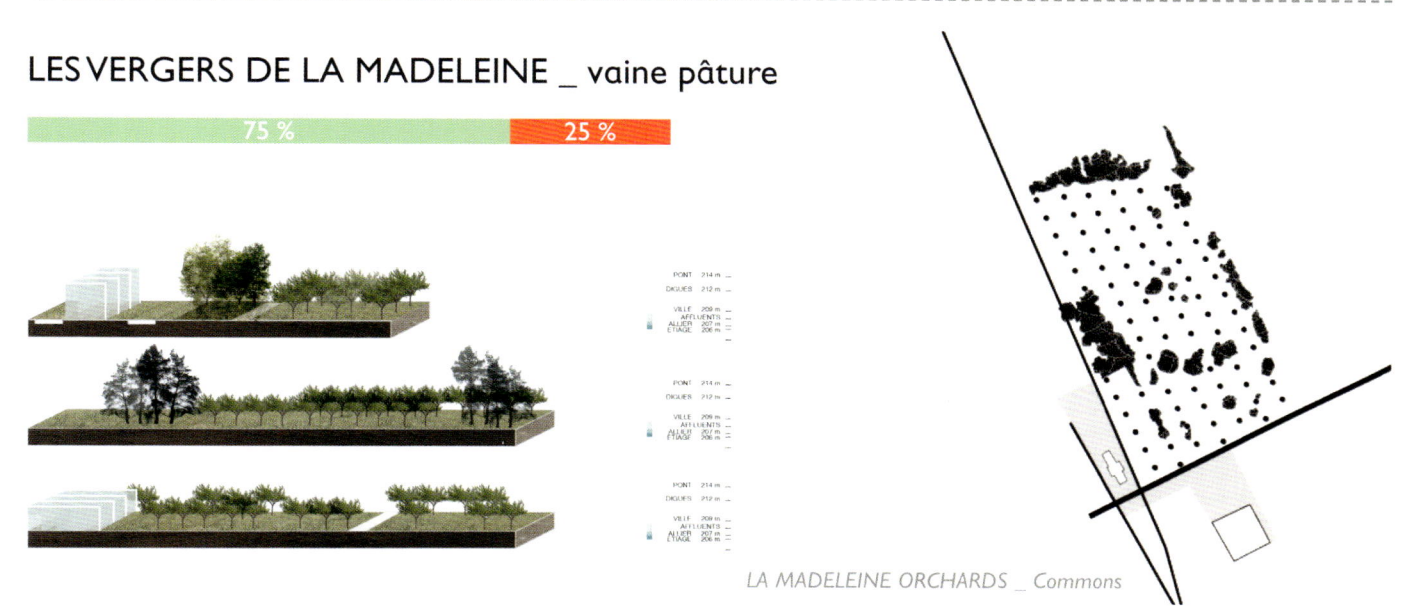

ALLIER   RIPISYLVE   DIGUE   MAISON SUR PILOTIS   3EME FRANCHISSEMENT   FRAYÈRE À SAUMON   QUARTIER AMPHIBIE   71

LES VERGERS DE LA MADELEINE _ vaine pâture

75 %   25 %

LA MADELEINE ORCHARDS _ Commons

12 - MOULINS (FR), WINNER - THE THEORY OF EVOLUTION > SEE MORE P.103

Revealing and modelling the specific potential of boundaries (fig.13)

So as we can see, each of these winners, in its own way, devises other forces of development with the capacity to overcome the real, symbolic or imaginary obstacles that urban dynamics can encounter. And, insofar as they were able to consider the proposed themes of "self-organisation" vs. "welfare state" and "object" vs. "project", they constitute entities that reveal new project trends and practices in Europe.

Finally, a third category of responses invites analysis. These consist of the winning proposals for the sites in A Coruña (ES), Palma (ES), Seinäjoki (FI) and Marne-la-Vallée (FR). In their consideration of the specific architectural and urban potentials associated with boundaries (whether a coast, a motorway or a railway line), these projects seem to have the capacity to devise distinctive arrangements suited to the site concerned and their problems.

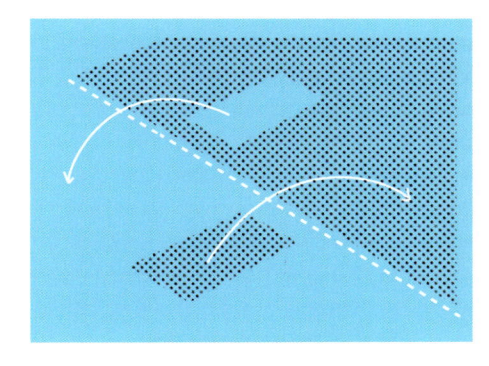

13 - REVEALING AND MODELLING THE POTENTIAL

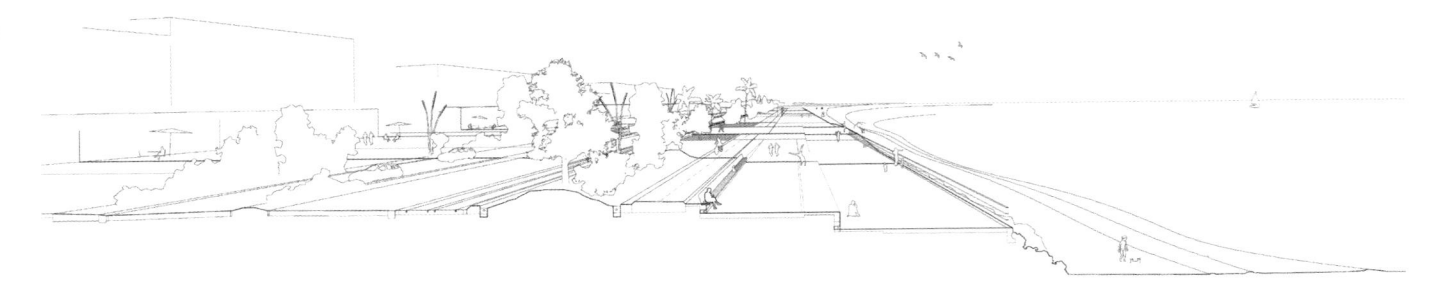

14 - PALMA (ES), WINNER - SALVEMOS EL HORIZONTE > SEE MORE P.111

In Palma, the task was to rethink the city's relationship to the sea. What urban arrangements could replace the current major road to accommodate a set of more sustainable and desirable forms of mobility, better able to connect the built fabric with the seafront? The winning project *Salvemos el horizonte* (fig.14), chooses to work with the site's distinctive feature: the horizon. Arguing that one of the objectives lies in the "non-construction" of the site, the project redraws street profiles that are more hospitable to walking and suitable for the creation of a genuinely shared public space.

For this session, the town of A Coruña proposed a complex site, a large heterogeneous fabric between a major road infrastructure and a waterfront. The question was what status and future should be devised for this territory with its multiple identities, and what crossings to introduce in order to make access easier. The *Nice to 'Sea' You* project won the competition by proposing a phased process in which this "unproductive" zone would be converted into a "productive" territory. Drawing on this leitmotif to enhance the area's capacities to host leisure, production, housing or mobility systems, the proposal also sought to show the economic credibility (notably in terms of attractiveness and therefore the potential for public-private partnerships) of such ideas in stimulating "productivity".

In Seinäjoki, the potential of the boundary revealed by the winning project (fig.15) was quite different; *Notch* sees a site that calls for a remodelling of the relationship between a station and its surroundings as an invitation to architectural invention: what does it mean to live and work every day by the railway line, and how can architecture itself be open to this specific situation? The winning team responds, in particular, with a set of hexagonal geometries as a matrix for new housing typologies perhaps more suited to the conditions of life by a railway line.

In response to the discontinuity caused by the divisive road infrastructures in Marne-la-Vallée, the winning project *Ville N(M)ature* (fig.16) explores the history of the location to highlight the great strength of this territory located at the interface between city and nature. Developing the multiple ways in which this boundary situation could be better presented, it seeks to introduce a more resilient urban form, with better managed interfaces, by proposing new uses (housing, "observation places", arrangements of public space, etc.) for the "green lane" produced by this metamorphosis. Also an opportunity to reinitiate the architectural experiments that may have accompanied the creation of these new towns, argues the team. In short, combating powerful processes of compartmentalisation through a revitalisation strategy that once again entails the highlighting and development of the particular situations created by the physical obstacle, rather than necessarily crossing it at all costs.

Adaptable urbanities, between ambition and practicality

One may begin by concluding that although the winners propose to introduce built structures to regenerate the city, they do not see these structures as finished objects but rather as projects that progress in stages. In other words, this is less about fixed objects than projects that evolve, adapt, are constructed gradually.

In fact, the awareness of economic uncertainties, but also of the difficulty of implementing "turnkey" projects on sites containing obstacles and therefore involving numerous actors (road companies, rail companies, river management bodies…) encouraged the winners not only to develop phased implementation processes, but also to propose solutions that recruit the various existing and potential actors of urban production, to devise innovative participatory processes, and finally to create new openings for possible catalysts for implementation (establishment of alternative economic arrangements, development of management structures, etc.).

Therefore, although all the projects propose spatial solutions to the crossing of physical obstacles, they also combine these solutions with nonphysical strategies.

In all this, the projects often consider more than the spatial framework alone, acquiring a social, economic and even ecological dimension. Similarly, the notion of adaptability has not been understood simply in its functional sense, but has been employed more broadly by the teams, to encompass the temporal, structural, or even symbolic dimension. Each of these axes constitutes a new approach to the understanding and conception of human settlements and their metamorphoses.

By way of conclusion, we would note that these projects are (in the large majority) extremely modest and pragmatic: no big engineering or architectural gestures, instead frugal and contextualised strategies… Something that was undoubtedly much appreciated by the municipalities present for the discussions at the Cities and Juries Forum. However, in these gloomy times, one may perhaps regret the absence of fantasy and ambition, a hint of folly that could give us food for dreaming in the future? More than ever, it is important to argue – perhaps a little too loudly – in favour of ambition for quality of life, openness and freedom for the "European city", It is our task to imagine and implement urban spaces that are ethically committed to what constitutes the strength of our shared urban virtues: their capacity to accommodate both the singularity of the individual and the breadth of the universal.

[1] OVINK, H, INTERVIEW VAI, 2015

15 - SEINÄJOKI (FI), WINNER - NOTCH > SEE MORE P.119

16 - MARNE-LA-VALLÉE (FR), WINNER - VILLE N(M)ATURE > SEE MORE P.99

A CORUÑA
ESPAÑA (ES)

CATEGORY: **URBAN – ARCHITECTURAL**
LOCATION: **A CORUÑA. RÍA DEL BURGO**
POPULATION: **245,293 INHAB.**
STRATEGIC SITE: **42.06 HA**
PROJECT SITE: **AREA 1: 6,743 SQM / AREA 2: 6,863 SQM**
SITE PROPOSED BY: **A CORUÑA CITY COUNCIL**

OWNER(S) OF THE SITE: **PUBLIC AND PRIVATE**
COMMISION AFTER COMPETITION: **INCLUSION IN THE TEAM THAT WILL COORDINATE THE PARTICIPATORY PROCESS TO DESIGN TOOLS AND PLANS. POSSIBLE PARTICIPATION IN AN AFTERWARDS PROJECT**

Interview of the site's representative
Department of Urban Regeneration and Right to Housing, Municipality of A Coruña

The ria is a paradigmatic unit of the Galician geography. Its strong identity lies on its shape and milieu. The coast unfolds in a repetition and sequence of rias.

The ria spatial profile –which could also extend to any other Galician geographical form (hence its condition as a paradigm)– is nothing like a river mouth or an estuary. Its space is more than a mere transition as a passage between two milieux: this transit space is also an enclosure in itself, a territoriality. The indication of the way out is shaping this enclosure.

Just like in any other periphery the intervention area of the Ria del Burgo unveils its biases and raises a lot of questions.

Interpreting it as a periphery means that the void –defined by water– imposes itself to the heterogeneous superposition of the urban systems; that continuity is not characterised by the coherence of its look, but rather by its contrast; that it gathers many social exhibition and exclusion; or that no single characteristic stands out, as all the marks on the territory overlap and criss-cross.

We assume that this space accumulates a strong concentration of accidents while the urban systems are constantly mutating after the resolution of so many singularities. The New or the Vernacular almost always emerges this way. As long as we cannot understand it, we will only see disorder.

JUAN MIGUEL SALGADO (ES)
YAGO LISTE (ES)
LUIS SANTALLA (ES)
VANESA VEIRA (ES)
ALBA GONZÁLEZ (ES)
ARCHITECTS

ANDER BADOS (ES)
ANTONIO ANTEQUERA (ES)
DAVID MARIÑO (ES)
ARCHITECTS

ÁNGEL REBOLLO 88, BAJO
15002 A CORUÑA, ES
T. +34 881993083
MAIL@FLU-OR.COM

WINNER - A CORUÑA (ES)
Nice to 'Sea' You

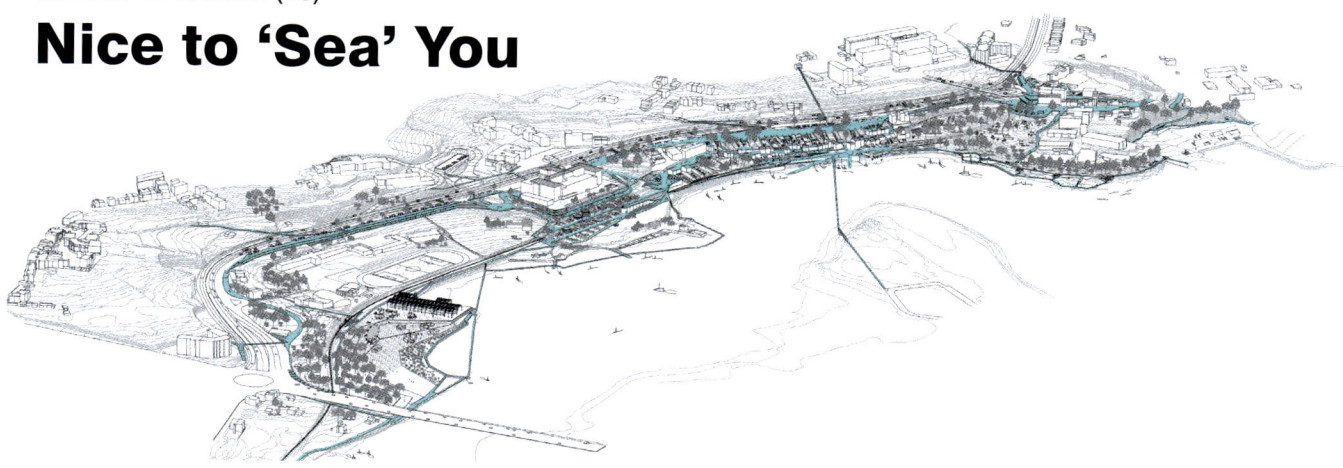

TEAM POINT OF VIEW "Nice to 'Sea' You" is an activation program with public and private initiatives focused on a sphere of actuation with both neighbourhoods of As Xubias and A Pasaxe, including 2% of the city population. It converts the area into a productive neighbourhood.
The area where the sanitary buildings are placed senselessly is defined by an abrupt topography and three lines –highway, train/tram and water border. This space of opportunity is a coastal ecosystem with good capabilities for crops and a periurban field between growing urban areas. Interconnected phases are based on a needed step: public initiatives about enhancing public transports and a strip to solve the highway border and the traffic and parking problems.
The activation program starts with some primary operations: the bridge to Oleiros as a new urban link; the new train/tram public transport with stations both at the new park and square; several transversal connections; a new incentive parking. These measures transform As Xubias in a free-car new urban node.
Public subsidies improve the housing conditions and attract population as irregular settlements are relocated. Building is associated to production, greenhouses, ground cultivation and shell fishing. The productive park is the space for new events and the restored building is a new activity focus. The borderline is turned into a water treatment pond, with a more pleasant sea loch approach.

JURY POINT OF VIEW This project is proposed as a tour of a territory in which small-scale actions trigger the reactivation of various points identified as problem areas. The project does not propose a set of actions. Instead, the actions are related to the itinerary: the sense of transit. The places that are generated are much more than spaces. They are regarded as the result of the joint action of individuals with other individuals or with the space. The project inserts space, time, memory and movement into a single action.

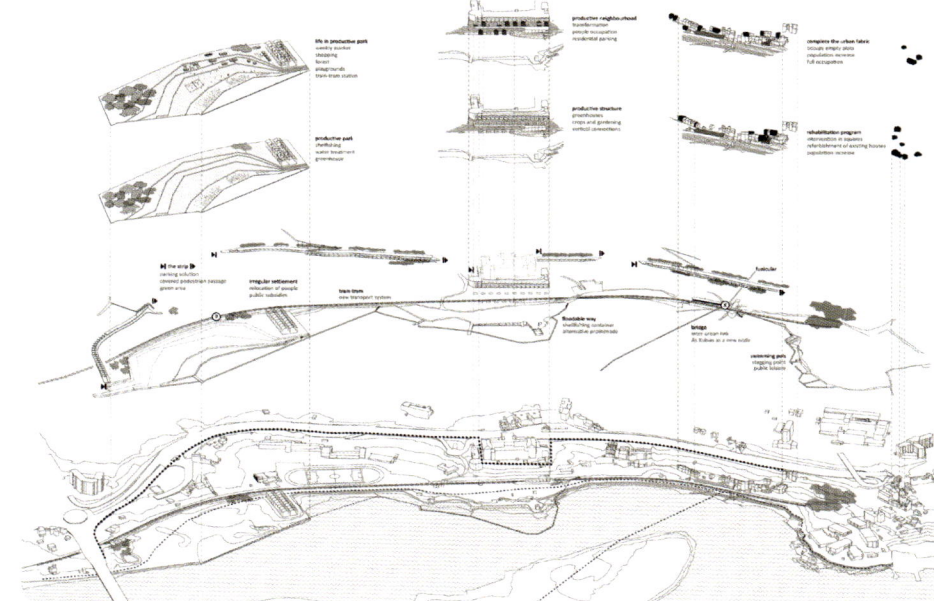

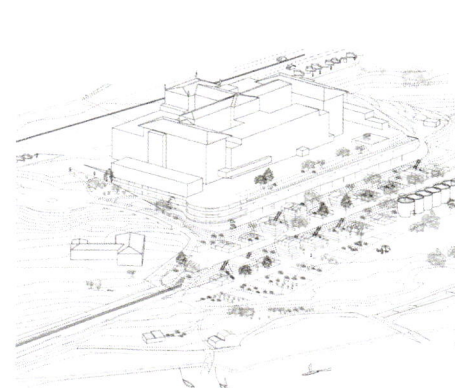

NURIA PRIETO GONZÁLEZ (ES)
ÁNGEL MONTERO PÉREZ (ES)
HUGO MALVAR ÁLVAREZ (ES)
DIEGO LUCIO BARRAL (ES)
OMAR CURROS SIMÓN (ES)
ARCHITECTS

RONDA DE NELLE 144
15010 A CORUÑA, ES
T. +34 661825665
FROM1984TO1989@GMAIL.COM

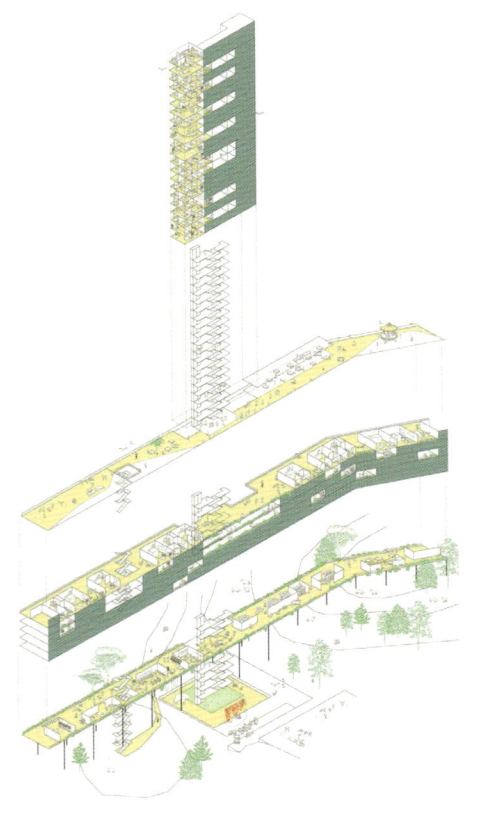

RUNNER-UP - A CORUÑA (ES)
Embroidering the Edge

TEAM POINT OF VIEW "I said: the horizon is a complex of Cartesian lines. Then, he said: because we live in a box over another box, and I said: Life has finally made an impenetrable labyrinth, and he added: Where to know each other is a great adventure, nevertheless, I said: There will always be a place to meet up" (Gallego,1999)
The competition area is an amalgam on the coast border creating a profile. This horizon of complexities has become inflamed, disrupted and entangled over time. At first sight the wounds are visible: disconnection, high speed, marginality. A territory that the city has tried to phagocyte imposing a range of scales that collides with the identity. A place where the landscape sets clues of its open sea condition, tamed in an organic way to find human scale. Four conceptual interventions materialize the project: REstructuration, REorganization of connections and mobility, REactivation of the coastline and REarrangement of the residential fabric.
"In a line the world comes together/With a line the world is divided/Drawing is beautiful and terrible." (Chillida, 2003). Drawing this territory reflects what is worth, only with a few more lines from an architectural project, it shows its nature. Beautiful and terrible, the project in this site is a line that tries to divide the obstacle to make it disappear and to join men and sea nature. A sea that is the main character of a project conceived in a town sculpted by water.

JURY POINT OF VIEW The project uses the observer's personal experience as an activating element for the landscape. This perception helps the project recognize the territorial structure and reconnect it by reorganising the mobility infrastructure and the connections. It also includes a well-though-out revision of the residential fabric with controlled growth adjusted to the operation scale and the proposal of an interesting morphological solution. Doubts subsist about the imposing size of the proposed building and the excessive pressure on a landscape, which the project itself acknowledges as harbouring fragile memories.

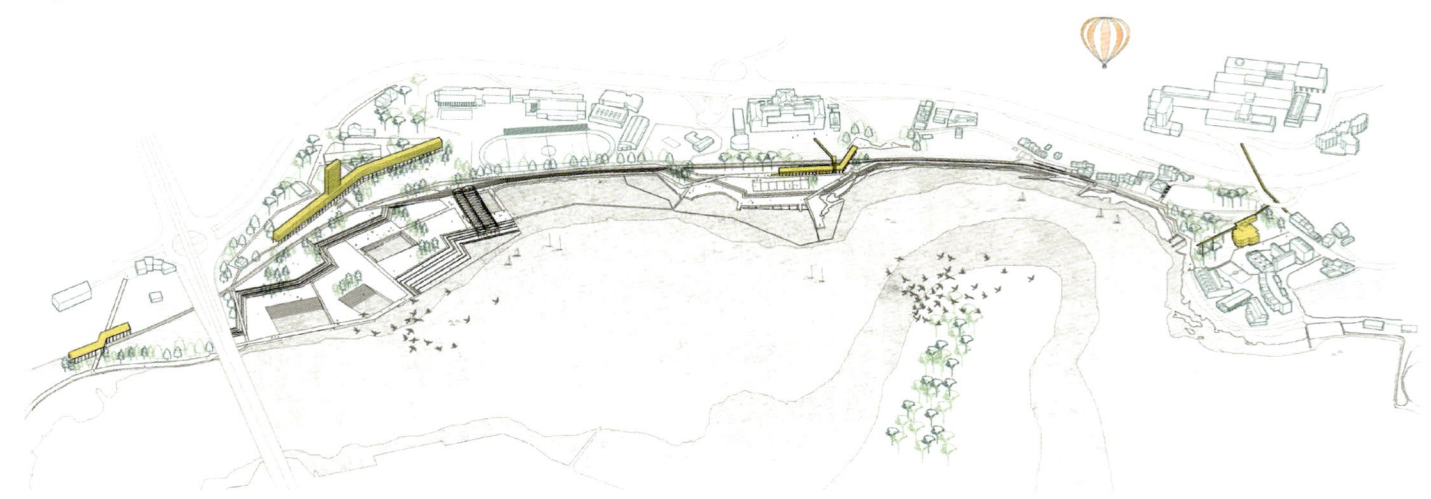

MARÍA MESTRE GARCÍA (ES)
IGNACIO MOREU FERNÁNDEZ (ES)
ALMUDENA MAMPASO CERRILLOS (ES)
GIAMMATTIA BASSANELLO (IT)
ARCHITECTS

MADRID, ES
M3@MOREUMESTRE.COM
WWW.MOREUMESTRE.COM
ROMA, IT
MAMBA.OFFICE@GMAIL.COM
WWW.MAMBAOFFICE.COM

RUNNER-UP - A CORUÑA (ES)
Walk along Burgo's Estuary

TEAM POINT OF VIEW The project proposes a way of working in the environment keeping its own character. It operates recognizing critical situations that can be understood as an obstacle in the landscape.

These situations recognized as operators of the tool, depending on a context that is not visible, abstract and changing, and decisive for the development of the city. This context is considered in a parametric form, generating solutions according to the context. All this allows linking solutions to the public space, generating a connected and constantly renovated landscape, without forgetting the character or basic structure of the territory.

The consideration of this context and the implications of private collective, cooperatives, associations… allow the city to faster and better respond to current needs. The administration has a shared responsibility with citizens in the development of the city, in some cases working as manager or arbitrator.

All these situations or operators are articulated around a common link. The routes organizing the area –the road pasaxe, the pedestrian street, the railway train and the estuary– can generate unity and cohesion in the land regardless of the solution developed. It is possible thanks to the transition spaces-elements-uses that put together each solution with the routes, allowing the understanding of the identity and unitary character of the area.

JURY POINT OF VIEW The project assumes the extreme fragility of the proposed study area and clearly reflects the need to minimize initiatives involving new housing blocks. It proposes a catalogue of initiatives focusing on what already exists and striving to improve it. The result is a detailed sum of local and regenerative interventions entrusted with the task in a possible method of revitalization, aiming to engage private agents as managers of the space under the arbitration of the Administration. The large number of operations entrusted to different stakeholders carries the risk of a complex management of this space as a unitary body.

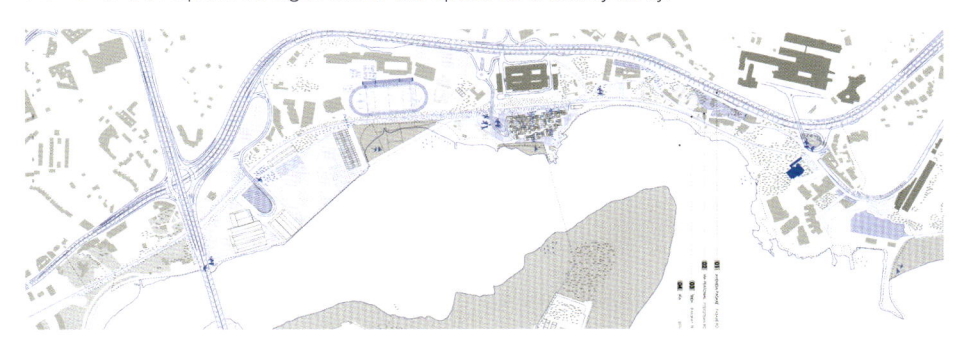

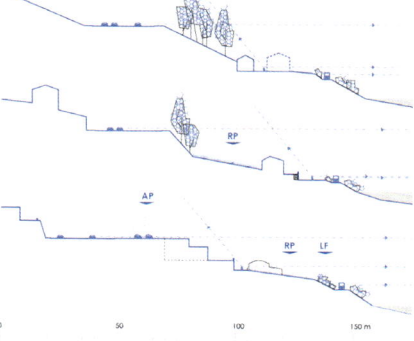

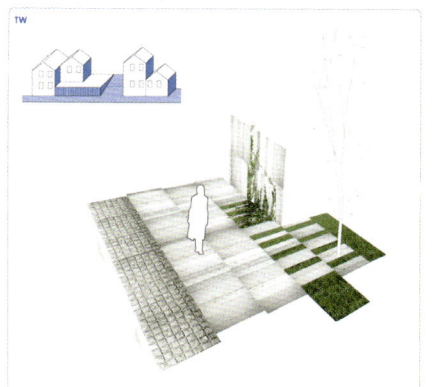

BAMBERG
DEUTSCHLAND (DE)

CATEGORY: **URBAN – LANDSCAPE – ARCHITECTURAL**
LOCATION: **BAMBERG EAST**
POPULATION: **71,000 INHAB.**
STRATEGIC SITE: **200 HA**
PROJECT SITE: **A 5.5 HA / B 18.1 HA / C 6.5 HA**
SITE PROPOSED BY: **BAMBERG CITY COUNCIL**

OWNER(S) OF THE SITE: **BAMBERG CITY COUNCIL, VARIOUS OWNERSHIP (PRIVATE AND PUBLIC) CONVERSION AREAS: FEDERAL REPUBLIC OF GERMANY (BIMA), ACQUISITION BY BAMBERG CITY COUNCIL PLANNED**
COMMISION AFTER COMPETITION:
OUTLINE OR LOCAL DEVELOPMENT PLAN

Interview of the site's representative
Andreas Burr, Municipality of Bamberg, Head of the Urban Planning Authority

PRESENTATION OF THE SITE WITH REGARDS TO STRATEGY
The development of the site should not only contribute to prevent the former military area from isolated development, but also set an impulse for the entire Oststadt. Urban planning interventions should upgrade the existing residential areas and streetscape and improve the link between Bamberg's Oststadt and the town centre.

HOW IS THE SITE CONNECTED TO THE SESSION TOPIC - THE ADAPTABLE CITY?
The site is forced to change and undergo further structural development. Besides classic urban planning tasks such as subsequent densification and the conversion of commercial wastelands into dwellings, conceptual, urban planning, and creative ideas should contribute to strengthen and better link the district. This should result in strengthening the Oststadt and provide impetus for changes. The characteristic special features of the district should, however, not be negated, but the development of an independent identity enhanced instead.

DID YOU DEFINE A SPECIFIC PROCESS FOR THE URBAN DEVELOPMENT OF THE SITE AFTER EUROPAN COMPETITION?
To foster the urban planning development of the site, the residents of the district should be involved in the planning. Information events were already held in the lead-up to the competition and the goal is now to go on with an exhibition. Preparations are already being made for talks with the different property owners, in which the individual aspects of the different tasks will be presented and discussed. In the process, we should also determine the potential subareas available for implementation.

CHRISTIAN EICKELBERG (DE)
ARCHITECT

PLAUENER STRASSE 9
44139 DORTMUND, DE
T. +49 17623756766
EYCKSBERG@GMX.DE

WINNER - BAMBERG (DE)

Tradition : Adaptation : Verknuepfung

TEAM POINT OF VIEW A wide area of railway tracks is dividing the Eastern side of Bamberg –with large barracks to convert into a residential area– from the Western – with the UNESCO World Heritage.

The project proposes a network of small districts with different levels of privacy in combination with new and existing public spaces connecting cycle- and footpaths between the barracks, the adjacent green space of Hauptsmoorwald and the inner city.

Special care is given to the area along the railway. The development is strengthened by the renovation and widening of the Zollnerstraße tunnel and a new direct cycle tunnel, both starting from the new bicycle parking house and the railway station. New buildings are proposed along the railway tracks to adapt and represent the local traditions of gardener culture and baroque style. The baroque principles of overlapping, plasticity and moving observer are translated into contemporary forms. Planted atriums and vertical green walls are references for the gardener culture. Office buildings and parking garages are set along the railway tracks as an acoustic noise barrier for the residential buildings. The design shows how to adapt traditions and to connect it to a subtle network.

JURY POINT OF VIEW The work convinces as a result of a coherent urban development and open space concept characterized by generous interconnections of green areas and paths, precise urban development links via small squares, and structural additions to-scale. The design is distinguished above all by the unorthodox, small-scale construction along the railway tracks. This building structure has the potential to give rise to a new quality at the entrance to the Oststadt, allowing development in small steps and facilitating realization by smaller enterprises and private developers.

BERNARDO GRILLI DI CORTONA (IT)
FRANCESCO CORONA (IT)
FRANCESCA ERRICO (IT)
MARCO MIOTTO (IT)
ARCHITECTS

67 QUAI DE VALMY
75010 PARIS, FR
T. +33 659995374
BEGRILLI@GMAIL.COM

RUNNER-UP - BAMBERG (DE)
CT*Bamberg

TEAM POINT OF VIEW "CT*Bamberg" aims at revitalizing Bamberg East by reinforcing its identity and connecting it to the city. Taking into account the UN post-2015 development agenda –"make cities and human settlements inclusive, safe, resilient and sustainable"–, the project focuses on pedestrians and establishes car-free zones and tramway lines. The 3 areas are seen as parts of the same body –with different functions and abilities, but complementary and moving together in a common direction.
A. Connective Boundary: A multifunctional structure is set close to the railway as a noise barrier, a connection to town, a landmark to attract the tourists and a meeting point for the inhabitants from both parts of the city;
B. Domestic Core: Regeneration of the area through densification and creation of a new public green path and semi-public green spaces opening up some private green spaces set within buildings;
C. Cultural Core: The centre of attraction of the area is contemporary music. The urban tissue is opened to insert new students or young couples houses.

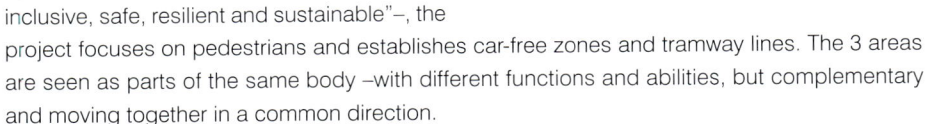

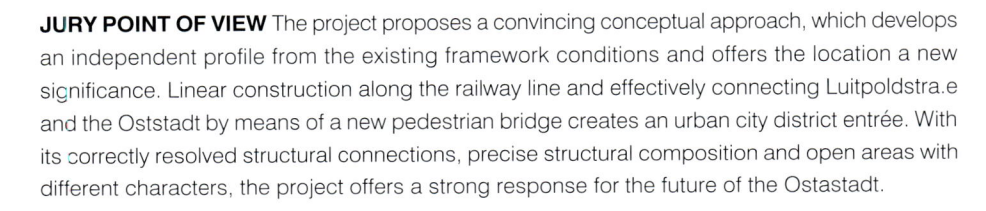

JURY POINT OF VIEW The project proposes a convincing conceptual approach, which develops an independent profile from the existing framework conditions and offers the location a new significance. Linear construction along the railway line and effectively connecting Luitpoldstra.e and the Oststadt by means of a new pedestrian bridge creates an urban city district entrée. With its correctly resolved structural connections, precise structural composition and open areas with different characters, the project offers a strong response for the future of the Ostastadt.

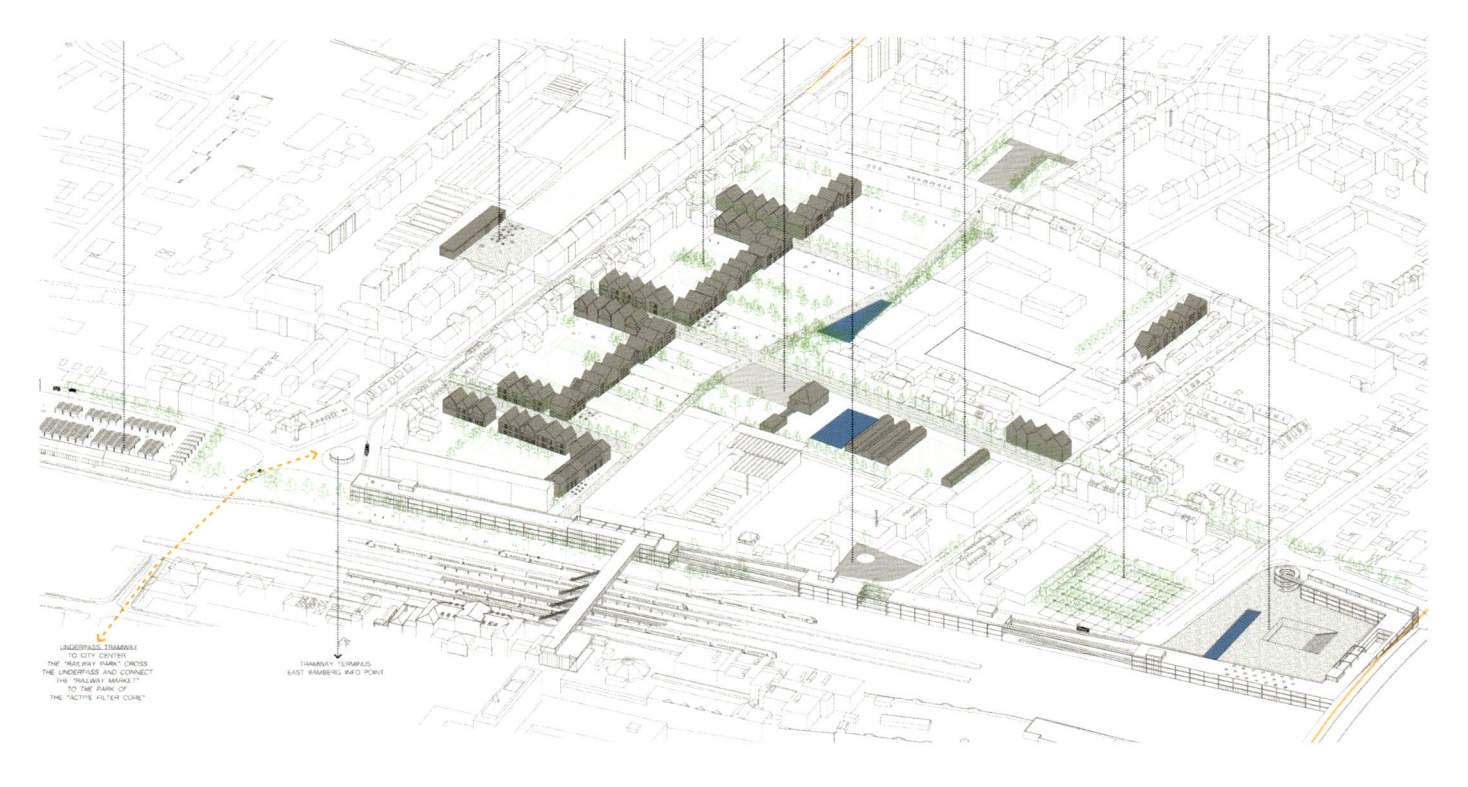

GJAKOVA
KOSOVO (KO)

CATEGORY: **URBAN – ARCHITECTURAL**
LOCATION: **GJAKOVA**
POPULATION: **96,000 INHAB.**
STRATEGIC SITE: **40 HA**
PROJECT SITE: **7 HA**
SITE PROPOSED BY: **MUNICIPALITY**
OWNER(S) OF THE SITE: **CITY OF GJAKOVA**

COMMISION AFTER COMPETITION:
URBAN PROJECT MANAGEMENT ROLE, DESIGN OF PUBLIC AND LANDSCAPE AREAS; REVITALIZING OF THE RIVERBANK AND TRANSFORMATION OF CENTRAL PUBLIC ZONE; RECONNECTING THE AREA TO CITY CENTRE

Interview of the site's representative

Mimoza Kusari Lila, Mayor of Gjakova
Elida Bejtullahu, Acting Director of Urban Planning and Environment Protection

PRESENTATION OF THE SITE WITH REGARDS TO STRATEGY

The site is located in the centre of the city development and stretches on both sides of the Krena River; the river creates a restrictive barrier between the old and new part of the city through natural elements, a chain of public and private buildings of cultural and natural heritage, and abandoned public spaces, therefore leaving the area as a passive development area. The strategy aims to eliminate the barriers and establish new approaches, which should end up interlacing both riverbanks in one single compact urban space.

HOW IS THE SITE CONNECTED TO THE SESSION TOPIC - THE ADAPTABLE CITY?

The current area implies the idea of being evaluated as potential area to transform –through suitable treatment, re-destination of its use, enrichment with public functions and social services, urban and architectural redesign, adaptation to current needs and requirements with stable economic and social activities– from a restrictive area to a bridging one between the surrounding spaces. The city is ready to adapt the area through the ground configuration and alignment on a variety of destinations to develop –like self-sustaining economic activities–, to improve its attractiveness, the activity and the dynamics of its use.

DID YOU DEFINE A SPECIFIC PROCESS FOR THE URBAN DEVELOPMENT OF THE SITE AFTER EUROPAN COMPETITION?

The city will engage in composing a detailed project for execution and a strategy of implementation, including the previous financial evaluation of the implementation cost and the analysis of the budget and financial possibilities for implementation. Depending on the project, the possibilities to implement in phases and the Municipal Budget and other potential financial sources, the Municipality plans to start the project implementation for the following year, involving the winning team.

ERBLIN BUCALIU (KO)
RRITA PULA (KO)
DEA LUMA (KO)
ARCHITECTS

KOMPLEKS AVALLA, B1 NO.13
10000 PRISTINA, KO
T. +386 49178567
ERBLINBUCALIU@GMAIL.COM

WINNER - GJAKOVA (KO)
SEAMbiosis

TEAM POINT OF VIEW Active society. Identity. Public transportation. Clean air and water. Community participation. Decentralization. Happiness. Cultural heritage. Flow. Children. Regulated sewage. Public realm. Artisans. Local stories. Religious harmony. Industry. Shared spaces. Education. Four seasons. Wellbeing. Bike lanes. Micro-economy. Organic farming. Lush nature. Green parks. Sustainability. Adaptive reuse. Technology. Traditions. Free movement. Diversity. Play. Accessibility. Tourism. Smokers' corners. Weddings. Hospitality. Dignity. Connections. Safety. Pedestrian-based. Good will. Equality. Free spirituality. Arts and crafts. The old and the new. Opportunities. LED street lighting. Farmers market. City landmarks. Hybridity. Bridges. Water collectors. Solar energy. Vibrancy. Awareness. Day and night. Relaxation. Coexistence between generations. Sharing and caring. Blurred boundaries between public and private space. The seam/network between these essentials make the city of Gjakova a living organism; an urban SEAMbiosis.

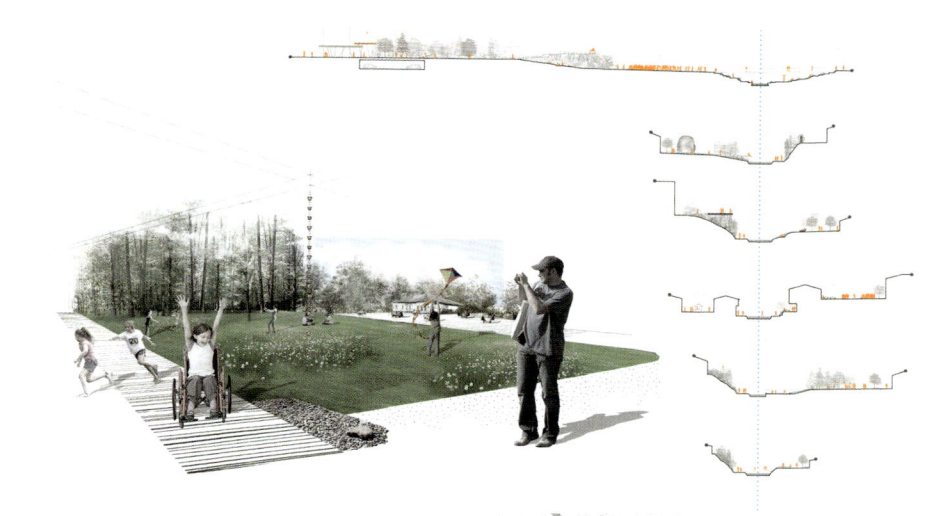

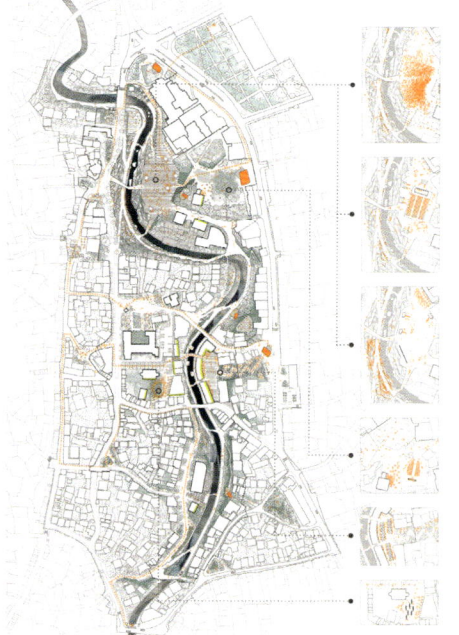

JURY POINT OF VIEW The project introduces a large publicness; it starts with what is there and works with it to create additional qualities. It does not invent anything but the simplicity of smaller interventions creates a diverse proposal. The project is very well elaborated and works with the current landscape. The authors created 2-3 crossing systems. They didn't introduce a lot of bridges but they created connections to bring more people to the area. The proposal of biking paths strengthens the idea and creates diversity of activities. The project overlooks the ecology of the city.

CARLES ENRICH (ES)
ARCHITECT

ADRIANA CAMPMANY (ES)
ANNA DE CASTRO (ES)
ARCHITECTS
CAROLINE FOULON (BE)
INTERIOR ARCHITECT
LAURA BELENGUER (ES)
RAFEL CAPÓ (ES)
STUDENTS IN ARCHITECTURE

C/ FRATERNITAT 38, PB
08012 BARCELONA, ES
T. +34 649769786
CARLES@CARLESENRICH.COM
WWW.CARLESENRICH.COM

RUNNER-UP - GJAKOVA (KO)
Caravanserais

TEAM POINT OF VIEW Gjakova has a strong tradition as a commercial town. The old groups of mercantile caravans that used to cross Gjakova triggered the construction of a bunch of bridges over the Krena River that became identifying meeting points for inhabitants and traders.

To maximize urban cohesion and empower the city's identity, the intervention focuses on the existing bridges and their immediate spaces, becoming strong urban reference spots and recovering the spirit of the ancient Caravanserais by introducing new program related to sports, music, leisure and market. The new Caravanserais are a piece of structure acting as a bicycle stop, street furniture, lighting and allowing public accessibility to the riverbanks. At the same time we propose the subversion of the actual river condition from a residual space to a reclaimed and sanitized natural area, by adding restorative nature and canalizing sewage water. Then, we bring forward an urban environmental strategy that consists in a green ring along the rivers and three green arteries structuring the city.

Thanks to the re-activation of the bridges and their surroundings, we can reinforce the existing streets to define an urban network that connects Qabrati Hill with the Erenik River, linking the architectural heritage and the cultural and educational areas of the city with the nature. The proposal is complemented by targeted interventions in existing buildings on both sides of the river.

JURY POINT OF VIEW The proposal has landscape continuity. It creates two arteries along the river. More dedicated to a bicycle path, bridges are the social centres of the project and they are bringing back their own importance. Interventions are very light. Proposal for urban furniture is lacking. The proposal is concentrated on the definition of current uses of existing roads for business clusters. What is interesting is that it is bringing the bazaar near the river. Even with light interventions the authors achieved to read the city and its functions correctly. By adding particular values to certain areas they created an interesting approach.

PAUL CETNARSKI (PL)
MIRABELA JURCZENKO (PL)
WOJCIECH MAZAN (PL)
RAFAŁ ŚLIWA (PL)
ARCHITECTS

STRIPETHECOMMON@GMAIL.COM

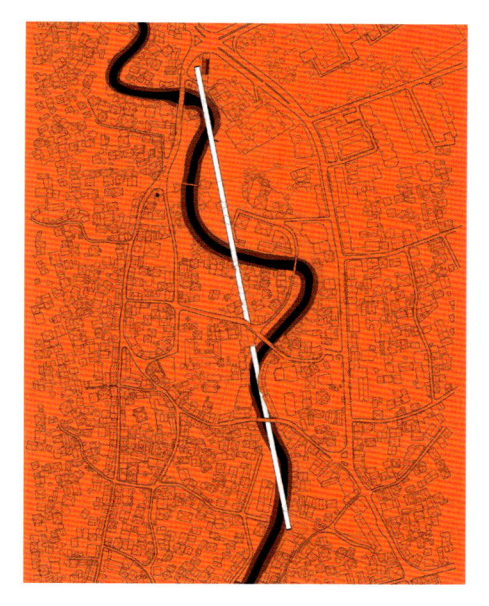

SPECIAL MENTION - GJAKOVA (KO)

Strip(e) the Common

TEAM POINT OF VIEW "There is a tendency to look at large pictures from a distance. The large pictures in this exhibition are intended to be seen from a short distance."
This is how Barnett Newman explained his enormous painting "Vir Heroicus Sublimis" back in1951 that elevated abstract art to the highest level. This is how we see the ———. A sublime, abstract urban concept. From a distance it is paradoxically perceived as urban frontier and connection. On the other hand, if someone is curious enough to have a closer look, they will immediately understand the variety of details that are provoked by the ——— appearance.

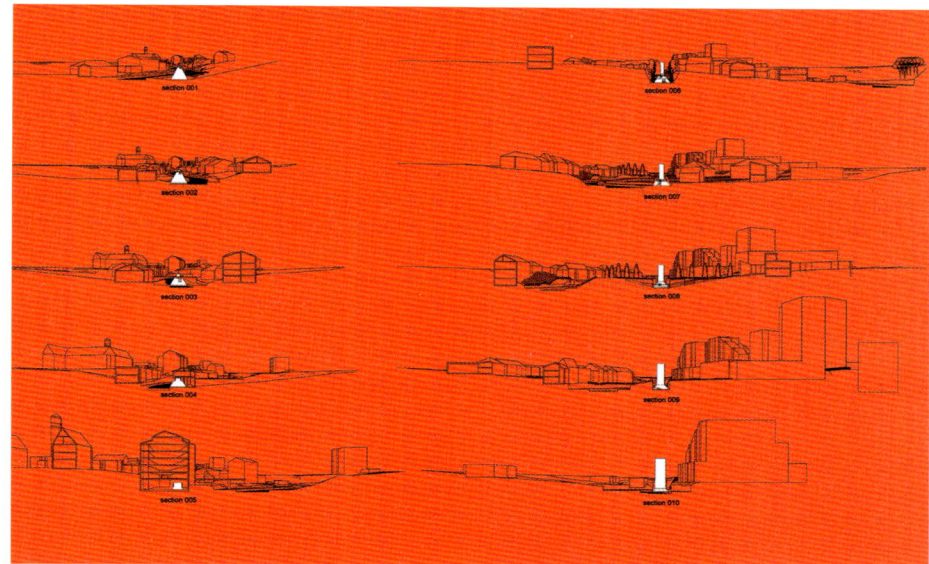

GRAZ
ÖSTERREICH (AT)

CATEGORY: **ARCHITECTURAL**
LOCATION: **GRAZ**
POPULATION: **280,000 INHAB.**
STRATEGIC SITE: **3.2 HA** / PROJECT SITE: **1.6 HA**
SITE PROPOSED BY: **CITY OF GRAZ AND ÖBB (AUSTRIAN RAILWAY COMPANY)**

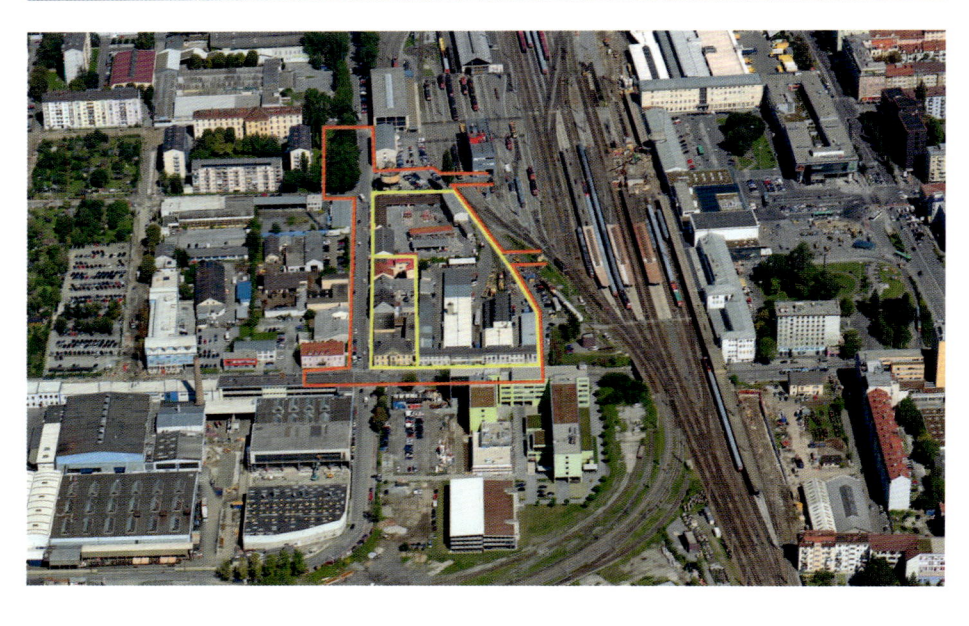

OWNER(S) OF THE SITE:
ÖBB & HANSCHMANN GMBH
COMMISION AFTER COMPETITION:
DESIGN OF ARCHITECTURAL PROJECT, POSSIBLY IN PARTNERSHIP WITH OTHER ARCHITECTS

Interview of the site's representative

Christopher Kreiner, ÖBB-Real Estate Management GmbH
Eva Benedikt, Department of Urban Planning, City of Graz

PRESENTATION OF THE SITE WITH REGARDS TO STRATEGY

The central location in the West of Graz is a "Europan Konkret". With a mixed-use neighbourhood (housing, work, commercial and sociocultural facilities), the aim is to build a bridge to the West and formulate a "West Entrée" for the main railway station. The project area and the Bahnhofsviertel West development area bordering it to the West are two of several future city districts. The development of former industrial areas into mixed city districts plays an important role. A main strategic aim of the ÖBB is to make the station area more attractive for travellers. The Southern pedestrian tunnel is to form an additional essential West-East axis that will create an attractive public area.

HOW IS THE SITE CONNECTED TO THE SESSION TOPIC - THE ADAPTABLE CITY?

The desired mix of use, the emphasis on solutions that create high quality living spaces near the noisy main train station, the approach to public space and the design of a centre around the main train station and close to the sensitive axis leading to Schloss Eggenberg to reflect urban planning-related and architectonic concepts – all these aspects are relevant and reveal that cities need to be adaptable in the future.

DID YOU DEFINE A SPECIFIC PROCESS FOR THE URBAN DEVELOPMENT OF THE SITE AFTER EUROPAN COMPETITION?

Before the concrete project development can begin, it is compulsory to present a development plan for the area, meaning that an urban planning concept needs to be created, which is then ordered by the municipality. Proprietors ÖBB / Hanschmann, the City of Graz and the winning team will discuss any potential optimisation in a workshop to examine how the project can be used as the basis for the development plan.

MIHAI BUȘE (RO)
MÁRTON TÖVISSI (RO)
ARCHITECTS

TAMÁS FISCHER (HU)
ARCHITECT-3D RENDERINGS

159 AVENUE D'ITALIE
75013 PARIS, FR
T. +33 753305966
INFO@A-PLATZ.COM
WWW.A-PLATZ.COM

WINNER - GRAZ (AT)
Walzer

TEAM POINT OF VIEW A new identity should be given to the site for it to become the pair of the train station as well as a gate to the city centre. The railway is a connection on a regional scale but also a physical barrier within the city. Changing the attitude towards it is important, so instead of hiding it, why not exploiting it? Underground tunnels are a functional but poor way to connect city parts. We propose a strong visual connection and the gate to the station needs to become a place on it own. We use the building mass to define a strong public space –a square– connected to the urban context yet also protected. Secondary courtyards are cut into the building mass, bringing in natural light and creating semi-public spaces. Special care is given in defining the good relations between these public and private spaces.
The building as an urban artefact works on different scales –towers on the city scale, building base on the district scale, colonnade on the human scale. As programs are in constant change the adaptable structure proposed will host a large range of functions and the diverse uses and users will grant the site a great chance to become a place full of life.

JURY POINT OF VIEW The project proposes a very clear strategy: the implementation of positive and negative volumes (high points and noise-protected courtyards), the differentiation of the building heights, the idea of a generous open space as a central plaza-like courtyard and the adaptable integration of the existing neighbouring buildings are convincing design elements. The project gives too much weight to the closure of the square, a fact that could be easily improved due to the robustness of the structure.

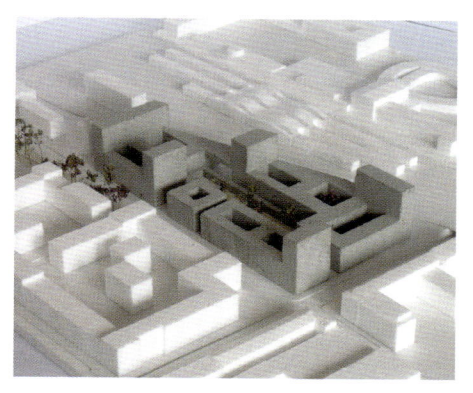

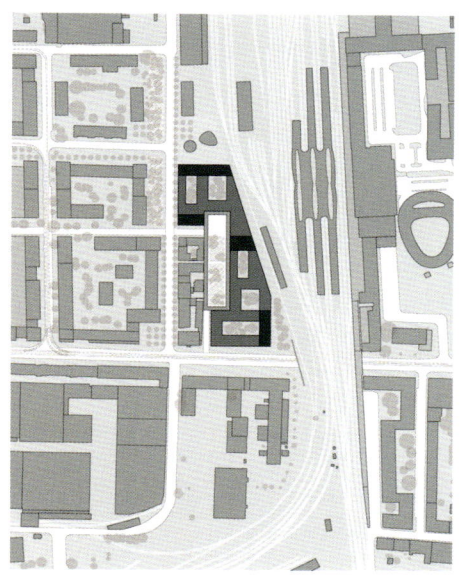

INGOLSTADT
DEUTSCHLAND (DE)

CATEGORY: **URBAN – LANDSCAPE – ARCHITECTURAL – TRAFFIC – SOCIOLOGY**
LOCATION: **TOWN CENTRE NORTH**
POPULATION: **130,000 INHAB.**
STRATEGIC SITE: **42 HA** / PROJECT SITE: **6.4 HA**

SITE PROPOSED BY: **CITY OF INGOLSTADT**
OWNER(S) OF THE SITE: **CITY OF INGOLSTADT, FREE STATE OF BAVARIA**
COMMISION AFTER COMPETITION: **URBAN MASTERPLAN/PRELIMINARY DESIGN STUDY**

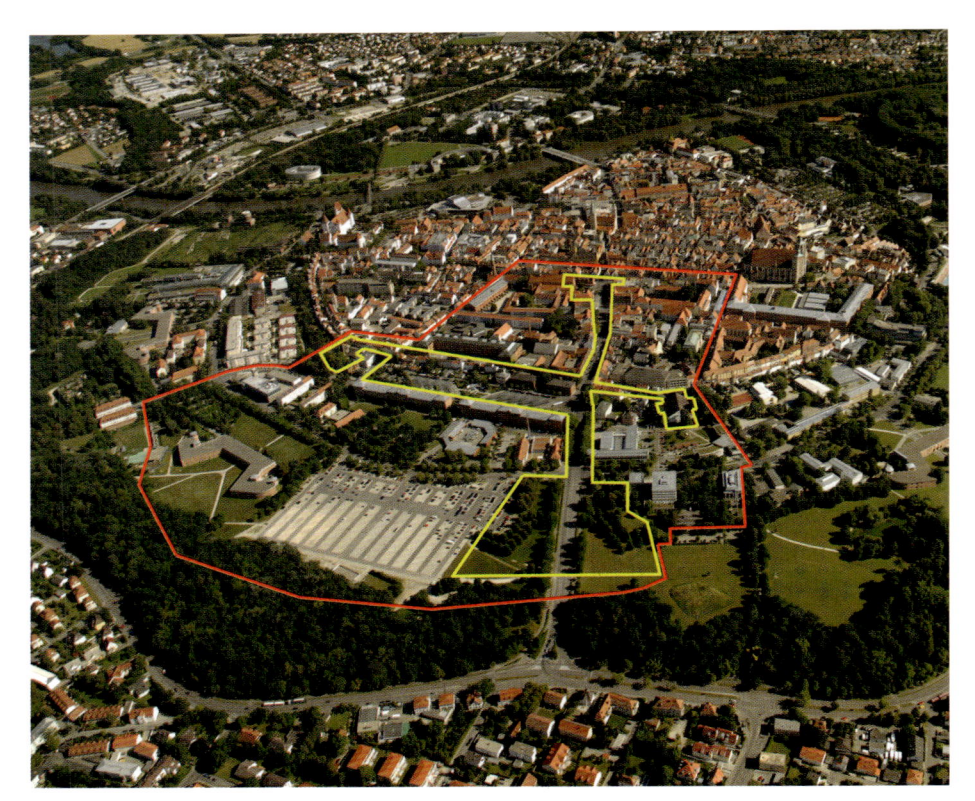

Interview of the site's representative
Renate Preßlein-Lehle
City Building Councillor of the City of Ingolstadt

PRESENTATION OF THE SITE WITH REGARDS TO STRATEGY

The goal of the urban planning is to preserve the historically evolved old city with its distinctive character, but nonetheless understand it as an urban space that is open to change and transformation processes and has to adapt to changing demands and needs. The necessary upgrading and redefining of the public space and the potentials of individual areas in the project area in the North of the old city of Ingolstadt allow for fundamental reflection on the identity and future of this urban space.

HOW IS THE SITE CONNECTED TO THE SESSION TOPIC - THE ADAPTABLE CITY?

Within the framework of the Europan competition, what should be considered here are the interventions that are suitable to generate an attractive living space, involve the different actors in the use of the spaces, create new interest points that enliven the old city as a whole, and ensure a perceptible link between locations via the public space. In connection with the Central Bus Station (ZOB) –which is located in the area–, new mobility concepts should also be taken into consideration.

DID YOU DEFINE A SPECIFIC PROCESS FOR THE URBAN DEVELOPMENT OF THE SITE AFTER EUROPAN COMPETITION?

The results of the Europan competition offer a wide range of ideas for the still pending public and political discussion of the future of the Northern section of the old city. Up to now, the development approaches have focussed on a restructuration of the North-South axis and subsequent densification in the area of the ZOB. The competition also provided interesting contributions relating to these points. A specific planning process has not yet been determined.

ÁLVARO CARRILLO (ES)
ADRIÀ ESCOLANO (ES)
GONZALO GUTIÉRREZ (ES)
ARCHITECTS

DRST
C/GREGORIO MARAÑÓN, 4. 1-1
29602 MARBELLA, MÁLAGA, ES
T. +34 952860827
WALDSTRASSE2015@GMAIL.COM
WWW.DRST.ES / INFO@DRST.ES
WWW.ALVAROCARRILLO.ORG

WINNER - INGOLSTADT (DE)
Waldstrasse

TEAM POINT OF VIEW Through an urban interior reform plan, we balance the North and South poles of the old town to atomise the occupation, using the green ring as the origin of the intervention and the absence of vegetation in the old town as an opportunity.
The HarderStrasse is turned into equipment with a unique identity communicating with the centre of the old town with the glacis, which acts as a walkway to the ring and the NEW-ZOB –relocated in the North access of the wall as a large technified green space in the main North-South axis. This way, a new element can be created to strengthen quotidian identity. The street becomes a lineal park and pedestrians not only have a public way, but also a nucleus of activity where they can enjoy a comfortable public space at street level. The new green axis is articulated in the North with the inherited esplanade from the OLD-ZOB, which can host events controlled by the city council via a cultural agenda. The urban space mutates into a public scenography. When expanding the activity to the North, new residential and civic opportunity spaces open (supported by the current public spaces), which can be occupied by permanent residents.

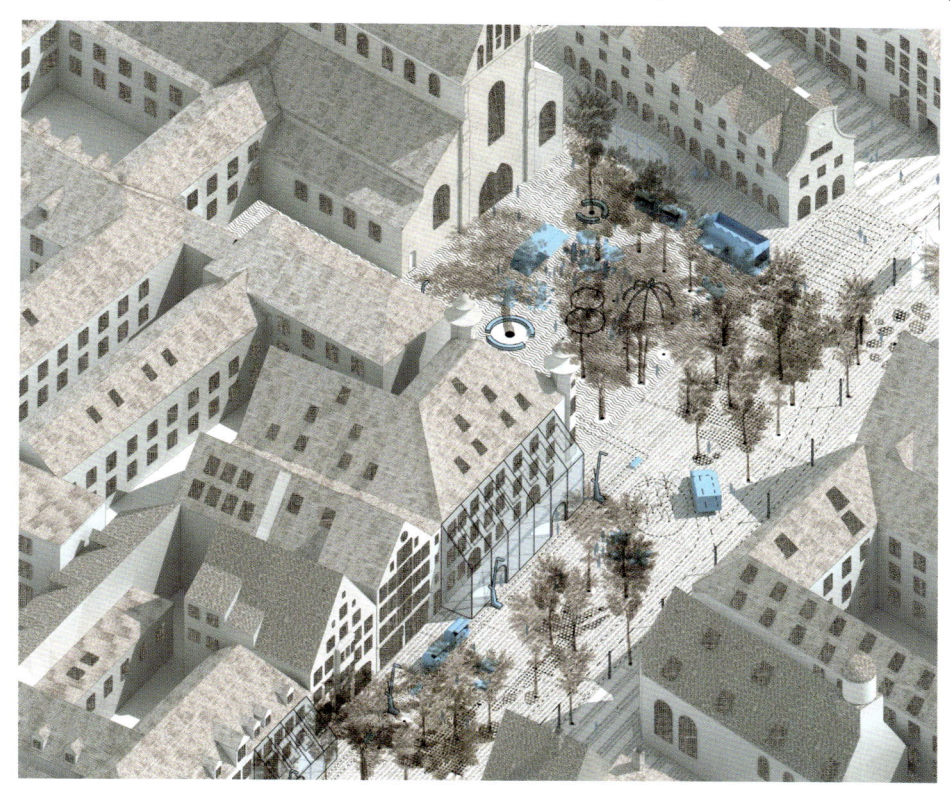

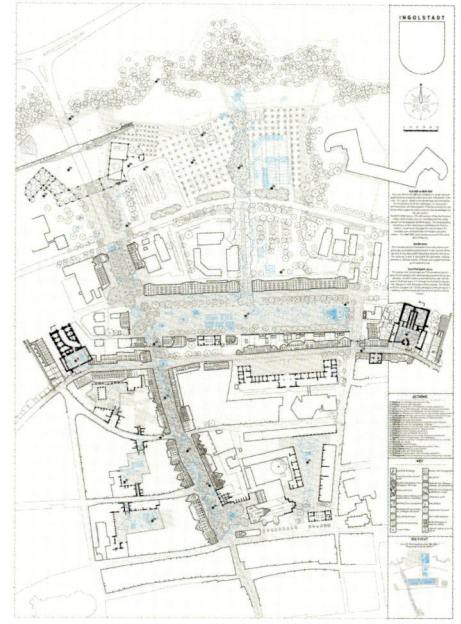

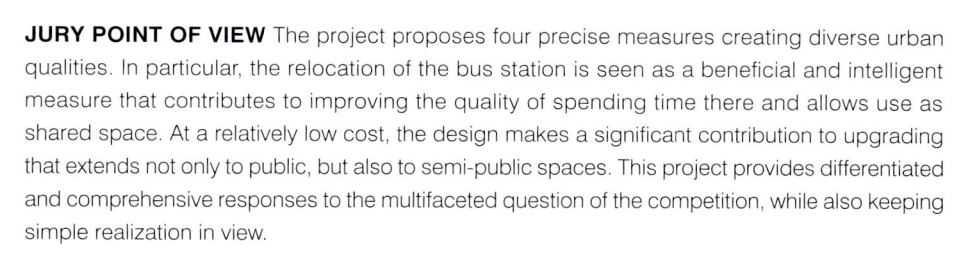

JURY POINT OF VIEW The project proposes four precise measures creating diverse urban qualities. In particular, the relocation of the bus station is seen as a beneficial and intelligent measure that contributes to improving the quality of spending time there and allows use as shared space. At a relatively low cost, the design makes a significant contribution to upgrading that extends not only to public, but also to semi-public spaces. This project provides differentiated and comprehensive responses to the multifaceted question of the competition, while also keeping simple realization in view.

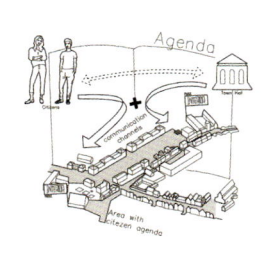

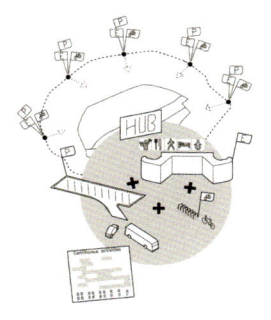

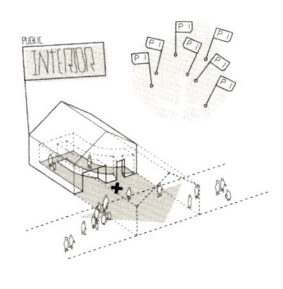

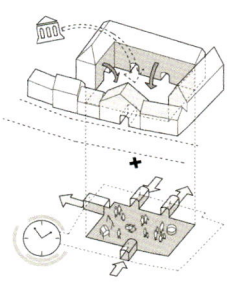

JO-NIKLAS DODOO (DE)
EROL SLOWY (DE)
ARCHITECTS

HOHENZOLLERNRING 121
22763 HAMBURG, DE
T. +49 1636331828
DODOO@2D3O.COM

RUNNER-UP - INGOLSTADT (DE)

Re-Connect

JURY POINT OF VIEW The project chooses to reactivate the public space by increasing the number of people who use it and proposes a building development with twelve freestanding residential buildings on the ZOB site. The provision of new residential spaces in a central location is expressly welcomed, but the concrete formulation is questioned, especially the open semi-public and private areas that will have difficulties developing qualities in a densely urban city even if they are elevated.

TEAM POINT OF VIEW The site is situated in the historic centre in which urban living and development are key characteristics. Prerequisite for a vital urban area is a heterogenic environment with high density, diversity and frequency of protagonists and their usage options.

We propose to establish a new mixed district close to the ZOB-area and use the area in the historic centre to increase density and vitalization. We focus on the provision of common area and new forms of sharing and living for diverse age groups and modi vivendi within the historic centre. A new "Quarter of Generations" then emerges and enables participation in the new urban living, ensuring a high user frequency and purchasing power. The vivid Quarter is a counter pole to Ingolstadt's mono-functional housing developments. The ZOB is transferred to the North and the exploration of the centre begins at its initial interface. A multifunctional green bridge builds identity, as a landmark, and act as a prelude for the historic centre, supplying access to the glacis and merging the disconnected green area.

IRÚN
ESPAÑA (ES)

CATEGORY: **URBAN**
LOCATION: **RAILWAY STATION ZONE; IRÚN, GUIPÚZCOA**
POPULATION: **61,847 INHAB.**
PROJECT SITE: **36.22 HA**

SITE PROPOSED BY: **IRÚN CITY COUNCIL**
OWNER(S) OF THE SITE: **PUBLIC (ADIF) AND PRIVATE**
COMMISION AFTER COMPETITION: **MANAGEMENT OF URBAN DEVELOPMENT PROJECT**

Interview of the site's representative
Mikel Gargallo Fernández, Director of Planning and Environment of the City of Irún

PRESENTATION OF THE SITE WITH REGARDS TO STRATEGY

The new Irún masterplan advocates rational, intensive land use with dense, compact and complex urban structures. It prioritizes foot, bicycle and public transport mobility. One of the aims is to recover the railway zone, reduce its current impact on the town and encourage the insertion of its remaining infrastructure into the urban area. The main goals are:
- To reorganise the railway zone, adapt its facilities to the requirements arising from the incorporation of the city in the TGV network;
- To build a new intermodal station with business, tertiary, recreational and other uses;
- To define a program for housing, businesses and public facilities on this released land;
- To build road links across the railway area to overcome the current physical barrier.

HOW IS THE SITE CONNECTED TO THE SESSION TOPIC - THE ADAPTABLE CITY?

These initiatives aim to streamline the operation of the railway area. They are expected to significantly reduce the major barrier created by the railway infrastructure, release land to complete the existing urban fabric and thus improve road and functional communication between both sides of the railway land. A new hub is expected to be created on the basis of a void with a major impact on the town centre and produce new living spaces with uses that generate activity.

DID YOU DEFINE A SPECIFIC PROCESS FOR THE URBAN DEVELOPMENT OF THE SITE AFTER EUROPAN COMPETITION?

A dialogue and consultation process has begun amongst the various public stakeholders with a view to defining a comprehensive masterplan. The planning proposals for the Europan competition will facilitate the production of a tool that will generate the masterplan for this area once the railway study is completed. The proposals will also permit the partial conversion of the former Customs precinct into university facilities.

GERARD DURAN BARBARÀ (ES)
ARCHITECT

ANNA CASADEVALL SAYERAS (ES)
JOANA TRIL QUERALT (ES)
ALBA FERNANDEZ RELLA (ES)
STUDENTS IN ARCHITECTURE

C/MARQUES DE MULHACEN 53
08034 BARCELONA, ES
T. +34 619283589
GDB@XPLUSX.EU
WWW.XPLUSX.EU

RUNNER-UP - IRÚN (ES)
Ura Eta Natura

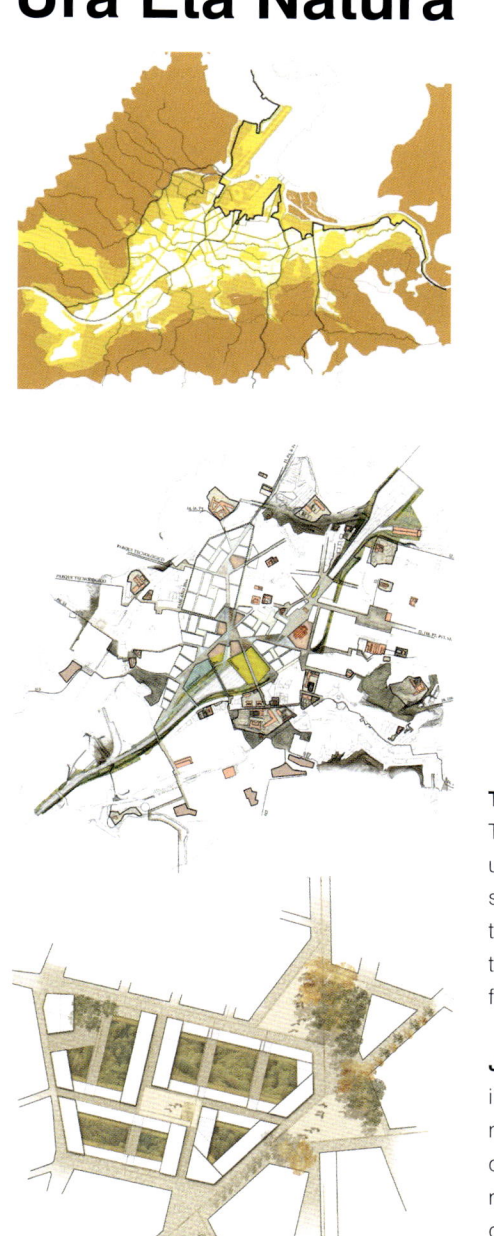

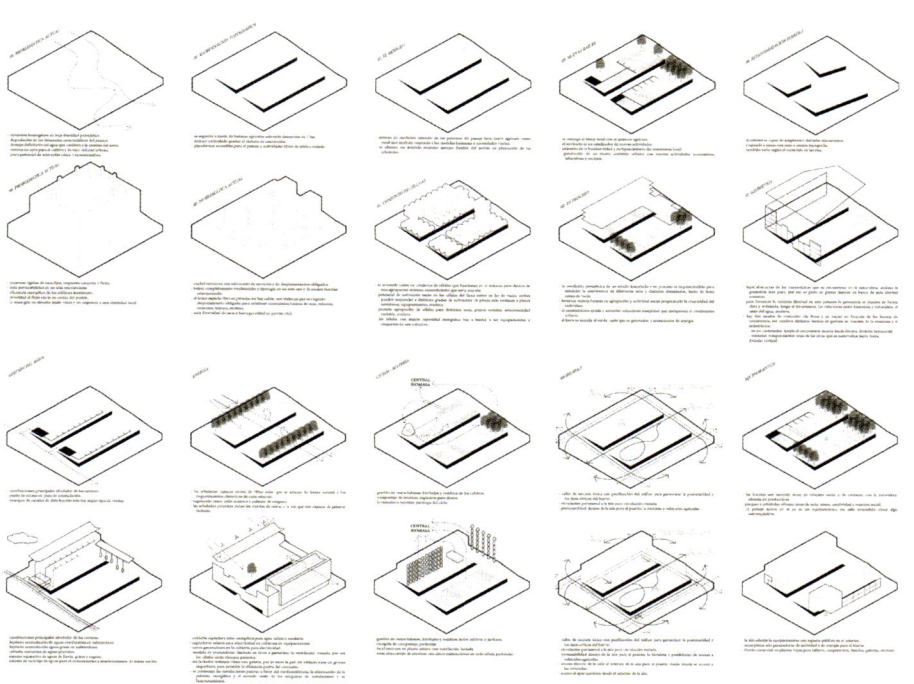

TEAM POINT OF VIEW "There is nothing permanent except change." Heraclitus of Ephesus The city is an image that transforms from the first instant and never materializes. It should be understood as a dynamic entity, where nothing remains the same over time, where everything is sequential. It flows governed by the laws of nature and human being. It is therefore impossible to concrete, as laws in constant transformation determine every city. Nevertheless, the architect, through study, is able to understand their development logics and act accordingly, allowing the future to flow in harmony.

JURY POINT OF VIEW The project proposes an interpretation based on the territorial dimension, in which great importance is placed on the geography and a relatively dense, cohesive urban model, with a grid defined by regular and irregular components by means of a reinterpretation of the value of the street block as a unit condensing city life. It investigates new alternatives to reconcile urban and rural environments, including the natural values remaining around Irún. It could be an ideal tool to reappraise the future development of this area and its implications for the rest of the town.

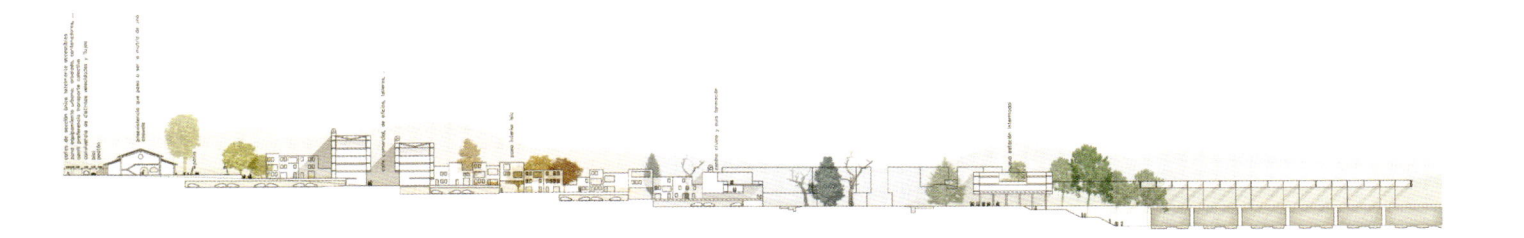

SPECIAL MENTION - IRÚN (ES)
Mugaz Gaindiko – Over the Border

TEAM POINT OF VIEW The arrival of the high-speed train will once again reshape Irún and its economy. The project proposes to keep the railway as a visual quality in the city, yet reducing the physical barrier. To do this the site is terraced – one side is elevated as a "pier" overlooking the tracks, while the other is lowered as a parallel street with activity on both sides. Together with new connections over and under the tracks, these elements make a station that is an integrated part of the city. Surrounding districts are weaved together with the new by continuing existing streets and public spaces.

ELI GRØNN (NO)
ARCHITECT-URBANIST

JUAN BERASATEGUI (ES)
LANDSCAPE ARCHITECT, JURIST
MARIT ØHRN LANGSLET (NO)
ARCHITECT
ANJA STANDAL (NO)
ARCHITECT, ENGINEER
TOM DAVIES (GB)
ARCHEOLOGIST

T. +47 41542767
ELIGRONN@GMAIL.COM

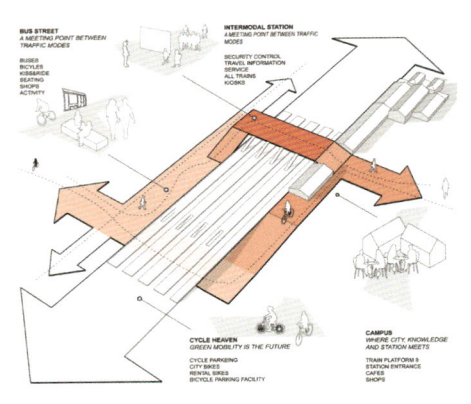

SPECIAL MENTION - IRÚN (ES)
United Uses of Irún

TEAM POINT OF VIEW The proposal is based on an analysis of the area to draw up four potential lines of action: nature, society, economy, history. We propose to generate a new central hub valuing the existing city, opting for a sustainable urban model growth for the urban revival, and at the same time to propose actions, which are also considered as indispensable in any urban strategy – urban symbiosis, green infrastructure, sustainable mobility, superblock, automated parking system, rehabilitation and adaptability, sustainability and adaptability, participation and elimination of urban barriers.

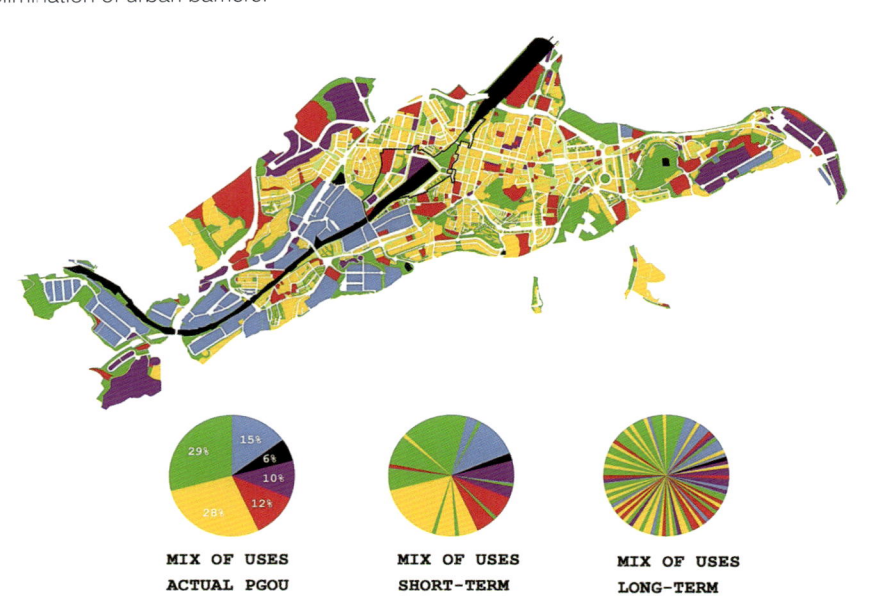

JORGE A. RUIZ BOLUDA (ES)
NICOLA CORVASCE (IT)
JORGE LÓPEZ GONZÁLEZ (ES)
TANIA NAVARRO APARICIO ES)
ARCHITECTS

C/ MÚSICO HIPÓLITO MARTÍNEZ 16-43
46020 VALENCIA, ES
T. +34 620931946
ESTUDIO@JORGERUIZBOLUDA.ES
WWW.JORGERUIZBOLUDA.ES

LIBRAMONT
BELGIQUE/BELGIË/BELGIEN (BE)

CATEGORY: **TOWN PLANNING AND ARCHITECTURE**
LOCATION: **LIBRAMONT-CHEVIGNY, TRAIN STATION DISTRICT**
POPULATION: **10,947 INHAB.**
STRATEGIC SITE: **32 HA**
PROJECT SITE: **10 HA**

SITE PROPOSED BY: **MUNICIPALITY OF LIBRAMONT AND BELGIAN RAIL (SNCB)**
OWNER(S) OF THE SITE: **MOSTLY SNCB, THE MUNICIPALITY AND PRIVATE INDIVIDUALS**
COMMISION AFTER COMPETITION: **TOWN PLANNING STUDY, ARCHITECTURAL DESIGN OF PUBLIC SPACES AND CERTAIN BUILDINGS**

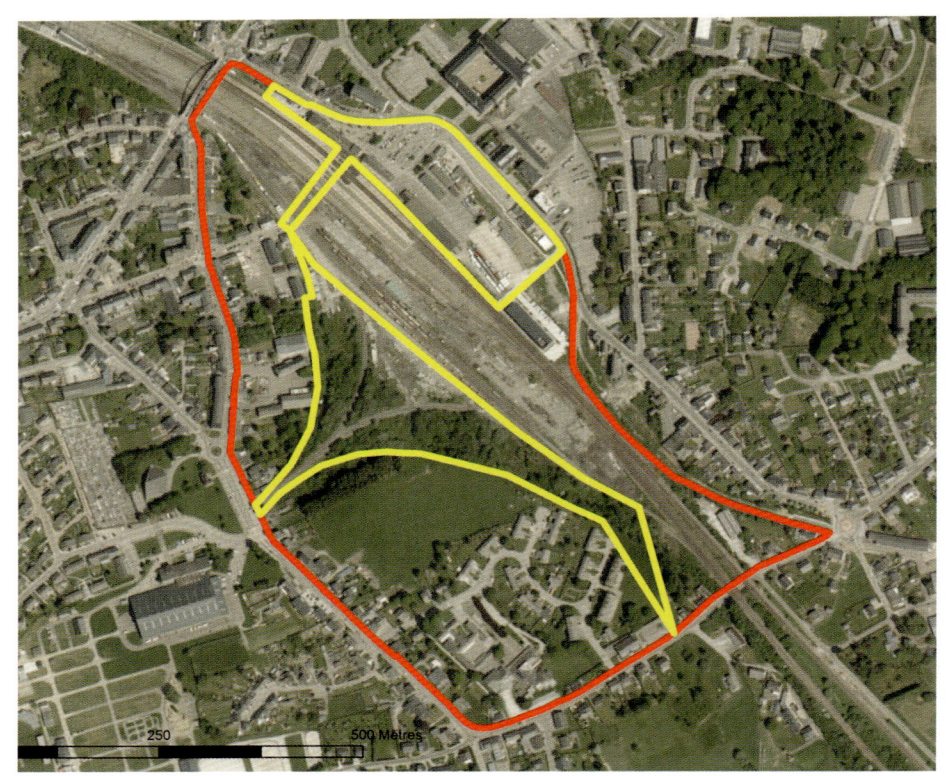

Interview of the site's representative
Pierre Arnould, bourgmestre

PRESENTATION OF THE SITE WITH REGARDS TO STRATEGY
Libramont-Chevigny is the pole of a rural region at the heart of the Belgian province of Luxemburg. The town developed around the railway – the North-East area hosts an intermodal and services pole while many public buildings lie the South-West –all around the main square. The municipality wishes to create a new dynamic for the train station district with the project "Cœur de Libramont" ("Libramont's Heart"). The main issues are the improvement of the station functionality to turn it into a 21st cent. station, and the restructuration of both sides of the railway.

HOW IS THE SITE CONNECTED TO THE SESSION TOPIC - THE ADAPTABLE CITY?
The creation of Libramont's Heart is planned in 3 steps: linking both railway sides; planning of the station district; and implementation of buildings for housing, offices, shops, services and parking lots on the area South-West of the railway. Each step should be planned in a flexible and progressive way, and should specifically consider the spacing out and modularity of the parking lots as well as the reversibility of housing and offices. Finally, one has to take into account the progressive liberation of lands and insure the continuity of the site's features.

DID YOU DEFINE A SPECIFIC PROCESS FOR THE URBAN DEVELOPMENT OF THE SITE AFTER EUROPAN COMPETITION?
As the site is the attractive feature to develop its centre, the Municipality is looking for a masterplan for the whole area. The Europan 13 winning team could be granted a collective mission by the SNCB (the Belgian railway company) and the local and regional authorities.

MARIA TERESA NESTÁREZ NARVÁEZ (PE)
LORENA TRINIDAD PHANG (PE)
MARILYNE SOUCHE MORENO (BR)
ARCHITECTS

41 BOULEVARD SAINT JACQUES
75014 PARIS, FR
T. +33 695361584
MML@EUROPE.COM

SPECIAL MENTION - LIBRAMONT (BE)

50 Shades of Green

TEAM POINT OF VIEW The vision of the project reinforces the development of urban agriculture within the urban tissue. It provides the neighbourhood with a specific activity improving the quality of life and encouraging community participation, becoming the city's tourist attraction.
Our proposal is organic and open, but also logical and staged. Within the organic grid of green and blue, we generate a spatial hierarchy and zoning allowing the user to easily understand space distribution and functions. The project aims at developing a way of life where the community could manage shared outdoor spaces.

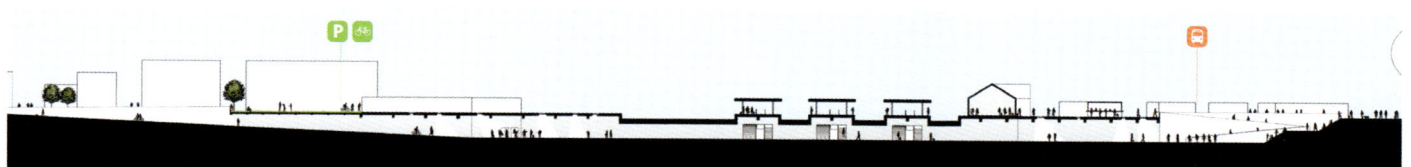

MARNE-LA-VALLÉE
FRANCE (FR)

CATEGORY: **URBAN - ARCHITECTURAL**
LOCATION: **VAL MAUBUÉE, NOISIEL AND LOGNES MUNICIPALITIES**
POPULATION: **291,132 INHAB.**
STRATEGIC SITE: **120 HA**
PROJECT SITE: **15 HA**

SITE PROPOSED BY: **ÉTABLISSEMENT PUBLIC D'AMÉNAGEMENT MARNE-LA-VALLÉE**
OWNER(S) OF THE SITE: **STATE, EPA MARNE, GENERAL COUNCIL, MUNICIPALITIES, PRIVATE**
COMMISION AFTER COMPETITION: **MANAGEMENT OF THE ARCHITECTURAL AND/OR URBAN PROJECT AND STUDIES**

Interview of the site's representative

PRESENTATION OF THE SITE WITH REGARDS TO STRATEGY

Fourty years after the creation of Marne-la-Vallée, the Val Maubuée territory is facing societal challenges of a new kind and is actively pursuing the urban changes and transformations to enhance its metropolitan attractiveness: revisiting the free public and private spaces that structure the neighbourhoods and blocks, and adapting them to modern uses and human practices; appropriately and inventively acting to foster new uses and the socio-economic balances of the town; making the links between neighbourhoods and the relations between housing and jobs more legible, facilitating residential movement, enhancing the spaces within housing estates.

HOW IS THE SITE CONNECTED TO THE SESSION TOPIC - THE ADAPTABLE CITY?

The Route de la Brie –which runs from the A4 motorway to the central part of the new town of Marne-la-Vallée– raises the question of urban divisions and the future of residual spaces around the centres and neighbourhoods it crosses. Roads and successive roundabouts separate the neighbourhoods, organised around parks, artificial lakes or green strips, which are the trademark of the new town. They sometimes seem to be juxtaposed. The brief is to think about boundaries, residual interstitial spaces with uncertain purposes, the recycling and re-adaptation of these spaces, which suffer from a lack of legibility and appropriation. These spaces have significant potential, to exploit in order to devise new places of life and activity, and offer possibilities for densification or urban intensification.

MAIA TÜÜR (EE)
YOANN DUPOUY (FR)
ARCHITECTS-URBANISTS

TU-DU ARCHITECTURE URBANISME
95 RUE DE LA ROQUETTE
75011 PARIS, FR
CONTACT@TU-DU.FR
WWW.TU-DU.FR

WINNER - MARNE-LA-VALLÉE (FR)
Ville N(M)ature

TEAM POINT OF VIEW Since its inception, Le Val Maubuée was conceived as a city-park. The framework was supposed to generate new relations of habitat to the nature. Unfortunately, it is now obvious that despite the impressive amount of public green areas the different forms of interfaces between habitat and nature are limited. The built-up areas on the site are full of closed systems that turn their back to the surrounding green areas. Our project suggests revealing the potential of mutation of the interfaces in the very centre of sector 2 by uniting the existing line of ponds and the residual spaces of infrastructures into a central figure that becomes a connecting green heart of the area. In our opinion the ideation of project is necessarily territorial as it reveals to be an appropriate scale to envision the densifications of the Val Maubuée. The strategy of densification is not seen as a formal process, proceeding by juxtaposition of the new territories "won by urban", but as a tool to work on the connections and the resilience of the existing neighbourhoods. We propose a linear discontinuous densification by small built areas connected to their green and built environment. The first identification of the possible project areas along the interface reveals that the potential of the residual spaces is more important than one might think. The advantage of this approach is the existence of the road-network and its flexibility of implementation in time, operation by operation.

JURY POINT OF VIEW The project offers a forward-looking vision of the nature-city which concentrates on the interface between the landscape areas and the exiting built spaces. It is an intelligent and original project which extends beyond the set perimeter and pursues the experimental work initiated on the territory through a resolutely contextual territorial and landscape approach. This strategy of scattered interventions brings out the infrastructures perceived as obstacles in the territory, leading to the emergence of a large-scale inhabited landscape that has turned its back on experiments with the juxtaposition of mutually disconnected built components.

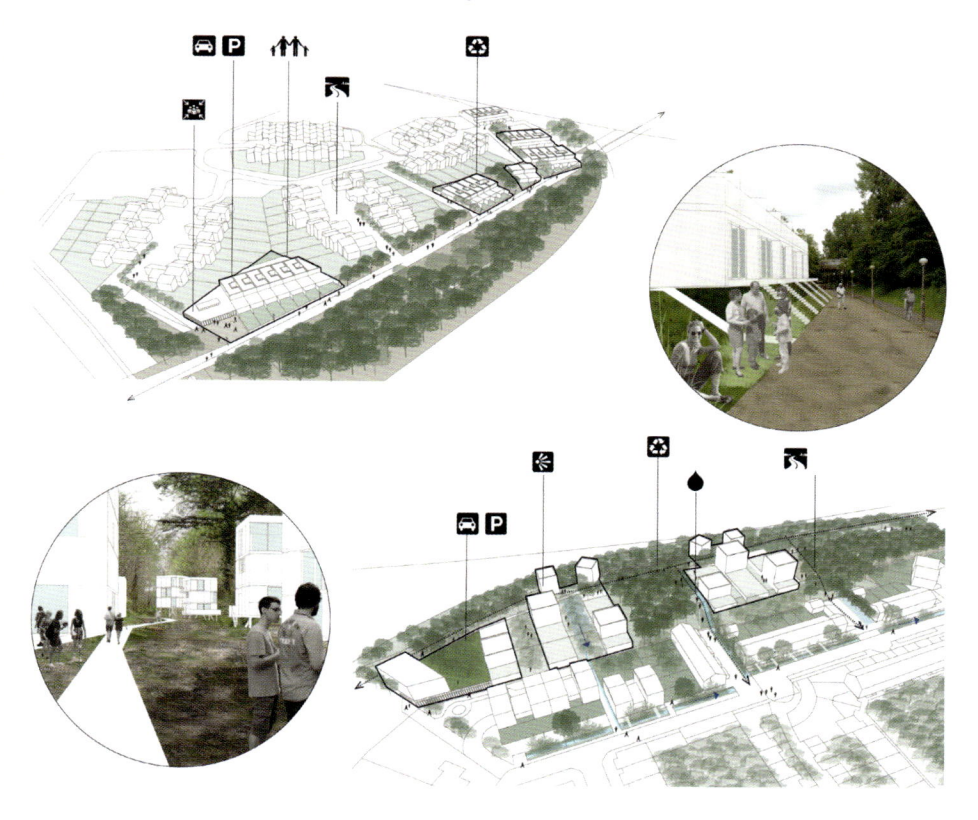

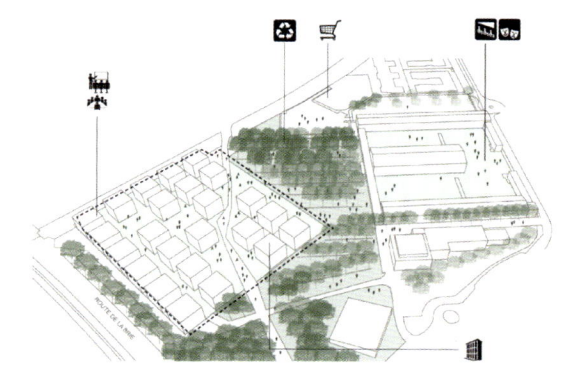

JONATHAN CACCHIA (FR)
CÉCILE FRAPPAT (FR)
CLAIRE GIRARDEAU (FR)
LOUIS MEJEAN (FR)
ARCHITECTS

PIERRE-YVES BLEVIN (FR)
ECONOMY MANAGER
MÉLANIE CARRATU (FR)
TRANSLATOR
ADRIEN PIU (FR)
VIDEO MAKER

CONTACT@TOHU-BOHU.EU
WWW.TOHU-BOHU.EU

RUNNER-UP - MARNE-LA-VALLÉE (FR)
La déprise

TEAM POINT OF VIEW New towns are the symbol of a peculiar era: a generous and complete vision matching the hopes of that time. Whether it was imposed or wanted, this model still survives. Yet, we question it especially when confronted to an uncertain ecological, economical and social territory on which it depends.

We think that keeping cities entrapped in such a system is unbearable. Indeed, we are looking for means to guide cities towards resiliency and the ability to adapt to its transitory needs. But where and how is such a mutation possible? We choose to adopt a "back up" posture towards these New Towns model, and particularly towards its main feature –"Green Spaces".

Instead of pursuing a pressuring, entrapping logic, we explore a backing up strategy to generate the urban project. Its starting point is a movement of emancipation to give room to one chocking self before being put back together. This backward rush creates enough room, like a fertile vacant field, so back and forth movement can start again. Unpredictability can happen again: here are the necessary folding and unfolding waves to the constitution of such a territory.

Moreover, we advise city-makers to re-evaluate their ability to control, manage, handle and live such a territory: we propose instead a humble tactic to settle the basis of "mastered uncertainty" in space and time.

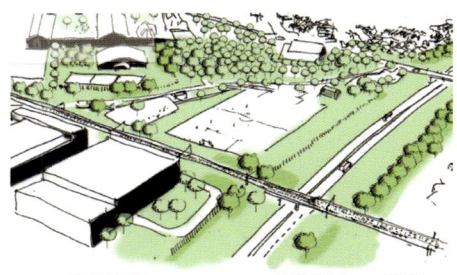

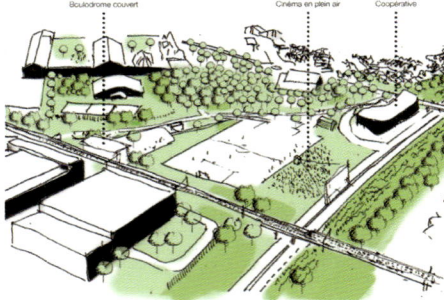

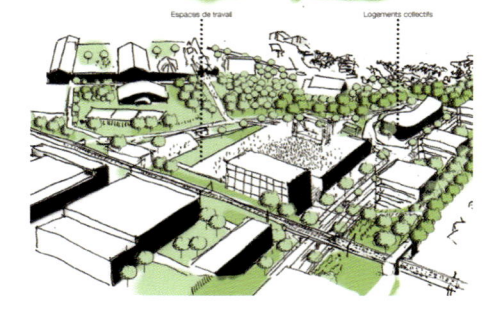

JURY POINT OF VIEW The project ideas focus on the role of nature in the New Town, which is seeking a new identity but is limited in its resources given the current economical and political context. The proposal develops a strategy of intensification and deactivation on certain spaces. This differential treatment is linked to the local economy and backed by a network of multiple local actors organised in the form of a cooperative. Decline gives resilience to the spaces, identified in consultation.

BORIS VAPNÉ (FR)
ARCHITECT-URBANIST
MAR ARMENGOL (BE)
LANDSCAPE ARCHITECT

93170 BAGNOLET, FR
BV@V-OLZ.EU
WWW.V-OLZ.EU

SPECIAL MENTION - MARNE-LA-VALLÉE (FR)

Relational Landscape

TEAM POINT OF VIEW The urban fabric is remeshed and punctually densified to evolve into a grid from its existing fractal organisation. Those actions allow renegotiating the dominant position of cars and a new relation to the public space can emerge. Yet, such plans can only be completed in collaboration with local residents. To involve them, a triennial is organized on the theme of the landscape of new towns, allowing the promotion of this common and the transformation of these ornamental parks in a relational and active landscape. The strategy mixes the physical transformation of infrastructure with a curatorial approach.

MOULINS
FRANCE (FR)

CATEGORY: **URBAN - ENVIRONMENTAL - ARCHITECTURAL**
LOCATION: **MOULINS - NEUVY**
POPULATION: **22,667 INHAB.**
STRATEGIC SITE: **570 HA** / PROJECT SITE: **105 HA**
SITE PROPOSED BY: **MOULINS COMMUNAUTÉ AND THE TOWN OF MOULINS**

OWNER(S) OF THE SITE: **MOULINS COMMUNAUTÉ, TOWN OF MOULINS, SOCIAL LANDLORD**
COMMISION AFTER COMPETITION: **URBAN STUDY, URBAN PROJECT MANAGEMENT, PUBLIC SPACE PROJECT MANAGEMENT, SOME ARCHITECTURAL PROJECT MANAGEMENT MISSIONS COULD BE INTRODUCED**

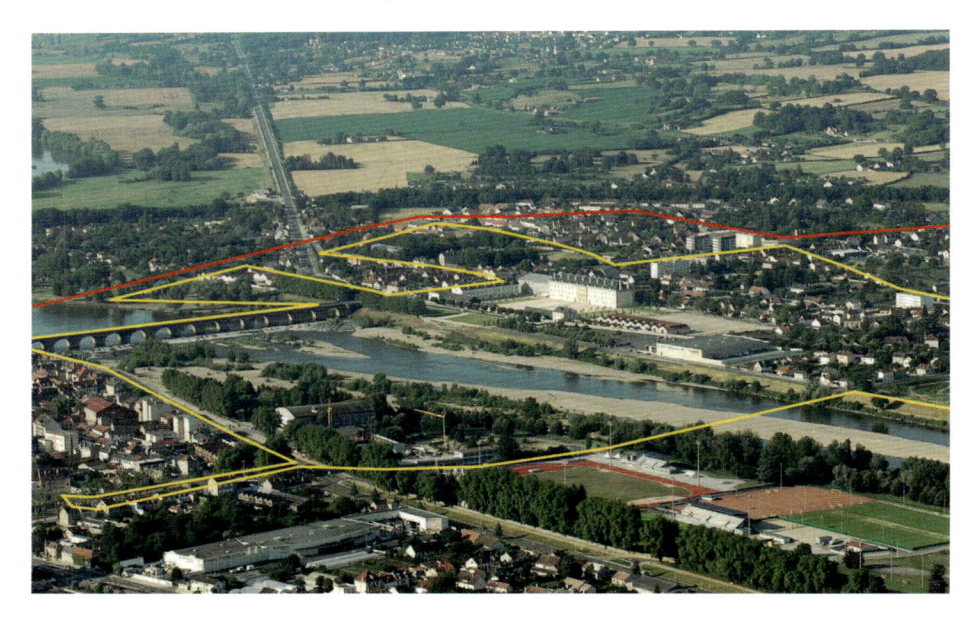

Interview of the site's representative
Sandrine Masquelet, Director of the Planning, Urban Planning, Habitat department

PRESENTATION OF THE SITE WITH REGARDS TO STRATEGY
The site is set around the banks of the Allier River that goes through the town of Moulins and federates the territory of the Moulins Community. The creation of a new building to relieve the unique bridge submits the site to major urban evolutions – the right bank, as the heart of the old town, and the left bank –a.k.a. La Madeleine– more salvage and representing a potential support of new urbanity. The Community wishes to boost an overall development dynamic on this bank through a rebalance that advantages the whole conurbation.

HOW IS THE SITE CONNECTED TO THE SESSION TOPIC - THE ADAPTABLE CITY?
We meant to receive innovative scenarios of mutation for the sector, integrating the dimension of nature in town, presenting an adaptable management of the project and adding value to the River while integrating the constraints –environmental (floods), rules and on the short-term (urbanize without growth). The scenarios should also allow boosting the conditions for economic and social attractiveness of the heart of the urban area and helping recapture the town in its human dimensions through the creation of a new mobility offer.

DID YOU DEFINE A SPECIFIC PROCESS FOR THE URBAN DEVELOPMENT OF THE SITE AFTER EUROPAN COMPETITION?
The Moulins Community wishes to go on with the dynamic and the partnership with Europan by organizing a workshop with the winning teams and all the local partners to allow the emergence and coproduction –in link with the structuring projects of the community territory– of an overall project shared by all the actors.

BENOÎT BARNOUD (FR)
LANDSCAPE ARCHITECT, ARCHITECT
CLARA LOUKKAL (FR)
GEOGRAPHER-URBANIST,
LANDSCAPE ARCHITECT

LAND
28 RUE DU CANAL
93200 SAINT-DENIS, FR
T. +33 683374612

WINNER - MOULINS (FR)
The Theory of Evolution

TEAM POINT OF VIEW A town is an evolving living structure. In which way can we anticipate future changes? What lingers on in spite of changes and what does not survive changes in a town? We looked for answers in natural sciences in which concepts about adaptability, transformation or evolution are developed. According to Lamarck, if the living conditions of a species are altered, then the individuals must make their organs evolve to guarantee their survival. An active participation is imposed. Behaviours imply adaptation. Then a town is the coproduction of its whole inhabitants. Darwin's theory is based on the idea that individuals composing the same species are all different from one another. The only surviving individuals are those casually equipped with the most optimized characteristics for a specific environment. The struggle for living can be interpreted as an economic competition. Then a town seems to be the sum of individual patterns.

These postulates are additional for the analysis of urban dynamics and constitute tools in the development of a sustainable town, though scientifically opposed. The town of Moulins, crossed by the Allier River, suffers from macrocephaly – the right bank developed at the detriment of the left one. But this bank already has the necessary organs for its survival. Irrigating, hybridizing and stimulating the good organs allow urban development and keep on offering a possibility for organs to evolve depending on the residents' need.

JURY POINT OF VIEW The project considers the development of the city over the long term, with respect to natural or anthropogenic alterations to the river system. By identifying the parts that reflect natural evolution and those that reflect human alterations, the project divides into nine territories related to specific types of action. The cartographic layering of these territories reveals a fluid landscape structure, reflecting a set of deliberate transformations that do not prevent the natural evolution of the milieus.

SIMON GUILLEMOT (FR)
CHARLY CROCHU (FR)
JEAN-BENOÎT BOCCAREN (FR)
ARCHITECTS

CAMILLE SERRES (FR)
ARCHITECT

PROJET 08
12 RUE CHRISTIAN DEWET
75012 PARIS, FR
T. +33 699244706
CONTACT@PROJET08.COM
WWW.PROJET08.COM

RUNNER-UP - MOULINS (FR)

When the Allier Becomes City

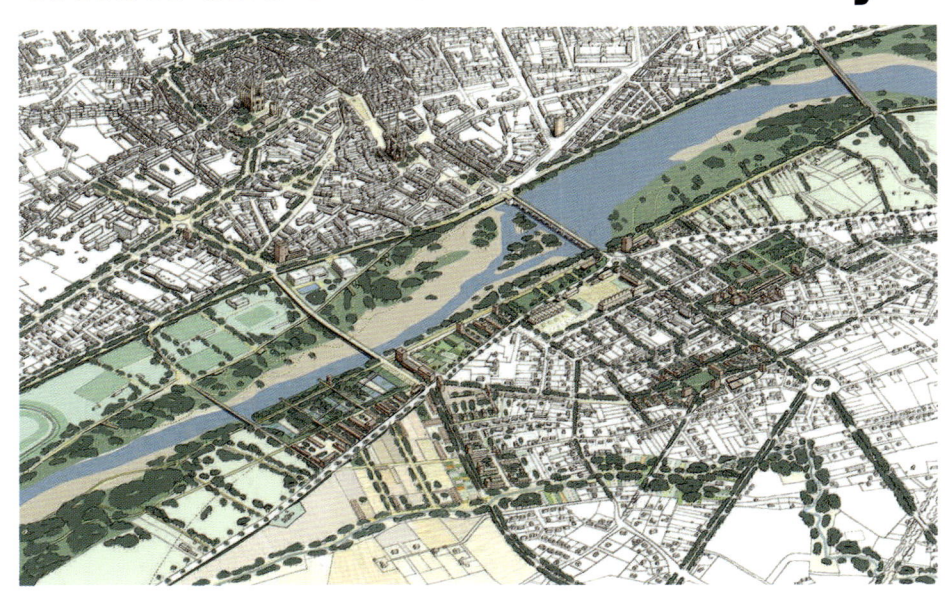

TEAM POINT OF VIEW Reconsidering the relation of the city with the river is to make it part of a territory. Starting from the heart of Moulins, the project connects the departmental park of the Valley of Allier, linking the various natural spaces of the riverbed to the surrounding cities. New pedestrian and cycle routes, on both sides of the stream, shape a vast network running through beaches, floodplains, undergrowth and fields, participating in the new urban system. If the city gradually turned away from the river, this one can nevertheless become her main asset. Because it was not channelled, it keeps its natural and tempestuous character, where the flora and fauna compose a landscape that the project suggests valuing. Connecting the city and the river is restoring the geographical space within the urban fabric itself. The whole suburb of Madeleine is thought as an extension of the Allier Park. A weft of planted ways and walks connect the river to the new public places in heart of the lots. Our intervention is set up in a process of densification of the urban fabric and the creation of public space. Basing ourselves on the potential represented by the hearts of the lots, we propose a reinterpretation of the enclosures of the diocese and the CNCS open spaces and their progressive systematization. The reconquest of the hearts of the lots gives way to floodplain meadows, around which the new forms of habitat are implanted.

JURY POINT OF VIEW The project treats the town of Moulins as an inflection point in the Vallée de l'Allier departmental park. The thickness of the major bed outlines an open space of contemplation staged by developing viewpoints and belvederes, pontoons and walking areas, architectural emergences echoing the spires of the religious buildings on the right bank. In urban terms, the project is based in a network of pathways and a web of public spaces interconnected between the two banks.

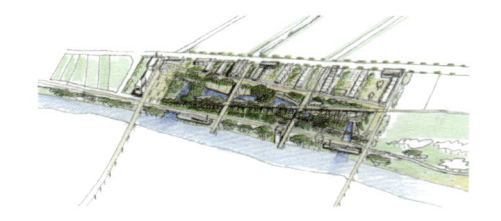

ERNESTO APOLAYA CANALES (PE)
CLAIRE SÈZE (FR)
ARCHITECTS-URBANISTS
SÉBASTIEN HARLAUX (FR)
URBANIST
CAROLE PLAGNOL (FR)
ARCHITECT

T. +33 619713360
ALLIES2MOULINS@GMAIL.COM
WWW.APU.COM.PE

SPECIAL MENTION - MOULINS (FR)
Les Alliés de Moulins

TEAM POINT OF VIEW The objective is to redefine the core of Moulins by balancing both banks and to connect it to its large territory resuming the dialog with the Allier River. The project proposes two frameworks of actions based on Moulins's natural and cultural assets. One consists in a network of immediate strategic interventions: "les Alliés de Moulins". Each "Allié" favours citizen participation, changes the area's perception and is the beginning of future developments. This strategy of urban acupuncture is guided by "les Lignes de Front": 6 axes of long-term interventions lead by the public authorities.

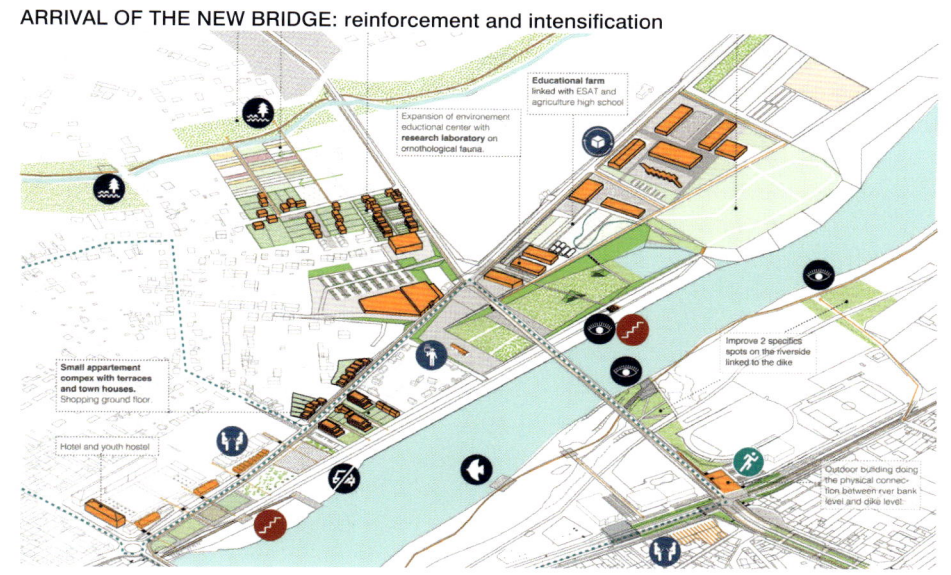

ARRIVAL OF THE NEW BRIDGE: reinforcement and intensification

OS
NORGE (NO)

CATEGORY: **URBAN - ARCHITECTURAL**
LOCATION: **OSØYRO, OS**
POPULATION: **19,000 INHAB.**
STRATEGIC SITE: **90 HA**
PROJECT SITE: **4.5 HA**

SITE PROPOSED BY: **OS MUNICIPALITY (IN COLLABORATION WITH HORDALAND COUNTY)**
OWNER(S) OF THE SITE: **OS MUNICIPALITY AND ESSO NORGE**
COMMISION AFTER COMPETITION: **PLANNING AND BUILDING COMMISSION**

Interview of the site's representative

Henning Wenaas Ribe, Architect,
Planning Department
Europan Norway

PRESENTATION OF THE SITE WITH REGARDS TO STRATEGY

Os is facing rapid change due to population growth and the opening of a new infrastructure increasing connectivity in the region. The county has identified Osøyro as one out of five regional centres around the city of Bergen that will have to accommodate this growth. Forecasts predict a doubling of the population in Os by 2040, which will put into question Osøyro›s identity as a village.

HOW IS THE SITE CONNECTED TO THE SESSION TOPIC - THE ADAPTABLE CITY?

The site proposed for the Europan 13 competition is the last remaining undeveloped strip of land with access to Osøyro's harbour basin. The site has the potential to work as a connecting element in the fragmented centre divided by natural elements, such as the river and substantial height differences, and manmade barriers such as infrastructure and roads. The site can become a mediator between the old and new, water and land, and locals and visitors.

DID YOU DEFINE A SPECIFIC PROCESS FOR THE URBAN DEVELOPMENT OF THE SITE AFTER EUROPAN COMPETITION?

The municipality has actively engaged itself in the development, investing in property and coordinating efforts to accommodate growth and increase and improve urban life. As of now, they are preparing work related to a new masterplan for the town centre as a whole, starting fall 2016. As part of this work they will invite the winning team, together with a wide range of local actors, to contribute with innovative ideas and enrich the planning process.

DIANA CRISTÓBAL OLAVE (ES)
ALICIA HERNANZ PÉREZ (ES)
GONZALO JOSE LÓPEZ GARRIDO (ES)
TANIA ORAMAS DORTA (ES)
ARCHITECTS

TEAM@KNITKNOTARCHITECTURE.COM
WWW.KNITKNOTARCHITECTURE.COM

WINNER - OS (NO)

Osurbia – Redefining Suburbia

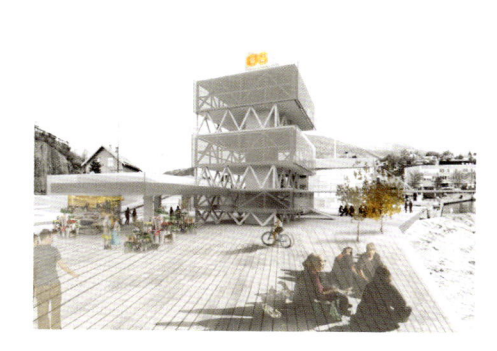

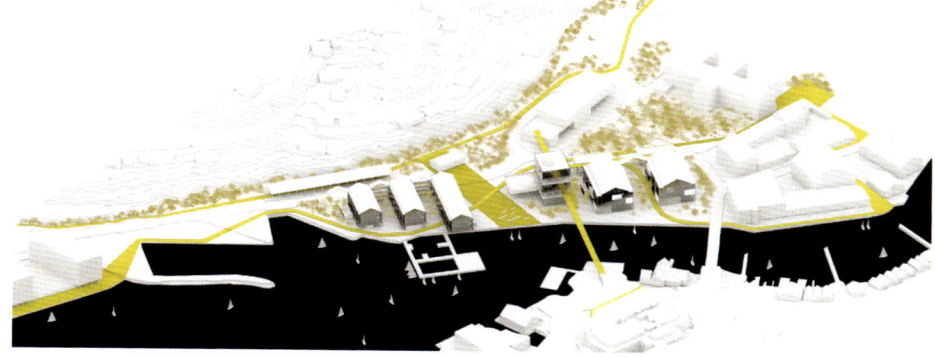

TEAM POINT OF VIEW Os is currently facing a major challenge in its history: how to become a new regional and urban centre while maintaining its own identity. This identity is mainly defined by its suburbia character (70% of households are single-family).

Our proposal stands up for the idea that this identity should be preserved and enhanced, while it advocates a redefinition of the concept of "suburbia" in the context of a new scenario where its traditional meaning is no valid anymore. The foreseen population growth or the construction of new infrastructures in the area, coupled with the need to conceive our cities in more sustainable terms, urges the exploration of new physical and socio-economic ways of development. Through our proposal we attempt to provide an answer to those emergent conditions by suggesting a shift from 'SUBURBIA' to 'OSURBIA'.

Our proposal explores the ideas behind the so-called 'suburbia' to understand the characteristics that underpin such a distinctive identity and unique way of living. To do so, 5 elements or types customarily associated with 'traditional suburbia' have been identified on the site: the single dwelling; the parking lot; the mall; the filling station; and 'suburbia beyond the dwelling'. A sixth type, 'the strip', has been defined as the element providing unity and coherence to all the rest. The project seeks to re-appropriate the complexities behind those elements to produce new meanings while maintaining its associated symbolism.

JURY POINT OF VIEW The project points at important issues at stake in the town centre and illustrates an effortless, but appropriate area plan addressing questions about disconnections and fragmentation. The historic buildings are given new importance, a new pedestrian bridge includes a public park and the shopping mall is integrated as an important activator of the riverfront. The project further illustrates a credible solution for private dwellings along the quay. In general all the re-appropriations and redefinitions show an in-depth understanding of Os and its future potential in a surprising and refreshing way.

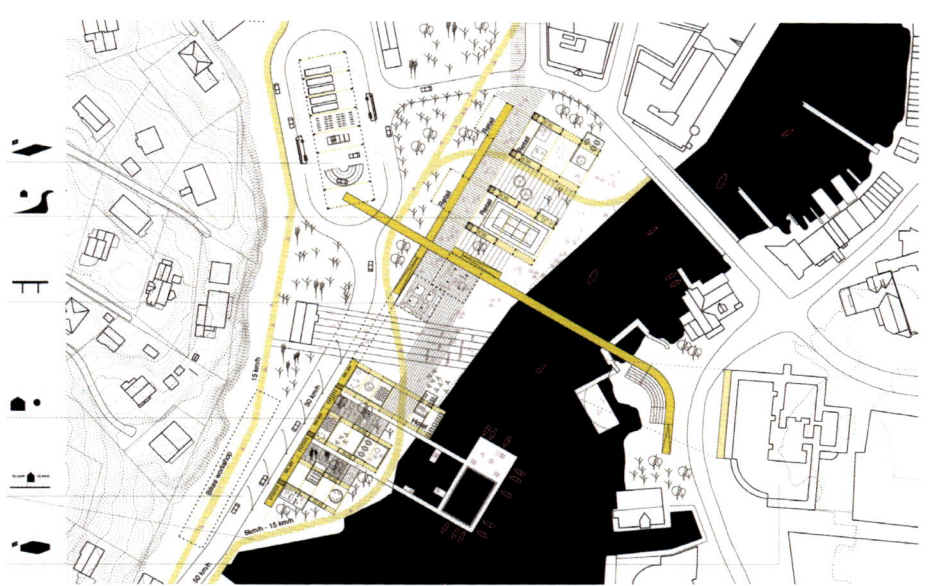

BOGDAN DEMETRESCU (RO)
ARCHITECT

OANA SIMIONESCU (RO)
ARCHITECTS
ADA OPREA (RO)
ALEX VOICA (RO)
BOGDAN TUDOR (RO)
DENIS POLOCA (RO)
DRAGOS NISTOR (RO)
STUDENTS IN ARCHITECTURE

D PROIECT
UNIRII SQUARE 5, AP19
300085 TIMISOARA, RO
T. +40 722540448
DPROIECT@GMAIL.COM
WWW.FACEBOOK.COM/D.PROIECT

RUNNER-UP - OS (NO)
Preparing Density

JURY POINT OF VIEW The project challenges a conventional type of development and the planned densification of Os. It argues that a traditional densification would harm the Os community and proposes instead a strategy of densifying social, cultural and economic interactions. It introduces a pavilion structure on site to promote temporary activity in the centre of Osøyro, ensuring large parts of Os city centre to become dedicated to the public and not to private market forces. As a result, a generous urban space with "unrestricted mobility" is created. The project promotes a system of empowerment where the inhabitants can directly participate in developing the town centre.

TEAM POINT OF VIEW In order to create a complete living experience for the inhabitants, Os does not need more built structures, but an increase in the number and diversity of functions and social interactions, making it a vibrant and active space of the community.

Our proposal uses different mechanisms to soften the strong limits bounding the site. We aim to create events on their paths, to perceive them not as obstacles but as opportunities to connect with natural elements or people.

In architectural terms, the site is a straight, man made platform. We devised a process to regenerate the space for public use, which starts by introducing the people to the site and asking them to participate. Most of the existing buildings are to be relocated. A complete overhaul of the square and its infrastructure will set the premises for further development, covering the area with a texture of pavement, green patches and wooden deck surface.

To activate the stage, prefabricated wood pavilions are proposed in strategic positions, configurations and densities. The modules can be rented for small businesses or left open and transparent to host temporary functions. The development plan includes specific rules over how people choose to extend the constructions on the site to follow a desire character. The final layout and aspect of the square remains for the people to decide.

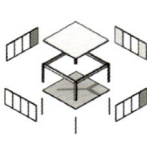

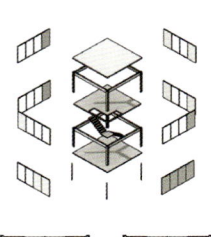

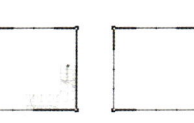

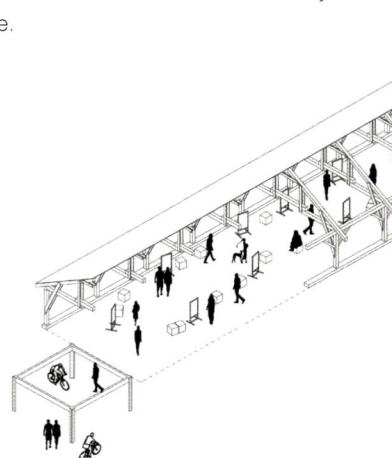

EMANUELA ORTOLANI (IT)
MICHELA ROMANO (IT)
EMILIA ROSMINI (IT)
DAVID VECCHI (IT)
ARCHITECTS

ELISA CECCHINI (IT)
NICOLA DONATI (IT)
STUDENTS IN ARCHITECTURE

ULTRA ARCHITETTURA
VIA GIULIO BERNASCHI 22
00044 FRASCATI, ROMA, IT
T. +39 069424015
INFO@ULTRAARCHITETTURA.COM
WWW.ULTRAARCHITETTURA.COM

SPECIAL MENTION - OS (NO)

Limelight

TEAM POINT OF VIEW The proposal for the future development of Os is designed to promote a growth model that not only aims at increasing densification but that is able to launch the city especially from an economic point of view, taking its identity and its intrinsic qualities into account. The insertion of the film industry is one of the focal points of the strategy designed for the renewal process of the city. Os must provide complementary functions to the ones already present in the region. The decision to include a creative industry represents a possible activation tool in the development of networks and relationships on a regional scale.

PALMA
ESPAÑA (ES)

CATEGORY: **URBAN - ARCHITECTURAL**
LOCATION: **PALMA, MALLORCA, BALEARIC ISLANDS, SEAFRONT PROMENADE**
POPULATION: **400,000 INHAB.**
STRATEGIC SITE: **38.5 HA**
PROJECT SITE: **6.4 HA**

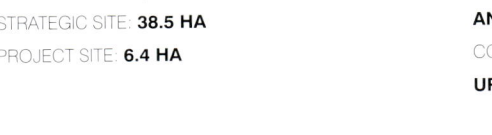

SITE PROPOSED BY: **DIRECTORATE-GENERAL OF ARCHITECTURE AND HOUSING. BALEARIC ISLANDS REGIONAL GOVERNMENT**
OWNER(S) OF THE SITE: **PALMA CITY COUNCIL AND HARBOUR AUTHORITY**
COMMISION AFTER COMPETITION: **PRELIMINARY URBAN STUDIES**

Interview of the site's representative

Óscar Canalís, Head of the Department of Urban Projects, Accessibility and Disclosure of the General Direction of Architecture and Housing, Balearic Government

PRESENTATION OF THE SITE WITH REGARDS TO STRATEGY

The aim of this competition was to seek ways to adapt Palma City to the new needs and desires for better quality lifestyles and tourist services, focusing the work on the seafront promenade. The city is now immersed in an adaptation process to reconcile its current structures with today's trends in uses and practices, which for citizens and tourists alike have evolved towards a need for physical exercise and the use of the seafront terraces. These uses should therefore be prioritized, while at the same time catering proportionally to the local need for mobility and facilitating access to alternative uses.

HOW IS THE SITE CONNECTED TO THE SESSION TOPIC - THE ADAPTABLE CITY?

Palma's seafront is a 5.5-km-long road from Manuel Azaña Street to the ferry terminal. Part of it borders the old town and the city walls, and another part runs beneath densely occupied districts with hotels, apartment blocks, restaurants, nightlife and nautical recreation facilities. The sense of a human scale and the proximity of the sea are greatly diminished by access problems and conflicts with traffic experienced by residents and visitors alike. It is now impossible to restore its physiognomy to its state prior to the changes brought about by the tourist boom in the second half of the 20th century, but we can try to evoke it with a successful adaptation project.

DID YOU DEFINE A SPECIFIC PROCESS FOR THE URBAN DEVELOPMENT OF THE SITE AFTER EUROPAN COMPETITION?

The aim was to receive idea proposals for the renewal of the Palma seafront promenade. Participants were asked to take into account the planning provisions, although they could present ideas for the development of these plans and also propose improvements and alternatives.

JUAN SOCAS (ES)
MURIELLE CLAIR (FR)
ARCHITECTS

37 RUE DU STAND
1204 GENÈVE, CH
T. +33 686653491
JUAN.SOCAS@JUANSOCAS.ES
WWW.JUANSOCAS.ES

WINNER - PALMA (ES)
Salvemos el horizonte

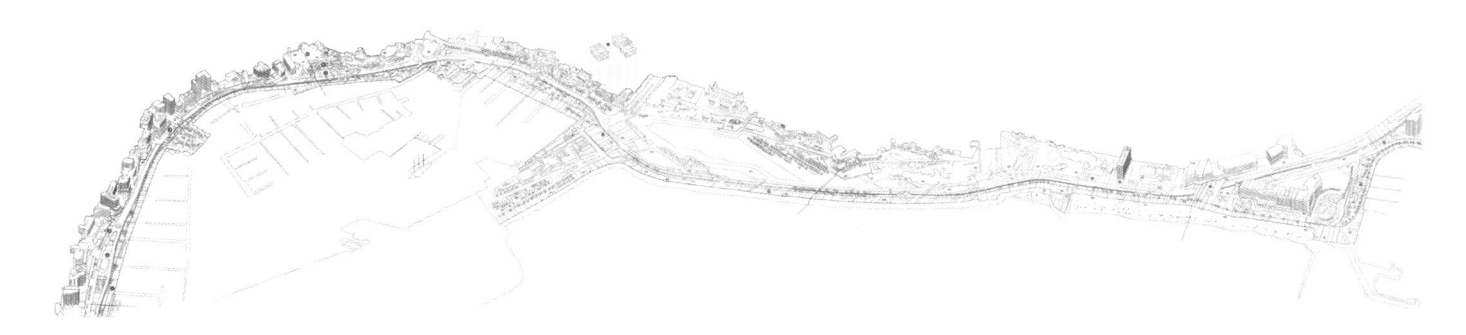

TEAM POINT OF VIEW We applied an external and independent variable as a pattern, able to organise and assume the form of the site. The insertion of these bands –that are able to integrate multiple problems in one gesture– implies a series of mutations generating various public spaces that, without adding new built elements, allow solving the problems of connection, changes of altitude, vegetal densification, compatibility of uses, integration of furniture, insertion of equipment as well as incoherence of flow.

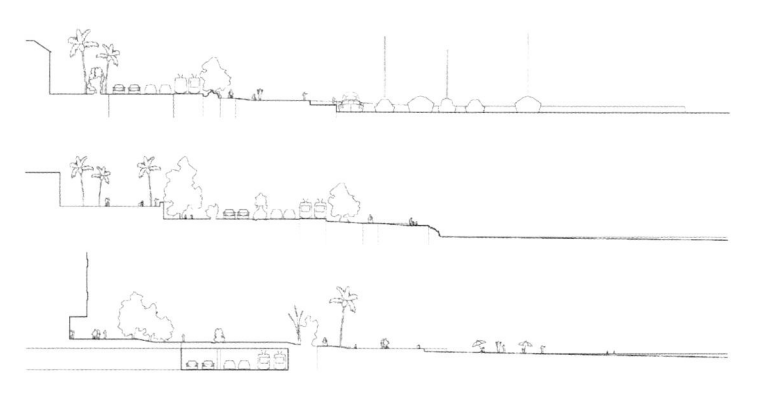

The project is in fact the result of making compatible an open system, abstract and generic able to adapt itself to the singularities of the site and the premise of "no construction".

Still, can a project adopting a decisive attitude of "no construction" be economically sustainable? Along the maritime front pockets of land appear that could receive uses generating financial profit. With the goal of sustainable management we activate and connect these fields to the study area so that the generated income finances other aspects of the project. At the same time, we propose to strengthen the local SLC; in exchange for the exploitation of these spaces we insert green areas in parking zones, uses of vantage point, etc. thereby decreasing the maintenance costs for taxpayers.

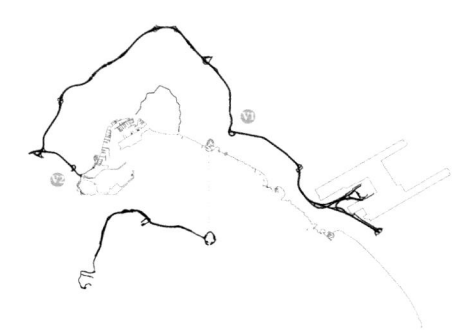

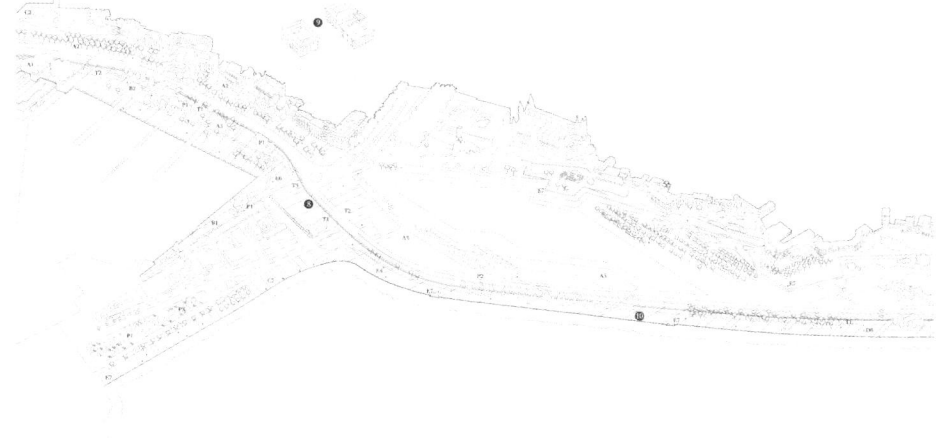

JURY POINT OF VIEW This confident project suggests a section containing serial solutions running perpendicular to the sea to be applied to the multiple circumstances of the city's coastal strip. It presents "non-construction" as an interesting operating method. It tackles the issue of the interface between the city and water throughout this area with five major cuts, each of which including seven repeatable solutions adapted to the traffic requirements, the topography, the various types of flow and the landscape.

FRANCISCO CIFUENTES UTRERO (ES)
LUZ MYRIAM DUQUE TARDAGUILA (CO)
SEBASTIÁN MARTORELL MATEO (ES)
CARLES GABRIEL OLIVER BARCELÓ (ES)
ARCHITECTS

ERNEST BORDOY ANDREU (ES)
LARA FUSTER PRIETO (ES)
ANA ROCA MORA (ES)
STUDENTS IN ARCHITECTURE
MIGUEL CAÑELLAS GINARD (ES)
CRISTINA LLORENTE ROCA (ES)
ARCHITECTS
PERE BENNASSAR (ES)
BIOLOGIST
MARIA RAZUMOVA (RU)
ECONOMIST
EDUARD CUADRADO DE JUAN (ES)
ENVIRONMENTALIST
LLUÍS GÓMEZ-PUJOL (ES)
GEOGRAPHER
RAFAEL VELASCO FERNANDEZ (ES)
MARINE ENGINEER

AULETS
LOCAL 16, 17 SANT FELIU STREET
07012 PALMA DE MALLORCA, ES
T. +34 971723498
AULETS@AULETS.NET
WWW.AULETS.NET

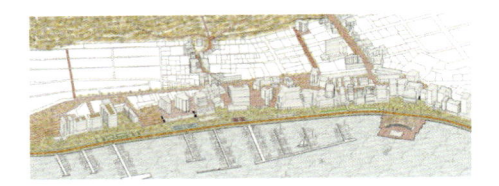

TOMEU DURAN GELABERT (ES)
JOSE M. ROS MATHEU (ES)
ARCHITECTS
JORGE GIMÉNEZ IBÁÑEZ (ES)
LARA GARCÍA GIMENO (ES)
ENVIRONMENTALISTS
CARLES F. BAEZA SERVER (ES)
SOCIOLOGIST

DANIEL IPPOLITO ALOMAR (ES)
LLUÍS BORT I CEREZO (ES)
ARCHITECTS

SISTEMESOPERATIUS@OUTLOOK.COM
WWW.SISTEMESOPERATIUS.COM
JROSMATHEU@GMAIL.COM
JORGEGIMIB@GMAIL.COM
LARA.GARCIAGIMENO@GMAIL.COM
CARLESFRANCESC@HOTMAIL.COM

SPECIAL MENTION - PALMA (ES)

Grace, Let's Go Swimming

TEAM POINT OF VIEW The project proposes to transform the waterfront into a green infrastructure. Beyond the coastline, the proposal rethinks the entire city. Through a new mobility model and the reorganization of the different uses we propose to enable the restoration of existing ecosystems and public space. The strategy is based on the environmental connection between the Tramuntana Mountains and the sea; a sustainable water management by recovering the soil permeability; and the enhancement of the heritage and environmental value of the adjacent consolidated urban areas.

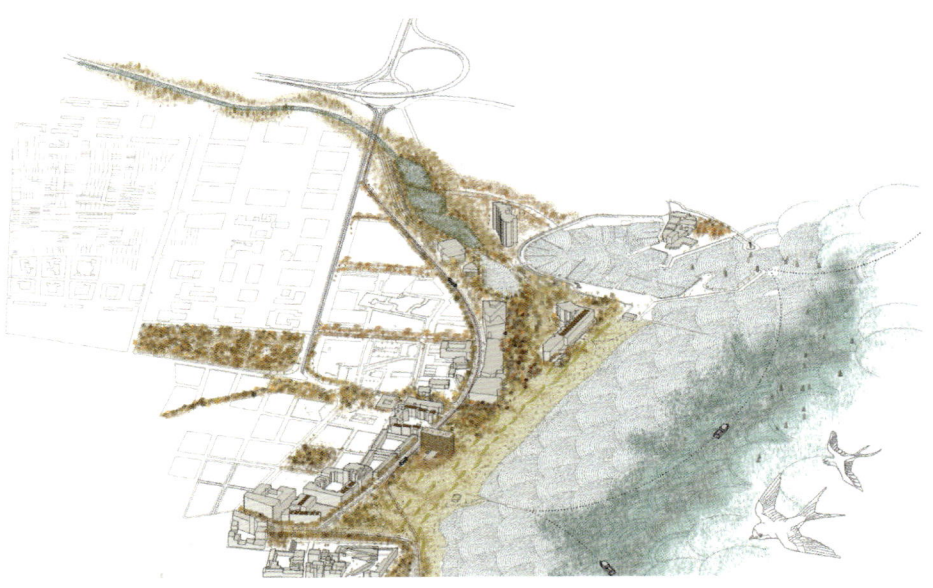

SPECIAL MENTION - PALMA (ES)

Seambiosis

TEAM POINT OF VIEW Our proposal extends the area of consideration far beyond the strip of the waterfront. The main idea of the project is to recover the symbiosis that existed between Palma and the sea by strengthening the linkage between the waterfront and the city behind. Palma's waterfront should be reconsidered within the context of the street spaces and squares that connect the urban tissue and the sea. Giving depth to the strip of the waterfront by means of articulating the links to the urban network may be a way to absorb the pressure on the waterfront and to "urbanize" the seafront at the same time.

SAINT-BRIEUC
FRANCE (FR)

CATEGORY: **URBAN - ARCHITECTURAL**
LOCATION: **SAINT-BRIEUC - BRITTANY**
POPULATION: **46,000 INHAB.**
STRATEGIC SITE: **350 HA**
PROJECT SITE: **70 HA (CITY CENTRE) + 6 HA (LÉGUÉ AREA)**

SITE PROPOSED BY: **MUNICIPALITY OF SAINT-BRIEUC, WITH SUPPORT OF EPFB (ÉTABLISSEMENT PUBLIC FONCIER DE BRETAGNE)**
OWNER(S) OF THE SITE: **VARIOUS**
COMMISION AFTER COMPETITION: **PROJECT AND STUDY MISSIONS ON ONE OR SEVERAL MUTABLE SITES FOLLOW-UP OPERATIONS CAN BE INITIATED WITH PRIVATE PARTNERS**

Interview of the site's representative

PRESENTATION OF THE SITE WITH REGARDS TO STRATEGY

The Saint-Brieuc Municipality wishes to undertake a strategic reflection on the organisation and future of the territory, underpinned by the highlighting of several geographical and cultural pairings: town land/town sea, man-made town/nature town, plateau town/valley town. In order to organise the urban, economic and tourist development, the municipality is looking at Europan for an overall vision that will notably explore the continuity of its urban and natural public spaces and the quality of the routes from town to sea. All this raises questions about mobility and public spaces, the possibility of projects in interstitial spaces, and a reflection on combining access to and use of the valleys with the protection of their landscape and environmental quality.

HOW IS THE SITE CONNECTED TO THE SESSION TOPIC - THE ADAPTABLE CITY?

In proposing a large study area, the Saint-Brieuc Municipality is raising a question of geographical scale for the implementation of a strategy of urban transformation through a new relationship between land and sea in terms of landscape, urban routes and public spaces. The overall urban and landscape vision should reinforce the heart of the conurbation and propose project processes appropriate to the town's specific historical and geographical features: the land relief and the slopes, the protection of nature, the town's identity and relationship to the sea, the interweaving of functions and uses, the presence of large infrastructures, the organisation of mobilities.

IRIS CHERVET (FR)
ARCHITECT, LANDSCAPE ARCHITECT

PARIS, FR
T. +33 677733770
IRIS.CHERVET@GMAIL.COM
WWW.CARGOCOLLECTIVE.COM/IRISCHERVET

WINNER - SAINT-BRIEUC (FR)
Landscape Focus

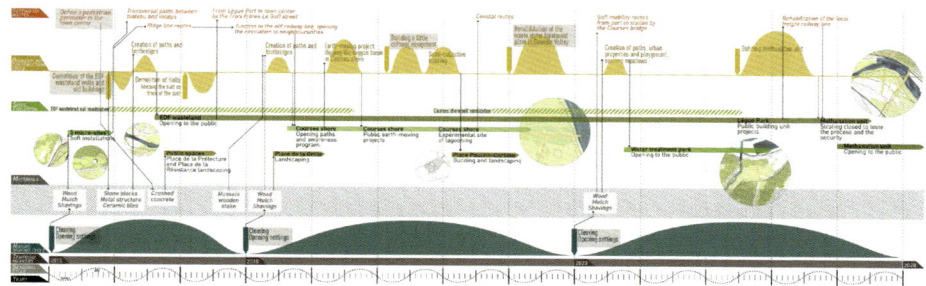

JURY POINT OF VIEW The project combines perceptual, physical, temporal and economic approaches to the landscape. It recognises the ambivalence of this landscape and invites us to qualify the quest for the sea in order to open up to the multiplicity of Saint-Brieuc's landscapes. The strategy divides into two phases: showing and providing access. In the first phase, the handling of the landscape, and in particular the partial deforestation of the valleys, has the effect of opening up new views, creating new routes and beginning a cycle of production and valorisation of materials. In the second phase, the estuaries are identified as potential project locations, bringing a special relationship with the sea

TEAM POINT OF VIEW The project makes the question of the proximity of the sea relevant by opening Saint-Brieuc to the multiplicity of landscapes composing it. In a play of contrast, the development of town identity as "mountainous" helps to reaffirm the difference in sea landscape. In this way different manners to recover a relationship between Land and Sea can be explored:
- opening of views showing the potent geography of this territory,
- through a gradient of landscape patterns making the transition between natural valleys and inhabited plateaux,
- through uses, evolving in the centre of a dense and attractive urban framework;
- by routes connecting the railway station to the harbour and opening upon broad landscape;
- through the relationships between stake-holders involved in environmental industry, on 3 emblematic sites in estuaries from valleys.
The approach lies on a horizontal view of territory based on perception through sight, vertical vision through the appearance of buildings from the ground upwards and a temporal view that articulates projects. The strategy consists of assessing a collection of possible projects through a long-term vision, then placing them in time by order of priority. The territorial project is put into place through landscape management, initiating a virtuous cycle for material re-use to develop public space. The material thus creates the link in space and time between each site in the project.

116

CYRIL BRETON (FR)
PIERRE-OLIVIER CARPENTIER (FR)
ARCHITECTS
MAXIME GENÉVRIER (FR)
ENGINEER, URBANIST

STUDIO ITA (C. BRETON, P.-O. CARPENTIER)
CONTACT@STUDIO-ITA.COM
WWW.STUDIO-ITA.COM
MG|URBA (M. GENÉVRIER)
MAXIME.GENEVRIER@MGURBA.FR
WWW.MGURBA.FR

WINNER - SAINT-BRIEUC (FR)
Seaside Boulevard

TEAM POINT OF VIEW Saint-Brieuc gave its name to a broad bay, based on a lively ecosystem in which the tidal range always rules the settlement of men's and town's life. Forward of the bay, where deep sea is permanent, towns have naturally grown around the shores and beaches, whereas at the end of the bay towns has settled few kilometres from sea in the inner lands. This situation is a key issue in the project. With the LGV extending (French high speed train) Saint-Brieuc is given the opportunity to become the only city of the bay directly accessible with high-speed trains and tightly linked to the sea. The old and still existing railway (for freight transport and tourism between Le Port du Légué and the train station) is reshaped as a seaside Boulevard. The latter is the matrix for urban interventions that fit the encountered landscapes, topographies, programs and to land owning opportunities. The project gathers multiple contextual issues and answers them using so-called "tools". In order to better adapt to these characteristics, tools are combined and also act as the scope of interventions just as much as the guiding principle of the project. This course across the city is the area where experiments come up and provide an opportunity to offer promising prospects to the surrounding environment.

JURY POINT OF VIEW The quality of this project lies in its capacity to combine a territorial strategy with situated projects. The authors describe the Saint-Birieuc landscape as a "puzzle". Their strategy is to draw on the existing infrastructure in order to introduce local interventions along a "trail of opportunities" and provide a "panoramic and continuous" interpretation of the landscape. They identify nine project themes (described as tools) that are combined and applied appropriately to the different sites.

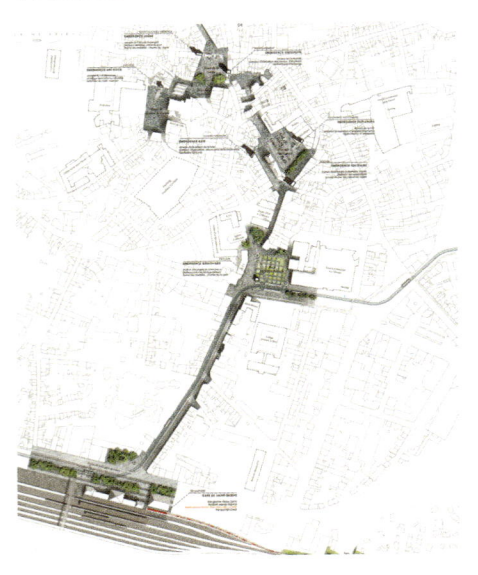

NICOLAS PINEAU (FR)
MARIE-EVE TURPEAU (FR)
NOÉMIE SCHMIDT (FR)
GAYLOR CHIARI (FR)
ARCHITECTS
JEAN CHEVALIER (FR)
ARCHITECT, LANDSCAPE ARCHITECT

ALEXANDRE RENIMEL (FR)
ARCHITECT

T. +33 698508520
NICOLASPINEAU@GMX.COM

RUNNER-UP - SAINT-BRIEUC (FR)
Versants Versatiles

TEAM POINT OF VIEW We suggest approaching the territory of St-Brieuc from a formal singularity: the topographical 80 meters NGF line that integrating the city centre in the Gouët valley. The general strategy consists in working on the relationship between both entities separated by this line: on one side the urbanized plateaus and on the other the deserted hillsides.

In terms of mobility, we propose a 2-speed network allowing increasing the connectivity between plateaus and hillsides by the crossing of a loop of public transportation situated on the axis station-harbour with a transverse pedestrian network arriving from the hillsides. These are therefore considered as connection spaces rather than remote putting.

On this weft, punctuations formed by mobile uses are situated in the junction of the various districts to connect and activate the connections. These uses take the form of small trucks proposing services such as cinema, library, or food truck.

In terms of landscape, the project suggests qualifying the binary report between plateaus and valleys 3 three modes of actions: interpenetration of natural spaces and built spaces (derelict industrial sites); conversion of natural spaces in food-producing spaces (hillside of Notre-Dame); and transposition of landscape (city centre).

This set aims to define a more diffuse landscape system, including the meshing of the landscapes and the uses and questioning the reappropriation of hillsides.

JURY POINT OF VIEW The quality of this project lies in its capacity to reinforce the multipolar nature of the town. The authors noticed that the 80 m long line that separates the plateau from the valleys means that the town centre is part of the latter entity. Their strategy consists in reinforcing the mutual connectivity of the spaces by working on mobility and landscape. They propose establishing a new bus loop from the station to the sea, combined with the enhancement of the hillside tracks. Along this axis, areas are set aside for service vans and mobile shops.

SEINÄJOKI
SUOMI-FINLAND (FI)

CATEGORY: **URBAN - ARCHITECTURAL**
LOCATION: **SEINÄJOKI**
POPULATION: **60,000 INHAB.**
STRATEGIC SITE: **70 HA**
PROJECT SITE: **33 HA**
SITE PROPOSED BY: **CITY OF SEINÄJOKI**

OWNER(S) OF THE SITE: **CITY OF SEINÄJOKI, STATE OF FINLAND AND SEVERAL PRIVATE OWNERS**
COMMISION AFTER COMPETITION: **COMMISSION AT THE LEVEL OF URBAN STRUCTURE AND URBAN PLANNING**

Interview of the site's representative

PRESENTATION OF THE SITE WITH REGARDS TO STRATEGY

Seinäjoki is one of Finland's fastest growing cities, with an annual growth of 1,5%. The city is the regional centre of southern Ostrobothnia and strives to be an attractive and viable choice for residence and businesses. The city strategy is to develop the quality of the environment in the centre and improve its commercial viability. This can partly be done increasing the housing density in the city centre and its immediate surroundings.

The competition area is the railway station with its railway yards and station buildings. It is an important junction of five railway lines halfway between Helsinki and Oulu. Those were originally built between 1880 and 1913 and the city grew up around the station. The old cargo railway yard has become obsolete and is currently an urban fallow. Many of the warehouse buildings as well as a large part of the tracks on the Pohja side will be removed in the future and the area will become available for new development. It is hoped that a variety of diverse mixed functions and housing will be created in the area, including work places, services and public functions.

HOW IS THE SITE CONNECTED TO THE SESSION TOPIC - THE ADAPTABLE CITY?

The objective is to develop Seinäjoki railway station area into a versatile centre where multiple functions, commercial services and housing come together. The station's location in the very centre of Seinäjoki is ideal and it is hoped that the new functions will be closely linked to the centre and enliven the surrounding areas. Developing the railway station area will offer an opportunity to complement and expand the city centre and bring the city a much needed new urban quality.

TAPIO KANGASAHO (FI)
ARCHITECT

JONNA HEIKKINEN (FI)
INTERIOR ARCHITECT, STUDENT IN ARCHITECTURE

T. +358 503444438
TAPIO.KANGASAHO@HEIKKINENKANGASAHO.FI
T. +358 407641465
JONNA.HEIKKINEN@HEIKKINENKANGASAHO.FI
WWW.HEIKKINENKANGASAHO.FI

WINNER - SEINÄJOKI (FI)
Notch

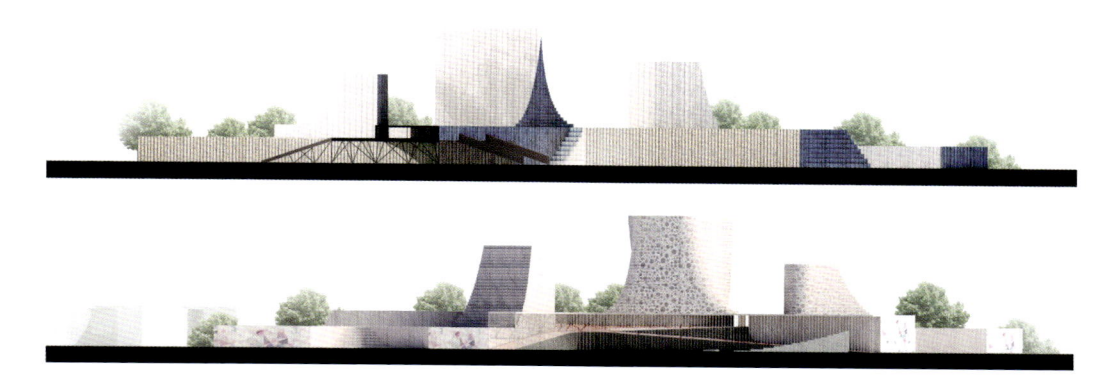

TEAM POINT OF VIEW "NOTCH" creates a new dense urban core for Seinäjoki. The new station structure is the heart of the design, creating a new landmark for Seinäjoki and acting as a visual welcome for passengers. The station forms a new node in the city, acting as a bridge between Pohja district and city centre and simplifying cycling and walking around railway tracks. Two new underpasses also make the connection to Pohja district even easier.

The station area is linked to the city centre by continuing city centres street lines and block structures still maintaining distinctive visual design, which gives the new area its own character. The station building has a wide range of functions, from bus and railway station to retail, office and hotel.

The urban fabric close to both sides of the tracks visually and functionally reduces the barrier effect of the tracks. The new area on Pohja side of the tracks is mainly focused on housing with a few retail spaces. It is created as dense housing area with enough porosity due to the shape of the building blocks.

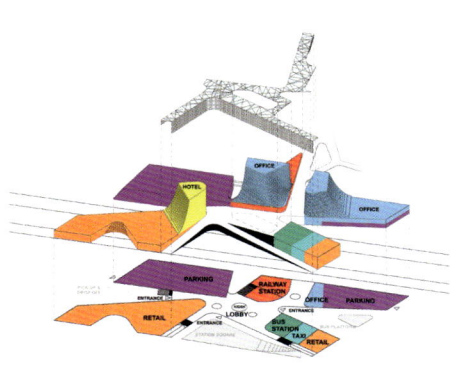

JURY POINT OF VIEW The proposal has a successful grasp of the competition area as a whole, creating a strong identity for the different areas. The approach to the urban structure is beautiful and the new connections work well. The functions have been successfully outlined. The block typology is novel and the design is bold. The blocks of the Pohja district are typologically the most interesting part of the proposal. There are many options available in the communal yards, even though no functions have been indicated for them. The form itself steers towards communal living. The buildings can easily be built in stages.

LOTTA KINDBERG (FI)
LAURA NENONEN (FI)
ARCHITECTS
MIIKA VUORISTO (FI)
ARCHITECT-URBANIST

TAAVI HENTTONEN (FI)
STUDENT IN ARCHITECTURE
JOONA HULMI (FI)
ARCHITECT

LOTTA.KINDBERG@GMAIL.COM
LAURA.MARIA.NENONEN@GMAIL.COM
MVUORISTO@GMAIL.COM

RUNNER-UP - SEINÄJOKI (FI)
Semaphore

TEAM POINT OF VIEW A new travel centre is placed one block South-East of the old building to shift the city gravity centre Southwards, establishing better connections to the locomotive stables and the Aalto centre. The new travel centre is a central node directing flows and becoming a metaphorical "semaphore", an old railway signal system. A cycling bridge connects the Pohja district to the travel centre. A new park South of the station extends the axis to the Lakeuden risti church. A pedestrian bridge connects the travel centre to the locomotive stables. All this is connected with train and bus travellers, a hotel, offices, commercial functions and dwellings. The Northern part of sub-area A consists in 3 different hybrid block typologies, all of which create a strong wall-like border against the railway and a weaker more open border against the street. Courtyards are located between both borders. Sub-area B is developed as a place for events, recreation, small businesses, pop-up activities and culture serving both visitors and local residents. Proposed functions include a microbrewery, a summer theatre, urban farming and different rental spaces. Sub-area C consists in a long, meandering ribbon of apartment blocks protecting the rest of the area from the railway. A public park is formed between the buildings and the railway. The area behind the ribbon is a dense small-scale setting with a network of diverse spaces.

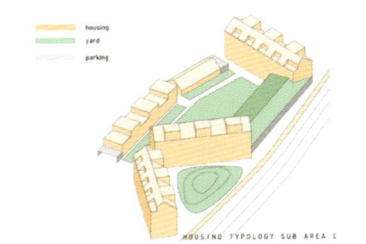

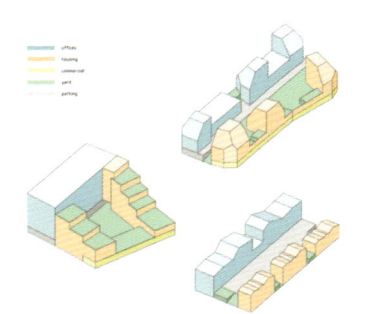

JURY POINT OF VIEW The proposal recognises and is successfully connected to the most important elements in the urban structure of Seinäjoki: the commercial centre and the Aalto Centre. A skilful totality has been weaved together around the axes, connections and landmarks. The new urban structure is influenced by its surroundings, and it changes in accordance with the surrounding existing structure. The orientation, functions and disturbances shape the character of the parts, ranging from a wall-like and enclosed structure all the way to a small-scale and breathing structure.

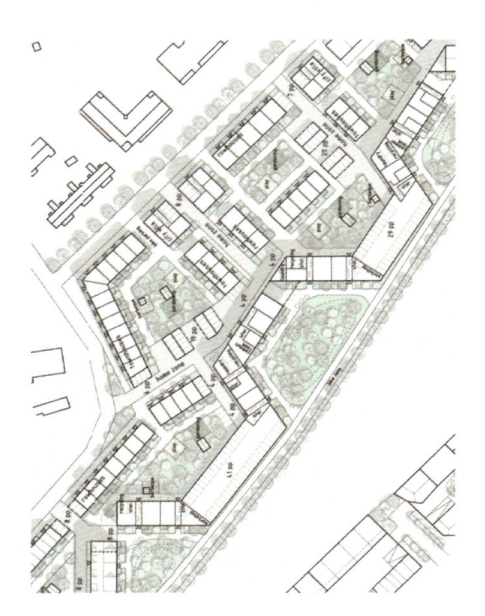

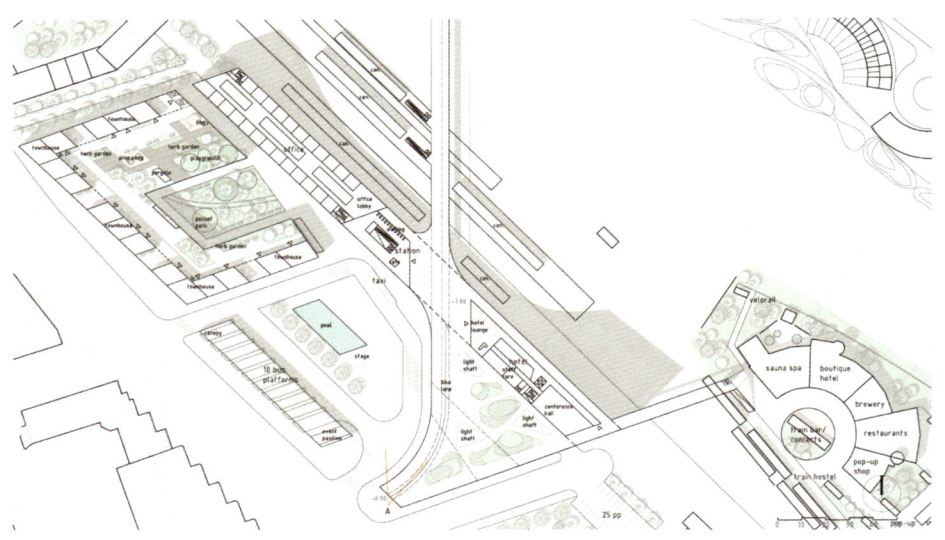

GUILLERMO DÜRIG (CH)
MATTHIAS WINTER (CH)
ARCHITECTS

G.DUERIG@DUERIG.ORG
MATIWINTER@ICLOUD.COM

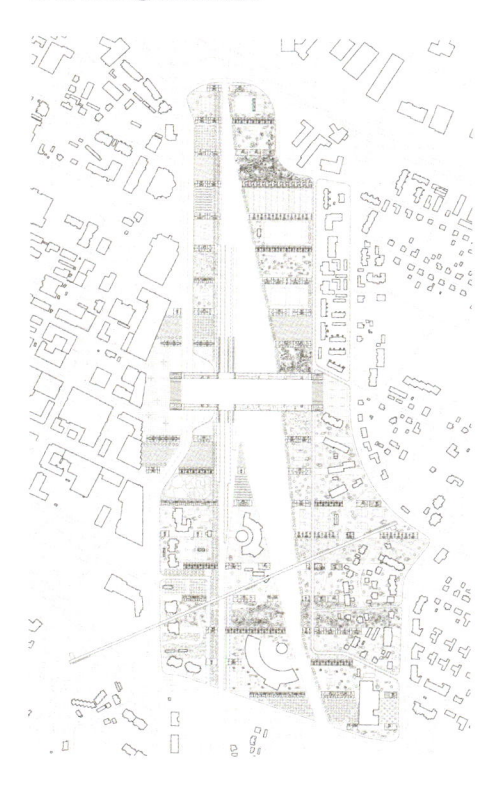

SPECIAL MENTION - SEINÄJOKI (FI)

Intermezzo

TEAM POINT OF VIEW The proposal establishes clear hierarchies in favour of sharply defined, unbuilt rooms-public spaces. These common rooms are used for leisure, sports or agriculture. They are equally open to both city districts and serve as a connecting tissue. The clear structure of the built space allows a super-density within the emptiness. Programmatically creating extremely diverse and dense common spaces. The built structure is not a border between the clearances but a frame and a catalyst for singularity and uniqueness of the rooms. The buildings are permeable and allow connections perpendicular to the spaces.

LAURA HIETAKORPI (FI)
TOMI JASKARI (FI)
ARCHITECTS

MESSENIUKSENKATU 3B 15
00250 HELSINKI, FI
T. +358406526206
LAURA.HIETAKORPI@GMAIL.COM
T. +358 405278050
TOMI.JASKARI@GMAIL.COM

SPECIAL MENTION - SEINÄJOKI (FI)

I Went Down to the Crossroads

TEAM POINT OF VIEW The project creates an urban fabric with Ostrobotnian identity in the heart of Seinäjoki and expands the pedestrian area in the centre. The existing train station is replaced with a travel hub/innovation centre that consists of dense blocks with pedestrian human-scale spaces in between. The pedestrian bridges on both sides of the train station act as gates when approaching the city. An underpass connects the locomotive event park to the innovation centre. On the Eastern side of the rails there is a modernized village of "Ostrobotnian" housing, a retreat within the city.

SISKO HOVILA (FI)
JENNI LAUTSO (FI)
ARCHITECTS
SUVI SAASTAMOINEN (FI)
JUN YANG (CN)
LANDSCAPE ARCHITECTS
RIIKKA ÖSTERLUND (FI)
TRAFFIC ENGINEER

ANNA AF HÄLLSTRÖM (FI)
ENNI OKSANEN (FI)
STUDENTS IN ARCHITECTURE
OTTO-WILLE KOSTE (FI)
STUDENT IN URBAN PLANNING
ANNINA VAINIO (FI)
ARCHITECT

SITO LTD, TUULIKUJA 2
02100 ESPOO, FI
T. +358 207476000
JENNI.LAUTSO@SITO.FI
WWW.SITO.FI

SPECIAL MENTION - SEINÄJOKI (FI)

Somewhere over the Railway

TEAM POINT OF VIEW All main directions lead to a unique hub of mobility. Residential, commercial, office, culture and leisure functions boost the liveliness of Seinäjoki. Valtionkatu Street is an urban boulevard with human scale milieu including spacious pedestrian environment and high quality bicycle lanes. Public spaces and connections, including four attractive pedestrian and bicycle accesses, weave through the city structure. Railway Park adds to the larger landscape structure. Development phases show a variety of temporary functions during the long construction process.

HOW TO USE NEW INPUTS TO CHANGE URBAN SPACE?

Point of views:

"Negotiate as You Go Along":
Infrastructures for Shared "Hybrid" Territories p. 126
by Socrates Stratis

New Inputs, New Public Spaces p. 130
by Carlos Arroyo

Bondy (FR) p. 134
Espoo (FI) p. 138
Landsberg (DE) p. 144
Lund (SE) p. 148
Molfetta (IT) p. 152
Montreuil (FR) p. 156
Santo Tirso (PT) p. 160
Schwäbisch Gmünd (DE) p. 164
St Pölten (AT) p. 170
Stavanger (NO) p. 174
Trondheim (NO) p. 178
Vernon (FR) p. 182
Wien (AT) p. 186

How to profit from new inputs to transform urban space and disperse the incoming positive dynamics to adjacent areas to create new urbanities? How to manage potential tensions between the local and translocal activities? These inputs are related either to new public transport network connections or to new programmatic developments. The scale of these incoming urban dynamics varies from the urban agglomeration to the whole world.

SOCRATES STRATIS, Doctor in Architecture, urbanist, associate professor at the department of Architecture, University of Cyprus. He is one of the founding members of the collaborative structure 'AA & U for architecture, art and urbanism' and a member of Europan's Scientific Council.
www.socratesstratis.com
www.aaplusu.com

Point of view

"Negotiate as You Go Along": Infrastructures for Shared "Hybrid" Territories

1 - BONDY (FR)
2 - STAVANGER (NO) 
3 - SCHWÄBISCH GMÜND (DE) 
4 - VERNON (FR) 
5 - MOLFETTA (IT) 
6 - ESPOO (FI) 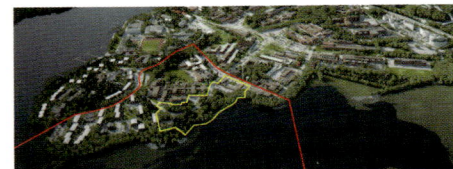
7 - SANTO TIRSO (PT) 
8 - ST PÖLTEN (AT) 

The article is an investigation about the infrastructural role of Europan 13 winning projects in enhancing shared "hybrid" territories. Such territories have multi-geographic realities resulting from urban transport network connections and incoming programs while transformed by all sorts of on-site localities. The projects unfold their political virtue by proposing gradual change of relations amongst the projects' actors, hence influencing how new incoming urban dynamics –inputs– may transform the competition sites into shared "hybrid" territories. The tensions may arise due to potential conflicts between on-site urban actors' agendas and those of the incoming ones. Europan projects' challenge is therefore to become negotiation apparatus in the hands of the urban actors for the adaptable city in, first fostering the presence of the public domain when there is decreasing absence of the Welfare State; second, promoting sharing within an increasing segregated world; and third, allowing for new relations and negotiating moments between the urban actors during project making where urban fragmentation is growing. In fact, this article departs from the last objective to shortly revisit the other two.
The Europan 13 hosting sites of such new inputs are grouped in three categories. The first one is about large mono-functional areas, of big box urbanism (fig.1) –Bondy (FR), Wien (AT)–, of fossil fuel industries (fig.2) – Stavanger (NO)–, or of former military camps and actual teachers' and school centre (fig.3) –Schwäbisch Gmünd (DE); most of them with reduced public presence and need of community spirit. The second category is about areas part of large territorial figures, such as riverbanks (fig.4)–Vernon (FR)–, former industrial waterfronts (fig.5) –Trondheim (NO), Molfetta (IT)–, or natural landscapes (fig.6)– Espoo (FI), Landsberg (DE)–, pressured by increasing private development and threatened by decreasing local community role. The third group is about rather isolated areas, some with community activity (fig.7) –Lund (SE), Montreuil (FR), Santo Tirso (PT)– confronted to potential overwhelming metropolitan flows due to imminent connections to agglomerations' transport networks (fig.8) –St Pölten (AT).

The Europan project in changing times: from participation to negotiation

The expression "Negotiate As You Go Along" could draw references from practices back in the 1960s and 1970s, such as that of Cedric Price collaboration with Inter-Action, an alternative theatre collective, to build the Inter-Action Centre, allowing him to investigate the role of architectural practice in changing times with the emergence of mass media, mass consumerism and mass housing. In fact, Price attributed negotiating capacities to architecture by opening up the design process into a collective platform, inviting for participation. According to Tanja Herdt[1], he found himself exposed in a rather broadened architecture's shift in terms of communication, project development and project outcome. Price invested in participatory moments thanks to the adaptable nature of Inter-Action's infrastructure based on a flexible technical building system. However, the results were rather questionable due to the incompatibility of the high-tech building infrastructure with the low-tech labour contribution intended by the "Inter-Action" collective[2].
Going back to Europan 13, the winning teams are investing in participatory moments thanks to the invisible technology of the urban project as well as to the visible one of the architectural object, both being quite decisive for the co-production of shared "hybrid" territories.

"The task at hand involves working in different scales and with a diverse set of mechanisms blending urban planning, programming, operative and recreational landscapes, infrastructure and communication."

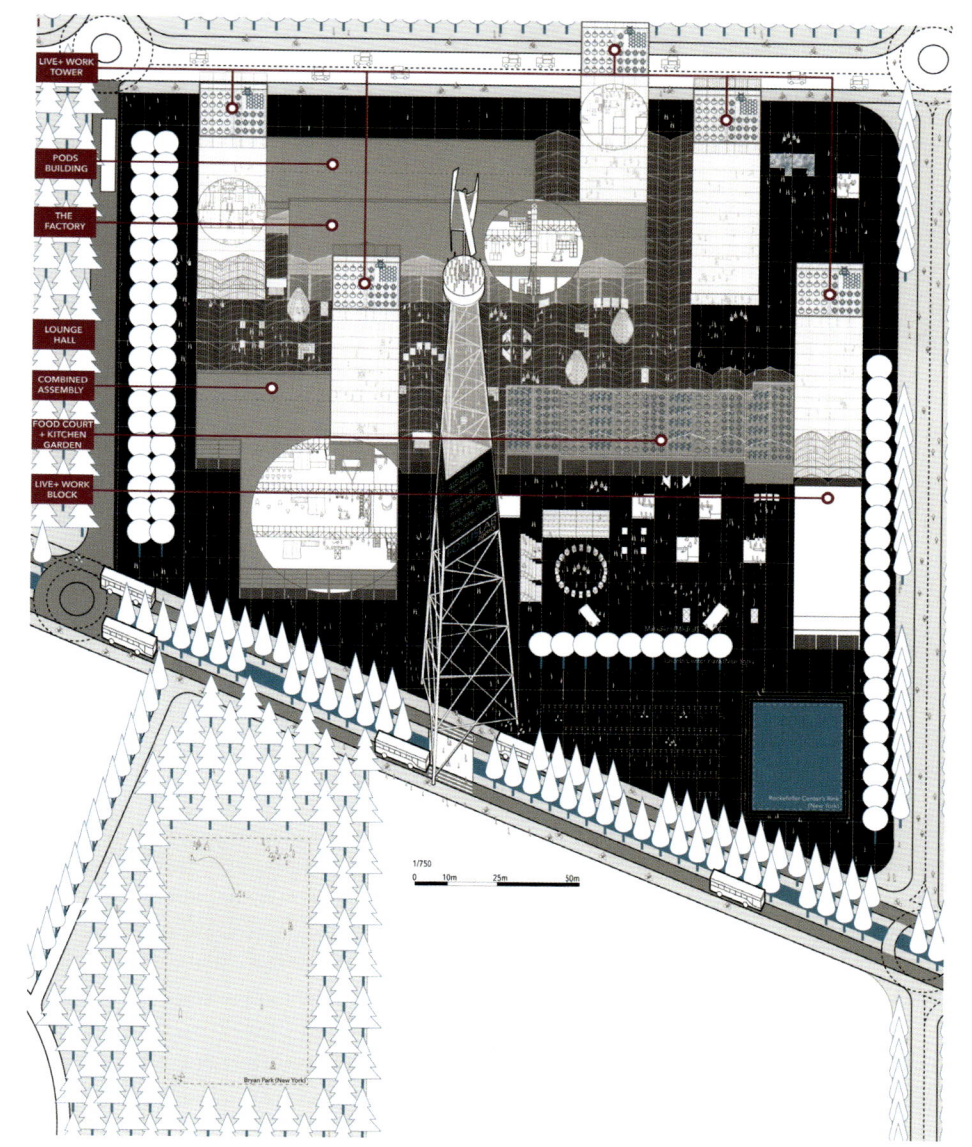

9 - STAVANGER (NO), WINNER - FORUS LABING > SEE MORE P.175

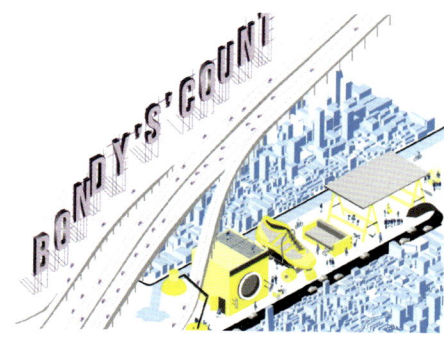

10 - BONDY (FR), WINNER - BONDY'S COUNT > SEE MORE P.135

Third, he refers to agents who, on the name of neutrality, are called to articulate the demand of citizens' participation without making their own stance explicit. He goes on to state that successful citizenship demands reorganization of institutions to have participation imbedded in their decision making, such as the recent case of Barcelona Municipality.

A multiagency approach to enhance the public: between strategies of infiltration and tactics of revalorization of the existing

in fact, the winning projects under study employ a multiagency approach to cope with such dilemmas and set up negotiating frameworks to initiate sharing within "hybrid territories". The point of departure of the projects depends on the state of things in regards to the competition sites and briefs. In some cases when the incoming global flows of people and activities are dominant, as in the first group of sites of mono-functional uses, the projects are about strategies of infiltration to enhance public and collective uses – winners in Bondy and Wien (fig.10 & 11). In other cases, where there is community life which may be

Reading the abovementioned excerpt from Stavanger's competition brief, quoted by winning team *Forus LABing* (fig.9), we are witnessing a shift of architectural practice such as the one confronted by Price. The new shift however demands for complex operations and alliances beyond the architecture's field. By using the concept of "negotiation" we are bringing forward the aspects of participation that are internal to design processes and contain a level of power shift among the project actors. In fact, we aim to surpass pitfalls of the participatory paradigm being used in neutralizing conflict and diminishing the risks of investment by limiting public protest, as Jeremy Till mentions[3]. In fact, we embrace his claim that participation should be about distribution of power in the co-production of the city. Further on, geographer Erik Swyngedow[4] addresses the myths of participation of which we need to be aware of. He first argues that the call for participation is a symptom of democratic dysfunction – institutions do not work and they therefore call citizens to find a solution. Second, he refers to a misunderstood concept of citizens' participation that addresses a specific set of people, since bankers and developers –who are citizens too– have plenty of access to decision making unlike many others; besides, they would not be very happy of sharing power.

11 - WIEN (AT), WINNER - PUBLICQUARTIER > SEE MORE P.187

12 - LUND (SE), RUNNER-UP - MONSTER PLANNING > SEE MORE P.150

13 - MONTREUIL (FR), SPECIAL MENTION - OULIPO > SEE MORE P.158

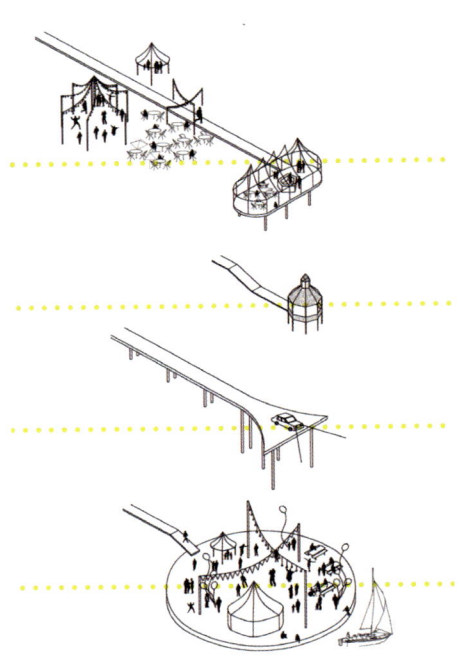

14 - VERNON (FR), WINNER - INSÉCABLE DISTANCE > SEE MORE P.183

challenged by the incoming metropolitan flows –Lund, Montreuil– the project teams choose to concentrate on tactics of revalorization of the unseen virtues of the local everydayness and show how they could play a new role in such "hybrid territories" –*Monster Planning* runner-up in Lund (fig.12); *OuLiPo,* special mention in Montreuil (fig.13); *Insécable distance,* winner in Vernon (fig.14). Further on, we can see projects that consider the new transport nodes as initiators of such hybrid territories –*Culture Symbiotic,* winner in Lund (fig.15); *Navigable Collections,* runner-up in Vernon. In some other cases, the project teams hold on the presence of agglomeration mobility networks to discourage the creation of isolated communities –*Serendipity of Fields,* runner-up in Montreuil (fig.16); *Living With(In)Nature,* winner in Landsberg; *Nodes,* runner-up in Schwäbisch Gmünd (fig.17)–, or create additional hosting space for incoming immigrant communities –*The Elastic City,* runner-up in St Pölten.

Emerging modes of collective practices thanks to synergies between process- and object-oriented approaches

To encourage collective practices –the main ingredient of shared "hybrid territories"– we may need to rely on new ways of negotiation, initiated thanks to synergies between object- and process-oriented approaches. We may then avoid what Swyngedow mentions in regards to the neverending processes usually employed by urbanists as well as to the authoritarian object placing by architects, unaware of its political implications. Amongst the E13 winning projects, we can see a diversity of approaches that employ new relations between processes and objects to achieve sharing within "hybrid territories", by departing either from an object placing or a process initiating and suggesting exchanges among them during design processes.

In some cases the architectural object gets a central role in defining the space of collective practices, either through its uniqueness or its repetition –*The False Mirror,* winner in Trondheim (fig.18). In other cases it gets a symbolic value of the community's presence along territorial figures such as rivers –*Insécable distance,* winner in Vernon – and seacoasts –Espoo–, opening up new kinds of sharing. The winning project in Molfetta, *Hold the Line,* employs a sort of stripped down urban Inter-Action centre to accommodate a community's everydayness along a public waterfront. In the case of the runner-up project in Trondheim, *More Trondheim!* (fig.19), we see existing industrial buildings as shelters for public activities. In the same project, the reorganization to medium size plots becomes another way to ensure the presence of city-scale activities, keeping out big box interventions. In the case of Wien the winning project, *Publicquartier,* reestablishes the role of public space as the enactment of any city

15 - LUND (SE), WINNER - CULTURE SYMBIOTIC > SEE MORE P.149

16 - MONTREUIL (FR), RUNNER-UP - SERENDIPITY OF FIELDS > SEE MORE P.157

17 - SCHWÄBISCH GMÜND (DE), RUNNER-UP - NODES > SEE MORE P.166

centre by proposing the gradual demolition of a city block by the train station, adjacent to a dominating shopping mall. *Publicquartier* initiates creative synergies between public and collective by strategically locating a "habitat" to negotiate the district's urban future.

Process initiating by the project teams may get a playful mode. This is the case of *Bondy's Count*, winner in Bondy, where a game-like negotiation takes place, during which the city should gain infiltration into the competition site by gradually acquiring left-over spaces as well as "left-over times" from the big box operational everydayness. The community would initially emerge by the ephemeral activities and on a second "game round", by a reorganization of the ground inviting big box actors to address the intermediate scale and the introduction of a diversity of activities. To empower a structured negotiation process, a special mention on the same site, *Les nouvelles dynamiques*, offers a well-devised methodology to infiltrate public and community activities within the site, encouraging the big box urbanism to adapt. The team offers a "precedence catalogue", very handy to support controversial dialogues (evidence based urbanism). In Stavanger, the winning project, *Forus LABing*, encourages the development of a networked collectivity guided by a complex strategy of management and design into visualizing transformative processes for urban futures of the actual mono-functional fossil industry area. "Innovation Palaces" is the name of the "habitat" for negotiation processes. The ground gets "super-surface" characteristics to maximize flexibility, where plug-in towers increase the critical mass of inhabitants to yield new communities.

Negotiation thresholds for gradual increase of sharing in co-producing the adaptable city

"Negotiate as You Go Along the Process of Making the Europan Project" is a notification to all actors for the gradual increase of sharing of project making. Their passage through many negotiation thresholds would alter their initial agendas towards a common final outcome. Such approach seems to be frequent among the winning teams, which have delivered complex packages of proposals, full of negotiating moments. Negotiation is ready to take place when the project teams revalorize the existing site's assets –*Monster Planning* in Lund–, and redefine the competition brief's priorities –*Forus LABing* in Stavanger. Negotiation is imminent when they propose roadmaps to the project actors for assisted itineraries through processes with uncertain outcome – *Les nouvelles dynamiques*, special mention in Bondy– or when they make visible the complex networks of relations and powers of the actors at stake –*Bondy's Count,* winner in Bondy.

"Negotiate as You Go Along" is an urge to rethink the technology of architectural practice and its contribution in the urban project operating in complex "hybrid" territories. Issues of communication, project development and outcome are indeed at the heart of architectural practice's shift. Europan is a pertinent platform to study the tendencies of change but also of reappearance of approaches. Addressing the challenge of participation through the concept of negotiation has shown that the Europan 13 projects could operate as platforms to change relations among divergent urban actors in creating shared "hybrid" territories.

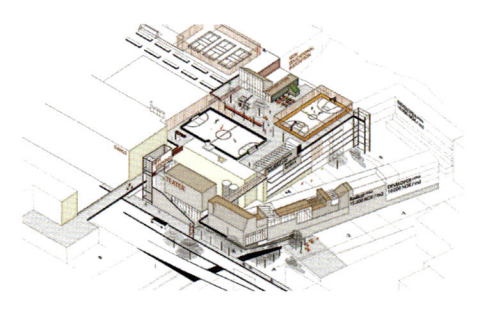

19 - TRONDHEIM (NO), RUNNER-UP - MORE TRONDHEIM! > SEE MORE P.180

[1] "ARCHITECTURE AS NEGOTIATION: THE INTER-ACTION CENTRE OF CEDRIC PRICE", IN CONFERENCE *ARCHITECTURE AS MATTER OF CONTENTION*, AACHEN, 2015
[2] ID.
[3] INTERVIEW PUBLISHED IN *MONU MAGAZINE* (NO 23, 2015)
[4] AESOP CONFERENCE, PRAGUE, 2015

18 - TRONDHEIM (NO), WINNER - THE FALSE MIRROR > SEE MORE P.179

CARLOS ARROYO, linguist, architect, urbanist, teacher in Madrid (ES).
and member of Europan's Scientific Council.
He is the founder and director of Carlos Arroyo Arquitectos.
www.carlosarroyo.net

New Inputs, New Public Spaces

1 - BONDY (FR)

3 - ESPOO (FI)

New inputs, game changing new infrastructures, new connections, renovated economic forces, strategic implementations, or simply new considerations in an existing and functioning area, offer an opportunity for negotiation between the new and the existing that can generate innovative contexts for interaction, new kinds of public spaces.

In the resulting transformation, the existing adapts to accommodate the new input, and a richer, denser, more elaborate constellation emerges.

The interior of an industrial building turned into a covered piazza

Consider the site in Bondy (FR), a strip of land between the canal and a parallel line of more modern infrastructure. Known as the "furniture road", it had been evolving from light industry to a combination of production and commercial (fig.1). Now, new bus lines will bring a different kind of public, populating a strip of canal side which, at the larger scale, is being transformed into a pedestrian network of semi-urban areas.

The special mention project Re_Bondying (fig.2) identifies an industrial building that can easily be transformed into a covered public space. This is a relatively new way to understand public space, which we have seen implemented in other similar contexts with a high degree of success (e.g. Île de Nantes). If the structure was not there in the first place, the idea of a covered but open public space might not be financially viable. On the other hand, a piazza sheltered from the rain and protected from the wind is an ideal meeting point in this kind of latitude.

The team takes this further by proposing reused wood for the cladding, as part of a holistic strategy that works with wood and the canal, both as productive resources and as material textures that are able to create an identity. Furniture production is combined with its commercial lines; the canal is a working means of low carbon transportation for the wood, at the same time as it provides a linear pedestrian leisure area; the covered piazza provides a node, and encourages people to visit the place regardless of the weather; the resulting is a rich mix of productive urbanity.

Introverted intermediate spaces

In the site in Espoo (FI) a natural society of "birds, squirrels and trees", quoting from the city's documents, will need to absorb a growing program of university buildings, including student housing (fig.3). The new buildings need to respect a bird sanctuary and squirrel habitats, with which they will need to integrate.

Many of the answers are based on a number of introverted buildings, dotted amongst the trees, with a minimum of interaction with the surroundings via a pedestrian connecting line, like a path in the forest. In the case of the winning proposal, Wild Synapse (fig.4), the buildings are indeed like trees, self-centred, their volumes made up of a myriad small branches. In the runner-up project Pärske (fig.5) the buildings are rather more mineral,

2 - BONDY (FR), SPECIAL MENTION - RE_BONDYING > SEE MORE P.136

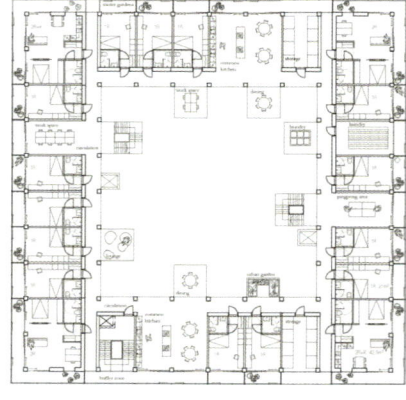

5 - ESPOO (FI), RUNNER-UP - PÄRSKE > SEE MORE P.140

4 - ESPOO (FI), WINNER - WILD SYNAPSE > SEE MORE P.139

6 - LANDSBERG (DE)

8 - SANTO-TIRSO (PT)

like abstract crystal cubes in the landscape. In both cases, the question is where to foresee the necessary intermediate shared spaces, so important for student housing, without interfering with the existing natural society. The ground floor, or the space between buildings, must be free of public functions as this would mean too much of a disruption in the ecosystems where the constructions are erected. The response of both proposals is introverted, and separated from the ground.

In *Pärske,* the mineral project, the intermediate spaces are in the core of the hard geometric volume. The strictness of the cubic form is broken up towards the isolated, defended, interior space, with elements of domestic life such as kitchens or dining rooms protruding inwards, like the crystals inside a geode.

In *Wild Synapse* the branch-like trellis partly screens the shared spaces from view, and these fly over from tree-building to tree-building, separated from the ground, linking the various constructions at the level of the canopy. The partial screening allows for a restrained integration of the human environment in the forest, as an optimized compromise between the need to restrain construction in the wildlife and at the same time enjoying the outstanding position of the tree houses.

Fragmented nature

The challenge in Landsberg (DE) is also about widening the footprint of an existing human settlement (fig.6). The new constructions are expected to find a balance with the natural cycles of the surrounding area, but in this case the target is not focused on the preservation of a specific ecosystem, but in the added value that an intensification of local ecosystems may offer to the new development.

The winning proposal, *Living With(in) Nature* (fig.7), creates an interface between the currently built-up area (former barracks turned business centre) and the new development (housing and recreation related to the former) which could be described as a fragmentation of the green infrastructure associated with an existing flow of water, breaking it up with a new geometry, so that it can be used as a collection of public spaces with different scales: from the garden, to the park, to the landscape.

The line of water becomes a succession of rectangular pools, maintaining the continuity while becoming perfectly permeable; the pools are staggered to one side and the other, defining a variety of open spaces, sometimes towards the business centre, sometimes towards the housing.

The transversal pedestrian lines that run through the new housing and across the alignment of pools will be populated with trees, to reconnect the patches of forest that were razed down over the past times to clear land for farmland.

A hybrid landscape emerges, with the centrality of a public space between work and residence, but integrated in the natural cycles and infrastructure of the territory; with a fragmented geometry that defines the proximity of the urban, but with the continuity and variability of a meandering flow of water.

Fragmented park

The question in Santo Tirso (PT) runs in the opposite direction (fig.8). The site is a very large area in a central urban context, formerly a large market square and building, which has lost its original function, and is now part of a wider strategy of transformation of the inner

7 - LANDSBERG (DE), WINNER - LIVING WITH(IN) NATURE > SEE MORE P.145

9 - SANTO-TIRSO (PT), WINNER - FOODLAB SANTO TIRSO > SEE MORE P.161

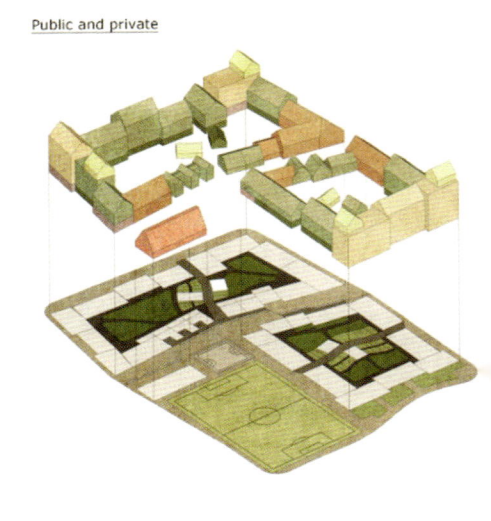

10 - LUND (SE), SPECIAL MENTION - PLAYFUL PATH! > SEE MORE P.151

city. How to take advantage of the size and centrality of this vast open space?

The winning proposal, *FOODlab Santo Tirso* (fig.9), is based on a simple but efficient device, a pergola that covers the whole open space, but is cut out in organic forms to create smaller areas. The double scale of this device ensures the continuity of the intervention while offering individuals, collectives or entrepreneurs –through the fragmentation into almost domestic-sized enclosures in varied oval forms– different opportunities to find their place.

Playful path

The title of one of the special mentions in Lund (SE), *Playful Path!* (fig.10), describes an interesting way to relate to the new input, in this case a railway station (fig.11). Rather than focusing on the infrastructural node, the project proposes a collection of clusters running parallel to the tracks, and threaded by a pedestrian zig-zagging line that goes in and out of the clusters, turning them into open courtyards or enclosed piazzas, creating a gradient from public to private with a rich collection of intermediate spaces that combine commercial and collective uses.

The relation with the station is tangential; it barely touches the playful path halfway, but on the side of its cross section. Walking or cycling to the station from any of the clusters can be envisaged as a pleasant and entertaining experience, with plenty of different scales and functions in the buildings and spaces along the way.

On the other hand, the clusters are protected from the noise of passing trains by an embankment which builds a landscaped horizon for the taller buildings along this side. It is interesting to note that the station access is understated, a small cabin in this landscaped horizon, highlighting the connectivity factor versus the heroic infrastructure approach of other proposals.

Double landscape

In Molfetta (IT) the city brief states that "The activities that were supporting the local economy, especially those referred to the sea activities, are now downsized" and the waterfront needs to be reconsidered as a place to live in, for locals, but also as a base for a new economy based on innovative formats for tourism (fig.12).

The winning design, *Hold the Line* (fig.13) addresses this issue in a literal manner, establishing a framework for relations between locals and visitors on two levels that overlap without mixing. A landscape of "fishing town" is enhanced, while an abstract landscape of clean geometry is traced above it.

The intervention is a lightweight structure of fine straight lines that runs along the waterfront, barely touching the ground, serving as an elevated promenade, pedestrian and bicycle connection on a platform level, but also framing and activating the ground level for more static activities.

11 - LUND (SE)

12 - MOLFETTA (IT)

13 - MOLFETTA (IT), WINNER - HOLD THE LINE > SEE MORE P.153

15 - ST PÖLTEN (AT), WINNER - JU(MP) IN THE WATER - KISS THAT FROG > SEE MORE P.171

14 - ST PÖLTEN (AT)

16 - STAVANGER (NO)

Temporary public landscapes

In St Pölten (AT) the news is that a former reserve of land is now ready to absorb a rising demand of housing, which will be well connected to public transport and city services (fig.14).
The winning proposal, *Ju(MP) in the Water - Kiss that Frog* (fig.15) is based on the logical assumption that the development of this large piece of land will not happen all in one go, and proposes a strategy to ensure that the intermediate situations are attractive. A series of foundational clusters are scattered over the terrain. The intermediate land is developed as a landscape of temporary public use, until the time comes for it to be built up, with strategically planted vegetation which will grow in the process to be incorporated in the housing development in the future.

Tempered intermediate space

Several kinds of new public space appear in the winning proposal *Forus LABing*, the winner in the site of Stavanger (NO), where the question is how to use the resources generated by oil to generate a viable lifestyle for the post-oil economy (fig.16).
One example is the covered space connecting different buildings, a lightweight greenhouse-like construction, part of a strategy they define using Reyner Banham's paraphrase *The Well Tempered Environment*. This is an inexpensive way to create a viable public square in this cold latitude, but it is also a buffer to facilitate climate comfort in the entrances of the buildings themselves; a lively public area can be expected to thrive, even in the coldest periods (fig.17).
At the scale of landscape, management of post oil industrial archaeology through colour (white) can change a collective perception of gloom into a desirable landscape identity (fig.18).

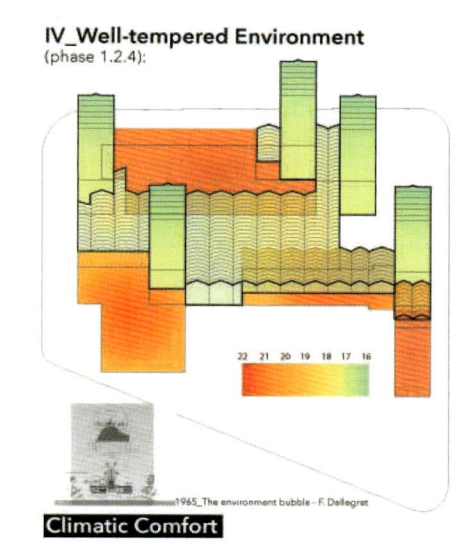

17 - STAVANGER (NO), WINNER - FORUS LABING > SEE MORE P.175

Conclusion

With the above examples we can see how the negotiation between a new input and an existing situation can generate a new condition, a new context for interaction, new kinds of public spaces.
It is important to be alert and identify such new conditions of the public, as they are the mainstay of the development of our societies. When societies evolve, the written or unwritten rules governing intermediate spaces become richer and more sophisticated. The development of a civilization depends on its ability to find contexts to share and exchange in deeper and safer ways, for successful civilizations are those that achieved a balance between the individual and the collective.
These projects have the potential to contribute to the development of our societies by exploring further fields for public exchange.

18 - STAVANGER (NO), WINNER - FORUS LABING > SEE MORE P.175

BONDY
FRANCE (FR)

CATEGORY: **URBAN – ARCHITECTURAL**
LOCATION: **BONDY, CA EST ENSEMBLE**
POPULATION: **53,053 INHAB.**
STRATEGIC SITE: **74 HA**
PROJECT SITE: **10.6 HA**
SITE PROPOSED BY: **BONDY MUNICIPALITY + ÉTABLISSEMENT PUBLIC FONCIER D'ÎLE DE FRANCE (EPFIF)**

OWNER(S) OF THE SITE: **BONDY MUNICIPALITY, EPFIF, SOCIAL LANDLORDS, PRIVATE LANDOWNERS, SIGNATURE OF A LAND INTERVENTION AGREEMENT WITH ÉTABLISSEMENT PUBLIC FONCIER D'ÎLE DE FRANCE (EPFIF) (MONITORING PERIMETER ON AVENUE GALLIENI)**
COMMISION AFTER COMPETITION: **URBAN AND/OR ARCHITECTURAL PROJECT MANAGEMENT**

Interview of the site's representative

PRESENTATION OF THE SITE WITH REGARDS TO STRATEGY

The site is characterised by the presence of Canal de l'Ourcq and the former RN3, which divide the town of Bondy. The Northern edge consists of areas of detached housing, apartment block estates and activities linked with the presence of the canal. There is little communication between here and the town centre to the South, even in terms of day-to-day operation. The construction of ZAC des Rives de l'Ourcq (1,300 dwellings + businesses and shops) near the cement works, planned for completion in 2020, marks the first stage in the reclamation of the canal at this Northern edge. On the Southern edge, the urban fabric becomes tighter and constitutes the Northern boundary of the historical centre of Bondy. Several apartment block projects (6/7 storey) with ground floor commercial premises are currently planned for 2006-2018, and should start the urban reclamation of the avenue.

HOW IS THE SITE CONNECTED TO THE SESSION TOPIC - THE ADAPTABLE CITY?

Both infrastructures on the site are currently under consideration for urban regeneration projects. The introduction of the "T Zen 3" BRT bus service linking Paris to Livry Gargan, will lead to a complete remodelling of the Avenue by 2020, notably with the demolition of the road bridge in Bondy. There are currently numerous urban projects for the banks and surroundings of the Canal de l'Ourcq at the scale of the Est Ensemble Conurbation. Finally, the arrival of Metro line 15 (in 2025), interconnecting with the "T Zen3" and the existing T1 tramline give this site a new territorial embeddings and strong development potential. The Municipality is therefore looking for process-projects capable of involving all the stakeholders, private and public, around a vision.

NICOLAS BARNAVON (FR)
GUILLAUME BARNAVON (FR)
CHARLES BOUSCASSE (FR)
DENIS BROCHARD (FR)
LOÏC DANIEL (FR)
JACQUES IPPOLITI (FR)
MARION LACAS (FR)
QUENTIN L'HÔTE (FR)
ARCHITECTS

STUDIO DIESE
37 RUE BOBILLOT
75013 PARIS, FR
STUDIODIESE@GMAIL.COM
WWW.STUDIODIESE.COM

WINNER - BONDY (FR)
Bondy's Count

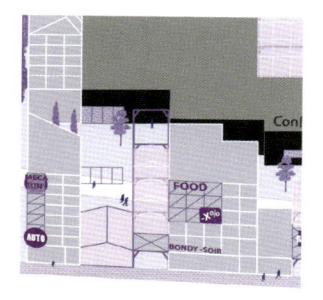

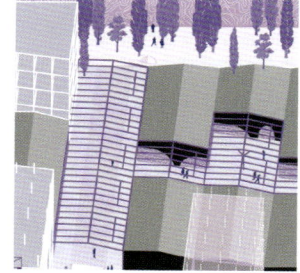

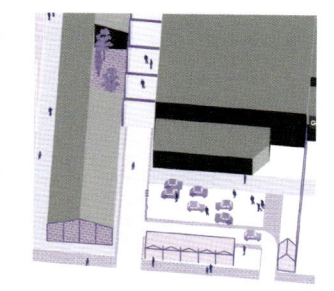

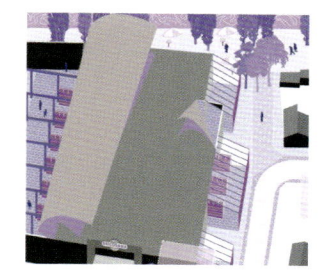

TEAM POINT OF VIEW Counters of Bondy "Bondy's'count" gathers the forces in presence to put in motion the transformation of the city from the inside. It allows increasing and diversifying the activities of the zone, adding services and spices to the franchised boxes, using the different times of the city. We plan to progressively modify the all-car structure of the area in order to create a neighbourhood opened towards the canal. The area is stimulated through a game of actions, using the progressive capacities of the industrial warehouses and the parking lots. The project looks under the skirts of the warehouses to unveil the richness of the commercial landscape. "Bondy's'count" takes the road towards post-commercialism, using warehouses as scenery, taking the time of prefiguration to step forward in designing and debating the city.

JURY POINT OF VIEW The project accepts the quality of this generic shopping area which the team calls a strip. It enhances its characteristics while transforming it and ultimately converting it to a post-commercial landscape, in which the shed, the typical typology of such fabric, becomes the decor for a new habitat. The proposal undertakes a gradual renewal of the area on itself, retaining its economic programme but diversifying its activities and services. The simplicity of the project's constitutive idea, based on small interventions, can lead to stimulating results that are open to future changes in retail patterns.

GUILLAUME BARON (FR)
ARCHITECT

3 RUE SOUFFLOT
75005 PARIS, FR
OFFICE@BARON-ARCH.EU
WWW.BARON-ARCH.EU

SPECIAL MENTION - BONDY (FR)

BoNDy Nouvelles Dynamiques

TEAM POINT OF VIEW Bondy becomes Bo.N.Dy, a paradigmatic private and public place exploring all the New Dynamics of space a 21st century suburb-city can promote. We therefore suggest a realistic roadmap to work with various actors on this common territory: a "pilot-project" to approach the retailers, a couple of controversies to share the territory and finally, the building of the results. Our theoretical background associates the "controversies maps" (Latour), which analyse individual concerns to build collective answers, and the "evidence-based design" (O'Cathain).

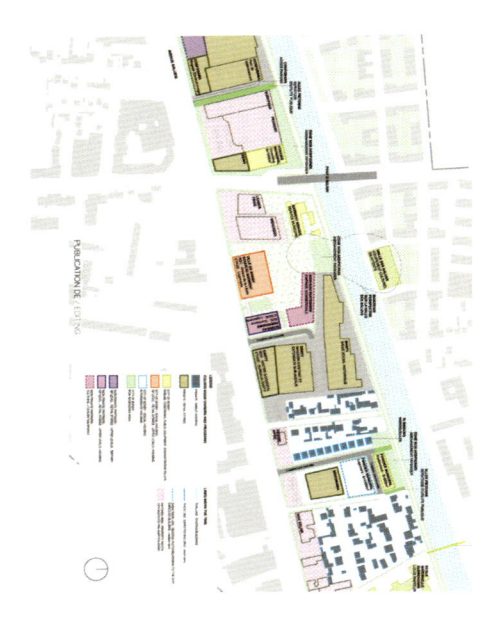

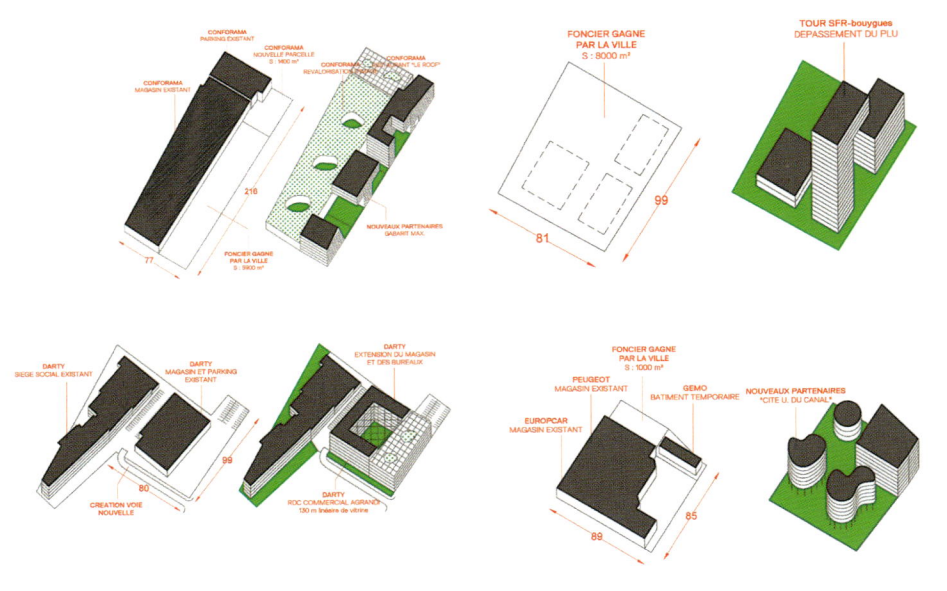

ALEXANDRE LAHYANI (FR)
ANGEL MENENDEZ (ES)
MIGUEL JIMENEZ (ES)
SYLVAIN EUSTACHE (FR)
ARCHITECTS

2 IMPASSE GIRARDON
75013 PARIS, FR
T. +33 643219434
ALEXANDRELAHYANI@ATELIERLAME.COM

SPECIAL MENTION - BONDY (FR)

Re_Bondying

TEAM POINT OF VIEW "Re_Bondying" is conceived as an evolution, a sequence of activities developing and enriching the canal in different stages. The proposal calls for actions based on the appropriation of the canal, reinterpretation of its identity and remembrance of the history of wood in the area. We propose to re-enliven the area through: creation of green entertainment spaces, designed meeting areas, different learning and assistance centres and creative workspaces that encourage innovation and ingenuity. The actions proposed create opportunities using existing elements and maintaining successful local business that will further be regenerated to create a more attractive, innovative site.

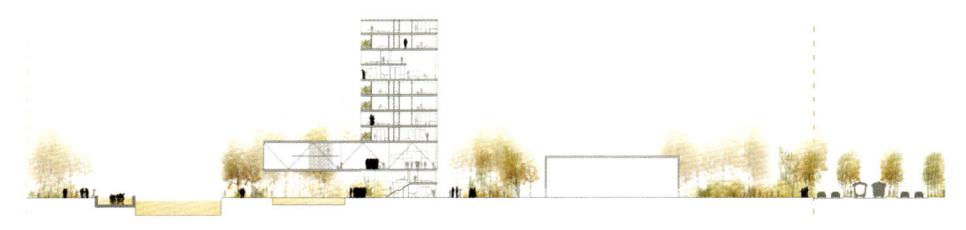

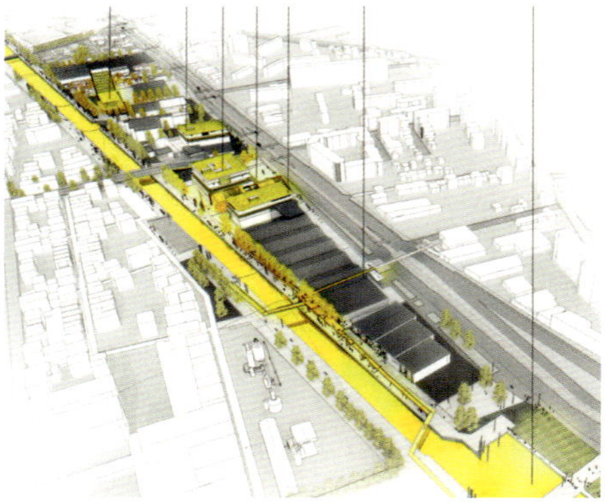

ESPOO
SUOMI-FINLAND (FI)

CATEGORY: **URBAN – ARCHITECTURAL**
LOCATION: **OTANIEMI, ESPOO**
POPULATION: **265,000 INHAB.**
PROJECT SITE: **5 HA**
SITE PROPOSED BY: **SENATE PROPERTIES**

OWNER(S) OF THE SITE: **SENATE PROPERTIES, CITY OF ESPOO, AALTO UNIVERSITY PROPERTIES LTD**
COMMISION AFTER COMPETITION: **COMMISSION AT THE LEVEL OF CONCEPT DEVELOPMENT AND URBAN PLANNING**

Interview of the site's representative

PRESENTATION OF THE SITE WITH REGARDS TO STRATEGY

Espoo is the second largest city in Finland and part of the Helsinki metropolitan area. Otaniemi, in the South-Eastern part, is only 6km away from Helsinki city centre. The new metro line will strengthen the logistic connections within the metropolitan area and the strategy is to develop the Otaniemi - Tapiola - Keilaniemi area into an attractive and innovative city district of science, art and business.

The vision of Espoo is to be a responsible and humane city. The most important resources of Espoo are its active inhabitants, educational institutions, communities and businesses. The city is developed in interaction with various partners. The goal is to make Espoo a pioneer in the municipal sector and a good place to live, learn and work in as well as engage in entrepreneurship.

HOW IS THE SITE CONNECTED TO THE SESSION TOPIC - THE ADAPTABLE CITY?

Otaniemi is best known for being the home of the Aalto University campus as well as several high tech research and business facilities. A new metro line will connect Otaniemi to Helsinki city centre in 2016. That, in addition to Aalto University's decision to move the School of arts to Otaniemi in 2017, has increased the interest to develop and densify the area. New university and commercial buildings will be planned in the area in the future as well as housing.

To the North of Otaniemi there is a "Natura 2000" nature preserve area, which is a significant bird sanctuary. Otaniemi also hosts a population of protected flying squirrels. One of the objectives is to find innovative ways to build and densify the area without disrupting the bird or squirrel habitats.

BORJA SALLAGO ZAMBRANO (ES)
ALAN CORTEZ DE LA CONCHA (MX)
MANUEL PINILLA FERNÁNDEZ (ES)
ARCHITECTS

ANA GEORGINA HERNANDEZ (MX)
GRAPHIC DESIGNER
FRANCISCO CRESPO BURGUEÑO (ES)
FERNANDO BASURTO GALLEGOS (MX)
VISUALIZATION AND RENDERING
ALBA SOSPEDRA ARRUFAT (ES)
LUISA DAZA REYES (ES)
STUDENTS IN ARCHITECTURE

BAMMM
MADRID, ES
T. +34 636121299
INFO@BAM-MM.COM
WWW.BAM-MM.COM

WINNER - ESPOO (FI)
Wild Synapse

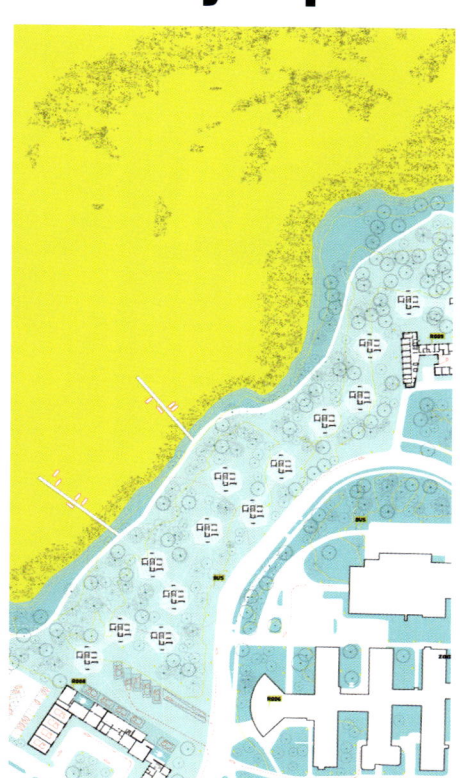

TEAM POINT OF VIEW Wild Synapse is not a project. It is an attitude. // Wild Synapse is a sudden spark in the friction between human beings and nature. // Wild Synapse is a way of living in radical contact with nature. // It is a Synapse linking multiple realities concepts we cannot see, but can feel and live. // It is Wild to let nature run its course.

Wild Synapse comes as an answer to multiple conditions. It builds a shelter, a home, a meeting point... but it also fades in the presence of ever changing nature. It is timeless and complex, adaptable to the inhabitants of today and tomorrow.

Adaptable Living – Our programme comes from the mixture of different agents in Espoo´s territory: PLAYERs + TOYs + GAMEs = WILD CODE

The goal is to link players with a toy and finally with a game. When you coagulate this algorithm, a code appears and "Wild Synapse" takes place. The mixture of all the codes represents the adaptability that the pieces provide, built or not, to our site.

On each building, the strategy is the same: two floors are proposed for regular housing and two other for collective housing. It allows the users feeling in touch with nature, because they can enjoy extra space outdoors out of their comfort space and in harmony with Espoo´s Campus.

JURY POINT OF VIEW The most important objective of the competition was to find the means to integrate housing and the nature values of the protected shoreline. The tower blocks in the proposal have been placed as if scattered in the forest, the buildings resembling tree houses growing out from the forest itself, and they sit well in their location. The solution minimises the construction footprint in the area. In addition, the facades of the buildings were designed so that they endeavour to facilitate the common paths of movement of the flying squirrels. Construction adapts to the surroundings and also serves the needs of nature.

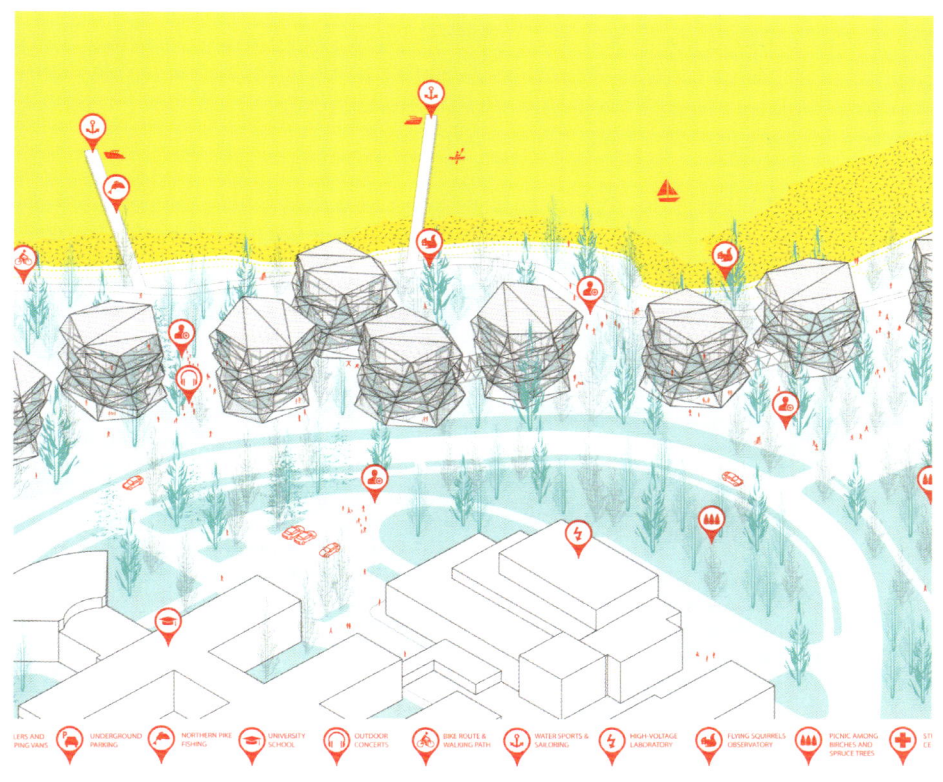

MARIA KLEIMOLA (FI)
ARCHITECT

HANNELE CEDERSTRÖM (FI)
INKA NORROS (FI)
KIRSTI PALOHEIMO (FI)
SINI RAHIKAINEN (FI)
STUDENTS IN ARCHITECTURE

JÄÄKÄRINKATU 8 A 18
00150 HELSINKI, FI
T. +358 503779987
MARIA.KLEIMOLA@AALTO.FI

RUNNER-UP - ESPOO (FI)
Pärske

TEAM POINT OF VIEW Adaptability creating social and spatial sustainability
The historically valuable context requires maximum architectural quality while innovative and open atmosphere of the Aalto University calls for communal and vibrant living environment. The plan therefore creates a strong yet extremely adaptable framework to connect individual life patterns into a whole. Axial composition with buildings surrounding courtyards and squares create a connection to the architectural identity of Otaniemi. Unique natural conditions are integral part of the plan. Series of flowing spaces create soft transitions from nature to urban, from campus to dwelling and from exterior to interior.

New blocks continue the theme of courtyards and gardens in Otaniemi. Continuous green areas offer connections and nesting areas for flying squirrels and recreational paths with biodiversity. Mobility is based on public transportation and quality pedestrian and biking routes. Car traffic is thus minimized and parking is situated out of sight. Buildings are connected to a network of squares and gardens with varying private-public character.

The composition offers generous views to nature and seaside connecting spaces both visually and physically. Three different typologies offer three different ways of living with endless variations. Buildings are grouped to blocks with different characters.

JURY POINT OF VIEW In the proposal the authors have laudably analysed the most important principles of Otaniemi's urban context and the connection to the overall urban structure is skilfully designed. The scheme includes novel variations of the typical Otaniemi atrium house and its scale. The thoughts on the courtyard buildings are interesting and they produced spaces that enable social interaction. The building design is without a doubt the main strength of the proposal. The stairs and spatiality of the atrium yard create a strong image of communal living.

FERNANDO PEREZ DEL PULGAR MANCEBO (ES)
LEOPOLDO GONZALEZ JIMENEZ (ES)
JUAN FRANCISCO PARRILLA SANCHEZ (ES)
ARCHITECTS

JOSE JIMENEZ PEREZ (ES)
ANGELES MONTERO RODRIGUEZ (ES)
ARCHITECTS
ELENA GONZALEZ CASARES (ES)
STUDENT IN ARCHITECTURE

39 MADRE DE DIOS STREET, B-F
29012 MÁLAGA, ES
T. +34 952601543
INFO@969ARQUITECTOS.COM
WWW.969ARQUITECTOS.COM

SPECIAL MENTION - ESPOO (FI)
Piilokoju

TEAM POINT OF VIEW We bet on a vertical arrangement for residential fabric to reduce land consumption and energy losses envelope, optimizing layout systems – i.e. getting an optimum urban fabric. The forest is used as a dominant urban landscape. Taking advantage of existing gaps the towers are strategically placed enhancing the presence of the natural landscape inside houses. In a word, we use the path void to place a new horizontal connection infrastructure and forest gaps to puncture vertical towers, leaving the South area between the road and the existing buildings as a public space.

GUIOMAR MARTÍN DOMÍNGUEZ (ES)
JAVIER DE ESTEBAN GARBAYO (ES)
ARCHITECTS

ANA SABUGO SIERRA (ES)
JIMENA ALONSO DÍAZ (ES)
JOSÉ MANUEL DE ANDRÉS MONCAYO (ES)
MIRIAM MARTÍN SANTOS (ES)
STUDENTS IN ARCHITECTURE

FERNANDO EL CATÓLICO 47, 3ºIZQ.
28015 MADRID, ES
T. +34 646162970
GUIOMARMD@GMAIL.COM

SPECIAL MENTION - ESPOO (FI)
Tumbling Dice

TEAM POINT OF VIEW Otaniemi has preserved much of Aalto's modern dream: a green territory sprinkled by built volumes that freely interact in a magnetic dialogue and seems especially attuned to Espoo's natural landscape. Our project proposes to think beyond such scheme grouping the housing units into strategic clusters. Like a clever dice game, these pieces move away from the shore to fit into forest clearings. They are connected by open-air platforms that provide a symbolic and physical place for casual and planned gathering, calling for a further reframing of today's collectivity.

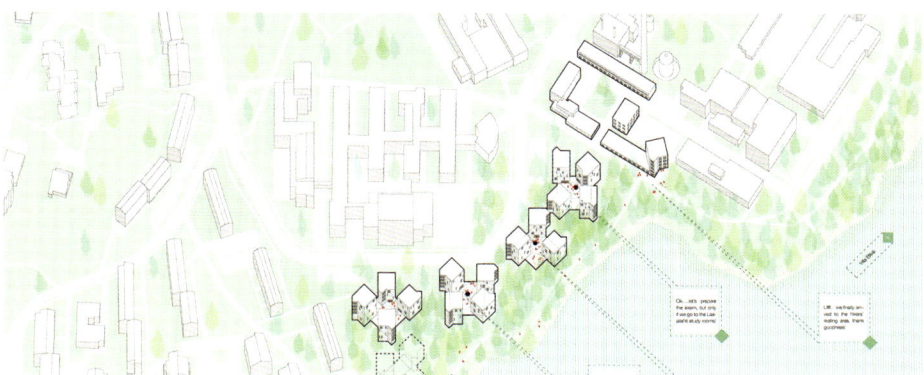

BEGOÑA DE ABAJO CASTRILLO (ES)
CARLOS GARCÍA FERNÁNDEZ (ES)
ARCHITECTS

ANDREA MUNIÁIN PERALES (ES)
LUIS LECEA ROMERA (ES)
ISMAEL LÓPEZ PORTILLA (ES)
STUDENTS IN ARCHITECTURE

AEADA 2, 6º-8
28013 MADRID, ES
T. +34 915466276
A@DEABAJOGARCIA.COM
WWW.DEABAJOGARCIA.COM

SPECIAL MENTION - ESPOO (FI)

Weaving the Woods

TEAM POINT OF VIEW The project negotiates with the existing, occupies the clearings and responds to an in-between situation that faces both nature and campus activity. Instead of a frozen unchanging solution, the units and the rules of assembly define an open-ended system that sets off a wide range of possibilities to be customized by developers, users and other agents. Adaptability is complemented by the technical definition of an industrialized system of pieces. The modulation and the use of new technologies lead to a list of prefabricated elements that build the whole structure.

LANDSBERG
DEUTSCHLAND (DE)

CATEGORY: **URBAN - LANDSCAPE - ARCHITECTURAL**
LOCATION: **LANDSBERG, FORMER LECHRAIN BARRACKS**
POPULATION: **28,000 INHAB.**
STRATEGIC SITE: **553 HA**
PROJECT SITE: **31 HA**

SITE PROPOSED BY: **LANDSBERG TOWN COUNCIL, 3C CARBON COMPOSITE COMPANY GMBH**
OWNER(S) OF THE SITE: **3C CARBON, LANDSBERG TOWN COUNCIL BIMA (INSTITUTE FOR FEDERAL REAL ESTATE), PRIVATE OWNERS**
COMMISION AFTER COMPETITION: **OUTLINE URBAN AND LANDSCAPE PLAN**

Interview of the site's representative
Birgit Weber, Director of urban planning and construction

PRESENTATION OF THE SITE WITH REGARDS TO STRATEGY
For the rapidly growing town of Landsberg, further development toward the South is of great importance. With its technically innovative production and research area, the company that is based there represents an extremely attractive offer in the commercial sector and has made a good use of the special local situation. The entire area under consideration should be developed to compile further development possibilities for the successful company need to expand and to find solutions between the concept of a work housing development and the (post-)modern idea of a "Google Campus".

HOW IS THE SITE CONNECTED TO THE SESSION TOPIC - THE ADAPTABLE CITY?
Located within the Munich metropolitan region the town benefits from its upward trend. Does the small town have to follow this upward trend, produce living space, expand its boundaries, create traffic axes or promote centres for technology? It does indeed have to do so with structured guidance. Whether and to what extent the competition area plays a role in this trend should be examined in detail – the framework conditions of nature conservancy and the development needs of the company based there should therefore surely be taken up in and around the competition area.

DID YOU DEFINE A SPECIFIC PROCESS FOR THE URBAN DEVELOPMENT OF THE SITE AFTER EUROPAN COMPETITION?
For Landsberg, it is important that the presented design ideas, even if they are hardly realizable in their current form, nonetheless provide important starting points. Revision while taking into consideration nature conservancy (e.g. ecological tourism and temporary dwellings with local recreation) and an innovative approach to subsequent densification of the company grounds is planned within the framework of a workshop with the prize winners.

PAOLO RUSSO (IT)
FABIANA LEDDA (IT)
ANNAMARIA GAITO (IT)
ANTONIO CUGUSI (IT)
ARCHITECTS

RICCARDO ONNIS (IT)
STUDENT IN ARCHITECTURE

VIA GIUSEPPE GIUSTI 4/A
07100 SASSARI, SARDEGNA, IT
T. +39 3486494827
PAOLORUSSO.AU@GMAIL.COM
WWW.PAOLORUSSOARCHITECTS.COM

WINNER - LANDSBERG (DE)

Living With(in) Nature

TEAM POINT OF VIEW The approach to the site requires time and study due to the complexity and the richness of the surroundings. The area is located between natural-artificial elements on all sides and the project site lies at the centre –both conceptually and geographically– of these opposing elements. The proposal should therefore not only answer the residential demand, but also a harmonious integration with the elements – defining a landscape front to the new area; creating the right relation between an industrial environment and a common and naturalistic one. Integrating both the natural and the human environment. The new buildings develop as they would flow from the new front, with a standard density at the beginning and then shading as they approach to the forest. This way residential, cultural and every day facilities are properly spread onsite. The North-South roads are mainly dedicated to cycling and walking to make the in-between streets the main common open spaces for the inhabitants social needs. On the other side the green of the forest penetrates the site and fades as it gets closer to the industry. The structure and the organization of the new living area consists with a balance of nature and artificial elements, creating an environment with very different and unique features that works in synergy with the deeply and strongly urban environment of the town of Landsberg.

JURY POINT OF VIEW A large, new structure merges different existing buildings into a single unit concentrating all public and communal services. This way, it physically separates housing from work and creates an interesting entrance plaza for the development. The development structure gradually dissolves towards the North, interweaving the built environment with a proposed extension of the forest and thus generating a wide variety of urban situations and spaces, which then constitutes the project's main potential.

MARCIN MARASZEK (PL)
MACIEJ KAUFMAN (PL)
ARCHITECTS

AGNIESZKA SZURAN (PL)
ARCHITECT
RADOSŁAW OBCZYŃSKI (PL)
LAWYER

WILANOWSKA 16/20 M.17
00-422 WARSZAWA, PL
T. +48 602490830
HELLO@CO-UP.PL
WWW.CO-UP.PL

RUNNER-UP - LANDSBERG (DE)

Forest First

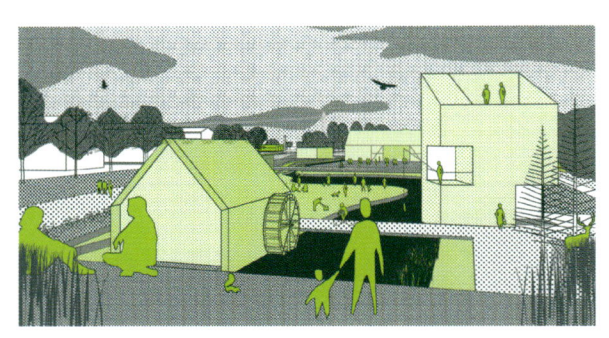

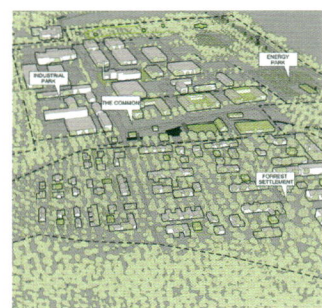

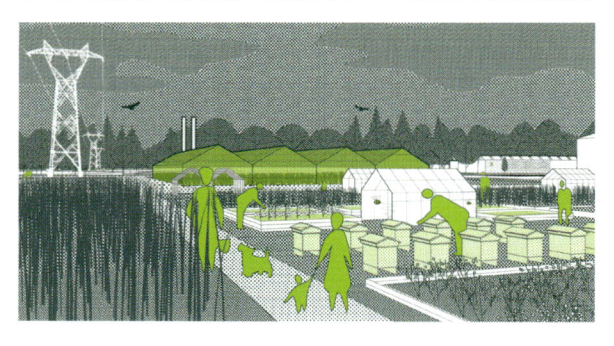

TEAM POINT OF VIEW "Forest First" establishes a sustainable forest ecosystem that people can gradually colonise over time and economical possibilities. The new development supports ecological functions expanding the forest onto the project site while public transportation network extends onto the site. The Wiesbach river is restored in a widened riverbed, the public transportation network is extended onto the site and energetic cycle can be achieved onsite. The project site is divided into 4 zones:
- A forest settlement: a new image of company housing immersed in a forest;
- The Common: a district civic centre with services and public spaces along the Wiesbach;
- An industrial park: a complex of the 3C Carbon production buildings; the factory develops inwards, the existing infrastructure is reused and the gross area doubled;
- The energy park: a hybrid space dedicated to recreation and energy production.

"Forest First" is a strategy rather than an ultimate project. The development always tends towards one of two extremes, from "Zero" to "Maximum Growth", from which it can be extrapolated at any given point of time. Notwithstanding the level of development, the spatial structure is always adapted.

JURY POINT OF VIEW The project proposes zoning the site into four completely differentiated areas included a buffer of public spaces and services in between them, called "the commons", although it has more of a public character than really being common facilities. The residential area ("forest development") is structured with a matrix of 13 green squares around which different types of housing are placed. The project proposes understanding the settlement as a forest, and filling it with trees. Although this idea serves to create interesting scenarios, it does not seem to take into account the long process involved in the growth of a forest.

LUND
SVERIGE (SE)

CATEGORY: **URBAN - LANDSCAPE - ARCHITECTURAL**
LOCATION: **LUND**
POPULATION: **115,000 INHAB.**
STRATEGIC SITE: **520 HA**
PROJECT SITE: **60 HA**
SITE PROPOSED BY: **MUNICIPALITY OF LUND, NORTH BRIDGE AND ESTANCIA AB**
OWNER(S) OF THE SITE: **MUNICIPALITY OF LUND AND PRIVATE LANDOWNERS**
COMMISION AFTER COMPETITION: **URBAN AND LANDSCAPE STRATEGIC STUDY. DEVELOPMENT OF PLAN PROGRAM AND MASTERPLAN IN COLLABORATION WITH MUNICIPALITY AND OTHER PARTNERS**

Interview of the site's representative
Vesna Vasiljkovic, Architect and urbanist at the municipality of Lund

PRESENTATION OF THE SITE WITH REGARDS TO STRATEGY

The site consists in mono-functional islands with recreational areas and leftover landscape in between, but it is less than 1km South-West from the medieval city centre. This vast unbuilt space is mainly due to the security zone between the wastewater treatment plant (WWTP) and housing. In the process ahead two interventions will take place within the strategic site, acting as catalysts: a new railway station on the line Lund-Malmö is planed for 2022. And the WWTP will either be transformed and updated according to modern technological solutions or removed from the site.

HOW IS THE SITE CONNECTED TO THE SESSION TOPIC - THE ADAPTABLE CITY?

A new train station and an updated WWTP will open up the site to densification and a possibility to redefine the whole area. The area that is today a bit detached will tomorrow be an integrated part of the city centre. Exploitation pressure will increase: how can today's use of green spaces be maintained in a densified situation and a future mixed urban pattern? The city wants to let the actual sports clubs, surrounding schools and neighbouring communities share this recreative space and let it be a kind of social cement for the surrounding mono-functional islands. A chain of activities can create a dynamic axis through the area.

DID YOU DEFINE A SPECIFIC PROCESS FOR THE URBAN DEVELOPMENT OF THE SITE AFTER EUROPAN COMPETITION?

The municipality of Lund agrees with the jury that no single proposal excelled in the important aspects of the problem and questions to solve on the site. Instead the municipality sees the rewarded projects as complementing each other. Lund is first going to invite all the rewarded teams to present their proposals and discuss the future development of the area. The process of involving the teams will be discussed within the municipality afterwards.

JOANNA HAGSTEDT (SE)
URBANIST

DAVID KISS (SE)
ARCHITECT

ERIK JANSSON (SE)
SIMON WALLQVIST (SE)
ARCHITECTS

JOANNAHAGSTEDT@HOTMAIL.COM

WINNER - LUND (SE)
Culture Symbiotic

TEAM POINT OF VIEW Man's longing for the ideal life is reflected in political ideology as well as in our myths and legends - from Atlantis to Heaven. So - is the adaptable city a utopia of our time? Lund's identity should nourish its citizens' creativity, not only at the university, but also in its various businesses and leisure activities. Therefore the key concept of this proposal is to complement Lund's identity with new a creative centre – a place where infrastructure development enables arts, culture, recreation, nature and cultural heritage to form the cityscape.

The focus point of our proposal is the intersection of infrastructure, culture, art, sports, housing and existing built structures. Culture & art occupy the station, an indoor hall under the rail tracks and existing industrial building as well as public space between the two. This gives these spaces a strong character and uniqueness creating identity of the whole new development. In this creative space professional artists meet amateurs – and commuters. A true makerspace aiming to encourage creativity through interdisciplinary collaboration is created.

JURY POINT OF VIEW The project's strength is that it interacts with all surrounding areas to create its own identity and that it marks –with a clear gesture– the station as a major asset in bringing the different characters together. The station roof is the centrepiece of the plan; an infrastructural device creating an abundance of space to host "culture" and at the same time linking the different sides of the track physically as well as visually. The jury asks for more realistic and sustainable ideas on how to invite future actors of the area.

LINUS MANNERVIK (SE)
ARCHITECT

ANDERS BENNRUP (SE)
FREDRIK LINANDER (SE)
KARIN LINDSTRÖM (SE)
KÄBI NOODAPERA RAMEL (SE)
MALIN SVENSSON (SE)
NICKLAS IVARSSON (SE)
NIELS PETTERSSON (SE)
PETRA SVENSSON (SE)
ARCHITECTS
DAVID FLYGAR (SE)
LANDSCAPE ARCHITECT

MOSAIK ARKITEKTER
C/O LINUS MANNERVIK
KULGRÄNDEN 7D
22649 LUND, SE
T. +46 736307731
INFO@MOSAIK-ARKITEKTER.SE
WWW.MOSAIK-ARKITEKTER.SE

RUNNER-UP - LUND (SE)
Monster Planning

JURY POINT OF VIEW "Monster Planning" celebrates an organic and gradual approach to urban development by focusing entirely on the underlying processes through which diverse human interests and expressions come together to shape the built environment. It outlines a way of understanding this process, as well as a set of concepts through which to look at it and support it. Yet, the level of abstraction of the overall project is likely to make it difficult to implement. The proposal is rewarded as an interesting and important intellectual perspective, rather than an easily implementable project.

TEAM POINT OF VIEW External interests and factors drive the development planned for the competition area. But what is the will of the area itself? Who asks for the opinions of those who spend time in the area everyday? How can their voices be a creative force in their own initiatives rather than a hindrance in someone else's project?

The proposal introduces the concept of the Monster into the realm of architecture to help us find new ways of seeing what cannot be defined or controlled. The Monster Plan is a method in pursuit of the pliable rather than something finite, such as a masterplan, and favours small-scale and critical projects to achieve something increasingly complex.

The wills and interests of the people in the area are established through Statements. These statements are expected to challenge each other, leaving some behind and letting some live on, but most often some kind of compromise will be generated. These conflicts and compromises are the seedbed for projects that further the investigations and development in the site. Three important roles for projects to take on are pointed out as: to be critical and open-minded when concerning what is and what is to be; to expand the insight in the values of the area; and to work as a test bed for the future form of the area. Development does not have to depend on slow, large-scale and pre-conceived planning, but can, instead, start today with the energy and knowledge of the people who are already a part of the area!

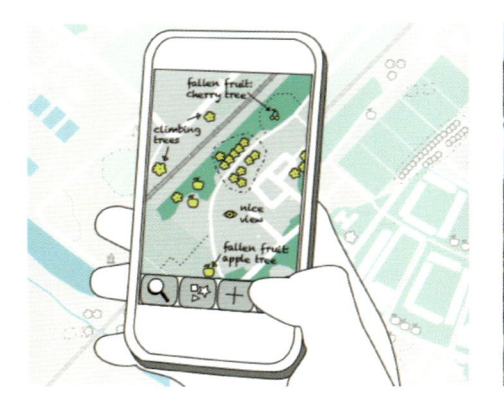

TADAS JONAUSKIS (LT)
JUSTINA MULIUOLYTĖ (LT)
URBANISTS
DŽIUGAS LUKOŠEVIČIUS (LT)
ARCHITECT

EDITA GUMAUSKAITĖ (LT)
ARCHITECT
JUSTINA SAKALAUSKAITĖ (LT)
STUDENT IN ARCHITECTURE

A.GOŠTAUTO 8-106
01108 VILNIUS, LT
T. +370 68818329
INFO@PU-PA.EU
WWW.PU-PA.EU

JOHAN NAVJORD (SE)
ARCHITECT

JONAS BERG (SE)
BENJAMIN GILLNER (SE)
ARON HÖGBERG (SE)
ARCHITECTS

A. VIKTOR RYDBERGSGATAN 29
412 57 GÖTEBORG, SE
T. +46 707423234
JOHAN.NAVJORD@GMAIL.COM

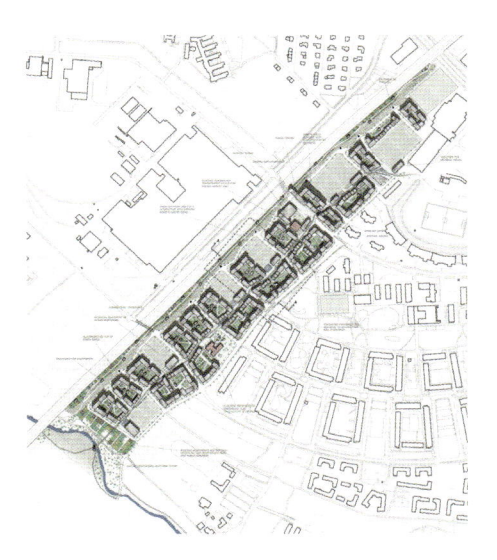

SPECIAL MENTION - LUND (SE)
Frontside

TEAM POINT OF VIEW Frontside is a new compact urban district with mixed-use environment and active public space facing rich natural landscapes with many sports and recreational activities. The train station, road network and structure of public spaces provide the robust framework. The rest of the urban fabric is an area for self-organization and community interaction. City users define design and function of the district by varying and adapting intelligent urban block rules. However, the highest quality of the district is its dense front-side edge looking to the vast landscapes – a unique natural resource of Lund.

SPECIAL MENTION - LUND (SE)
Playful Path!

TEAM POINT OF VIEW The proposal combines housing, business, sports/activities and cultivation in an innovative mix to create a new, adaptable neighbourhood typology: A dense, small-scale city that lives 24/7. The sport combined with small-scale cultivation profile will be unique to Lund. A green "activity path" is established to develop a credible connection between green recreational areas. The public profile of the path invites both neighbouring districts and greater Lund to take part in the activities that line it. In this way the new area shares its qualities with the rest of Lund and strengthens social integration.

MOLFETTA
ITALIA (IT)

CATEGORY: **URBAN – ARCHITECTURAL**
LOCATION: **MOLFETTA**
POPULATION: **60,000 INHAB.**
STRATEGIC SITE: **35 HA**
PROJECT SITE: **12 HA**
SITE PROPOSED BY: **MUNICIPALITY OF MOLFETTA**
OWNER(S) OF THE SITE: **MUNICIPALITY OF MOLFETTA AND STATE**

COMMISION AFTER COMPETITION: **IN ADDITION TO THE PUBLIC PRESENTATION OF THE PROJECTS, THE MUNICIPALITY SHOULD CONSIDER TO START A PROCESS, ALSO INVOLVING PRIZE-WINNING TEAMS, THROUGH WORKSHOPS, URBAN STUDIES ETC., AIMED AT THE DEVELOPMENT OF DETAILED PLANNING**

Interview of the site's representative
Paola Natalicchio, Mayor of Molfetta City

PRESENTATION OF THE SITE WITH REGARDS TO STRATEGY

The program aims at redevelopping the waterfront, from the Eastern beaches to the Madonna dei Martiri, to give back to the citizens a common good that has always been the best source of Molfetta: the sea. A deep regeneration where it is necessary to combine the urban space with the use of public beaches, creating bicycle paths and pedestrian areas for leisure. Through a better relationship of the city with its sea we can trigger the revival of tourism, commerce and production by promoting new forms of employment, development and attraction.

HOW IS THE SITE CONNECTED TO THE SESSION TOPIC - THE ADAPTABLE CITY?

The program required to the young architects the need to adapt the project to some existing urban scenarios. This led to a coherent response to the theme of sustainable city. The perspective offered by the young architects focused on the development of solutions to zero consumption of land, re-naturalization of the environment, use of local materials and street furniture renewable without upsetting but strengthening the identity of our city.

DID YOU DEFINE A SPECIFIC PROCESS FOR THE URBAN DEVELOPMENT OF THE SITE AFTER EUROPAN COMPETITION?

In the selected proposals, there are important ideas to be used. The opening of the exhibition will be the occasion to organize a workshop with the teams, invited for a public presentation of their projects. It will be a great opportunity for exchange between professionals and involvement in the city. By mid 2016 we want to get to a preliminary project on the new waterfront, starting from the Eastern part, that takes into account the ideas of this competition and grafts them on our urban identity in order to put the interventions in the programming of European funds 2014-2020.

NICOLA DARIO BALDASSARRE (IT)
PASQUALE CIPRI (IT)
SALVATORE DENTAMARO (IT)
NICOLETTA FACCITONDO (IT)
ANDREA SALVATORE (IT)
MARGHERITA VALENTE (IT)
ARCHITECTS

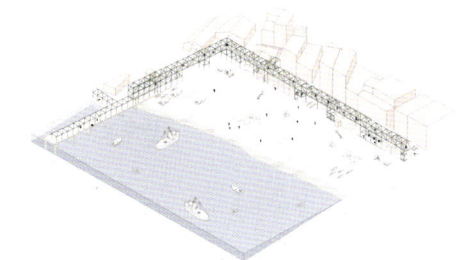

VIA ALFARANITI 19
70125 BARI, IT
T. +39 3925555792
NICOLA.BALDASSARRE@GMAIL.COM

WINNER - MOLFETTA (IT)
Hold the Line

TEAM POINT OF VIEW The project proposes a flexible system to help the site realize its full potential. It designs a new unified and compact waterfront with a single action, a line running through the entire site, made of a system of metallic portals with a base module of 3,60x3,60m; its repetition forms the road for bicycles and pedestrians. The module can be equipped in several ways, with shelters, little cafes or stalls.

Our main concern is to give the waterfront back to the citizens, making them live and inhabit the site. The entire area has to remain free, giving artisans and small business owners the possibility to open small commercial activities using the system of stalls provided by the project without privatizing the land or the access to the sea. The spirit is to involve and educate the population in a process of self-organization, self-maintenance and sharing of the waterfront.

There are six attractors: for the ex-Colonia, a place for children and a public shore; nearby the Inps building, a spacious square, overlooking the sea; for the waterfront till the old town, a constructed wetland, and three public pedestrian piers, with cafes and stalls; a walk running just above the sheds of the shipyards, giving people the opportunity to observe the workers; an administration office for the reception of tourists and some recreational areas; for Secca dei Pali, pools and an artificial beach.

JURY POINT OF VIEW The project fully responds to the theme of the Adaptable City through the idea of "modular portal" becoming a generating element of the entire waterfront and involving citizens in a process of self-management and sharing. The module lends itself both to customization, according to the different uses and to the reversibility, also using the characteristic features of Molfetta traditions. This aspect of the project will involve an action of shared planning in the development of the individual thematic areas.

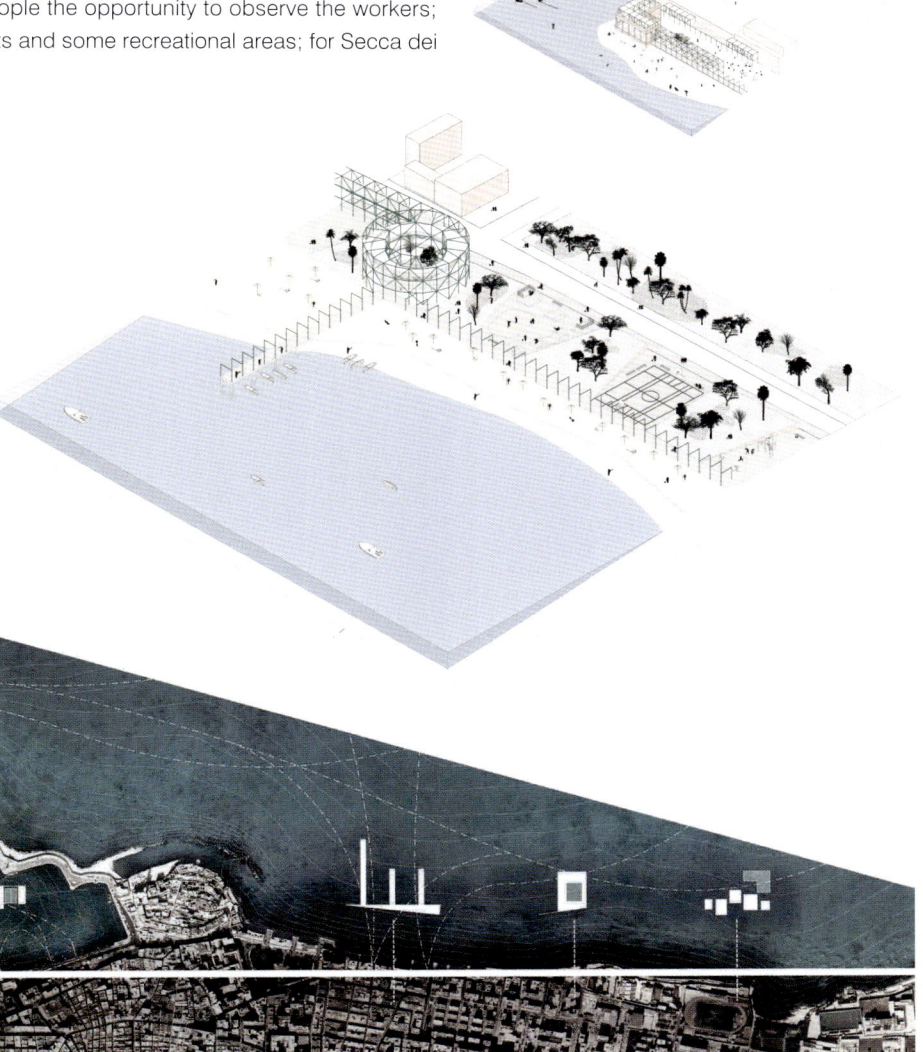

BARBARA PIONA (IT)
FERRAN VILADOMAT SERRAT (ES)
JOSEP NINOU CARMONA (ES)
LUIS JULIO PAREDA ARIAS (ES)
ARCHITECTS

CARLES ESQUERRA JULIÀ (ES)
GABRIEL CASALS SERRANO (ES)
STUDENTS IN ARCHITECTURE

ELEMENTS ARCHITECTURAL LAB
C/ CANONGE BARANERA 107
08911 BADALONA, ES
T. +34 678511506
STUDIO@ELEMENTS-ARCHLAB.COM
WWW.ELEMENTS-ARCHLAB.COM

RUNNER-UP - MOLFETTA (IT)

Molfetta, Terra e Mare

TEAM POINT OF VIEW The aim of the proposal is to bring back the city to the sea. The current relationship between land and sea, as well as the high traffic density and the poor parking organization, have transformed the coastal landscape of Molfetta in a variety of promenades unrelated to the historical identity and tectonics of the city.

The project is the regeneration and creation of a new promenade in order to get back the identity of the city. The proposal enhances the waterfront by adding activities in the most representative points of the promenade and decentralizing parking lots from the historical centre of Molfetta, reorganizing it along the entire promenade.

JURY POINT OF VIEW The project generates a system by critical elements along the waterfront through the widespread use of local limestone declined in the various design solutions. This limestone was identified as the dominant material in continuity with the structure of the old town. The result is a dynamicity of seafront through interesting design solutions developed in the most representative points.

MIGUEL FERNÁNDEZ-GALIANO RODRÍGUEZ (ES)
JOSÉ SANZ GORORDO (ES)
ALFONSO RENGIFO CAVESTANY (ES)
LAIA CERVELLÓ SABATÉ (ES)
REGINA VALLE VIUDES (ES)
ARCHITECTS

MARTA CRIADO DEL REY ARANA (ES)
LUIS GÓMEZ HERNÁNDEZ (ES)
JAVIER NÚÑEZ PÉREZ-SEOANE (ES)
STUDENTS IN ARCHITECTURE

MALTA ESTUDIO
MALTA@MALTAESTUDIO.COM
WWW.MALTAESTUDIO.COM

SPECIAL MENTION - MOLFETTA (IT)

A Walk to Re(New-Imagine-Activate)

TEAM POINT OF VIEW The proposal is divided in three main strategies.
First: to create a main axis along the waterfront, it is important to create new parking lots to free the condensed centre of cars, allowing a more pleasant experience of the coast and the city. Second: 7 areas of interest are identified along the coastline. Renewing, reactivating or reimagining these spaces will permit the pursued connection. Third: a multipurpose foundation is designed allowing the installation of every kind of new activity. The design of the stands will be open to competition every year.

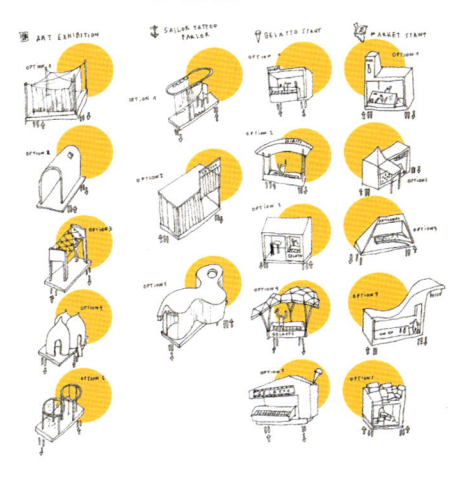

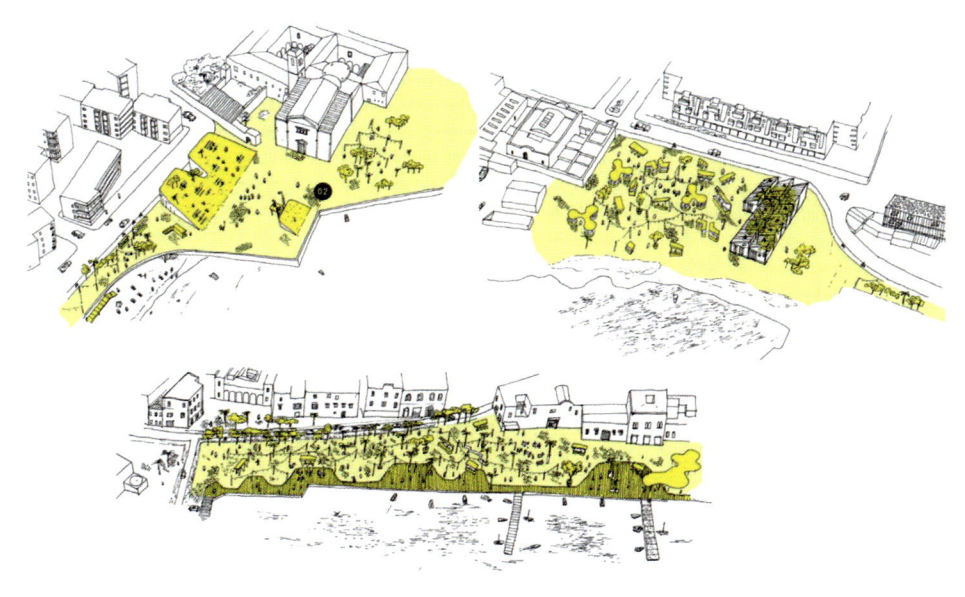

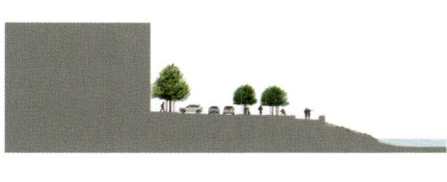

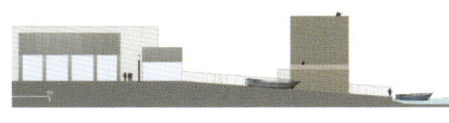

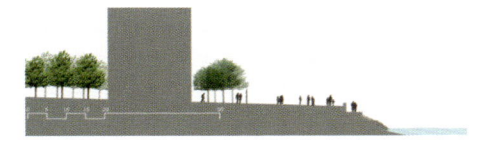

SERAFINO FIORIELLO (IT)
LORENZO LOIACONO (IT)
MARIA CONCETTA BUQUICCHIO (IT)
ARCHITECTS

ANDREA CAPUANO (SI)
ARCHITECT

60 VIA DEI 500
70027 PALO DEL COLLE (BARI), IT
T. +39 3405543970
S.FIORIELLO@VIRGILIO.IT
WWW.LAB-ARCHITECTS.COM

SPECIAL MENTION - MOLFETTA (IT)

SeaSide

TEAM POINT OF VIEW "SeaSide" aims to reconnect both waterfronts through the identifying element of the city –the sea– and valorise their identity: vocation for tourist, sports and seaside on the one hand, and religious, historical and productive on the other.
The re-naturalization of natural elements, the enhancement of historical buildings as ex-colony, shipyards and Basilica of St. Maria dei Martiri, and the realization of more permeable spaces connecting in a cross the sea-front with built fabric, define the project as functional and innovative, yet highly respectful of historical traditions.

MONTREUIL
FRANCE (FR)

CATEGORY: **URBAN – ENVIRONMENTAL – ARCHITECTURAL**
LOCATION: **MONTREUIL, SECTOR HAUT MONTREUIL - COMMUNAUTÉ D'AGGLOMÉRATION: EST ENSEMBLE CONURBATION, GRAND PARIS TERRITORY**
POPULATION: **103,000 INHAB.**
STRATEGIC SITE: **140 HA**
PROJECT SITE: **29 HA**
SITE PROPOSED BY: **MONTREUIL MUNICIPALITY, ETABLISSEMENT PUBLIC FONCIER D'ILE-DE-FRANCE (EPFIF)**
OWNER(S) OF THE SITE: **MONTREUIL MUNICIPALITY, EPFIF**
COMMISION AFTER COMPETITION: **A WORKSHOP WILL BE HELD WITH THE CHOSEN TEAMS, WHO WILL BE COMMISSIONED TO CARRY OUT A FURTHER STUDY LEADING TO URBAN DESIGN CONTRACTS (PUBLIC SPACES). ONE OR MORE ARCHITECTURAL PROJECT MANAGEMENT COMMISSIONS MAY BE AWARDED**

Interview of the site's representative

Marie Fourtane, Architect-urbanist Haut Montreuil, Urban Development Studies Department - Directorate for Urban Planning and Housing

PRESENTATION OF THE SITE WITH REGARDS TO STRATEGY

The combined arrival in 2020 of metro line 11 and tramline T1 will deeply transform the Haut Montreuil. The City proposed an extended reflection site to the teams. The urbanisation of this former horticultural plateau is heterogeneous with suburban areas, activity, major blocks and fallow lands. The City identified a project sector with 3 potential sites: Boissière, along the Boulevard and around the future metro station; Roches, a large activity and storage area to evolve; and Signac, along the A186 to reconnect with the new building sites along the tramway line.

HOW IS THE SITE CONNECTED TO THE SESSION TOPIC - THE ADAPTABLE CITY?

The site is on hold due to some delay in the agenda of the extension of tramway line T1; this avenue is due to replace a highway from the 1970's and should bring back dynamics on the plateau. The site should also face the uncertainty of the planning project around the future Boissière metro station and adapt to some sort of concern from the inhabitants who is legitimately claiming for a "living together" despite the lack of transportation and services. One major issue will be to graduate the mutation in steps: a city in transition.

DID YOU DEFINE A SPECIFIC PROCESS FOR THE URBAN DEVELOPMENT OF THE SITE AFTER EUROPAN COMPETITION?

We are currently defining an urban development process. The winning projects bring complementary approaches allowing the promotion of short-term actions as well as the federation of a prospective vision and the work on spatialization and land assembly processes.

MATHIEU GARCIA (FR)
FLORENT DESCOLAS (FR)
ARCHITECTS-URBANISTS
ADRIEN MONDINE (FR)
ARCHITECT

OYAPOCK ARCHITECTES
11 RUE MANIN
75019 PARIS, FR
T. +33 663063466
AM@OYAPOCK-ARCHITECTES.COM
WWW.OYAPOCK-ARCHITECTES.COM

RUNNER-UP - MONTREUIL (FR)
Serendipity of Fields

JURY POINT OF VIEW An approach essentially based on the integration of nature into the city through 2 green pathways, one in the heart of the blocks and the other in the footprint of the motorway: a linear forest of pines linking Romainville to Montereau Park. The 3rd landscape consists of cross-fields infiltrated between the existing buildings, providing gardens for the inhabitants. Transformation process: rehousing the existing activity, emptying the land, creation of superimposed structures providing a diversity of programmes, as well as changes through the addition of successive blocks.

TEAM POINT OF VIEW With the arrival of the metro and the T3 tramway line, we propose to extend the urbanization over the "Haut Montreuil" following 3 approaches:
- The first link at the city scale is the linear forest. This urban pine tree forest extending from Romainville to the Parc de Montreau is the missing link between the plateau and the town centre that arises from the opportunity created by the demolition of the highway.
- The second landscape, which spans over the "Haut Montreuil", is the nature corridor, North-South Pedestrian walking paths that go across the heart of the plots away from the car traffic. The natural shape of the North-South inclined topography gives place to a swale that irrigates the gardens and fields with rainwater all the way towards the linear forest.
- The third landscape structures the city blocks: the crossing fields infiltrate the existing buildings and ends up structuring the distributions of the plots for future constructions. Conviviality is allowed by a culture that favours local markets.

At a the time when Paris aspires to convert its roofs into urban gardens, it is imperative to conceive any periurban expansion by integrating " new vegetable gardens" as food supply parks of the future. Agriculture should not be considered as an element that blocks the growth of the city anymore, but as the real scheme of the Grand Paris.

MARION RHEIN (FR)
CAROLE CHEVALIER (FR)
LOUISE MAURICE (FR)
ARCHITECTS

82 RUE DE VINCENNES
93100 MONTREUIL, FR
MARIONRHEIN@GMAIL.COM

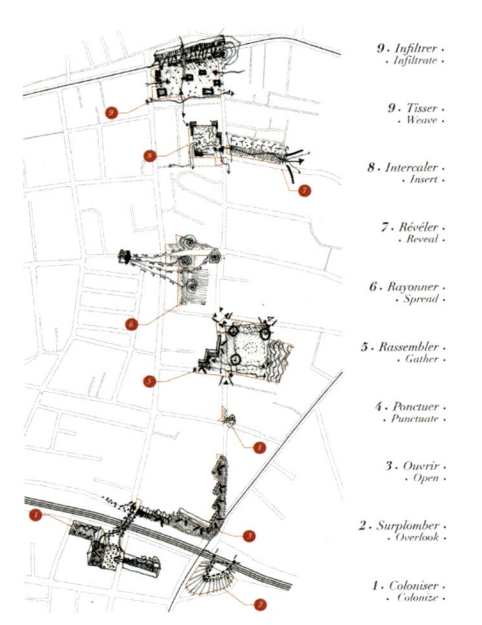

YVAN OKOTNIKOFF (FR)
JORDAN AUCANT (FR)
ANNE LEVALOIS (FR)
ARTHUR POIRET (FR)
ARCHITECTS-URBANISTS
THIBAULT BARBIER (FR)
MATHIEU DELORME (FR)
LANDSCAPE ENGINEERS
AURÉLIEN DELCHET (FR)
LOLA MARLHOUX (FR)
ARCHITECTS

JULIE-ALISSON DUCROS (FR)
ADÈLE ROCHE (FR)
ARCHITECTS
CLAIRE AQUILINA (FR)
ADÈLE SORGE (FR)
STUDENTS IN ARCHITECTURE

ATELIERGEORGES
WWW.ATELIERGEORGES.FR

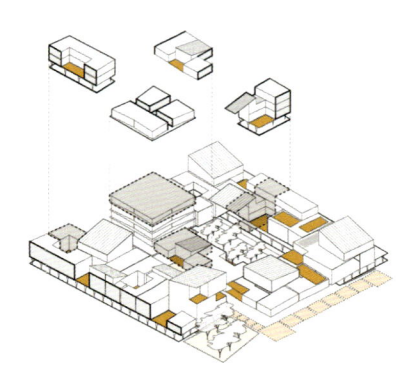

SPECIAL MENTION - MONTREUIL (FR)

From Punctual to Usual

TEAM POINT OF VIEW The future arrival of subway and tramway on the Montreuil plateau is going to disrupt the existing situation and offers an occasion to reconnect elements. To get the most of it we propose a strategy able to forecast, prepare and follow the mutation. We identified several situations and spaces as opportunities to link up the mutation to the existing city. We picked out different types of scopes of intervention. These types match nine sites and we set up a strategy for each. These strategies seize good conditions, increase potentialities, give access to hidden places and make good use of resources.

SPECIAL MENTION - MONTREUIL (FR)

OuLiPo

TEAM POINT OF VIEW In Montreuil, the amount of initiatives at work invites us to find a way to facilitate and coordinate their blooming rather than prepare an additional proposal.
Behind each project currently marking out the plateau there is a community project run by a singular way of looking at the world. We believe absorbing and allowing this plurality is the first City quality. We propose to establish a laboratory to encourage the maintenance and development of a differentiated city. Land strategy, consultation, planning, financial and administrative legal support, OuLiPo will carry a wide range of skills.

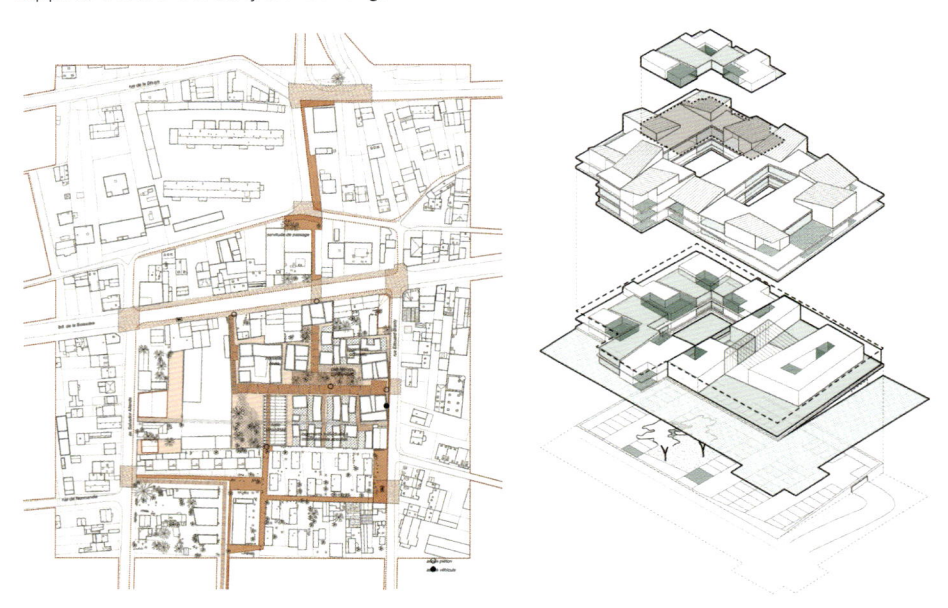

SANTO TIRSO
PORTUGAL (PT)

CATEGORY: **URBAN – ARCHITECTURAL**
LOCATION **SANTO TIRSO, MARKETPLACE AREA**
POPULATION: **27,000 INHAB.**
STRATEGIC SITE: **40.3 HA**
PROJECT SITE: **3.4 HA**

SITE PROPOSED BY: **SANTO TIRSO MUNICIPALITY**
OWNER(S) OF THE SITE: **SANTO TIRSO MUNICIPALITY**
COMMISION AFTER COMPETITION:
**ARCHITECTURAL PROJECT;
REDESIGN OF PUBLIC SPACE**

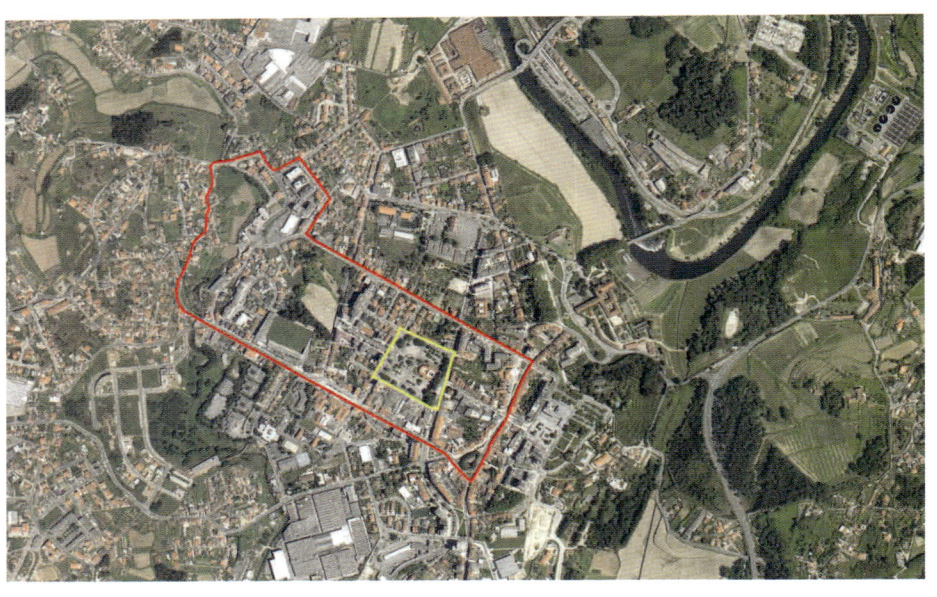

Interview of the site's representative

Conceição Melo, Director of the Department of Urban Planning and Environment, Municipality of Santo Tirso

PRESENTATION OF THE SITE WITH REGARDS TO STRATEGY

The strategy to make Santo Tirso more attractive and competitive as an urban centre is based in interventions that connect the civic and administrative centre to the riverside system. The Europan 13 site, just like the Europan 9 one, is part of ongoing projects focus on urban regeneration issues, in relation to built heritage, consolidation of central urban functions and public spaces improvement and smooth mobility solutions.

HOW IS THE SITE CONNECTED TO THE SESSION TOPIC - THE ADAPTABLE CITY?

The Market has been losing the role it once held in the everyday life due to changes in commercial retail offer. Its strategic location and recognition are important in urban and social life, and it is essential to counteract the current abandon trend through a commitment to a more adaptive strategy that links the market with city areas offering diverse uses and contributing to new possibilities for urban vitality.

DID YOU DEFINE A SPECIFIC PROCESS FOR THE URBAN DEVELOPMENT OF THE SITE AFTER EUROPAN COMPETITION?

The municipality is improving an agriculture policy to put dismissed agricultural areas in the production chain, refining them with new agricultural crops. The market will be the last link allowing the direct interaction between producers and costumers, offering new possibilities to show their products, creating new employment and increase local food culture. In order to renew the market it is also important to complement with other functions increasing urban life. The early involvement between the crew project and the users is the critical point of this project and the bound that can guarantee its success.

LAURA ALVAREZ (NL)
ARCHITECT

NIEUWE HEMWEG 2
1013 BG AMSTERDAM, NL
T. +31 615298655
OFFICE@LAURAALVAREZ.EU
WWW.LAURAALVAREZ.EU

WINNER - SANTO TIRSO (PT)
FOODlab Santo Tirso

TEAM POINT OF VIEW Santo Tirso is a great example for integration of landscape and architecture. The regeneration of the Ave riversides is a good prove of this. Built and unbuilt form in this area a harmonious amalgam, a beautiful green and cultural city belt. Still, the city centre needs a push further to achieve this balance. Potentially it also has good ingredients. But the urban tissue is very disconnected.

The first action is to create continuity. First, we need to reinforce the SE-NW axis by acting in the market square and also creating new housing area in the vacant plot along this new axis. The new axis will continue until the river and will be connected to the green belt surrounding the city. The market square should be a catalyst for the regeneration of the city centre – it should connect, gather and move people.

The new square creates a strong link with the existing market. And it therefore also needs a new impulse with new functions to support the new centrality created by the square. We propose to create a FOOD lab. A combination of a traditional market with uses related to food – a food court, restaurant, culinary school and artists-in-residence will complete the program of the new food centre.

JURY POINT OF VIEW A strong image envisions a combination between a "ludic" and iconic profile, centred on the plaza approach as a kind of architectonic concept, with partial covering and landscaping organization. Difficulties in implementation process should be carefully manageable.

IGNACIO GALBIS LLORÉNS (ES)
MARÍA GARCÍA BERNÁ (ES)
LUCÍA MARTÍNEZ RODRÍGUEZ (ES)
ARCHITECTS

CALLE CONDE DE COCENTAINA 18
03820 COCENTAINA, ES
T. +34 647945301
NACHOGALBIS@GMAIL.COM

RUNNER-UP - SANTO TIRSO (PT)

3tirsolines

TEAM POINT OF VIEW Nowadays Santo Tirso marketplace is an almost empty building surrounded by a wide-open space full of vehicles. We propose 3 strategies to attract more people to the area and fight against the lost of significance:

- Replace the parking lots with vegetation that will spread gradually, following smooth slopes to save the height difference, to the city centre and to the Sanguinhedo River. This will create a long green axis where new bicycle paths and pedestrian walks (connected with the currents itineraries), urban agriculture spaces and sport facilities will increase the local offer of outdoor-activities. Cars will be distributed in 3 car parks zones, promoted by Institutions.
- Renovate the marketplace, improving its access and acclimatization to incorporate new uses (restoration, exhibitions, specialized shops). The building work will be made in stages to avoid closing the market stands and to turn it into the first meeting point for the public participation, that will take part in the design process and organize shared activities with all the agents involved.
- Increase the building, merging public uses and facilities into a variety of sustainable dwellings. Studio houses, student housing and communal greenhouses will encourage the arrival of new neighbours that live and work there. In addition, the first shared ideas will consolidate in new institutions, community facilities will be needed overtime and new business will set up.

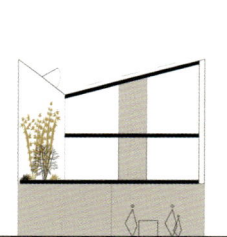

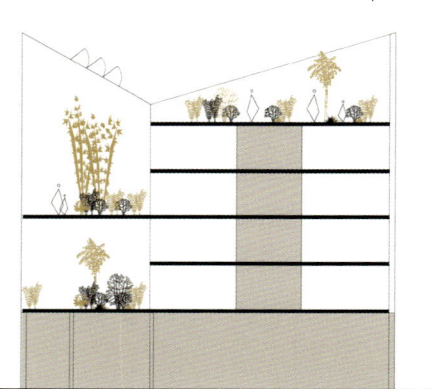

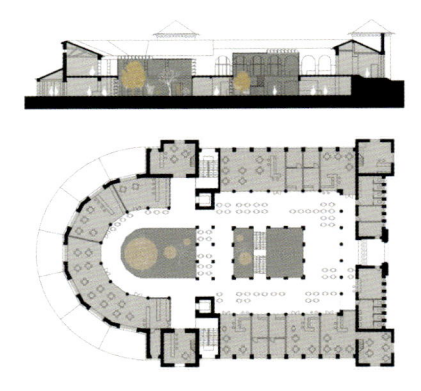

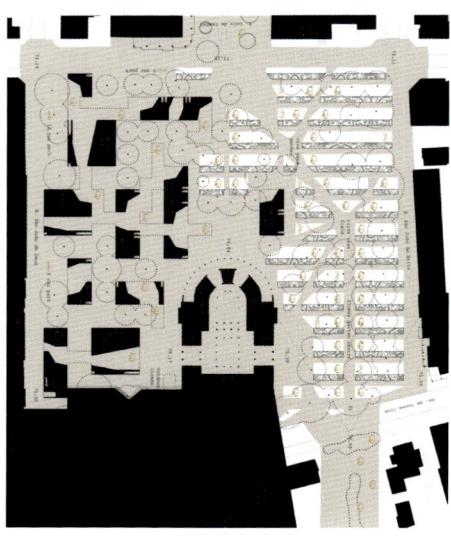

JURY POINT OF VIEW It is a complex diversification proposal with eventual difficulties in implementation of some parts, but strong in its interaction with the surrounding areas with an innovative approach to place-making through a strategy of urban morphological and activities motivation.

FERNANDO EIROA LORENZO (ES)
JORGE GARCÍA ANTA (ES)
ALBERTO SEOANE SESAR (ES)
ARCHITECTS

ALCALDE SALORIO SUÁREZ P1 L4
15010 A CORUÑA, ES
T. +34 981256020
INFO@LCGARQUITECTURA.COM
WWW.LCGARQUITECTURA.COM

SPECIAL MENTION - SANTO TIRSO (PT)
Play Time

TEAM POINT OF VIEW The proposal enhances the spot with accessibility, attraction, amenities and action. The building is changed into a more permeable one, maximizing the central patio with a new cover and creating another entry connecting the square. This open space should receive the weekly fair and all kind of events and can be covered by tarpaulins; there is also a car park under it.
Two small pavilions and pergolas demarcate the soft square with an open green space to foster the commercial life of the streets and even host new uses in the near future.

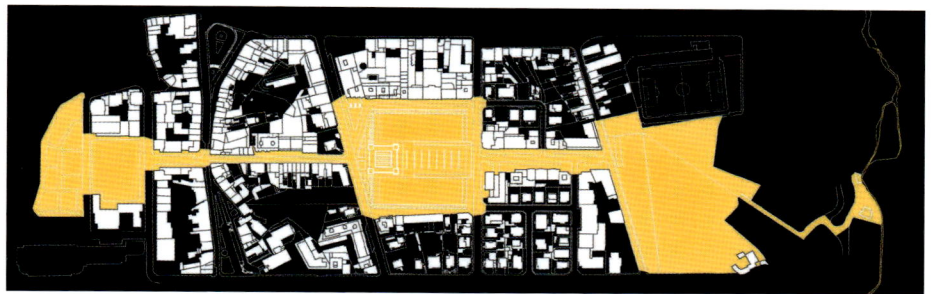

SCHWÄBISCH GMÜND
DEUTSCHLAND (DE)

CATEGORY: **URBAN – LANDSCAPE – ARCHITECTURAL**
LOCATION: **HARDT DISTRICT**
POPULATION: **59,700 INHAB.**
STRATEGIC SITE: **57 HA** / PROJECT SITE:
A 1.18 HA, B 1.20 HA, C 0.67 HA, D 0.56 HA
SITE PROPOSED BY: **CITY OF SCHWÄBISCH GMÜND**

OWNER(S) OF THE SITE: **CITY, VGW (SCHWÄBISCH GMÜND PUBLIC HOUSING AUTHORITY), SVG (SELF-HELP HOUSING SOCIETY), COUNTY, STATE, PRIVATE OWNERS**
COMMISION AFTER COMPETITION: **INTEGRATED URBAN PLANNING DEVELOPMENT CONCEPT, IMPLEMENTATION MODULES FOR SITES A–D AND THE IDEAS PART**

Interview of the site's representative

Julius Mihm, Mayor and Head of the Town Planning Department, Municipality of Schwäbisch Gmünd

PRESENTATION OF THE SITE WITH REGARDS TO STRATEGY

The Hardt district –the only part of the town centre situated as a satellite– goes back to a barracks of the 1930s to which isolated housing estate fragments (row housing in the 1950s, US Army housing area, teachers college, vocational school centre) have been added since the Second World War – a juxtaposition of autistic urban building blocks whose main thoroughfare deepens the separation between the parts of the district. The goal is to rescue the parts from their isolation, to interlink the different functional urban planning areas, and to supplement them in an integrated way.

HOW IS THE SITE CONNECTED TO THE SESSION TOPIC - THE ADAPTABLE CITY?

It relates to designing future requirements for the individual urban planning sections and for their relationship to the whole: adapting to the model of a lively town centre with diverse connections and possibilities for the parts to exchange with one another; adapting scopes for joint processes of growth and exchange in order to develop new urban planning syntheses that are more than the sum of the parts of their districts up to now; developing the inner structures and typologies of the individual urban building blocks towards the outside, and adapting them to one another and integrating them into a new higher-level whole.

DID YOU DEFINE A SPECIFIC PROCESS FOR THE URBAN DEVELOPMENT OF THE SITE AFTER EUROPAN COMPETITION?

The results of the competition contributed –on the basis of the winning ideas– to the developing of a concrete development framework plan for the application to be named as a redevelopment area (Soziale Stadt). Inclusion in the subsidized funding for redevelopment work of the State of Baden-Württemberg is expected for the beginning of 2016.

JOHAN LAURE (FR)
GUILLAUME GIRAUD (FR)
HADRIEN BALALUD DE SAINT JEAN (FR)
ARCHITECTS

NAS ARCHITECTURE
4 RUE DES TRÉSORIERS DE LA BOURSE
34000 MONTPELLIER, FR
T. +33 467671873
CONTACT@NASARCHITECTURE.COM
WWW.NASARCHITECTURE.COM

RUNNER-UP - SCHWÄBISCH GMÜND (DE)

Creative City

TEAM POINT OF VIEW The "Creative City" is based on the idea of tuning the whole area composed of various pieces ruling the life of the new city centre. The city cannot be made of autonomous juxtaposed and isolated entities. It can no longer grow with a simple hierarchy where centrality would only leave possible "peripheries". Beyond this positioning, it becomes necessary to think of the image of a connected network structure in terms of hyper-media and interdependent entities rather than one single environment dominating the other. The process of linking things together introduces a new type of dimension to practise inside each branch of the network. Fluctuation becomes part of the established dynamic involving a united and interrelated vision of the territory pockets, as "hyper-medias".

The main goal is to set up an urban fabric that wouldn't focus on one single point but develop around micro-districts as nodes able to grow their own particular identity.

The concept of "Creative City" represents a powerful proposal based on various scales, from daily needs to new ways of living. By setting up an aware approach of each site context and temporalities, the "Creative City" aims at becoming an adapted tool for a mutating city, providing a respectful architecture inside an adapted urban planning putting Mankind and Living conditions as its priority.

JURY POINT OF VIEW This design makes a valuable contribution to adapting structures originating in the open urban development of the 1960s to the demands of current cities without abandoning their large scale. Rather than densifying and detailing structures on open spaces in retrospect, it accepts the size and openness of the space and proposes a well thought-out open space concept linking new social focal points by means of a sequence of open spaces that are developed in detail. The detailing of the design with respect to urban development is not convincing.

HÉCTOR PEINADOR (ES)
SWASTIKA MUKHERJEE (IN)
THOMAS GAINES (GB)
ARCHITECTS

CALLE SANTA ISABEL 13, 4A.
40004 SEGOVIA, ES
T. +86 13520125761
HECTORPEINADOR@GMAIL.COM
WWW.HECTORPEINADOR.COM

RUNNER-UP - SCHWÄBISCH GMÜND (DE)

Nodes

TEAM POINT OF VIEW The project aims at knitting and weaving a very diverse community together and awaken the potential public spaces around the Hardt area. The schemes aim is to affect exchange between numerous ages and nationalities within the area. Creating a new identity, a sustainable community seeking to change its habits and to live differently.

The project tries to reconnect the Hardt area with a system of organized interventions of greenery, trees, plazas, streets, curbs and cycle routes. The most important being the green belt running from North to South, having a section of shared surface that cuts through the Oberbettringer strasse shifting the balance and producing an ease of movement. The green belt also creates a civic spine connecting all parts of Hardt area. In conjunction with the green belt the 4 interventions offer voids along which versatile and changing activities can take place.

JURY POINT OF VIEW The project accepts the size and openness of the space and –in a clever urban development way– inserts functions and structures at selected locations that enliven the open spaces and existing structures and link them together. Nodes unfold along this framework with different housing typologies and buildings.

The urban layout remains schematic and a detailed formulation of concrete structures and open spaces is lacking.

MICHAEL SCHOTT (DE)
ARCHITECT

ZIKESCH | ARCHITEKTEN UND INGENIEURE
LINDENSCHULSTR. 33
70327 STUTTGART, DE
T. +49 711331542
SCHOTT@ZIKESCH.AT
WWW.ZIKESCH.AT

RUNNER-UP - SCHWÄBISCH GMÜND (DE)
Un-Break my Hardt

TEAM POINT OF VIEW The proposed urban spatial structure aims at providing the framework for a development process taking social, cultural, environmental and economic issues equally into account.
"Un-Break my Hardt" serves as a model for uniting disconnected areas of the Hardt district on many levels. In addition to the given urban spatial barriers and caesuras, use-related and socio-cultural divisions must also be overcome to transform the district into a multifaceted and interwoven whole promoting coexistence and exchange between generations and nations. For this purpose 4 zones with different use priorities are derived from the existing structures: education, socio-cultural, commercial and administration. Strengthened and supplemented by new buildings each of them receives its own characteristic urban centre affiliated with specific uses that encourage social interaction and new sharing concepts and fill the urban space with life.
Pedestrian- and cycle-friendly promenades and paths interlink the centres and create sequences of diverse public spaces that facilitate synergies and exchange between the different uses. To reinforce cohesion a continuous ribbon structure is implemented that serves as street furniture to communicate and relax but also provides multifunctional services like Wi-Fi, open Internet and charging stations for e-mobility.

JURY POINT OF VIEW The project succeeds in providing hope for a comprehensive transformation of the problematic city district. It proposes a series of structural additions that transform the open urban landscape into more clearly readable building site squares. As a result, the existing spatial structure is given a stronger hierarchy. A correspondingly comprehensive transformation strategy is a conceptual as well as financial effort. Implementation requires a sensible examination of local and regional resources and actors, but also of small-spatial qualities already onsite.

FELIX EIFFLER (DE)
PABLO V. HILDEBRANDT (DE)
JULIA MAISCH (DE)
ARCHITECTS

VICTOR AOUIZERAT (DE)
SOCIOLOGIST

FELIXEIFFLER@AOL.COM

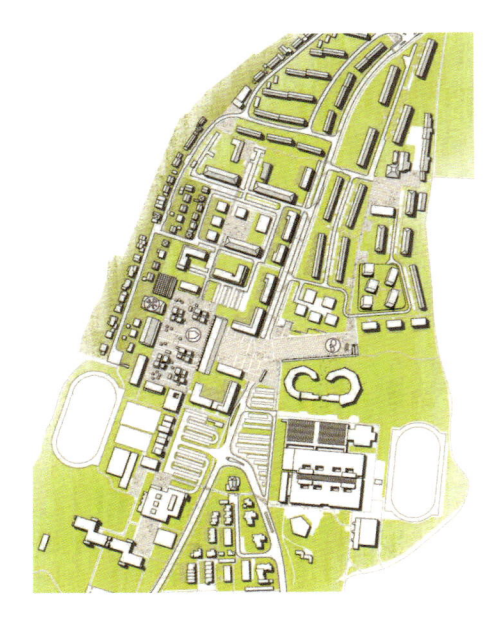

SPECIAL MENTION - SCHWÄBISCH GMÜND (DE)

Playful Hardt

TEAM POINT OF VIEW The concept assumes that collective actions and common projects are most suitable to encourage interpersonal exchange and thereby produce cohesion and social identity. Empty spaces in the urban fabric are reserved for common projects and a game of urban planning is initiated as a participation method. An agora is established to allocate game and planning. Unused storehouses are converted in public, self-organised workshops to support common projects with tools and media. The concept of Cluster Housing offers adaptable living space while implying again planning as a social factor.

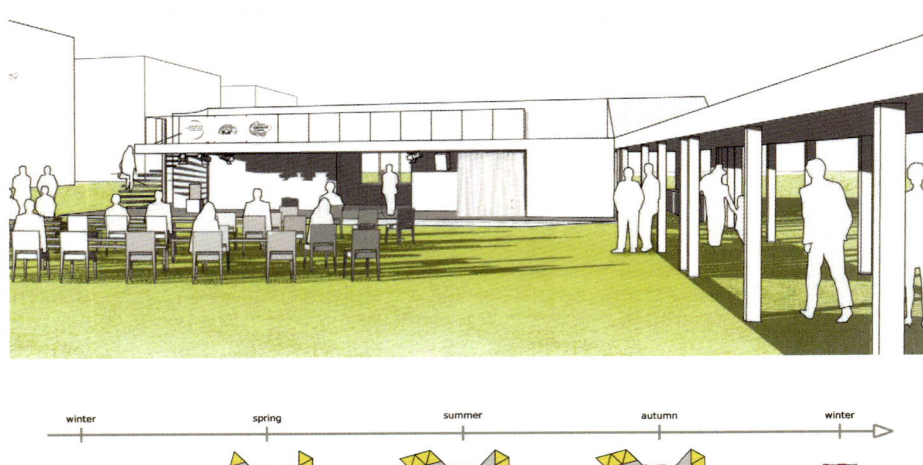

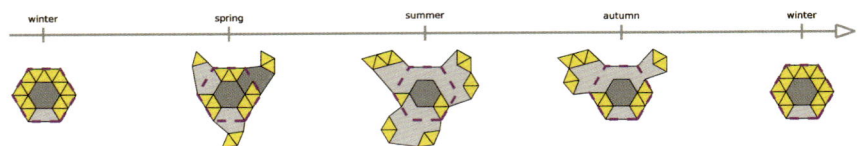

ST PÖLTEN
ÖSTERREICH (AT)

CATEGORY: **URBAN – ARCHITECTURAL**
LOCATION: **ST PÖLTEN**
POPULATION: **53,000 INHAB.**
STRATEGIC SITE: **21 HA** / PROJECT SITE: **8.7 HA**
SITE PROPOSED BY: **CITY OF ST PÖLTEN**

OWNER(S) OF THE SITE: **WWE WOHN & WIRTSCHAFTSPARK ENTWICKLUNGSGESMBH**
COMMISION AFTER COMPETITION:
URBAN PROJECT MANAGEMENT ROLE, FURTHER INVOLVEMENT IN ARCHITECTURAL FOLLOW-UP PROCEDURES

Interview of the site's representative

Jens de Buck, Head of Department of Urban Planning and Development, City of St Pölten
Peter Wondra, WWE Wohn- und Wirtschaftspark Entwicklungsgesellschaft m.b.H
Robert Hahn, Head of Project Development Bauträger Austria Immobilien

PRESENTATION OF THE SITE WITH REGARDS TO STRATEGY

A forgotten site, an urban wilderness in close proximity to the city centre, comes to the focus of urban development thanks to its links to the railway network, investigating new forms of "Living in the Green." Traces of the past, a feral landscape by the water and excellent local and regional links invite to discover a unique address for contemporary housing!

HOW IS THE SITE CONNECTED TO THE SESSION TOPIC - THE ADAPTABLE CITY?

Only 30 min. away from Wien by train, the adaption & implementation of landscape and the sensitive consideration of the historical context will establish a positive identity of the currently forgotten site. The transformation of the railway as a barrier into a linking element to the neighbourhood will put the site in a new and highly connected position as well as in the city and the metropolitan region. The discovery of the Genius Loci of the site is key to establish a new identity of qualitative housing, living & working. The implementation of a new concept of "housing with added value" will launch new types of housing with a well-balanced social and urban mix sensitively corresponding to the small-scale surrounding: Beyond worn-out modernist concepts of stacked single-family homes or multistorey housing typologies.

DID YOU DEFINE A SPECIFIC PROCESS FOR THE URBAN DEVELOPMENT OF THE SITE AFTER EUROPAN COMPETITION?

The four rewarded projects show a dense array of ambitious concepts with various degrees of practical realization. After a thorough review process, it is intended to cooperate with a rewarded team.

FRANCESCO MARRAS (IT)
FEDERICO ARU (IT)
ADRIANO DESSÌ (IT)
PHILIP GROSCH (IT)
SILVIA MOCCI (IT)
FRANCESCA OGGIANO (IT)
AURORA PERRA (IT)
ARCHITECTS

FEDERICO SERCIS (IT)
STUDENT IN ARCHITECTURE

19 VIA MONTE SABOTINO
09122 CAGLIARI, SARDINIA, IT
T. +39 3200837195
FRANCESCO.MARRAS@UNICA.IT
WWW.04401ARCHITECTS.COM

WINNER - ST PÖLTEN (AT)

Ju(MP) in the Water - Kiss that Frog

TEAM POINT OF VIEW The public space of the historic city of St Pölten is defined by compact blocks with buildings facing the street. As the compact urban tessera gets further from the urban centre it opens to the outside, toward the field. Rurality enters the city and fills the heart of the blocks in the form of private gardens and defining the living unit as element with a strong spatial tension between urban and rural areas.

The habitat of the project withdraws from the forms of the latest urban developments to reaffirm a dense aggregation system facing the road and finding roots in the local history. As urban areas weld the road fronts, the green spaces stitch the back of the living units in a systemic logic of park-wood linking the built compact blocks to small paths. The green system is developed as a public space – complementary to the urbanity – projecting the inhabitants towards the rediscovery of the community values of nature and open air.

The goal is to answer the question of the new urban settlement through an added value embracing a strong natural component, overturning the exclusive antithesis between urban and natural contexts through an adaptable inclusive proposal. The habitat is fed by future events and is able to absorb the changes of the place, shaping itself according to new needs which are still unknown.

JURY POINT OF VIEW The project features a poetic dealing with the subject of landscape as a refuge, and with water both in its representational and conceptive approach. Although the economic challenges of the task have not been met, the soft development of the proposal is interesting and sparks off discussion on housing quality in relation to landscape and considering wilderness as a public space. Urbanity in its classical sense will never be generated through this project, but it is exactly this contradiction and dealing with nature that are so innovative and valuable.

VERA SERIAKOV (AT)
NELA KADIC (AT)
ARCHITECTS-URBANISTS

WÄHRINGER GÜRTEL 7/18
1180 VIENNA, AT
T. +43 6601493007
VERA@SERIAKOV.COM
NELAKADIC@GMAIL.COM

RUNNER-UP - ST PÖLTEN (AT)

The Elastic City

TEAM POINT OF VIEW While the Austrian government is struggling with the accommodation of refugees, new strategies clearly have to be found. We –as urbanists– should at least contribute with a proposal dealing with a qualitative way of cooperation with people in need in a dignified way. 75% of Austrian municipalities do not provide shelter for refugees. Still, there seems to be less xerophobia among the local population of the ones hosting refugees. This might be due to the fact that knowing what you are confronted to can help you overcome most fears of contacts and lay the foundation to integrate people with different backgrounds and needs. The city's adaptability is its intelligence and sensitiveness to react on human and spatial requirements. We have to set a system as a base to achieve those mechanisms. By establishing a framework for a socially sustainable growth we contribute to St Pölten's capability to answer those future challenges. We believe in a clear yet flexible system allowing more freedom and urban variety. Today's urban planning strategies need to react on economic and societal challenges and be aware of their responsibility to prevent segregation and poverty.

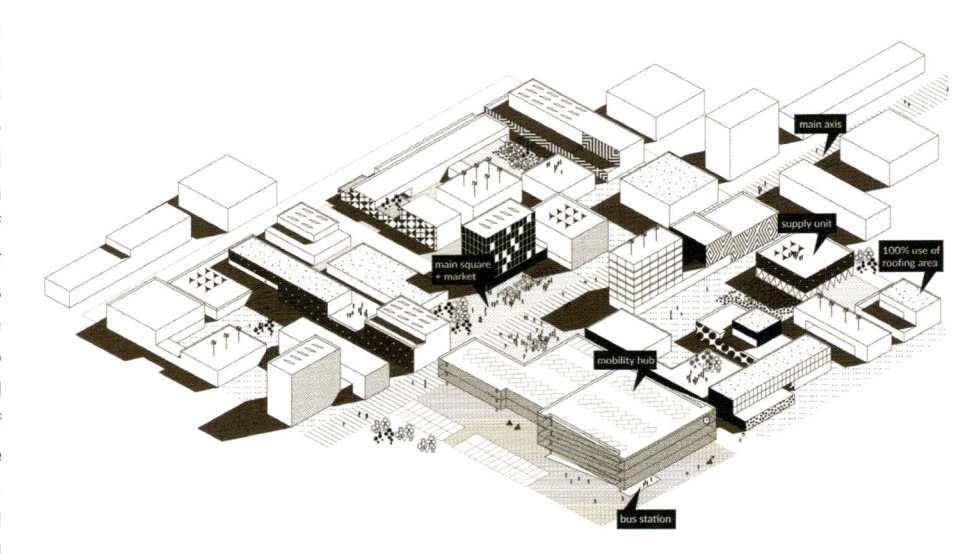

JURY POINT OF VIEW The project of an elastic framework of urban rules creating a socially diverse mix of 60-70% long term inhabitants to 30% short term inhabitants –like asylum seekers and other temporary stay guests– is appreciated as an essential political statement and interesting conceptual approach. The theoretical research, its representation and the positioning of St Pölten in a greater radius in Austria offers a vision of a new dense neighbourhood of the future and raises the question how to create society in adaptable times.

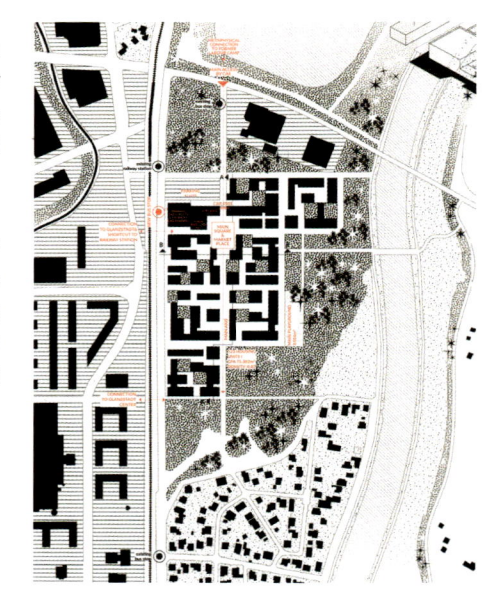

KONRAD BASAN (PL)
EWA ODYJAS (PL)
AGNIESZKA MORGA (PL)
JAKUB PUDO (PL)
ARCHITECTS

CONTACT@BOM.EU
WWW.BOM.EU

SPECIAL MENTION - ST PÖLTEN (AT)
A(US)trium

TEAM POINT OF VIEW The proposed urban scheme is a grid splitting the space into semi-public and semi–private areas, forming a hybrid of housing blocks. Semi-public zones host entrance areas. Semi-private zones contain common green spaces. The grid role is to mitigate the disadvantages of a noise pollution. The density of the housing structure decreases from the Northern part of the project site to the South to generate a seamless connection between single-family housing estate and the project site. A green outline of bike and pedestrian routes allows users to enjoy sport activities and soft mobility.

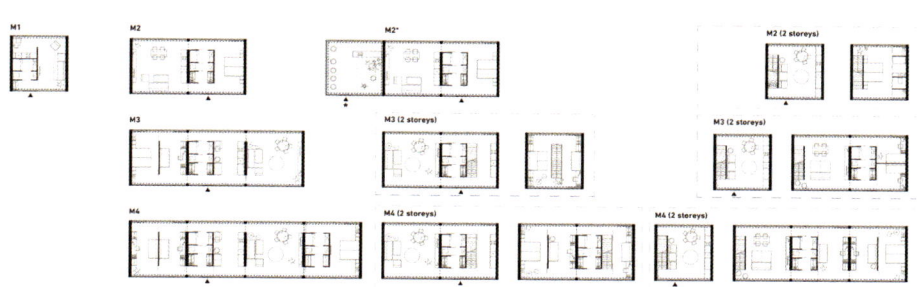

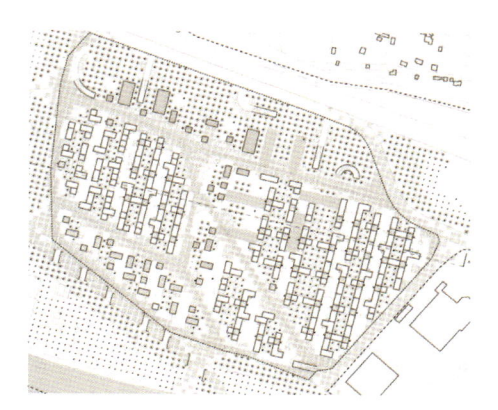

LUIS MASIÁ MASSONI (ES)
FABIO CAVATERRA (IT)
ARCHITECTS

CALMM ARCHITECTURE
14 RUE DES TAILLANDIERS
75011 PARIS, FR
CAVATERRAMASIA@CALMM.EU
WWW.CALMM.EU

SPECIAL MENTION - ST PÖLTEN (AT)
Osmose

TEAM POINT OF VIEW The aim of the project is to create a positive harmony between the different areas of the city.
The position of the site gives it the opportunity to become the entrance of Traisen's Valley into the city so we try to purchase the connection of natural corridor proposing structured plots around existing vegetation. We propose connections to establish continuity between the site and the existing activities in the surroundings. We suggest multi-functional life structures combining the existing St Pölten housing into an architectural hybrid that frames the semi-public spaces.

STAVANGER
NORGE (NO)

CATEGORY: **URBAN – ARCHITECTURAL**
LOCATION: **FORUS, STAVANGER**
POPULATION: **130,000 INHAB.**
STRATEGIC SITE: **102 HA**
PROJECT SITE: **4.5 HA**

SITE PROPOSED BY: **STAVANGER MUNICIPALITY**
(IN COLLABORATION WITH
FORUS NÆRINGSPARK)
OWNER(S) OF THE SITE:
STAVANGER MUNICIPALITY
COMMISION AFTER COMPETITION:
PLANNING AND BUILDING COMISSION

Interview of the site's representative

Fieke Verschueren, Project manager and Urban Designer, Development Department
Europan Norway

PRESENTATION OF THE SITE WITH REGARDS TO STRATEGY

Forus stretches across three municipalities: Stavanger, Sola and Sandnes. The Stavanger municipality owns a site at the very epicentre of Forus and is currently collaborating with its neighbouring municipalities on a common municipal plan including a new public transportation axis across Jæren intended to reduce car dependency in the region. The project site should in this respect serve as a case study for the way to pilot new urban developments and thus introduce a new narrative for Forus.

HOW IS THE SITE CONNECTED TO THE SESSION TOPIC - THE ADAPTABLE CITY?

The development of Forus as a business area started in the sixties. Fuelled by the postmillennial expansions of the fossil fuel industry, Forus has been subject to immense growth. An area of more than 110 ha was developed into a successful business area. The growth was based on an industry that is nowadays facing a highly uncertain future due to the extremely low oil prices. The region must therefore prepare for a less oil- and gas-dependent future and use its knowledge and knowhow as its main commodity.

DID YOU DEFINE A SPECIFIC PROCESS FOR THE URBAN DEVELOPMENT OF THE SITE AFTER EUROPAN COMPETITION?

The municipality believes that the winning project can inspire and be a catalyst for many initiatives and aspects of the local processes going on in the region. The winning team will be involved in the process of developing a strategy for the Forus site, starting with the establishment of a "living lab" at the site early February 2016. The municipality is not planning to make a fixed plan but embraces the ideas of the winning project to start with a management strategy, better connecting with the industry, to find different economic assets for the site. Later on, a design strategy will follow.

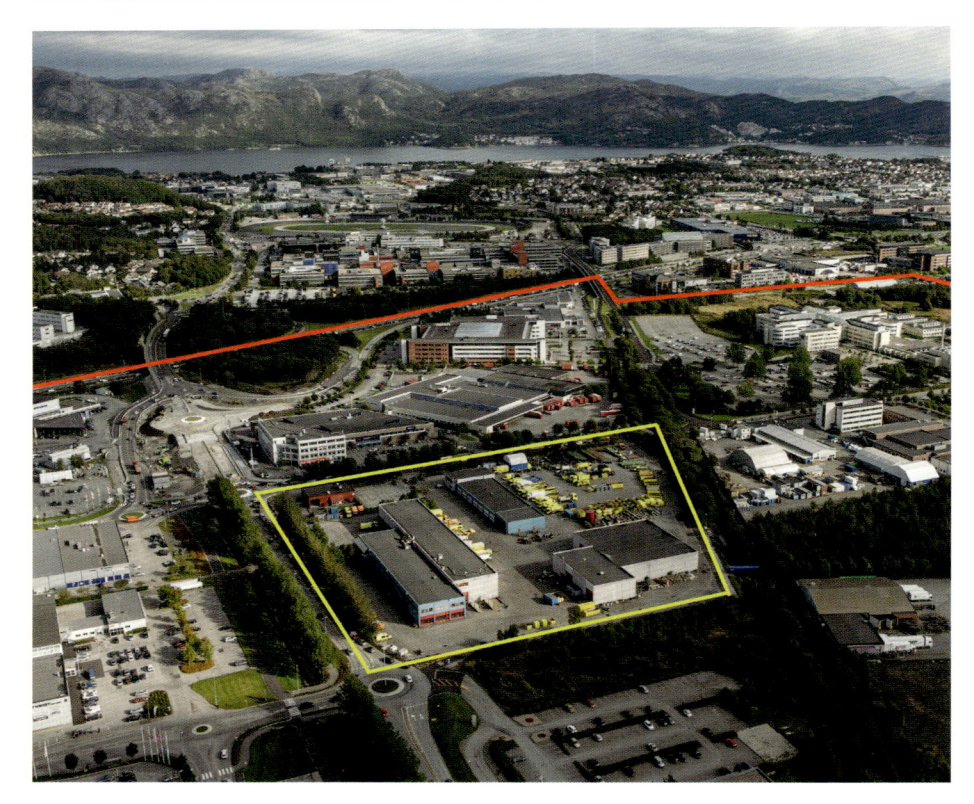

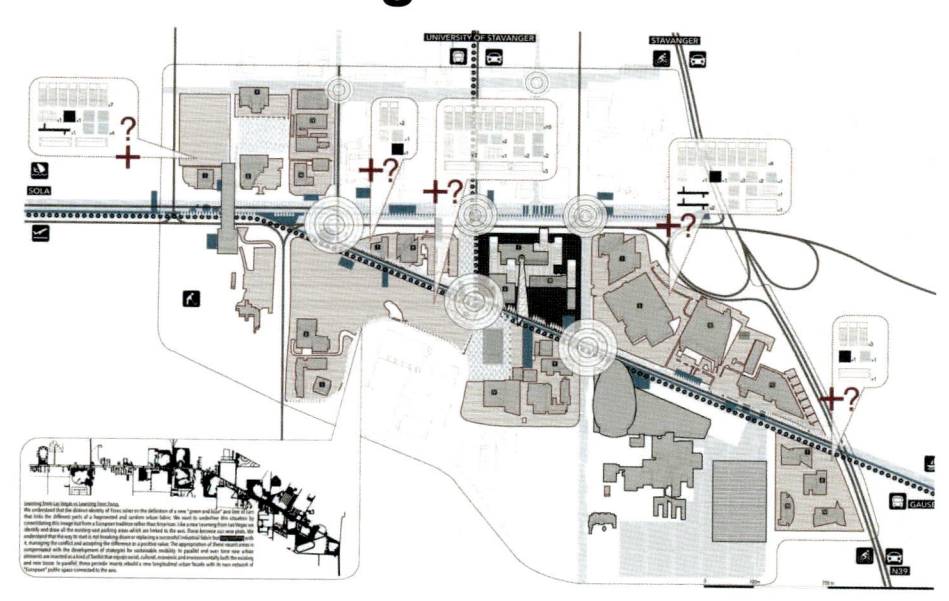

IVÁN CAPDEVILA CASTELLANOS (ES)
VICENTE IBORRA PALLARÉS (ES)
ARCHITECTS

JOSÉ ANTONIO GRÁS IÑIGO (ES)
SIMONA MIRÓN (RO)
ARCHITECTS

PLAYSTUDIO
PLAZA CALVO SOTELO 3, 8°A
03001 ALICANTE, ES
T. +34 965923392
TO@PLAYSTUDIO.ES
WWW.PLAYSTUDIO.ES

WINNER - STAVANGER (NO)
Forus LABing

TEAM POINT OF VIEW We see economic innovation not as an end in itself but as a means to the urban and social innovation. Our goal therefore is to propose a new model of society linked to a new urban model and promoted by a new economic model. This ideology will structure the project.

Therefore, as F. Ascher raises in "Les nouveaux principes de l'urbanisme" (2004) we do not propose the construction of a result but a kind of "middle-out" experimental process, which we call FORUS LAB, where top-down and bottom-up strategies intermingle. This suggests a horizontal approach by means of networks with a wide range of actors-mediators where processes are constantly renegotiated in an exercise that can be more inclusive and diverse to make conflicts visible. It is conceived as a comprehensive urban strategy –social, cultural, economic, and environmental– running in parallel to the process of change of the economic model in the region (20-30 years). It is structured into 3 groups of operations linked to 3 phases in time:
-1- Project site / Forus Hub; -2- Strategic site / Cluster_0; -3-Conurbation / Innovation Axis.
The production model to encourage innovation is the laboratory, since it allows the intersection between public participation and executive decision.

JURY POINT OF VIEW The project is not proposing a final result, but a process linked to a comprehensive new urban model based on participation of many actors, considering social, cultural, economic and environmental development. Public participation and executive decisions intermingle in the laboratory – the Foruslab. The pilot plot as a testing ground is described in a multi-layered design strategy that illustrates both reappropriation of existing structures, the use of the plot as a supersurface, and implementation of new structures.

176 **DACE GURECKA** (LV)
ARCHITECT

NORDBORGGADE 4, 3 TH
8000 AARHUS C, DK
T. +45 52673140
DACEGURECKA@GMAIL.COM

RUNNER-UP - STAVANGER (NO)
Rise of Nature

TEAM POINT OF VIEW The project proposal for the Green Axis consist of Six Park structures, Fifty Forests & Fields, which are both bound together by new regional mobility axis of BusWay 2020. Together they form a basis for the future of the Green Axis based on nature, clean technologies, agriculture, rural tourism and recreation.

Six Parks create artificial iconographic landscape types, which form basis for multipolar settlement structure and offers platform for a different way for densities to be structures. Parks outline various development areas, each with their unique programmatic and spatial identities, public spaces, relationship to the new mobility, potential for housing development.

Fifty Forests & Agriculture Fields are responsible for a regional level landscape strategy. They form an interconnected landscape connecting Sola Bay with Gand Fjord and Hafrsfjorden. The regional landscape strategy preserves and connects existing agricultural fields, small rural settlements, specific cultural landscape heritage sites (like Domsteinane), the slow network of green pathways, the existing scenery of the landscape and the main mountains and forests. Intervention in this level of landscape is proposed only through extremely small design or architecture gestures –a set of circular swings as a perfect viewpoint for mountain landscape or extension of the small local pathway to connect with one of the park settlement structures. The extremely big is supported by extremely small.

JURY POINT OF VIEW The strength of the proposal lies in its extension of the territory of the site and its understanding of the plot as part of a larger regional strategy which seems viable independent of any other future development of the Forus site. The project shifts the focus away from traditional development towards careful cultivation and definitions of existing qualities. Whilst suggestions for regional and urban scale pose interesting and critical questions for the overall development of Forus, the illustrated solution for the project site comes across as formalistic and almost contradictory to the rest of the overall ideas discussed in the project.

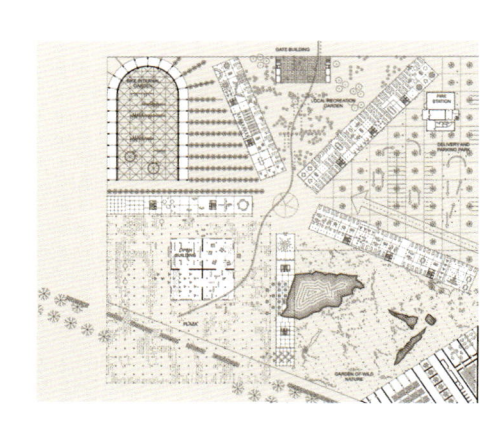

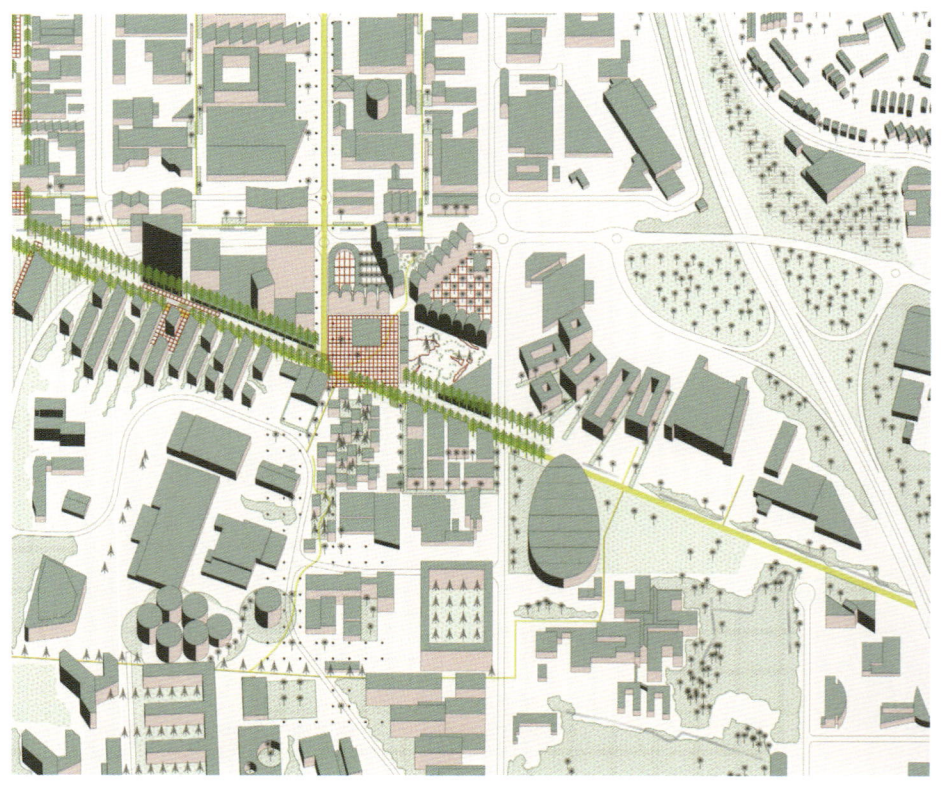

MIGUEL ZABALLA LLANO (ES)
ARCHITECT

ACHA ZABALLA ARQUITECTOS
SOTERA DE LA MIER 8,4º
48920 PORTUGALETE, ES
T. +34 944725734
ESTUDIO@ACHAZABALLA.COM
WWW.ACHAZABALLA.COM

SPECIAL MENTION - STAVANGER (NO)

Indigo

TEAM POINT OF VIEW The oil platform is seen as the symbol of identity that deserves to be recycled under a different way. This vision is related to the force of identity. With the possibilities brought by recycling. With the collective intelligence and social resilience capable to adapt to deep changes. It brings together identity, building technology and the logic of stacking up.

The introduction of the nature component facilitates the recovery by the community of the spaces from where it was excluded by the predominance of the non-human scale.

TRONDHEIM
NORGE (NO)

CATEGORY: **URBAN – ARCHITECTURAL**
LOCATION: **NYHAVNA, TRONDHEIM**
POPULATION: **180,000 INHAB.**
STRATEGIC SITE: **41.9 HA**
PROJECT SITE: **6 HA**

SITE PROPOSED BY: **TRONDHEIM HAVN**
(IN COLLABORATION WITH TRONDHEIM MUNICIPALITY)
OWNER(S) OF THE SITE: **TRONDHEIM HAVN**
COMMISION AFTER COMPETITION: **PLANNING AND BUILDING COMMISSION**

Interview of the site's representative

Per Arne Tefre, Head of the inner city department, Urban Planning Office
Europan Norway

PRESENTATION OF THE SITE WITH REGARDS TO STRATEGY

Nyhavna sits next to "Midtbyen", the city's urban core area. The municipality and the Harbour Authorities have collaborated and the newly developed masterplan points at the Europan site at Strandveikaia as a local centre for the residential zone of the greater Nyhavna area. The Strandveikaia site is strategic since it contains buildings that the Harbour Authority itself owns. The buildings also have short term contracts, meaning they can be easily be part of a first phase in the development of Nyhavna.

HOW IS THE SITE CONNECTED TO THE SESSION TOPIC - THE ADAPTABLE CITY?

Distinctive waterfront architecture including WWII structures characterize the area and provide a tremendous resource for a wide range of actors in culture, innovation and nightlife. The existing buildings and new buildings can contribute to the creation of a unique area in the city, mixing old and new architecture with an array of programs. A brewery on the neighbouring site, Ringnes, plans a national centre for beer that can be the starting point for a new ecosystem of urban life. How can the city create an urban space that acts as an engine for the transformation of the rest of the Nyhavna, adapting to sustainability and a growing Trondheim population?

DID YOU DEFINE A SPECIFIC PROCESS FOR THE URBAN DEVELOPMENT OF THE SITE AFTER EUROPAN COMPETITION?

A large potential can be realized at Strandveikaia as a first step of the larger Nyhavna development. There are plans to activate the area through events and temporary structures including local actors and the university this summer. The municipality is finalizing the new masterplan and the Trondheim Harbour Authority as landowner intends to continue the Europan process and establish dialogue with the winning team. The next step will be inviting the winning team to a workshop in Trondheim.

ANDREA ANSELMO (IT)
GLORIA CASTELLINI (IT)
GUYA DI BELLA (IT)
FILIPPO FANCIOTTI (IT)
GIOVANNI GLORIALANZA (IT)
BORIS HAMZEIAN (IT)
ARCHITECTS

MURA DELLA MALAPAGA 7/2
16128 GENOVA, IT
FALSEMIRRORPROJECT@GMAIL.COM
WWW.FALSEMIRRORPROJECT.COM

WINNER - TRONDHEIM (NO)
The False Mirror

TEAM POINT OF VIEW Against the 20th century superimposed approach, the idea of flexibility over permanence represents the new panorama of the adaptable. However, to what extent will this innovative approach –often based on standardized solutions– be able to represent the optimal response to our cities without falling in neutralization of the cities specificity?
To subvert such an overwhelming approach, "The False Mirror" envisages a profound shift in paradigm. Enlarging the field of investigation to a multi-perspective able to include matters such as morphology, typology and symbolism, we propose a new form of adaptability that categorically refuses the conventional approach to promote the inverted process: from global tools to site specific investigations.
We focus on what adaptable can mean: the rejection for neutrality becomes the adapted solution for Trondheim sustainable future. The project sets up a coherent strategy able to inform a new hybridity between the persistence of traditional forms and the flexibility of a rapid transformation process.
This new hybrid is conceived through the re-signification of 4 different and complementary archetypes steeped in the history of Trondheim: the traditional waterfront warehouses; the urban opening process through canalization; the site manufactured sea vessels fleet; and the adoption of land and water infrastructure such as ferries and new tram lines. The hybrid of past forms and future necessities is the "new" adaptability.

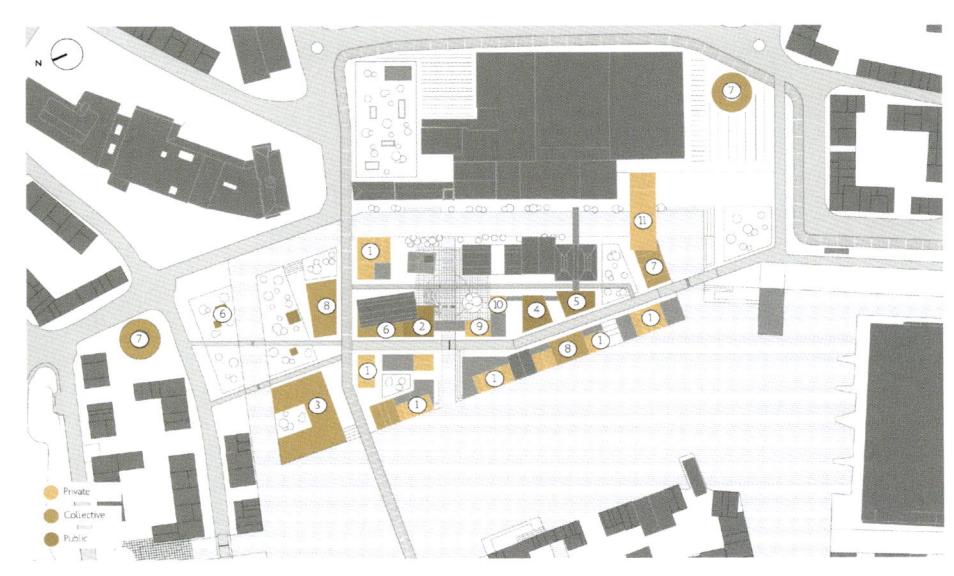

JURY POINT OF VIEW The team proposes a new form of adaptability based on an analysis of the local morphology, typology and symbolism. In the project this is exemplified with a reinterpretation of what the project defines as four local "archetypes": the warehouses, the canals, the sea vessels and the specific land and water infrastructure. The jury believes this project and the accompanying toolbox is an exciting new plan for Standveikaia – a plan that will work with time and against the generic city.

The evolutive process

1. Existing buildings to be demolished or renovated

2. Program displacement during renovation phases

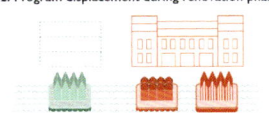

3. Program reinsertion in the finished buildings

4. Program upgrade through Barges utilization

DOMINIQUE HAUDEROWICZ
KRISTIAN LY SERENA
ARCHITECTS

STUDIO FOUNTAINHEAD
FREDRIKSBORGVEJ 64
2400 COPENHAGEN NV, DK
T. +45 20979923 / +45 60802087
INFO@STUDIOFOUNTAINHEAD.DK
WWW.STUDIOFOUNTAINHEAD.DK

RUNNER-UP - TRONDHEIM (NO)
More Trondheim!

TEAM POINT OF VIEW "More Trondheim!" sees the project site not as a place to establish its own constructed order, but as a place to embraces the true city, with all its complexities, contradictions and conflicts of space and interest, extending the existing urban fabric –unordered and unruly as might be– onto the harbour site.

Economy – The proposal recognizes the fact that urban planning today is conditioned by monetary interests of big developer companies. Rather than denying this truth the projects tries to see this as a latent potential. It embeds smaller fractions of "plots to be sold" throughout the project site – seeking to establish dense, spatial qualities at an urban scale. Creating coherent and co-dependent spatial relationships in disregard of economical ones.

Program – "More Trondheim" recognizes the self-grown variety of programs that populate the harbour site. As development goes on, the proposal mostly inserts everyday life program into the plan – kindergarten, supermarket, fitness-centre, housing for the elderly. The project seeks to challenge the spatial and architectonic possibilities of these mundane types. The consequence is a three-dimensional public sphere that lives and moves, disregarding the boundaries of volumes and institutions – the varied program of everyday life is woven into both new and existing buildings. "More Trondheim!" is just that –the qualities of the existing city brought together in 4 dimensions.

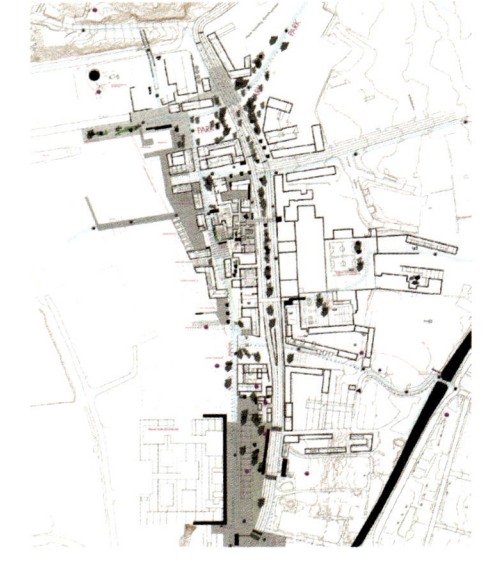

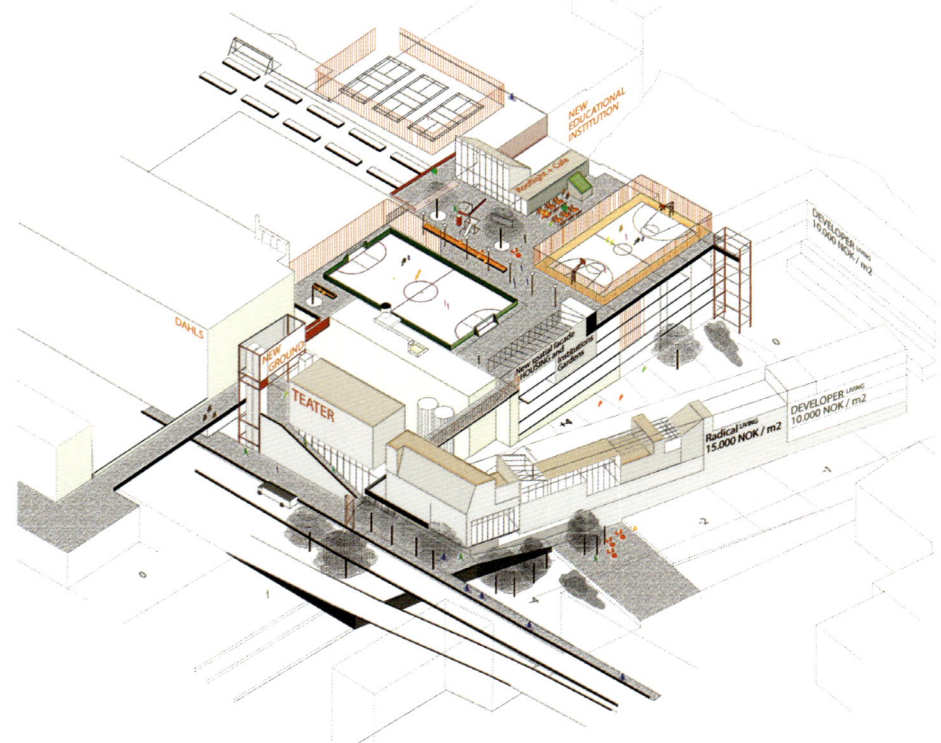

JURY POINT OF VIEW The project addresses fundamental discussions for spatial production in Norway and beyond by investigating the site in relation to topics such as the future of the welfare state and the role of institutions within it, the mechanisms of the real estate market, and demographic change. As a way to open the site up for a new, anti-speculative, development, the site is broken down into smaller units, allowing for the participation of other economic actors. Elsewhere, the reconsideration of specific functions is used to illustrate a rethinking of their current status and use.

JONATHAN LAZAR (IT)
GUILLAUME GUERRIER (FR)
FILIPPO MARIA DORIA (IT)
ANTONIO SANNA (IT)
ARCHITECTS

PROTOCOL COLLECTIVE
PROTOCOL.COLLECTIVE@GMAIL.COM

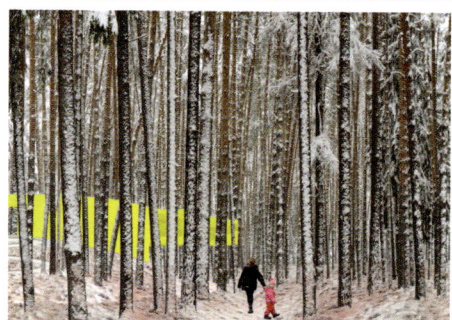

SPECIAL MENTION - TRONDHEIM (NO)
The Rim

TEAM POINT OF VIEW A limit is defined along the edges of the site to preserve a new urban forest and the existing activities. The architectural device is not a static frame: it is a porous public colonnade, dynamic infrastructure for both current urban life and future development.
This urban configuration for Strandveikaia adapts in a peculiar way to the progressive growth of Nyhavna. It is conceived as a centrality that remains a stable reference point: while the built volume on top of the colonnade progressively increases in time, the quantity of open space is kept constant and the quality is preserved.

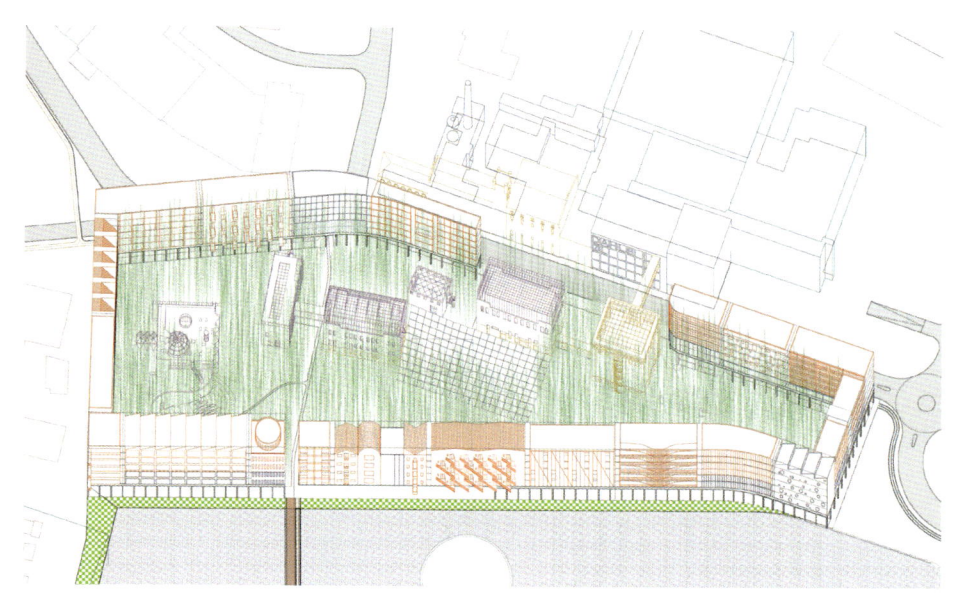

VERNON
FRANCE (FR)

CATEGORY: **URBAN – ENVIRONMENTAL – ARCHITECTURAL**
LOCATION: **VERNON**
POPULATION: **25,000 INHAB.**
STRATEGIC SITE: **1.770 HA**
PROJECT SITE: **220 HA**

SITE PROPOSED BY: **CITY OF VERNON**
OWNER(S) OF THE SITE: **VARIOUS**
COMMISION AFTER COMPETITION: **URBAN STUDY, MANAGEMENT OF ONE OR MORE ARCHITECTURAL PROJECTS**

Interview of the site's representative

PRESENTATION OF THE SITE WITH REGARDS TO STRATEGY

The municipality of Vernon lies along both banks of the Seine crossed by a bridge with heavy traffic. The River and its banks have very little impact on the life of inhabitants and visitors; it is strange how "the river runs through the city without stopping". The entry points to the city are being reorganized. The highways along the Seine and rail lines to the South-West produce continuous urban breaks. The recovery of the banks of the Seine and the transformation of the city centre neighbourhoods would have actual repercussions for lifestyle and activities proposed by the city. The station and the surrounding neighbourhood are to be rethought in an emblematic way. Reconstruction possibilities through original approaches adapted to the complex urban identity can renovate the too out-dated image of the centre.

HOW IS THE SITE CONNECTED TO THE SESSION TOPIC - THE ADAPTABLE CITY?

Today "traversed" for functional reasons – D6015, bridge, gardens of Giverny– the city is committed to a brave urban policy seeking, in a context of limited resources and means, a balance between housing, amenities, shops, leisure activities, in order to better attract a young and active population.
The location of Vernon on both banks of the Seine encourages a better sharing of identity, a more affirmed connection between neighbourhoods. Restoring through identity and uses an urban coherence to the city's motley grouping of neighbourhoods that public space barely manages to hold together, also means postulating on the future of open development proposals that include sociological developments and long-term innovation.

ADRIEN RÉRAT (FR)
LOUISE LE PENNDU (FR)
ARCHITECTS

27 BIS RUE CLAUDE LORRAIN
75016 PARIS, FR
T. +33 777073431

WINNER - VERNON (FR)
Insécable distance

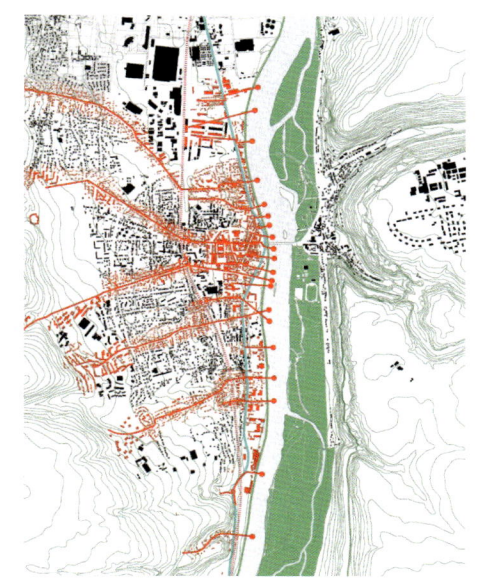

JURY POINT OF VIEW The quality of this project lies in way in which it proposes to reactivate leisure practices along the banks of the Seine. The team describes Vernon as a "ford-town" because of its river crossing, a "station-town" because of the railway lines and as a "dock-town" because of the riverbanks; in other words a town moulded by its nature as a passage. Their strategy is to reconnect the town to its riverfront and provide stopping points there. They propose extending all the transversal axes towards the Seine by means of a collection of "viewpoint-jetties", accommodating a wide variety of programmes.

TEAM POINT OF VIEW Ford-town, bridge-town, station-town, Vernon is a passing town crossed by numerous physical cuts: river, bank and rails. Consequently, it is about promoting the ability for Vernon to generate relations and exchanges. The project privileges crossings, encounters and reinforces local travels in relation to distant ones. As a ford town, Vernon has to become a river-town. Planning intends to develop and extend the existing routes to the Seine River to connect all the district to the banks. Enhancing this network of physical movements is crucial for the inhabitants to take over the fluvial space again and to become riverside residents. To forge a collective identity alongside the river, the physical bond is doubled with a programmatic one. Each continuum of the public space is extended with a pier-belvedere on the fluvial land. These structures anchor urban functions designed as extended homes. The temporality created is therefore ephemeral, collective and participative. As a framework to the town, the linear promenade offers various relations with water through succeeding events acting as landmarks. The urban transformation is thus structural, functional and social. Platforms like theatre trestles accordingly back up plays in which residents are the actors. Thanks to them, structures embedded in the soil of the Seine banks are urban bridges to bind the town and the Seine, an invitation to daydream for Vernon inhabitants and visitors.

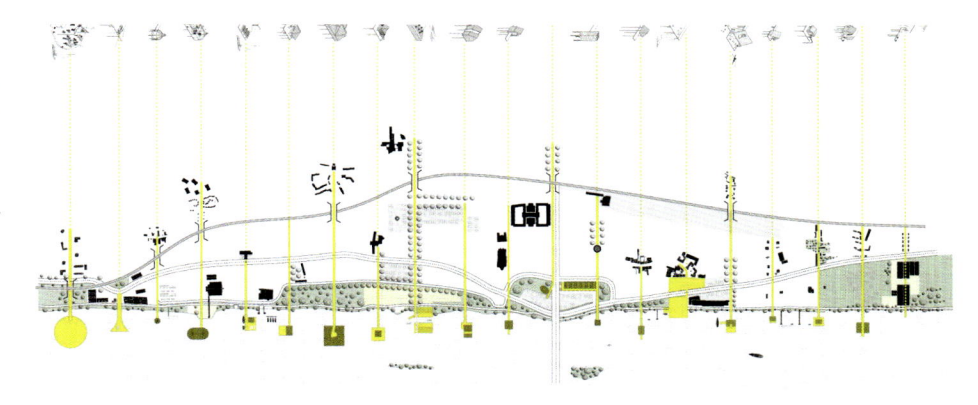

MAYA NEMETA (FR)
AMINE IBNOLMOBARAK (FR)
EMILIE MEAUD (FR)
ARCHITECTS
CHARLOTTE MEAUD (FR)
INNOVATION & ENTREPRENEURSHIP CONSULTANT

MAYANEMETA@GMAIL.COM

RUNNER-UP - VERNON (FR)
Navigable Collections

TEAM POINT OF VIEW Vernon is a city of paradoxes: a city with hybrid heritage where no one lingers; a city nested in a natural setting with public spaces turning their backs on it; a rather compact yet disjointed city; a city gaining inhabitants but lacking employment; a populated yet deserted city; a highly connected city, but where no one stops. Seemingly a peaceful town – in reality a city of passage. Vernon appears as a collection that seems to have been abandoned by its curator.
Beyond these paradoxes, a project for Vernon would be to reinstall the curator, or should we say "curators": policy makers, planners, residents, entrepreneurs, those whose experiences and visions feed on living Vernon.
In other words, reading Vernon with its inhabitants, reading the collection, connecting places, people and memory fragments, linking the familiar and the distant, the foreign and the local, the layers of nature, the common places, predicting the future, telling gestures and accents of this unique city line, is already making project, is already making culture.

JURY POINT OF VIEW The quality of this project lies in the richness of its spatial proposals. The authors describe Vernon as a town of paradoxes, a "loose collection that seems to have been deserted by its curator". Their strategy is to identify preliminaries that will trigger changes to the town. These preliminaries are the transformation of the station, the redesign of the transversal axes and the conversion of the foundry site. The team demonstrates a precise knowledge of the territory that they consider as a whole from the big high-rise estates to the opposite bank of the Seine.

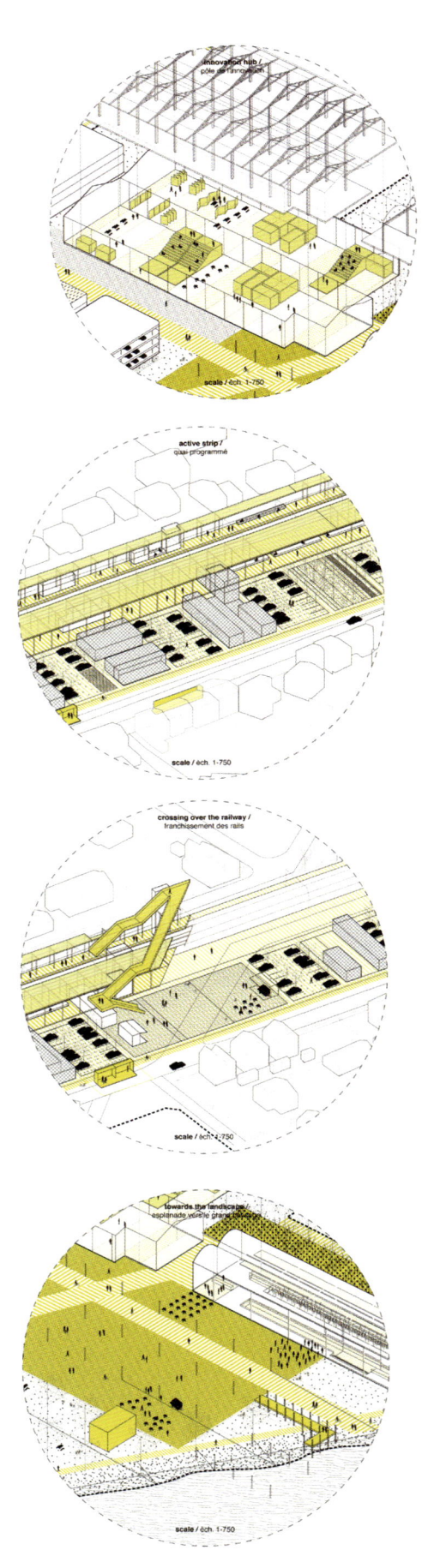

AURORE CROUZET (FR)
FABRICE DOMENECH (FR)
AURÉLIEN FERRY (FR)
JEAN-RENÉ MANON (FR)
ARCHITECTS-URBANISTS

1 RUE DE LA DHUIS
75020 PARIS, FR
T. +33 677642747
CONTACT@CROUZET-MANON.COM

SPECIAL MENTION - VERNON (FR)

Vernon sur Seine

TEAM POINT OF VIEW Opening the city on the Seine River begins with the activation of the city entrances, which continue by the multiple pole inter-connexions and to the larger territory of the town and its surroundings, in order to implement central areas that would allow growing density, networking and built in a mixed marriage, to serve the pertinent and adaptable city project for the habitants of Vernon of today and tomorrow. Once operating the main strategic levers, the North/South mesh will naturally thrive to join again the connections and the places, open the river town toward the Seine and make living in Vernon enjoyable again.

WIEN
ÖSTERREICH (AT)

CATEGORY: **URBAN – ARCHITECTURAL**
LOCATION: **WIEN KAGRAN, DONAUSTADT**
POPULATION: **1,765,000 INHAB.**
STRATEGIC SITE: **24 HA**
PROJECT SITE: **7 HA**
SITE PROPOSED BY: **CITY OF VIENNA**

OWNER(S) OF THE SITE: **CITY OF VIENNA AND OTHERS**
COMMISION AFTER COMPETITION:
URBAN PROJECT MANAGEMENT ROLE, DESIGN OF PUBLIC AND LANDSCAPE AREAS

Interview of the site's representative

Andrea Eggenbauer, MD21, Department of Urban District Planning and Land Use, City of Vienna
Georgine Zabrana, MD BD Gruppe Planung, Department of Urban Planning, City of Vienna

PRESENTATION OF THE SITE WITH REGARDS TO STRATEGY

Wien Kagran is experiencing a far-reaching process of transformation. Dynamic development in the centre of Kagran to the north of the Donau is to be used to redefine the public space between the Kagran underground station and Schrödingerplatz, and to activate the existing potential of current structures along this axis. The restructuring of Schrödingerplatz offers the chance to connect the surrounding heterogeneous areas by means of a spatial reorientation and additional forms of use as well as to make an important contribution to determining Kagran's identity.

HOW IS THE SITE CONNECTED TO THE SESSION TOPIC - THE ADAPTABLE CITY?

When public space is transformed, its edges and corners are affected, which in turn impact the public space as a whole. It is important to make use of this relationship to create a positive dynamic that enables high-quality public space to be formed, where buildings structures and usages interact with the space. The area in Kagran has the potential to create a lively centre – Europan is looking for ways to adapt to the demands on a city of the future.

DID YOU DEFINE A SPECIFIC PROCESS FOR THE URBAN DEVELOPMENT OF THE SITE AFTER EUROPAN COMPETITION?

Based on the radical approach of the winning project, the focus is on identifying the most important aims of the transformation of Kagran's centre and the desired qualities of the public spaces that are to be reconfigured. It is important to work closely with stakeholders in the area. Winners can both contribute their expertise to the process and provide an outsider's perspective.

BLAŽ BABNIK ROMANIUK (SI)
ANNA KRAVCOVA (SI)
ARCHITECTS
DUŠAN STUPAR (SI)
LANDSCAPE ARCHITECT

DRAGAN POPOVIĆ (RS)
3D DESIGNER

OBRAT D.O.O. + KRAJINARIS
JANEŽIČEVA 3
1000 LJUBLJANA, SI
T +386 41384764
INFO@OBRATDOO.SI
WWW.OBRATDOO.SI
WWW.KRAJINARIS.SI

WINNER - WIEN (AT)
Publicquartier

TEAM POINT OF VIEW Kagran will become one of main centres of polycentric Vienna. A shopping centre currently dominates Kagran centre, acting as a substitute for public space and its variety of uses. Still, it also presents the properties of a city centre – dense node of transportation nodes, spatial position in the centre of Donaustadt, surrounded by wide variety of uses. A long-term programmatic and physical restructuration is necessary for Kagran centre to become a city centre, but trajectories can be set today. The proposed changes will engender:
• the development of diverse, recognisable and accessible public space by changing built environment and offsetting current programmatic hierarchies; by concentrating Donauzentrum at Schrödinger Platz and establishing open public space between Wagramer Strasse and U-Bahn station this is achievable.
• a variety of uses and its democratic participatory administration in main public space, where new public space would be a rigorous testing ground for participatory politics;
• goals set by Smart City strategies securing long term liveability and possibilities for further development.
In open process of step-by-step restructuring, Kagran could become a city centre determined by a balance of public and private interests.

JURY POINT OF VIEW The project proposes a courageous and innovative strategy to shift the Donauzentrum shopping mall from the underground station to the direction of Schrödinger Platz in order to establish an open "publicquarter" for Kagran around the underground station. This radical proposal provides an essential tool for the city of Vienna to start a process-oriented dialogue with a grand perspective on the future public space of Kagran-centre. It represents an innovative contribution to the urban discourse in European cities, reflecting the future meaning of public spaces and the public space-relation of indoor/outdoor spaces.

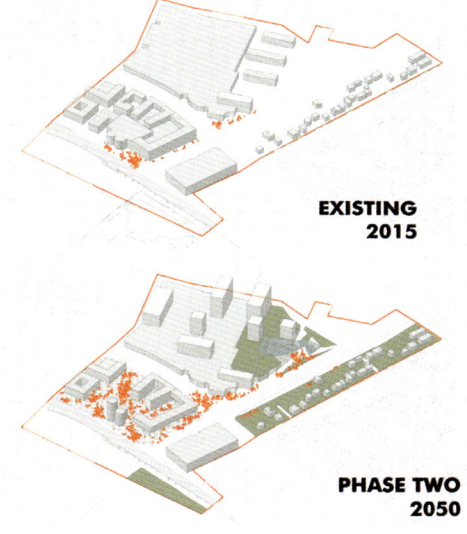

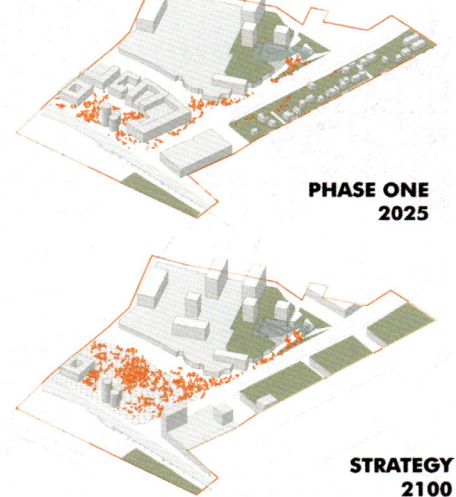

HOW TO CREATE POSITIVE DYNAMICS FROM A DIFFICULT SITUATION?

**Point of view: Regenerative Metamorphoses
of Inhabited Milieux and Project Culture**   p. 190
by Chris Younès and Julio de la Fuente

Azenha do Mar (PT)	p. 198
Barcelona (ES)	p. 202
Bruck/Mur (AT)	p. 208
Charleroi (BE)	p. 210
Gera (DE)	p. 214
Goussainville (FR)	p. 218
Jyväskylä (FI)	p. 222
La Corrèze (FR)	p. 228
Linz (AT)	p. 232
Marl (DE)	p. 236
Ørsta (NO)	p. 240
Selb (DE)	p. 244
Streefkerk (NL)	p. 248
Warszawa (PL)	p. 252

Many sites are faced with difficult urban situations. The origins of these difficulties are to be found in problems caused by urban, economic and environmental factors, as well as differing values and a lack of cultural understanding. Despite these difficulties, the sites nevertheless constitute a favourable ground for the creation of new dynamics which rely on scenarios of sharing and the adaptation of traditional architectural and urban tools.

CHRIS YOUNÈS, anthro-philosopher of inhabited milieux, teacher at Paris's Ecole Speciale d'Architecture (ESA) and member of Europan's Scientific Council. Founder and member of the Gerphau research laboratory.
www.gerphau.wordpress.com/presentation-du-laboratoire/

JULIO DE LA FUENTE, architect, urbanist, co-founder of Gutiérrez-delaFuente Arquitectos, Madrid (ES) and guest teacher in Spain and Germany. He is a member of Europan's Technical Committee.
www.gutierrez-delafuente.com

Point of view
Regenerative Metamorphoses of Inhabited Milieux and Project Culture

In situations of serious difficulty and disorientation, the need for metamorphoses of inhabited milieux is all the greater in problem situations and emphasises how the project can make use of the vitalising resources of the milieu. What it means is giving up predatory practices and devising mixed, immersive systems with the capacity to regenerate inhabited milieux, and which acknowledge the interactions between living organisms and their environments, an approach that runs counter to a toxic culture based on separation and the unlimited exploitation of resources.

In this move towards regenerative metamorphoses, a different way of managing resources is crucial: "A resource is as much for living as for thinking, it no longer separates them. So from this re-sourcing of the resource we could begin again, take our cues from it, in order to live and think at the same time."[1] Which relates to projects that seek to exploit or generate changes based in the interweaving of scales, while at the same time being anchored in elemental, agricultural and landscape resources.

Supporting emerging practices

By contrast with centralised and normative systems, at local level emergent alternative ways of inhabiting are developing, halfway between sharing and emancipation. These strategies, devised outside "planning" mechanisms, employ practical methods that are growing in scale: shared gardens, eco-production, permaculture, exchanges of knowledge and know-how, recycling, artistic practices... How can architecture participate in these lively practices?

For example, urban agroecology is emerging as a basis for reinventing human settlements from a necessarily eco-rhythmic and eco-political perspective.[2] This entails being on the lookout for approaches that redefine the places and interconnections not only of the urban and rural between them, but also of their common immersion in living nature: for living and elemental urban entities need to be envisioned with appropriate food-producing activities (market gardening, agricultural parks, woodland, meadows, vines, urban farms, green roofs, shared gardens...), directed at permaculture, short supply chains, protection of the water and soil systems, recycling, multiple energy sources, access to and preservation of cultivatable land...

While today, water, air and land are not intact because of human industries, the elemental remains a living force which speaks of the secret of the Earth and of life. In their material, imaginative and symbolic renaissance, the four elements seem even to regenerate matter and the poetics of inhabited milieux. Bachelard explored the oneiric power of earth, water, air and fire, which are primordial and renewable materials that have the property of taking us beyond ourselves. They have the imaginative force to "be one" with the world and to be "part of its living totality" through a "holistic and dynamic vision that is re-emerging in the epistemology of contemporary ecology".[3] The power of their material imagination – material because it is water or fire or air that governs images – which is strictly speaking unreal, surreal or hyperreal, has an equally substantive reality but one which differs in nature from that procured by scientific knowledge, one that combines with the evolution of ways of living. As a result, numerous possibilities are opened up:

- transformations of divided heritages through eco-systemic interconnecting between cultures, but also between the human and the nonhuman;
- the interweaving of spatiotemporal scales, between micro-places, city, metropolis, bioregion and globalisation;
- adaptations to the digital era, capable of linking vernacular cultures and innovations;
- implementations of socio-spatial processes able to encourage communality.

The Europan projects submitted under this theme propose other connections, global and local, urban and rural, other territorialised sociopolitical forms of organisation, moulded by dynamics of interweaving: the key is to be able to adjust to conditions, to adapt to local situations with their specificities, rather than making a *tabula rasa* or sticking to pre-established recipes. The combination of creating distinctive places, living milieux and political projects proved decisive in the reconfigurations that link scales, community equity and diversity, project and consultation. The challenge, therefore, is not to define the style of an object to be built from a fixed programme, but to respond to contemporary changes on the basis of priorities and lines of force in which accommodation and

1 - JYVÄSKYLÄ (FI)

2 - LINZ (AT)

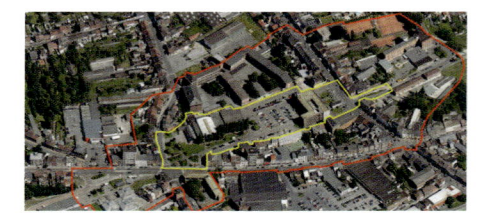

3 - CHARLEROI (BE)

4 - BARCELONA (ES)

consultation, territory and architecture, are interwoven. Today, the demand for frugality and for collaboration is making ground, both as a necessity and a value. Within this dynamic, the minor proves major and encounter is empowerment.

On the one hand the substance of this article addresses three different milieux, each with common goals: districts-intensity, islands-connectivity and shrinkage-resilience. On the other hand, three basic emblematic attitudes are shared by the winning teams: frameworks, inputs and pre-existences.

Intensifying districts

The first group of sites in the 13th edition of Europan share the common issue of how to intensify an urban district and thereby create positive impacts on the surroundings.

The district of Kortepohja in Jyväskylä (FI), featured as a large community of students living in a modernistic 1960s urban planning environment, aspires to be densified and revitalized through residential-led mixed-use development (fig.1). The same challenge appears in Linz (AT), in a large socially mixed neighbourhood, developed over the last 50 years as a "housing zoo" (fig.2). At Gilly, Charleroi (BE), the municipality is keen to create a multi-functional public square as a new attractor at the heart of the quarter (fig.3). The Barcelona (ES) site is located in La Marina district (fig.4), which is undergoing conversion from a former industrial site to a new mixed-use area with the associated challenge of attracting compatible economic and residential activity.

Reframing infrastructures as a procedure over time

The first attitude noted by several teams is the introduction of a new infrastructural framework to trigger social mixes and diversity. A cultural infrastructure is conceived as a procedure, as a platform for negotiation and urban discussion, a space for programmed uncertainty.

T. Sieverts[4] reflected on the socio-economic conditions required for a fine-grained mixed-use milieu, highlighting the "dimension of time" and "for the purpose of longevity and to save resources, the building must in future be capable of adjustments to changing demands". But how can a flexible infrastructural framework be developed at political level? Or at a level that will permit it to become the infrastructure of the infrastructures?

The winning project in Barcelona, *In Motion* (fig.5), as the name suggests, is a reaction against a static city model. The team proposes an urban infrastructure as an unspecialized collection of stacked slabs "with high resistance to municipal management", and flexible enough to allow for a wide range of uncertain uses throughout time.

In Charleroi, the runner-up *The Heterotopia Pool* (fig.6), also proposes a new infrastructure. This time the "social pool" spatially organizes the core of the district, attracting new users and consolidating the existing activities.

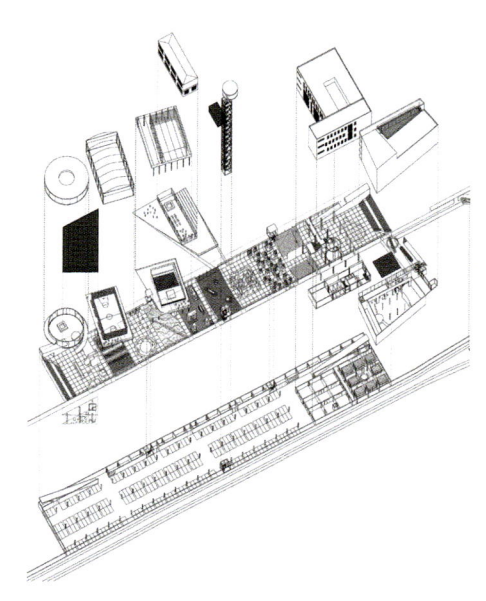

5 - BARCELONA (ES), WINNER - IN MOTION > SEE MORE P.203

6 - CHARLEROI (BE), RUNNER-UP - THE HETEROTOPIA POOL > SEE MORE P.212

8 - BARCELONA (ES), RUNNER-UP - SUSTAINABLE INTERFACE > SEE MORE P.205

Rethinking typologies as a mediator between public and private

Inventing new typologies to regenerate an urban fragment and to activate a cultural and social realm is another common approach. New typologies are able to articulate the potential of the spaces that are intermediate between public and private, sharing a promise to build a community. But which new types are needed to manage the interactions between the public, collective and private space?

In the winning entry in Jyväskylä, *The Nolli Gardens* (fig.7), the friction between street space and private space is explored and confronted with a modernistic urban plan in order to define what a community is. The proposed block is based on a sequence of co-inhabited and shared spaces at different levels and scales. A collective courtyard and a series of common uses – the "Nolli Gardens" – enhance the social interaction.

In Barcelona, the runner-up *Sustainable Interface* (fig.8), plans a typology called "The Workshop House for City Starters", a sustainable interface between the Green, the Productive and the Living City, that provides affordable housing and working spaces for a new socio-economic reality. A new relationship with the street is also established through productive and robust plinths.

The winning project *In-between* (fig.9), at Streefkerk (NL), also deals with the transition between the private, the neighbourhood and the territorial scales, and in so doing, develops a prototype. The brief calls for the reconstruction of a plot of land between the river Lek and its hinterland, a result of the installation of dike reinforcement designed to provide protection against rising water levels. The project takes advantage of the new artificial topography, and splits the intimate and public spaces into two levels, with a new shared space located in between them at dike-street level, which becomes "an open field of possibilities both for the inhabitants and for the development of the city".

7 - JYVÄSKYLÄ (FI), WINNER - THE NOLLI GARDENS > SEE MORE P.223

Reinterpreting heritage as the substance for the future

The third trend anchors the works to the site's existing values in order to promote a vibrant neighbourhood. The pre-existing cultural landscape and the reinterpretation of heritage are the two main forces used to trigger a process of densification. But which kind of new and existing values should guide the production of the city? And how can these values be transformed into the heritage of the next decades?

9 - STREEFKERK (NL), WINNER - IN-BETWEEN > SEE MORE P.249

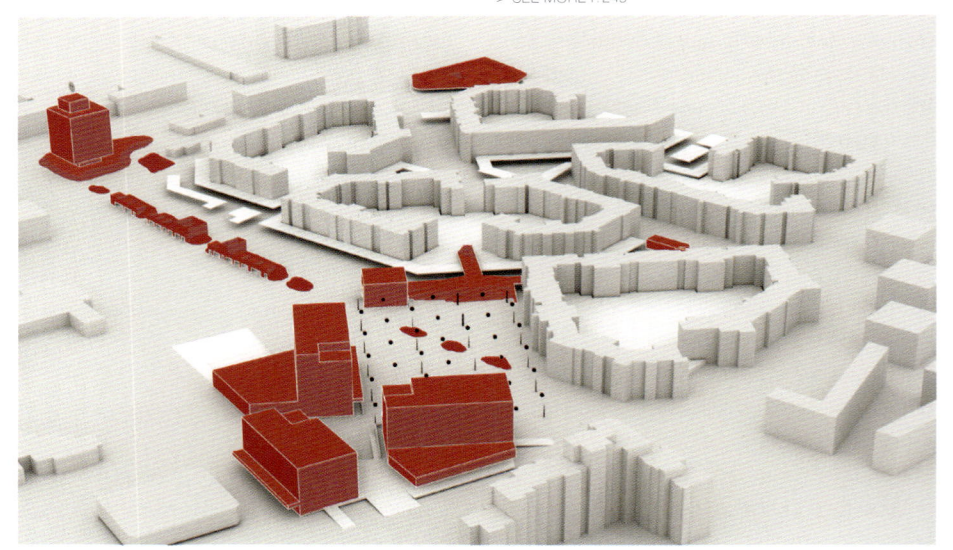

10 - LINZ (AT), WINNER - ALL TOMORROW'S PARTIES > SEE MORE P.233

All Tomorrow's Parties (fig.10), the winning entry in Linz, works at two different levels, on a series of projective interventions at the borders of the site, and on a participatory strategy around a series of workshops in the inner parts of the district. Both strategies are based in the local understanding of the neighbourhood as a "network of manifold collectives", which are converted in the urban substance for a future development.

Reconnecting islands

The second set of sites is characterized by the notion of insularity and the matter of how to reconnect urban islands at different scales, from global to local, from the physical to the cultural dimension.

In Ørsta (NO), the goal is to give the inner city a new central position in the region and better connections with its surroundings. At Bruck an der Mur (AT), a piece of land bordering the railway tracks and expressway, is similarly waiting to play a central role in the region and to be reconnected with the city, by way of the arrival of a new railway stop. In the case of Warsaw (PL), Cubryna Garden is isolated between the lanes of a new expressway, and aspires to open up to the riverside boulevards, buoyed by the design of the exhibition of stone treasures rescued from the Vistula. At Marl (DE), the large mining area of Auguste Victoria Colliery Shaft 3/7 is scheduled for closure in 2015, and the project brief therefore calls for new visions for a 21st century industrial site. The Azenha do Mar (PT) site is a recent fishing settlement located between the agricultural landscape and the ocean, looking for an economic model that combines responsible tourism and a unique local experience.

Shaping stimulants to welcome processes of interaction

Within this subtopic some teams work with the aim of shaping new spatial frameworks at an urban scale to host new programmes, to integrate existing uses and to reinforce connectivity.

11 - ØRSTA (NO), WINNER - CONNECTING ØRSTA > SEE MORE P.241

In their *Collage City*, C. Rowe and F. Koetter[5] listed a set of "stimulants, a-temporal and necessarily transcultural, as possible *objets trouvés* in the urbanistic collage", such as memorable streets, stabilizers, or splendid public terraces. But what kind of stimulants can help us to reconnect the different urban fragments, and how can these elements attract new economic and social processes of interaction?

At Ørsta, the winning project *Connecting Ørsta* (fig.11), plans to establish clear links and identities through three urban connectors, "the Urban, the Park and the Educational connection", that are anchored in a chain of new centralities and spaces of exchange, "the Squares". Public space is understood as the backbone of future development.

In a special mention in Marl, *The Spine* (fig.12), proposes the eponymous entity as a flexible spatial feature which allows the first steps of implementation to be taken without large-scale investment, addressing the uncertainty of how the area will evolve in the future.

12 - MARL (DE), SPECIAL MENTION - THE SPINE > SEE MORE P.239

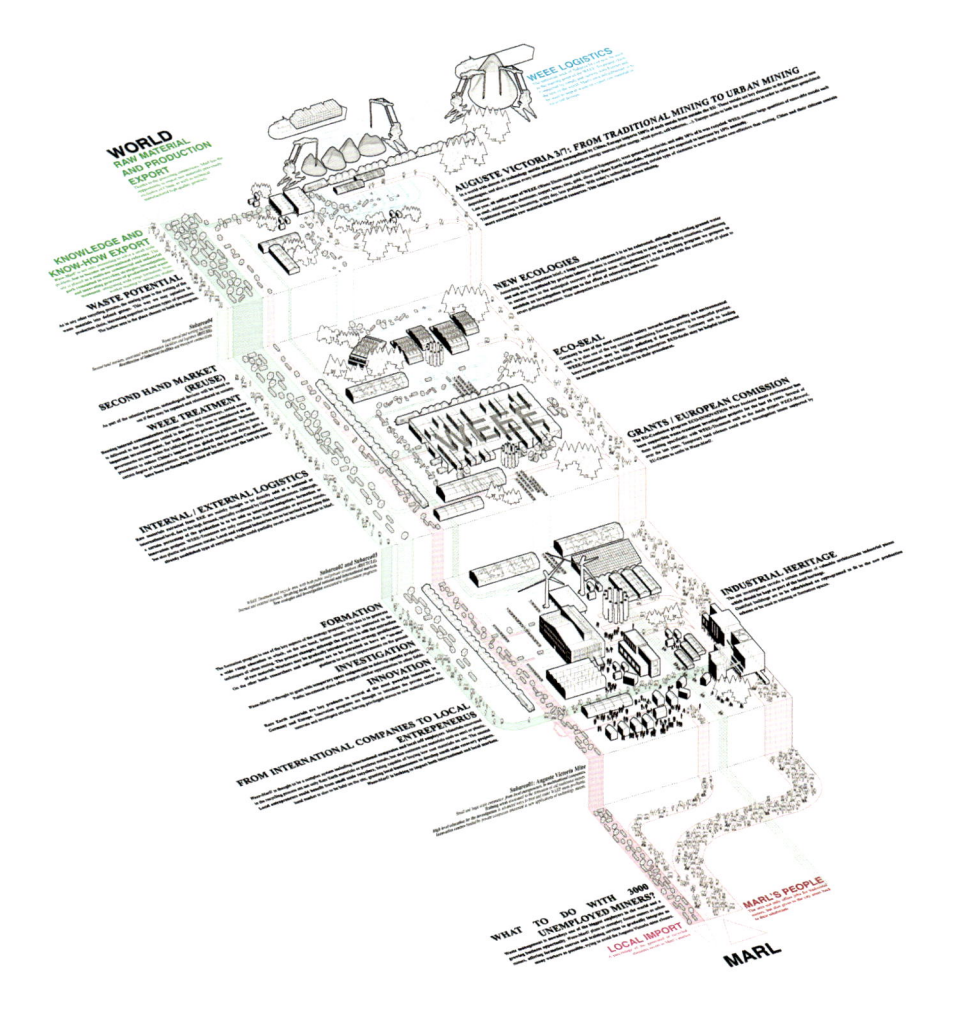

Devising programmes to reconnect the sites with their contexts

Introducing innovative programmes to reconnect the sites with their contexts is the most frequent response. The new links can be social, economic, ecological or cultural in nature, but all of them stand, as the French sociologist Alain Touraine suggested, between the extremes of "economic globalization" and "cultural orientation to a place". But what kind of new programmes can mediate between the local and the global, subverting the idea of proximity?

The winning project in Marl, *WEEE Marl!* (fig.13), is an economic and social strategy triggered by a new programme, a WEEE – Waste Electrical and Electronic Equipment recycling plant – that seeks to cushion the shock of the 3000 jobs lost with the closure of the mine. The transition "from traditional mining to urban mining" is anchored in geopolitical reasons and facts, such as recycling being the world's second largest employer after agriculture, or that a ton of soil from a gold-mine contains less gold than a ton of smartphones. The former mining site

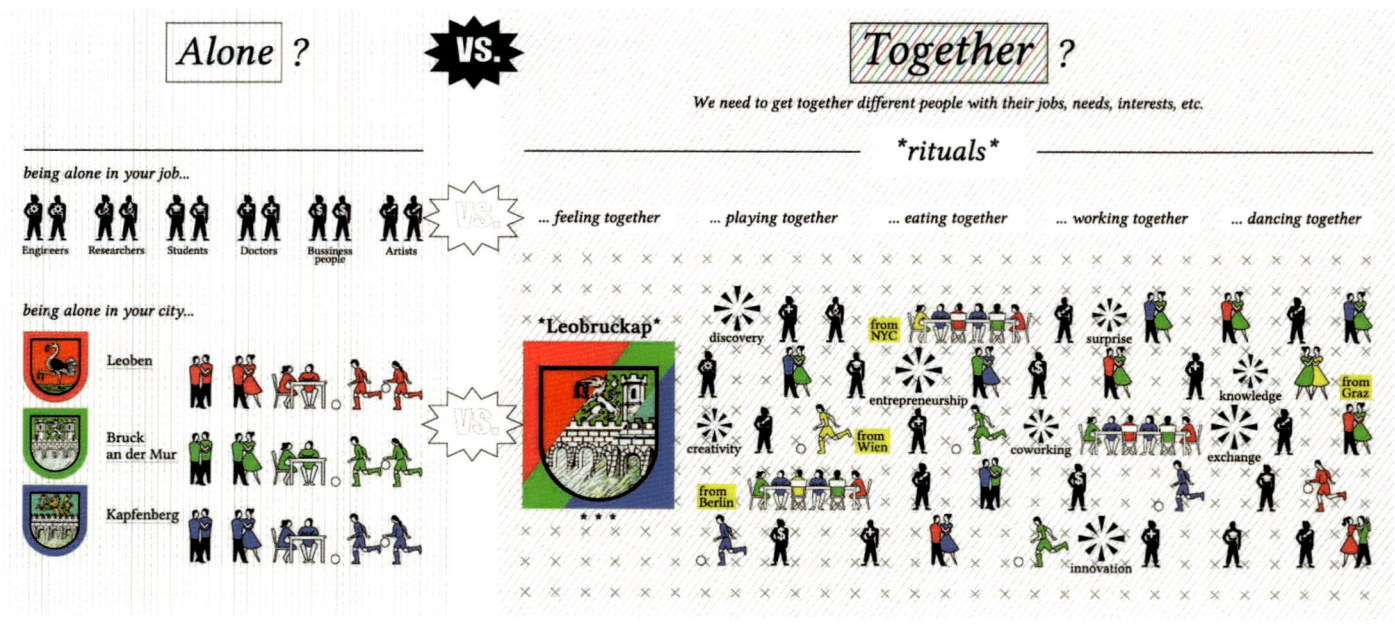

13 - MARL (DE), WINNER - WEEE MARL! > SEE MORE P.237

14 - BRUCK/MUR (AT), RUNNER-UP - TOGETHER > SEE MORE P.209

15 - WARSZAWA (PL), RUNNER-UP - APPORT PLUS SUPPORT > SEE MORE P.254

becomes a platform for research and knowledge exchange that seeks to strengthen the local environment as a complement to internationalization.

Decoding the environment to open up an enclave

Some teams put their faith in the values of the natural and social environment as levers to open up an enclave in the city-archipelago. O.M. Ungers and R. Koolhaas suggested that only through a "process of identification" will the potential of urban islands be preserved, and "for the city dweller, the environment will be legible again, and thereby endowed with human quality".[6] But how can the sites achieve a high degree of permeability through legibility?

While the runner-up in Bruck an der Mur, *Together* (fig.14), anchors the project in the communities from a regional perspective, channelling the citizens' voices into a strategy called "politics of spatial cooperation", another runner-up, *Apport plus Support* (fig.15), this time in Warsaw, re-integrates the site into the city by treating Cubryna Garden as part of a larger territorial-scale natural system.

The winning project in Azenha do Mar, *Limenochora* (fig.16), suggests specific interventions inspired by the logics of local economic models and the archetypal image of the traditional Portuguese house, in order to build a shared community identity.

Resisting shrinkage

The third collection consists of sites that are undergoing processes of urban shrinkage. The last decade has seen the launch of slogans in response to shrinkage, such as "the future is less", or "progress without growth", supporting the idea that "shrinkage will be in future considered as normal a process of development as growth".[7] The challenge now is to define which new alliances between city and society are needed to lead that process of normalisation.

The city of Selb (DE) is experiencing a process of continual shrinkage following the post-industrial collapse of the porcelain sector. The goal is to activate the inner city, with special attention to vacant properties. A similar situation, although originating in the reunification of Germany, is found in Gera (DE). An extensive city centre wasteland, a result of demolition, is waiting for an attractive mixed-use development. At La Corrèze (FR) a rural context outside metropolitan influence is proposed for the quest for new visions of rurality, to be tested in three different communities: Ussel, Argentat, and Turenne. In the site of Goussainville (FR), the historical village, affected by CDG airport, metropolitan and agricultural influences, is trying to find new forms of occupancy compatible with the constraints.

Infiltrating new rules to steer a regeneration process

A first shared position on the topic is the establishment of a new political framework, composed of new rules, to steer a process of regeneration over time. New rules become a platform for critical participation in order to allow new forms of societal organization. If the urban space can no longer be planned as before, what kind of societal rulebooks are needed?

16 - AZENHA DO MAR (PT), WINNER - LIMENOCHORA > SEE MORE P.199

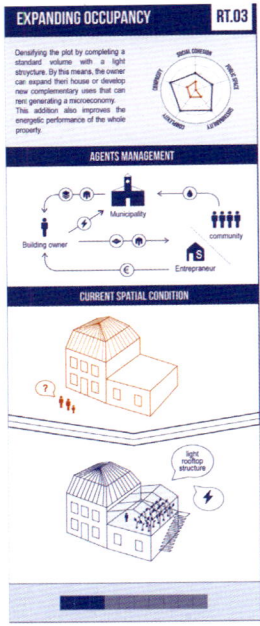

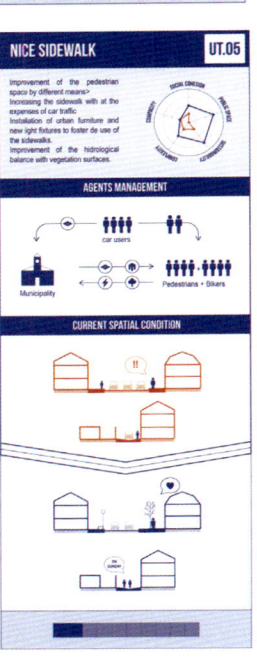

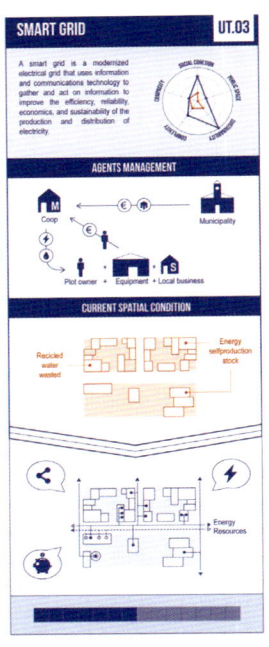

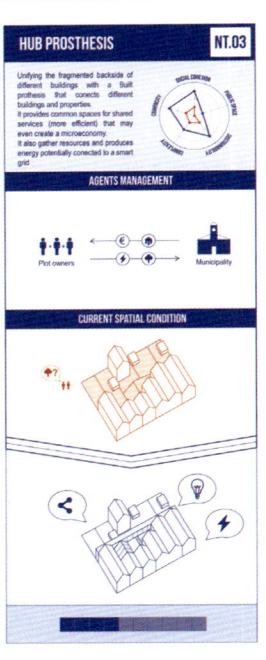

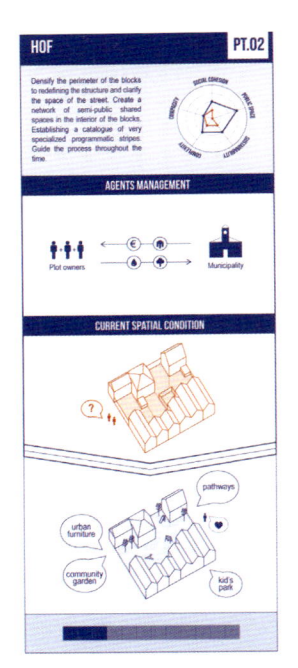

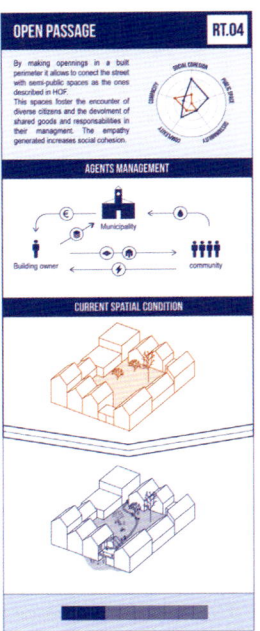

These new frameworks also update the role of the architect to that of a social agent between the three economic forces: state, private, civic. In the light of the disinvestment agenda, how can the involvement of private owners in the fabrication of the city be managed?
Urban Toolkit (fig.17), the winning project in Selb, is an open and never ending process based on a toolkit and a series of goals, "urban indicators", to deal with uncertainty and to offer an alternative to rigid plans. As a first step, the authors suggest the creation of an Office for Urban Regeneration to mediate between all the players. The system promotes small interventions that take advantage of previously hidden opportunities, including a wide range of hybrid funding modalities, from top-down to bottom-up, which blur the boundaries between the public and private.

Devising new landscapes to attract new inputs

The execution of preparatory work or interim projects, to keep a site alive while waiting for the arrival of investment, is a different approach. The question is, how can the first signs of transformation be triggered as one of the crucial moments of identification?
Vacancy is one of the features of shrinkage, "post-industrial landscapes become part of the city in the form of wasteland. Transitional situations between built-up and vacant land are productive zones, … experimental fields for a new type of urban landscape. A preference for life on the urban periphery can be realized in inner-city locations".[8] But which kind of new urban landscapes can attract new residents?
The special mention in Gera, *Das ist Gera* (fig.18), plans to colonise the inner city wasteland with a "Stadtgarten" in order to resolve the negative perceptions of a no man's land and to redefine the space of the street. In a second step, the garden will be programmed by pioneering entrepreneurs and public facilities. Once developed, the garden will be ready to welcome new investors and dwellers.

Revisiting the everyday life to build a community

The most common attitude in response to shrinkage is the development of pre-existing potential to create a different vision and positive prospects. If production of the city and the cultural landscape are organized around the inhabitants' own dynamics, instead of ambitious master plans or financial speculation, which inclusive narratives can provide the best operation fields?
"I will cut a bit of basil for dinner in the shared kitchen garden, and then I will have a look at the most recent table that Richard is making in his carpenter's workshop." This is a quote from one of the winning projects in La Corrèze, *Sharing Islands* (fig.19), which tries to improve the quality of "community life" through the infiltration of common programmes for everyday life.
The runner-up in Goussainville, *Des racines et des ailes* (fig.20), is likewise focused on local potential – the forest – understood as a unifying resource with a social, ecological and economic role. "As an apprentice carpenter, I was looking to settle down in the region. The consolidation of the forestry guilds in old Goussainville offers a solid network and excellent visibility to establish my own business," Mr Delorme states.

17 - SELB (DE), WINNER - URBAN TOOLKIT
> SEE MORE P.245

18 - GERA (DE), SPECIAL MENTION - DAS IST GERA
> SEE MORE P.217

Accommodating latent, local and trans-local resources

Other positive forms of health, solidarity and frugality can drive fertile projects for territorial transformation. Each will be a different way of stressing the importance of the micro but also of processes capable of contributing to the conception of broader intermediate scales as well as to the renewal of the conditions of possibility for living together. An ethics of care, of solicitude, of frugality and of reconnection, pathways that seek to reinvent other ways of making the city, making architecture, making the world. The challenges are simultaneously political, scientific, aesthetic and ethical, in the quest to establish the renewed conditions needed to create possibilities for eco-rhythms between human beings and living environments.

Each will define its possibility conditions in terms of diversities of practices and knowledge, of heritages and innovations, founded in a reversal of imaginative visions and value systems.

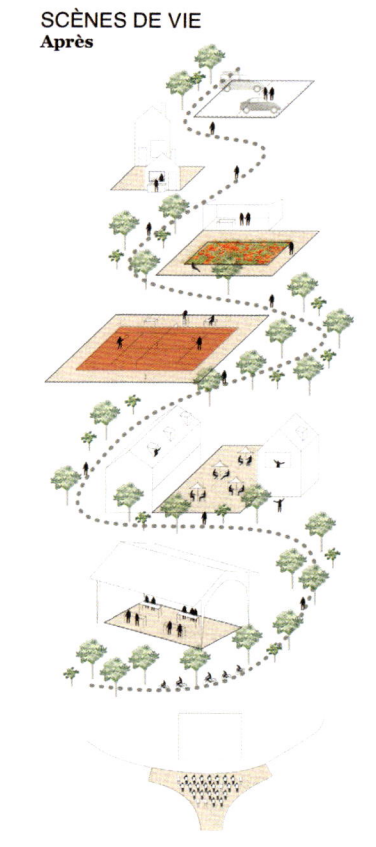

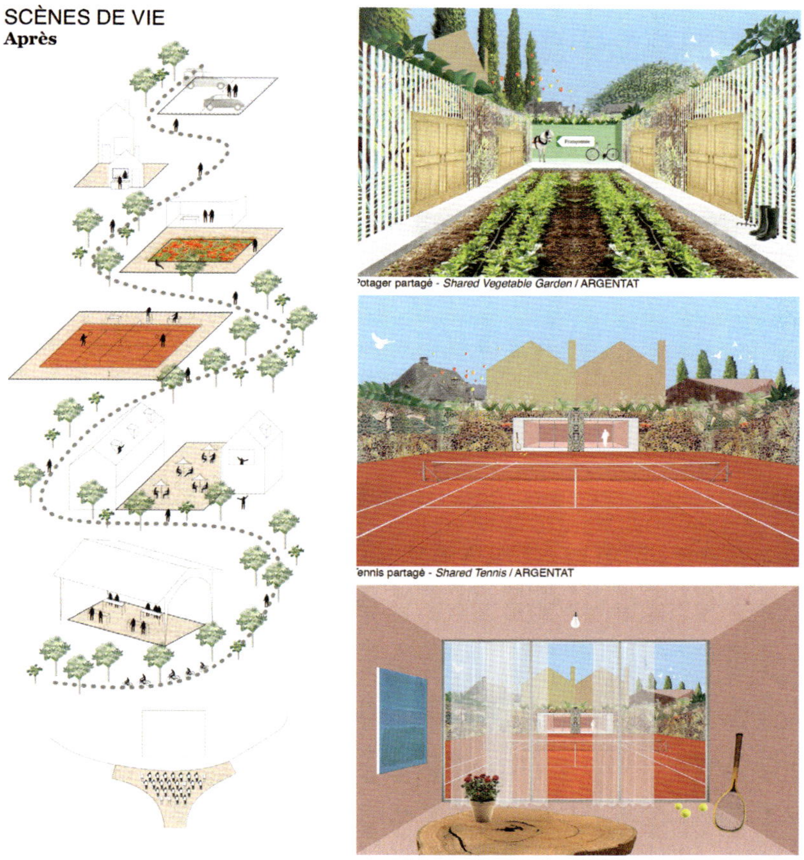

19 - LA CORRÈZE (FR), WINNER - SHARING ISLANDS > SEE MORE P.230

[1] FRANÇOIS JULLIEN, *DE L'ÊTRE AU VIVRE*, GALLIMARD, 2015
[2] ROBERTO D'ARIENZO, CHRIS YOUNÈS (DIR.), *RECYCLER L'URBAIN*, MÈTISPRESSES, 2014
[3] JEAN-JACQUES WUNENBURGER, "GASTON BACHELARD ET LA MÉDIANCE DES MATIÈRES ARCHE-COSMIQUES", IN *PHILOSOPHIE, VILLE ET ARCHITECTURE. LA RENAISSANCE DES QUATRE ÉLÉMENTS* (DIR. C. YOUNÈS ET TH. PAQUOT), LA DÉCOUVERTE, 2002, PP. 27-41
[4] THOMAS SIEVERTS, *CITIES WITHOUT CITIES, AN INTERPRETATION OF THE ZWISCHENSTADT*, ROUTLEDGE, NY, 2003. (FIRST PUBLISHED 1997 BY VIEWEG)
[5] COLIN ROWE AND FRED KOETTER, COLLAGE CITY, THE MIT PRESS, CAMBRIDGE MA, 1978
[6] OSWALD MATHIAS UNGERS AND REM KOOLHAAS, THE CITY IN THE CITY – BERLIN: A GREEN ARCHIPELAGO, LARS MÜLLER PUBLISHERS, ZÜRICH, 2013. (FIRST PUBLISHED, DIE STADT IN DER STADT – BERLIN: EIN GRÜNES ARCHIPEL, 1977)
[7] PHILIPP OSWALT, HYPOTHESES ON URBAN SHRINKING IN THE 21ST CENTURY, PROJECT SHRINKING CITIES, 2006
[8] IBA PRINCIPLES. GUIDELINES OF THE CABINET REGARDING THE SETUP OF THE IBA STADTUMBAU 2010, 2002

20 - GOUSSAINVILLE (FR), RUNNER-UP - DES RACINES ET DES AILES > SEE MORE P.220

AZENHA DO MAR
PORTUGAL (PT)

CATEGORY: **URBAN – ARCHITECTURAL**
LOCATION: **AZENHA DO MAR, ODEMIRA [SOUTHWEST COAST OF PORTUGAL, 230 KM FROM LISBON]**
POPULATION: **130 INHAB.**
STRATEGIC SITE: **25 HA** / PROJECT SITE: **6.5 HA**
SITE PROPOSED BY: **MUNICIPALITY OF ODEMIRA**

OWNER(S) OF THE SITE: **MUNICIPALITY OF ODEMIRA**
COMMISION AFTER COMPETITION: **CONCEPT AND DEVELOPMENT DESIGN FOR A URBAN STUDY THAT CAN EVOLVE TO INCLUDE PUBLIC SPACE URBAN DESIGN AND ARCHITECTURAL AND LANDSCAPE DESIGN**

Interview of the site's representative
Pedro Rebelo Ramos, Councilman, Municipality of Odemira

PRESENTATION OF THE SITE WITH REGARDS TO STRATEGY
The natural characteristics of the rocks "towards open sea", the green cliffs and picturesque fishing toil, make this conurbation a symbol of handmade fishing and shellfish activity. The site covers vacant areas of a former municipal allotment (that was never fully implemented) also integrating shed buildings that show a degraded urban image and accentuate the problems related to economic fragility and social exclusion. It is intended to counteract degradation and exclusion by transforming Azenha do Mar in a sustainable cluster. The perspective of structured development aims at responsible tourism, where tourism experience is to be diluted with the local experience and generates a demand for visitors throughout the year.

HOW IS THE SITE CONNECTED TO THE SESSION TOPIC - THE ADAPTABLE CITY?
Azenha do Mar is a recent fishing settlement. Its adaptability corresponds to a challenge regarding the dynamics of a contemporary society, related to a particular place's identity. It is aimed at urban complementarities articulating natural landscape and activities through the enhancement of local resources, and also to promote flexibility on these areas in a way that allows specific targets of hosting and providing greater diversification of economic, cultural and social activities.

DID YOU DEFINE A SPECIFIC PROCESS FOR THE URBAN DEVELOPMENT OF THE SITE AFTER EUROPAN COMPETITION?
Framing the winning project with the established goals; and then developing a preliminary study for the unfinished municipal allotment process, that can evolve with public space, architectural and landscape design.

ALESSANDRO LABRIOLA (IT)
ROBERTO CARLUCCI (IT)
GIUDITTA MATARRESE (IT)
ARCHITECTS
ANTONIETTA CANTA (IT)
SUSTAINABILITY ENGINEER
DANIELA MANCINI (IT)
URBANIST
MARIA PIEPOLI (IT)
LANDSCAPE ARCHITECT

VIA MARTIN LUTHER KING 37
70124 BARI, IT
T. +39 3384551111
INFO.LIMENOCHORA@GMAIL.COM
WWW.LIMENOCHORA.COM

WINNER - AZENHA DO MAR (PT)
Limenochora

TEAM POINT OF VIEW "There's never been any shortage of landscape in the world. Whatever else may be lacking, that's one thing that has never been in short supply, indeed its sheer abundance can only be explained by some tireless miracle, because the landscape clearly pre-dates man, and despite its long, long existence, it has still not yet expired." J. Saramago, "Raised from the Ground"

If there is anything of which Azenha do Mar owns plenty, it is landscape. The proposed development of this village is guided by landscape, where most of its unexpressed potential lies. The fishing seaport is implemented with facilities related to the sea, which become part of the cliff profile. At the edge towards the countryside new activities relink the urban tissue to the fields. These new poles trigger Azenha's socio-economic growth as a self-standing community based on a clever and sustainable use of disposable resources: fishing, agriculture, renewable energy and tourism.

Micro-scale actions on existing housing and new adaptable houses turn the existing uncompleted allotment into a new relationship system, where the sense of community is enhanced by small shared spaces and functions inside blocks. The new promenade looking at the sea becomes part of the Rota Vicentina, thus generating continuity between Azenha and the landscape. This connection, together with the rediscovery of traditional self-construction techniques and materials, will rebuild the identity of this small place.

JURY POINT OF VIEW It is a conceptualization of a minimalist and respectful approach with a logic regarding its development. The project offers a strong emphasis on a separation between the cliff area soft context, with independence from the urban grid area.

FRANCESCO MARRAS (IT)
FEDERICO ARU (IT)
ADRIANO DESSÌ (IT)
PHILIP GROSCH (IT)
SILVIA MOCCI (IT)
FRANCESCA OGGIANO (IT)
AURORA PERRA (IT)
ARCHITECTS

FEDERICO SERCIS (IT)
STUDENT IN ARCHITECTURE

19 VIA MONTE SABOTINO
09122 CAGLIARI, SARDINIA, IT
T. +39 3200837195
FRANCESCO.MARRAS@UNICA.IT
WWW.04401ARCHITECTS.COM

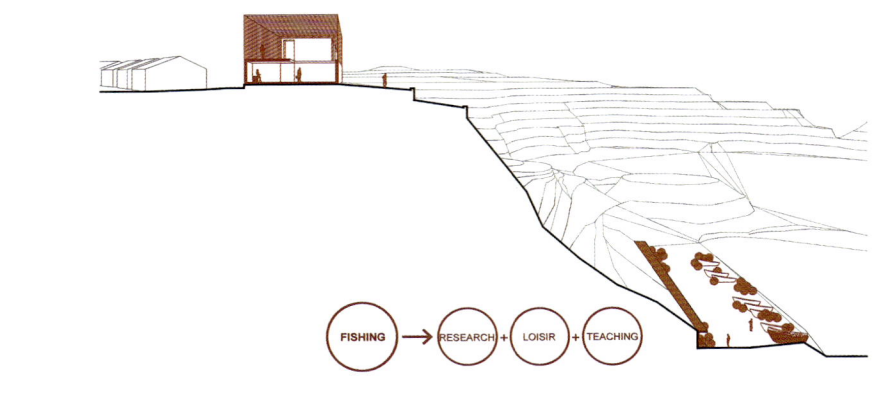

RUNNER-UP - AZENHA DO MAR (PT)

Second Lines

TEAM POINT OF VIEW The proposal strategy seeks to systematize the qualities of Azenha do Mar, with particular attention on strengthening the concept of community, starting with the individual inhabitants, and of landscape as the result of productive and above all cultural activities of the community in the territory. Starting from the hypothesis that the traditional practices and uses of the land must and should be enriched with new procedures, a multi-functional diversification process is put forward to create local development with the active participation of the inhabitants, who give full meaning to the idea of life in a community. In other words we are referring to new ways in which the established community can take the leadership and create new forms of contemporary and cultural niche hospitality and tourism linked to well-being, knowledge, discovery, sharing, uniqueness and the ability to support itself by its traditional activities in the area. The Sergio, José, Mariana families along with all the activities related to land or the sea that involve them are the primary goal of the process strategy; their homes and the spaces used for daily activities become the physical locations through which to flesh out those strategies. This is a project/process for the community in which new objects integrated with the existing ones find new potential, spaces for the carrying out of integrated activities and that can be adapted to those already in use.

JURY POINT OF VIEW The project offers a detailed urban development process articulating uses diversity. The role of central plaza, being somehow unclear, could obstacle uses appropriation and feasibility. The cliff intervention makes sense, although not strictly in line with brief's orientation.

STYLIANI DAOUTI (GR)
GIORGOS MITROULIAS (GR)
MICHAIL IOANNIS RAFTOPOULOS (GR)
ARCHITECTS

IASONAS HOUSSEIN (GR)
STUDENT IN ARCHITECTURE

AREA (ARCHITECTURE RESEARCH ATHENS)
LAMACHOU 3
10557 ATHENS, GR
T. +30 2107229302
INFO@AREAOFFICE.GR
WWW.AREAOFFICE.GR

DANIEL PEREIRA (PT)
FERNANDO FERREIRA (PT)
SARA FERREIRA (PT)
ARCHITECTS

RUA DO PINHEIRO Nº 95, NOGUEIRA
4715-225 BRAGA, PT
T. +351 916839661
SARA.CCARVALHO.FERREIRA@GMAIL.COM

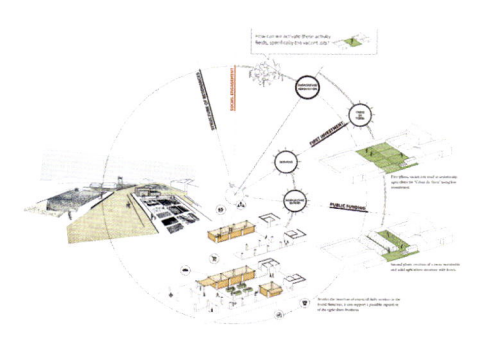

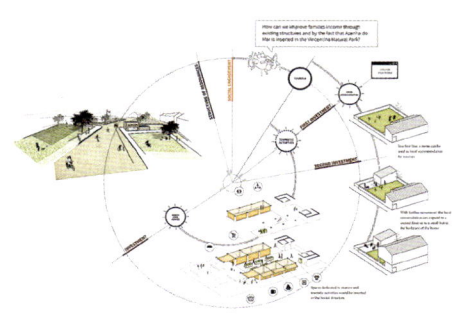

SPECIAL MENTION - AZENHA DO MAR (PT)
Amphibia

TEAM POINT OF VIEW To survive, Azenha do Mar must draw from its amphibian nature: its ability to adapt to both land and water. From the Greek "amphibios" –or "living a double life"– "Amphibia" is a flexible participatory strategy that allows Azenha do Mar adapting to changing social and economic conditions. The town's inhabitants form the proposal's starting point: identities drawn from a microcosm of economic and tourist activities are re-imagined as hybrid actors in a vastly expanded network of spaces. Communal and residential facilities are thus designed to be adaptable and accommodate multiple lifestyles.

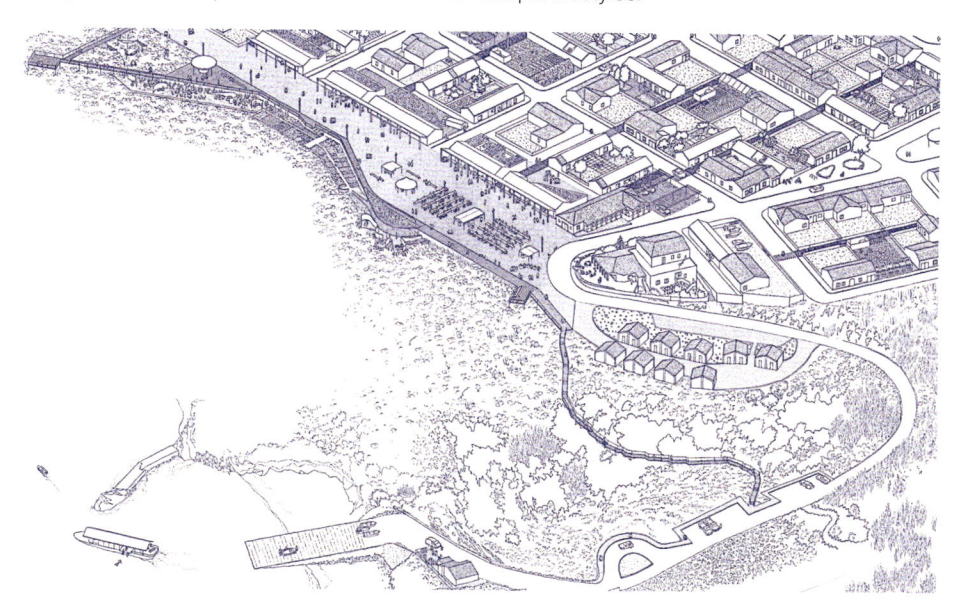

SPECIAL MENTION - AZENHA DO MAR (PT)
Resonance(s) as Chan(c)ge

TEAM POINT OF VIEW An alternative approach to Azenha do Mar selected the existing resonances of the place as catalysts to generate a structure of resonances: a complex process which aims to invite flexible and several activities. Three future scenarios are presented, considering two types of interferences over this structure: a social engagement interference and an investment interference. To finalise, we create chang(c)es – chance to integrate and engage specific agents, scales and constraints of the place; and change for a better and more meaningful future.

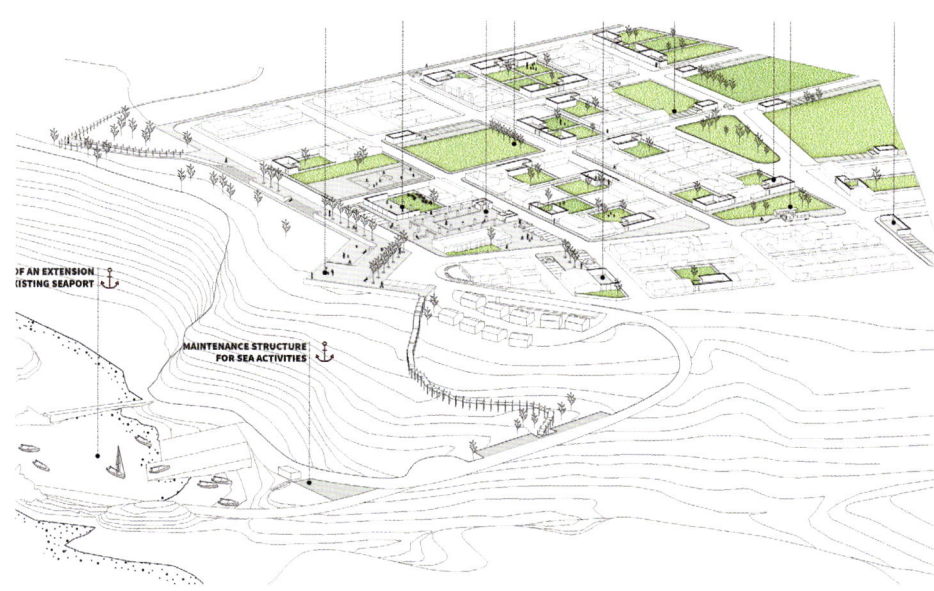

BARCELONA
ESPAÑA (ES)

CATEGORY: **ARCHITECTURAL**
LOCATION: **BARCELONA, SANTS-MONTJUIC DISTRICT, MARINA DEL PRAT VERMELL, SECTOR 10**
POPULATION: **1,600,000 INHAB.**
STRATEGIC SITE: **10.5 HA**

PROJECT SITE: **1,430 SQM**
SITE PROPOSED BY: **BARCELONA CITY COUNCIL**
OWNER(S) OF THE SITE: **BARCELONA CITY COUNCIL**
COMMISION AFTER COMPETITION: **BUILDING PROJECTS (HOUSING OR FACILITIES), OTHERS**

Interview of the site's representative
Sara Udina Armengol, Cap de Projectes. Gerència Adjunta d'Urbanisme. Ecologia Urbana, Ajuntament de Barcelona

PRESENTATION OF THE SITE WITH REGARDS TO STRATEGY
Marina del Prat Vermell is the area between Metal·lúrgia, Foc, Cisell and Mare de Déu del Port Streets. Under the Metropolitan Master Plan Amendment, this former industrial area is being turned into a new mixed-use district in which homes and businesses are perfectly compatible, making it one of the highest profile parts of Barcelona. The area covers nearly 80 ha, equivalent to 40 blocks of the Barcelona Expansion district.
The site was proposed for the Europan 13 competition to receive urban renewal proposals for the adaptable city, specifically a self-sufficient social housing project in this new district. A larger study area was also proposed for the competition in order to prompt ideas about the synergies between the different facets of the urban environment.

HOW IS THE SITE CONNECTED TO THE SESSION TOPIC - THE ADAPTABLE CITY?
The Marina del Prat Vermell district is in itself an example of a forward-looking adaptable city in transformation. The new social housing building included in the competition should also help to shape a social habitat for the society of today and tomorrow, i.e. taking into account the new personal and collective needs and the social changes that may occur in the future. The project is also facing the great challenge of adapting to the city's new environmental requirements.

DID YOU DEFINE A SPECIFIC PROCESS FOR THE URBAN DEVELOPMENT OF THE SITE AFTER EUROPAN COMPETITION?
Urban development in the Marina del Prat Vermell district consists of the application of the current Master Plan. In the current socio-economic context, it is particularly important and indeed urgent to implement social housing projects such as the building included in this Europan competition.

MARÍA LANGARITA (ES)	ANGELA JUARRANZ (ES)	LANGARITA NAVARRO ARQUITECTOS
VÍCTOR NAVARRO (ES)	RAMÓN MARTÍNEZ (ES)	CALLE GRIJALBA 8
ARCHITECTS	ARCHITECTS	28006 MADRID, ES
	JACOB KUMMER (UK)	T. +34 915645984
	GUILLERMO DIEGO (ES)	WWW.LANGARITA-NAVARRO.COM
	STUDENTS IN ARCHITECTURE	

WINNER - BARCELONA (ES)
In Motion

TEAM POINT OF VIEW "In Motion" is an architectonic strategy for an adaptable and self-sufficient city. An adaptable city is a city able to manage times of change and keep up with the speed of its inhabitants. A self-sufficient city is a city that thinks of its life cycles synchronized with the production of resources. Both objectives are applied at two scales:

- The Urban Plan: we reduce the prophylactic layer of hard pavements covering the city and more power is given to the porous and permeable floors to recover the cultural landscape of the Marina de Sants in the long-term. The objective is that the civic and natural cycles synchronously pass through time alongside the appearance of urban orchards, recollection systems and water treatments or the proliferation of native ecosystems.

- The Project: The building acts as a group of high resistance plots/slabs of municipal management. Each platform acts as an equipped plot with independent management and reprogramming. The high-capacity communication systems allow for the coexistence of diverse uses throughout the whole building breaking the usual public-private vertical gradient. The constructive and material solutions arise as the combination of local intelligence to make them easily transformable and they are thought to manage the obsolescence of the different layers (facilities, façades, partitions, etc.) that allow a sustainable and economic adaptation.

JURY POINT OF VIEW It is a clear, assertive project, which succinctly chooses three concepts to structure its architecture. -1- The town land should be more impermeable and better controlled; -2- The occupation and usage of the urban tapestry can be public-private by means of the implementation of strong inhabitable infrastructure; -3- Different technologies and methods are applied to different cycles and times. The result is a flexible and open building/structure. Its ability to replicate as a form of action is feasible throughout the district.

CARLOS GOR (ES)
ÁLVARO GOR (ES)
AGUSTÍN GOR (ES)
JOSÉ LUIS CONCHA (ES)
PABLO FERNÁNDEZ CARPINTERO (ES)
JOSÉ MARÍA DÍAZ (ES)
ÁLVARO GUTIERREZ (ES)
ARCHITECTS

GRX ARQUITECTOS
C/GRAN VÍA DE COLÓN 14B, 2ºIZQ
18010 GRANADA, ES
T. +34 675938095
INFO@GRXARQUITECTOS.COM
WWW.GRXARQUITECTOS.COM

RUNNER-UP - BARCELONA (ES)
Domestic Infrastructure

JURY POINT OF VIEW The project is presented as a large residential condenser, the main virtue of which is the interaction and condensation of public spaces, which can be used by residents and visitors alike. Here, activities, shops and technological development for local use can be implemented to foster social participation. The project does not aim to plan social participation. Instead it is proposed as a tool that encourages it through these spaces. The housing units are regarded as operators of this experimental management of environmental resources. Queries were raised about the use of the ground floor space.

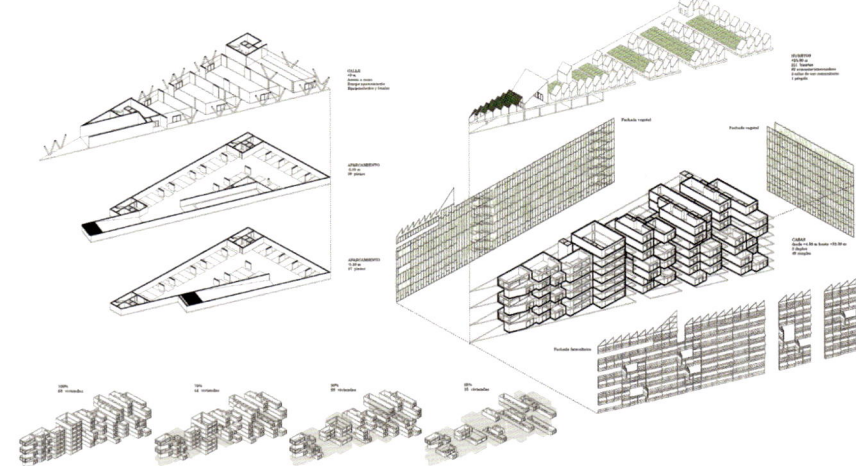

TEAM POINT OF VIEW Strategy with the environment – urbana simbiosis
The district of La Marina del Prat Vermell provides a perfect DNA to implement a centralized area for the management of natural resources and environmental technologies. The fact of the thermal application from the treatment of liquefied gas from Algeria from the port of Barcelona and supplying thermal energy to the area, possible joint implementation of other techniques such as water treatment, geothermal and solar energy. On the other hand, the district history linked to agriculture and industry allows the application of urban technologies and building, so that works successfully, just as they are doing elsewhere in Barcelona and the world.

Benergy park – environmental and social condensador
Experience shows that social participation cannot be designed from the planning process, but if you can make designs and strategies that favour. Further than a design, a way of managing environmental resources and a system of public spaces with the urban garden as a way to articulate and promote social interaction and participation is proposed.
In this context, the housing project will be a model to put in evidence the different environmental exchange systems that serve future architectural interventions in the area and the park as a place where symbolically these energy and human exchanges take part.

EDUARD BALCELLS (ES)
HONORATA GRZESIKOWSKA (PL)
ARCHITECTS-URBANISTS

TRAVESSERA DE LES CORTS 265, 6º2ª ESC. A
08014 BARCELONA, ES
T. +34 934304071
EDUARDBALCELLS@COAC.NET
WWW.EDUARDBALCELLS.COM
WWW.HONURB.COM

RUNNER-UP - BARCELONA (ES)

Sustainable Interface

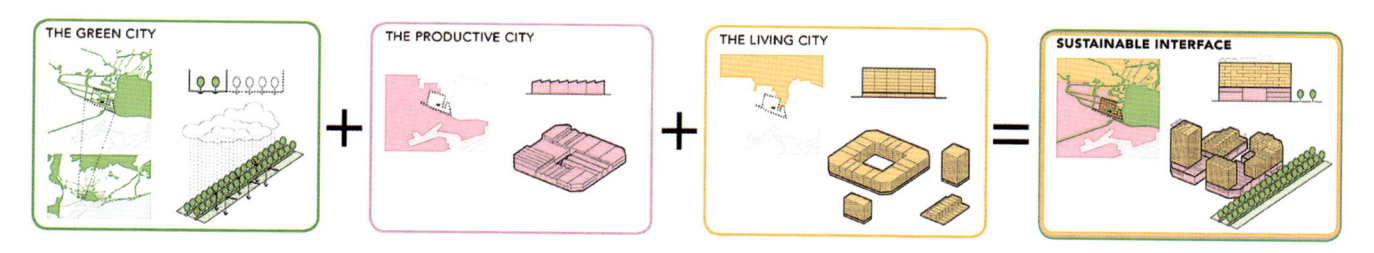

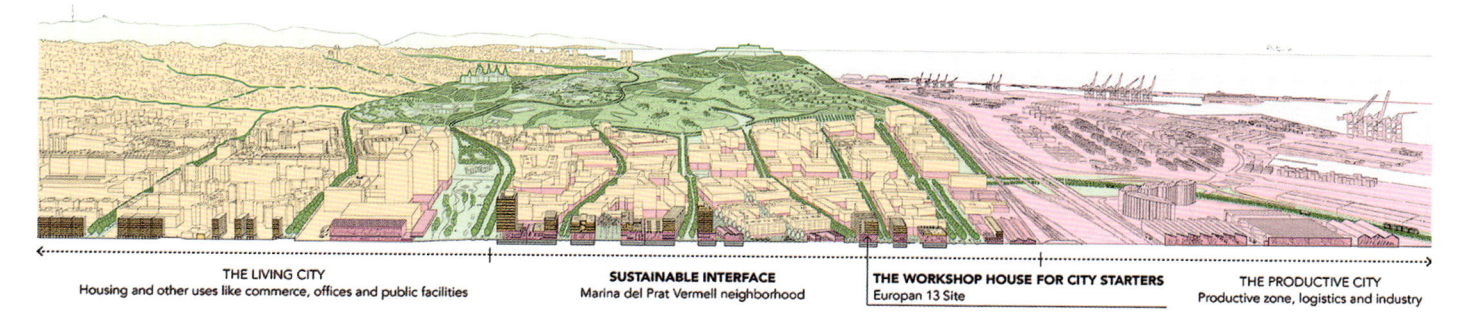

TEAM POINT OF VIEW With its unique location between the Green City, the Productive City and the Living City, the new Marina del Prat Vermell district has the potential to become a self-sufficient Sustainable Interface between them, expanding the possibilities of living and working within the city.
Green City – The existing streets with their Sustainable Urban Drainage Systems are extended and become Green Fingers reconnecting the district with the green lung of the Montjuïc mountain.
Productive City – The lack of adequate spaces for productive activities is tackled by introducing thick Robust Plinths that have the adaptability of the industrial spaces nearby and where any use is possible, including light urban manufacturing and local production making the city's economy more resilient.
Living City – On top of the plinths, Living Toppings enable any desired lifestyle encouraging a low ecological footprint and seeking to build a strong community.
Sustainable Interface – A mixture of these cities is developed in The Workshop House for City Starters, a new social housing typology providing affordable living and working spaces to start economic and social initiatives. Between 2 Green Fingers a Robust Plinth with workshops of all sizes proposes workspace for residents and neighbours, becoming a social focus. On top, a Living Topping of lofts offers living and working spaces while the roof hosts a large collective and productive garden with views to the sea

JURY POINT OF VIEW The project is developed at various scales. It combines a discourse of "territorial" connectivity with the idea of private and collective production cycles as efficient, closed circuit "sustainable interfaces". This is made possible by combining the coexistence of a precise, expert discourse for the site with an ambitious "manifesto" of hypothetical social transformations. "Sustainable interface" proposes the construction of a system of greenways to link the Marina del Prat Vermell zone to the Southern slopes of Montjuïc by means of optimised urban drainage systems.

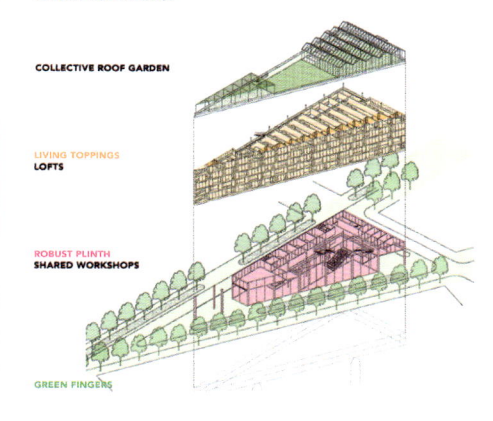

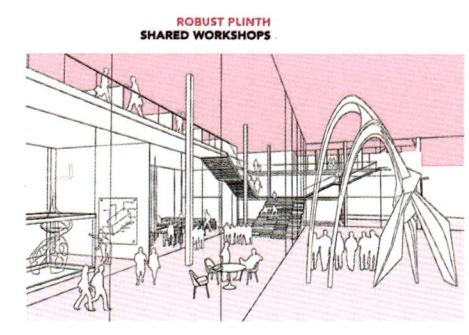

GREGORIO RAMÍREZ VILA (ES)
ENRICA SANTACRUZ SASTRE (ES)
ARCHITECTS

COWORKING FÀBRICA RAMIS
GRAN VÍA DE COLÓN 28
07300 INCA, ES
T. +34 659347616
INFO@RARQUITECTES.COM
WWW.RARQUITECTES.COM

CARLES ENRICH (ES)
ARCHITECT

ADRIANA CAMPMANY (ES)
ANNA DE CASTRO (ES)
ARCHITECTS
LAURA BELENGUER (ES)
RAFEL CAPÓ (ES)
MINERVA RAMÍREZ (ES)
STUDENTS IN ARCHITECTURE

C/ FRATERNITAT 38, PB
08012 BARCELONA, ES
T. +34 649769786
CARLES@CARLESENRICH.COM
WWW.CARLESENRICH.COM

SPECIAL MENTION - BARCELONA (ES)
Computers Aren't Food

TEAM POINT OF VIEW The project aims to blur the boundary between town and country by creating hybrid junctions, where both can coexist and interact. In this way, we eliminate the constant agricultural threat due to urban growth. Location strategy, along with an urgent update of industrial, production and trade models, is a social approach to economic and financial processes. To practice sustainable design not only in terms of buildings, but also at all levels: territorial, urban and domestic. The challenges ahead require global collaboration and the promotion of knowledge in the everyday citizens environments.

SPECIAL MENTION - BARCELONA (ES)
Gent del barri

TEAM POINT OF VIEW The Marina del Prat Vermell is located between geographical landforms as the Montjuïc mountain and the harbour area. The intense program of events in Fira 2 introduces a temporary user who actually does not integrate in the public space.
Our proposal is based on breaking these limits and mixing these realities to improve social cohesion to recover the origin of the place, preserving the existing tissue and promoting mixing of users, housing, industries and production spaces. With this goal we propose strategies to reactivate the public space for temporary and permanent users.

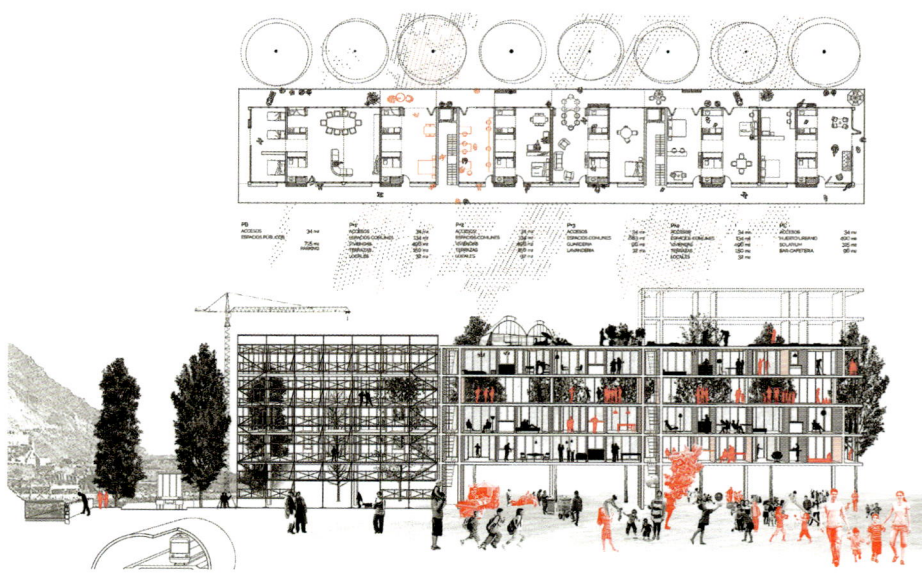

DANIEL DEL REY HERNÁNDEZ (ES)
ARCHITECT
SERGIO DEL CASTILLO TELLO (ES)
ELISA POZO MENÉNDEZ (ES)
COMPUTER GRAPHIC DESIGNERS

ALEJANDRO LONDROÑO (ES)
ARCHITECT
RAQUEL VILLA (ES)
CRISTIANA MARCU (ES)
STUDENTS IN ARCHITECTURE

T. +34 616295933
ZERCASTEL@GMAIL.COM
WWW.NANETWORK.NET
HTTP://INFOGRAFIA.AQ.UPM.ES/

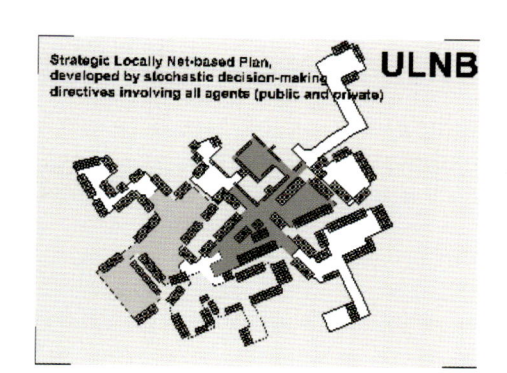

SPECIAL MENTION - BARCELONA (ES)
Urban Species Evolution

TEAM POINT OF VIEW The project analyses 3 possible geological stages, depending on the choices made by local actors: investments and decisions configure every stage and determine the adaptability of the project area according to an "Adaptability Urban Indicator" (AUI) based on land uses, metabolism, equipment, biodiversity, typology, open spaces and social cohesion. The 3 evolution paths are evaluated to qualify their adaptability through actions: the more options, the more AUI to invest, and therefore the more suitable the urban solution for the citizens.

BRUCK/MUR
ÖSTERREICH (AT)

CATEGORY: **URBAN - ARCHITECTURAL**
LOCATION: **BRUCK A.D. MUR**
POPULATION: **13,000 INHAB.**
STRATEGIC SITE: **20 HA**
PROJECT SITE: **1.5 HA**
SITE PROPOSED BY: **CITY OF BRUCK AN DER MUR & FEDERAL STATE STEIERMARK**

OWNER(S) OF THE SITE:
FEDERAL STATE STEIERMARK
COMMISION AFTER COMPETITION:
URBAN PROJECT MANAGEMENT ROLE, FURTHER INVOLVEMENT IN ARCHITECTURAL FOLLOW-UP PROCEDURES

Interview of the site's representative

Hans Straßegger, Mayor of the city of Bruck an der Mur
Robert Pichler, Director of Urban Planning, City of Bruck an der Mur
Günter Koberg, Head of Department 16 – Traffic & Construction, Federal state Steiermark

PRESENTATION OF THE SITE WITH REGARDS TO STRATEGY

Bruck an der Mur is a gateway to Upper Styria and the geographical centre of the city region Leoben- Bruck - Kapfenberg. The insular situation of the project site reflects Bruck as an urban landscape dominated by large infrastructures, potential and challenge in one. The aim is to establish the site as a centre in the local and regional context as well as in the awareness of society to open up the visionary path to become a city region with a sustainable leading project!

HOW IS THE SITE CONNECTED TO THE SESSION TOPIC - THE ADAPTABLE CITY?

Together with its neighbouring towns Bruck an der Mur is in the process of forming one of Austria's 38 city regions. For this transformation a number of strategic adaptations on both levels –regional and city– have to be made. Corresponding to Europan's subtopic "Segregation vs Sharing" within the coming years steps of intensified networking and development towards a cross-linked urban agglomeration on an administrative and infrastructural level will take place.

DID YOU DEFINE A SPECIFIC PROCESS FOR THE URBAN DEVELOPMENT OF THE SITE AFTER EUROPAN COMPETITION?

The City of Bruck an der Mur and the Federal State Steiermark intend to follow a workshop based structure with the Runner-up team and Europan Österreich.

JOSÉ MANUEL LÓPEZ UJAQUE (ES)
FRANCISCO GARCÍA TRIVIÑO (ES)
KATERINA PSEGIANNAKI (GR)
ARCHITECTS

C/ AMPARO 8, 3º A
28012 MADRID, ES
T. +34 628848995
JFK@KUNEOFFICE.COM
WWW.KUNEOFFICE.COM

RUNNER-UP - BRUCK/MUR (AT)
Together

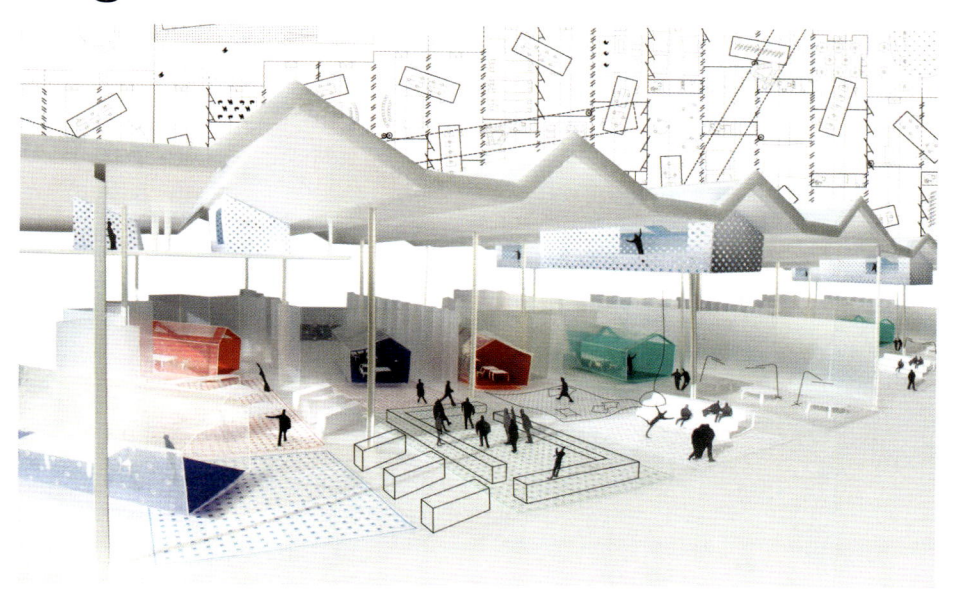

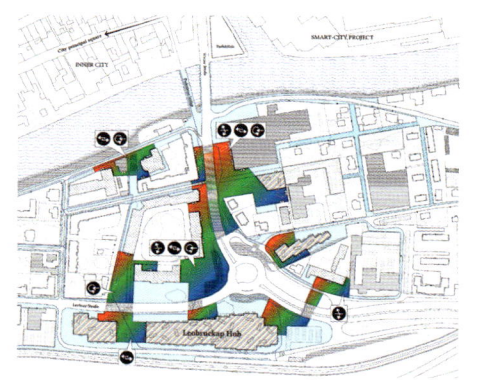

TEAM POINT OF VIEW "Being Together" is much more than a simple addition of single individualities. It is a way to cooperate within diversity, a way to create, grow and learn. Each designed layer of the project responds to everyday spatial politics with decisive interaction. The project identity is based on daily cooperation situations, which are necessary to innovate, develop and undertake the needs of the contemporary society. We propose 3 strategies of building relationships between different agents: superimpose spaces to provoke exchanges, create in-between spaces to share common infrastructures, and fill spaces with other spaces to get influenced by each other.

The resulting architectural system assumes the complexities of this necessary yet incomprehensibly weakened working mode of daily cooperation in many aspects of our life. A singular building becomes the place for cooperation and new public spaces are designed to bring together the disconnected pieces of the city.

Bruck/Mur and the nearby cities of Leoben and Kapfenberg have the geographical and infrastructural conditions needed to make the proposed joint project possible.

JURY POINT OF VIEW The proposal introduces a process and participatory development based on modular space structures on the site. It is considered to be the only submitted project that provides the requested time-puffer for the city to start a process on the site. Moreover "Together" could even work on a small scale and low-budget level as the first starting point to occupy the site and establish the first step of a strategy. However, the architectural formulation of the hall-structure with the roof is unanimously criticized.

CHARLEROI
BELGIQUE/BELGIË/BELGIEN (BE)

CATEGORY: **TOWN PLANNING AND ARCHITECTURE**
LOCATION: **CHARLEROI, GILLY, PLACE DESTRÉE**
POPULATION: **203,753 INHAB.**
STRATEGIC SITE: **11.4 HA**
PROJECT SITE: **2.5 HA**

SITE PROPOSED BY: **CITY OF CHARLEROI, CHARLEROI BOUWMEESTER**
OWNER(S) OF THE SITE: **CITY OF CHARLEROI**
COMMISION AFTER COMPETITION: **TOWN PLANNING STUDY, ARCHITECTURAL DESIGN OF PUBLIC SPACES AND SOME BUILDINGS**

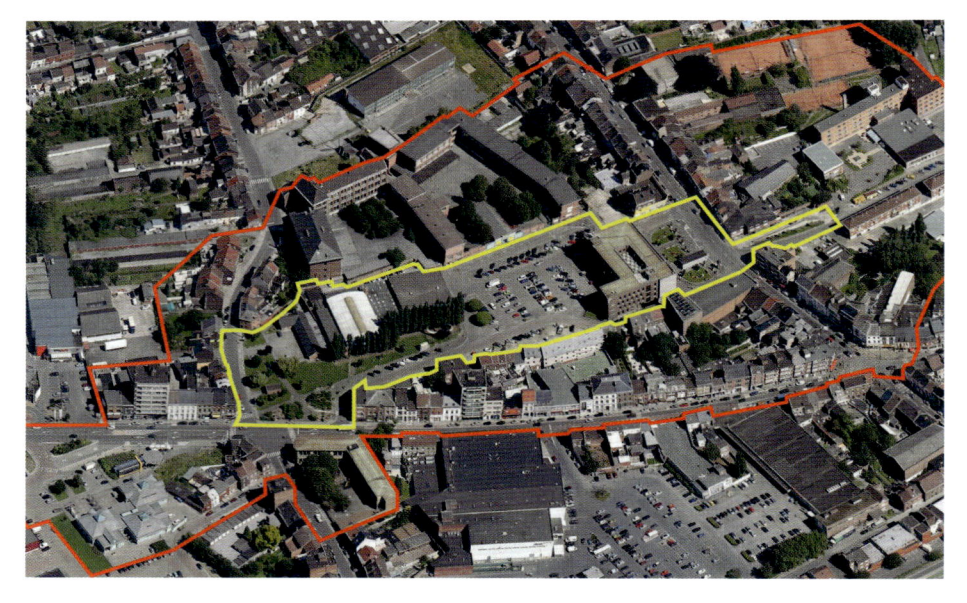

Interview of the site's representative
The City of Charleroi
& Charleroi Bouwmeester

PRESENTATION OF THE SITE WITH REGARDS TO STRATEGY
The choice of the site answers the strategy of the strategic development plan of the City of Charleroi. It is based on three axes: the ongoing requalification of the city centre; the redevelopment of the economic areas; and the development of the peripheral districts and ancient urban centres, the first step of which being the requalification of the place Jules Destrée in Gilly.

HOW IS THE SITE CONNECTED TO THE SESSION TOPIC - THE ADAPTABLE CITY?
The place Jules Destrée was built out of a series of accumulations and subtractions giving it its current flexible structure and non-frozen character compared to a classical square. The goal of the competition is to preserve this flexibility while shaping a project that preserves the existing activities, improves the attractiveness of the place and allows the emergence of a new usage mode thanks to the elaboration of a progressive development scheme.

DID YOU DEFINE A SPECIFIC PROCESS FOR THE URBAN DEVELOPMENT OF THE SITE AFTER EUROPAN COMPETITION?
The City of Charleroi wants to initiate a competitive dialogue between both Runners-Up and both Special Mentions in order to make the public space project evolve with regards to the expectations of the citizens and the stakeholders. After this competitive dialogue, we will name a winning project and implement it as soon as possible. The City of Charleroi has already planned a budget for the requalification of the public space of the place Destrée.

RADIM LOUDA (CZ)
PIERRE BURQUEL (BE)
PAUL MOUCHET (FR)
VALENTIN PIRET (FR)
ARCHITECTS

TINA JAVORNIK (SI)
ARCHITECT

CENTRAL OFFICE FOR ARCHITECTURE
AND URBANISM
28 RUE DU CONSEIL BTE 8
1050 BRUSSELS, BE
INFO@CENTRAL-NET.EU
WWW.CENTRAL-NET.EU

RUNNER-UP - CHARLEROI (BE)
Making Room for Gilly

JURY POINT OF VIEW Adaptable cities can be seen both as projects and as existing realities. The strong point here lies in bringing both visions together in a "complex building", the design of which revolves around re-using the sports centre but augmenting it with new developments. The project has the potential to weave an urban story maintaining the metropolitan quality of existing facilities while developing a whole new approach to the spaces and their roles.

TEAM POINT OF VIEW Re-qualifying the Place Destrée means considering the complexity and potential qualities of the site. Turning them into a strong urban experience means defining a strategy able to evolve and adapt in time –an urban strategy that strongly and directly transforms the uses of the site while preparing the ground for its ambitious future configuration.
We propose to structure the urban process around 5 principles:
- Emptying: A wide urban room for Gilly as the first step for an ambitious urban renewal;
- Defining: redefinition of the relation between the square and the surrounding buildings to activate its urban condition and shape;
- Processing/Re-Using: despite the actual lack of quality of the sport complex buildings, the existing layering logic is seen as an opportunity to develop a flexible building process able to define a characteristic public space, allowing a site transformation in time and need;
- Connecting: the site's public space and landscape logics are extended, creating a continuous promenade under trees punctuated by public space interventions;
- Share Refining: The redevelopment process of the Place Destrée district acts as an urban vision defined by clear principles able to produce strong yet adapted changes. More than defining an agenda for a design, we propose a development logic that settles the basis for a shared refining between the city, the citizens, the developers and the planners.

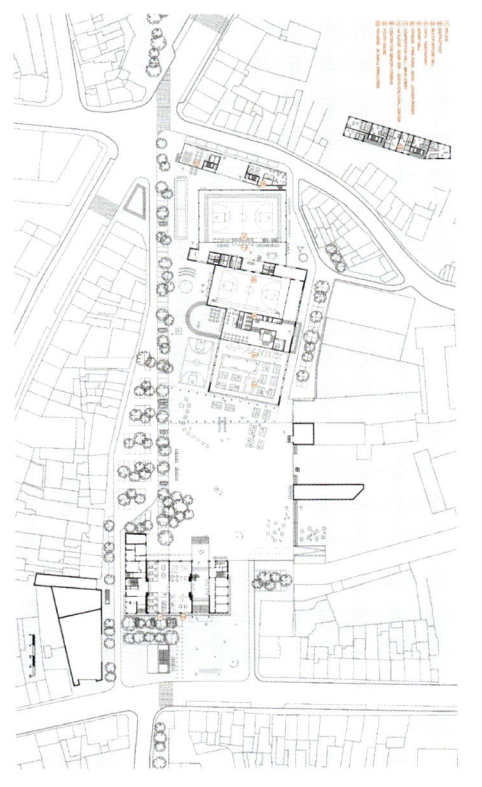

YAJUN CHEN (CN)
GAOFEI TAN (CN)
ARCHITECTS

JOZEF LIBERTSTRAAT 30
2140 ANTWERP, BE
T. +32 488120056
CHENKEABBA@GMAIL.COM
GAOFEI.TAN@GMAIL.COM

RUNNER-UP - CHARLEROI (BE)

The Heterotopia Pool

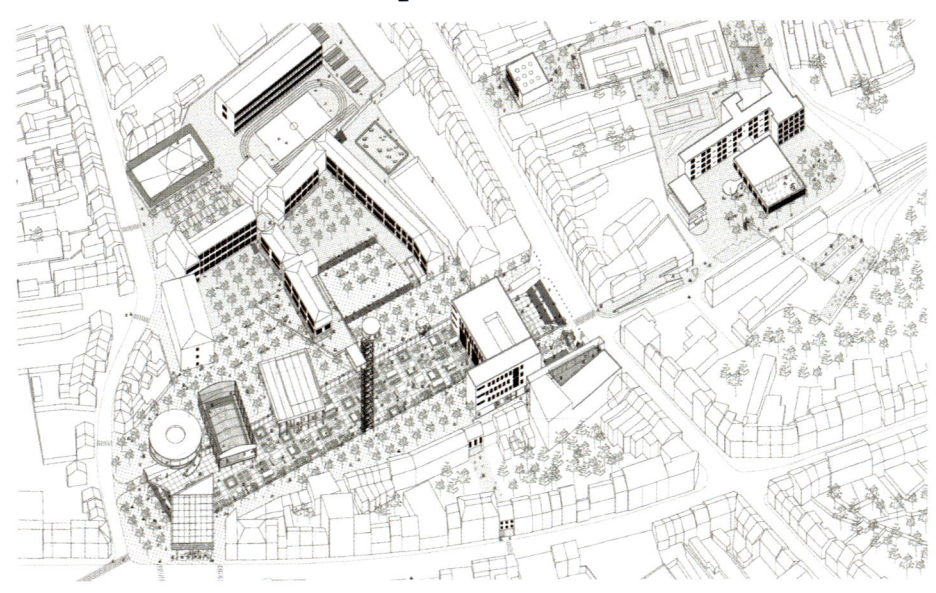

TEAM POINT OF VIEW "The Heterotopia Pool" holds all culture, all real, which is simultaneously mythic and real. It links every fragmented site, changes the functions within a single form, bridges the twisted and broken time and space under varying historical circumstances.

The overlapping of different periods brings a rich, yet unclear situation. But with the death of the mining industry, there is no self-evident activity taking place like the historical periods. The city space that is left became mixture, mist, mystery.

We propose a simple 3-step development:
-1- Form a simple void to have a clear spatial identity;
-2- Link the void with the nature and artificial landscape;
-3- Generate the net of public circulation

The Pool.
The Heterotopia.
The Space.
The City.

JURY POINT OF VIEW The overall concept draws upon elements that are central to the city's identity. It creates a public space using a gap dug between the "Jules Destrée" design and rue du Calvaire. This malleable space peppered by architectural features calls Charleroi's emblematic objects to mind. It generates a traffic network that goes beyond the proposed space.

It creates visual depth accentuated by trees around the platform, bringing nature into the city. The project does not set the design of the site in stone and can therefore be adapted to future changes in use.

EMMANUEL NGUYEN (FR)
ROBERT JANEZ (SI)
DELPHINE ALTIER (FR)
PAULINE MERLET (FR)
ARCHITECTS

25 RUE ETIENNE DOLET
75020 PARIS, FR
T. +33 983267510
NJAM.ARCHI@GMAIL.COM
WWW.JANEZ-NGUYEN.COM

SPECIAL MENTION - CHARLEROI (BE)
Gilly "Made It Yourself"

TEAM POINT OF VIEW Gilly "Made It Yourself" proposes to solve issues of an area by improving attractiveness through the place identity and cooperation of local citizens. The place identify is disclosed by making a distinct urban morphology. Four new-built front redesign the square and create a gathering place allowing all access to public facilities.

To develop and value the site, we propose a collaborative block based on inheritance of old urban block of Gilly. Block is promoted by the involvement of citizens. The principle is a weft of pedestrian path and plots to welcome different typology or uses.

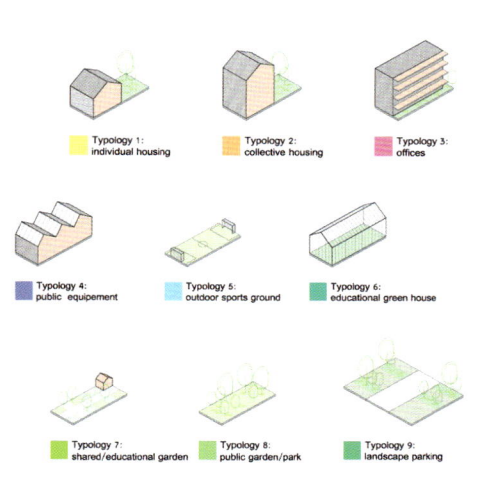

RÉMI VAN DURME (BE)
DENIS GLAUDEN (BE)
PIERRE-LAURENT RIGAUX (BE)
BRICE POLOMÉ (BE)
ARCHITECTS

1000 BRUXELLES, BE
T. +32 24242466
COLLECTIF@HORIZONTAL.CC
WWW.HORIZONTAL.CC

6060 CHARLEROI, BE
T. +32 71418153
INFO@GOFFART-POLOME.COM
WWW.GOFFART-POLOME.COM

SPECIAL MENTION - CHARLEROI (BE)
Sur les pavés, la place !

TEAM POINT OF VIEW Against the prevalence of generic, utilitarian public space, we propose a masterplan that celebrates collective public space by taking the pavestone as its iconic element – Gilly's very own pavestone. Its particular, yet quintessentially simple geometry allows the pavement to bend up and down in a hilly geometry that integrates public amenities into a continuous, active ground cover. This square of a new kind can be shaped to integrate mineral and vegetal spaces in a free composition that responds to the actors' input to create a diverse, unique urban landscape.

GERA
DEUTSCHLAND (DE)

CATEGORY: **URBAN - LANDSCAPE - ARCHITECTURAL**
LOCATION: **TOWN CENTRE, BREITSCHEIDSTRASSE EAST**
POPULATION: **95,000 INHAB.**
STRATEGIC SITE: **13 HA**
PROJECT SITE: **5.27 HA**

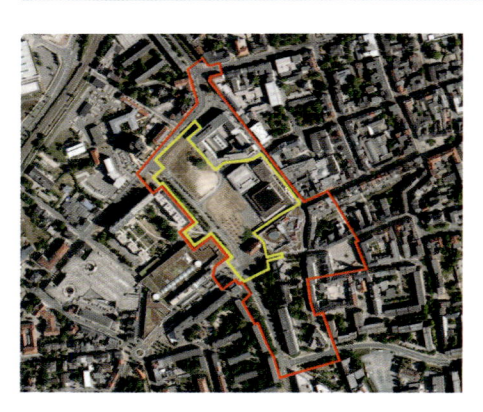

SITE PROPOSED BY: **GERA CITY COUNCIL/IBA THÜRINGEN**
OWNER(S) OF THE SITE: **GERA CITY COUNCIL AND GWB ELSTERTAL MUNICIPAL HOUSING ASSOCIATION**
COMMISION AFTER COMPETITION: **STRATEGIC OUTLINE PLAN FOR BREITSCHEIDSTRASSE**

Interview of the site's representative
Thomas Leidel, city of Gera
Dr. Bertram Schiffers, IBA Thüringen

PRESENTATION OF THE SITE WITH REGARDS TO STRATEGY
The competition area in Gera forms a five-hectare-large wasteland right in the middle of the centre of the third largest city in Thuringia. Despite the prominent location it has not been possible over the last 15 years to stimulate economic and simultaneously high-quality investments here. With the support of the International Bauausstellung (IBA) Thuringia, the City of Gera and the association Ja – für Gera have now jointly initiated a new process of development. As partners on an equal footing, they seek a coproduction of city administration and citizens for this location. What is desired is a new urban planning scale and a gradual appropriation of the area.

HOW IS THE SITE CONNECTED TO THE SESSION TOPIC - THE ADAPTABLE CITY?
Since the social upheaval of 1990, Gera has undergone a large-scale economic restructuring, a loss in importance, and a decline in population. Earlier structural references of the development of a metropolitan and industrial city are no longer viable as a bridge to the future. Due to budget shortfalls, conventional urban development as a mix of public and private investments does no longer function either. With its focuses on self-organization and participatory processes, the Europan 13 theme "The Adaptable City" precisely fits Gera.

DID YOU DEFINE A SPECIFIC PROCESS FOR THE URBAN DEVELOPMENT OF THE SITE AFTER EUROPAN COMPETITION?
The Europan site and the historical KuK culture and convention centre form the visible venue of awakening for Gera. The competition results will be exhibited in the KuK on the beginning of 2016 and the winning teams are invited to Gera to showcase their projects. The goal is to have a masterplan that defines the key urban planning points and also creates the framework for temporary and permanent uses.

MARC TORRAS MONTFORT (ES)
ANNELIE SEEMANN (DE)
ARCHITECTS

VINCENZA LA ROCCA (IT)
ARCHITECT

SEEMANN-TORRAS ARCHITEKTUR
HUFELANDSTRASSE 17
10407 BERLIN, DE
T. +49 177 3320576
INFO@ST-ARCHITEKUR.COM
WWW.ST-ARCHITEKUR.COM

WINNER - GERA (DE)
Colonization of the City Centre

TEAM POINT OF VIEW In Gera, large buildings –like the arcades, the KuK or massive precast buildings– are opposed to a new architecture design dividing the Breitscheidstraße district in small plots that should, in the future, combine different design elements and using structures.

To initiate the revitalization of the site – accompanied and supported step-by-step by the population– we develop the plots in several construction phases. The project only shows a still unfinished 1st development step. The area is first marked by basic orientation architectural structures connected by a footpath with a new lighting system –guiding people from the shopping street Die Sorge to the new quarter – and including a hotel with commercial spaces on the ground floor, a youth centre with a sports and skate park and a residential complex with private gardens. Temporary uses supplement basic architecture and offer the possibility of a low-cost upgrade of the area. Micro architecture –container garages, private gardens, playgrounds, etc.– complete the proposal. New development possibilities for the Breidscheids district will be presented in the future.

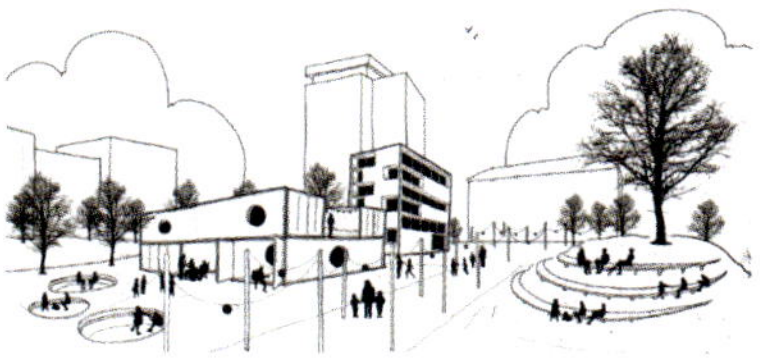

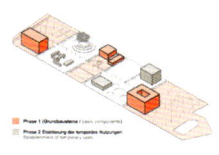

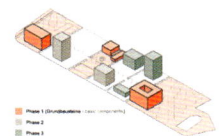

JURY POINT OF VIEW The design concept reacts to the site special situation proposing a phasing of temporary and permanent uses. A step-by-step "colonizing" of the central square is supposed to take place from a temporary micro-architecture. The design reacts to the dimensions of the neighbouring buildings and plots of land without succumbing to an inappropriately small scale. Public and private spaces are clearly distinct from one another and thus affect the spatial potentials of a development of gradual appropriation. A clever contribution to the theme of the Adaptable City.

GAUTIER DUTHOIT (FR)
ARCHITECT-URBANIST

20 RUE DES ROCHERS
67190 GRESSWILLER, FR

RUNNER-UP - GERA (DE)

Connected_Urbis

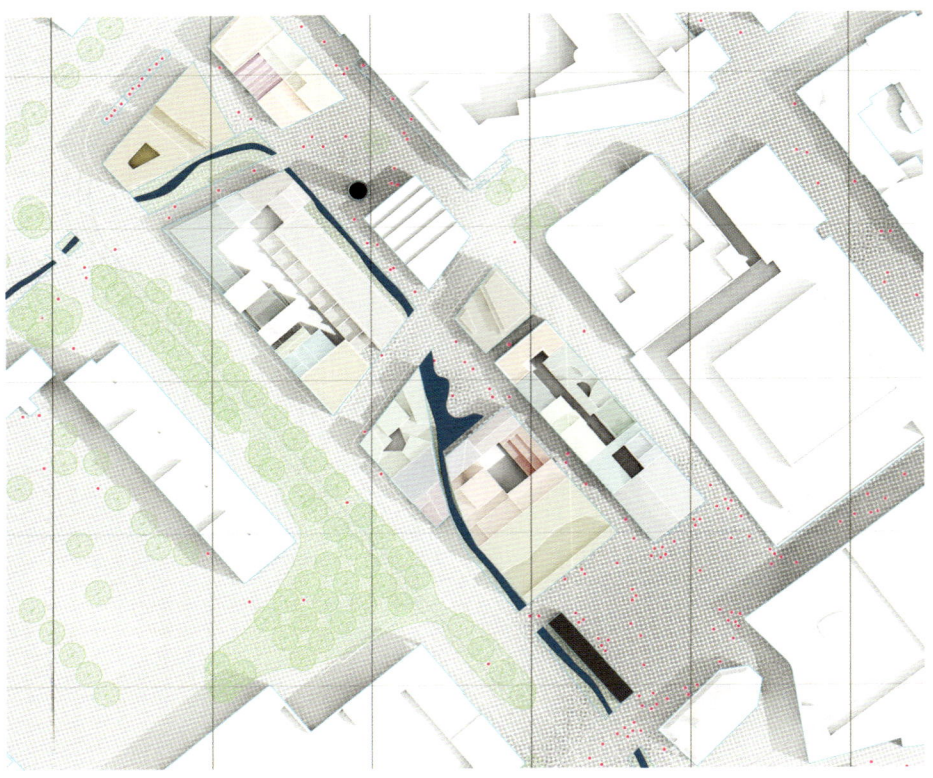

TEAM POINT OF VIEW In opposition to the principle of the polarizing archipelago, in the global economy, it is possible to apply a principle of balance and of isotropic distribution, and rethinking proximity and what is the "right distance". There is no relationship between individuals without space. Any territory has the ability to develop this mental image that one forges of a space providing a frame for accumulating knowledge. The digital world should not be seen as a revolution but rather as a transformation of the understanding of collective phenomena by increasing the visibility and the aggregation of singular collective events. It is possible to develop uses of the digital network that make the potential of territories visible by redistributing connection possibilities among actors within the networks of the mass production economical paradigm. The infinite reorganization of items composing the possible urban scenarios becomes an opportunity to promote participation of urban users to reintegrate them actively in the decision-making on territorial development. These digital tools forge links between individuals, inviting them to participate in a strategy of co-creation of value for their business. On the concept of crowd sourcing model such as Wikipedia, the urban institutions could develop this alliance with individuals in the co-production of the urban environment based on participation and continuous experimentation an different scales.

JURY POINT OF VIEW The development basis is a stable and well thought-out urban planning design that also contributes to the upgrading of the adjacent public uses. The path relationships are cleverly selected and strengthen the connections between the Western and Eastern centres of the city. The work also offers interesting experimental proposals for the development of the project. One weakness of the work lies in the lack of consideration of the conceivable uses; since the process proposed will take a lot of time, even in the case of positive conditions for investment.

TIMOTHY VANAGT (BE)
ARCHITECT

NICK ALBERS (NL)
PROJECT DEVELOPER

C/O NICK ALBERS
GAASTERLANDSTRAAT 30
7559LA HENGELO, NL
T. +31 645286890
NICK@MARATHONWORKS.COM
WWW.MARATHONWORKS.COM

SPECIAL MENTION - GERA (DE)
Das Ist Gera

TEAM POINT OF VIEW "New Gera" - a continuously evolving concept of being at home in the city.
Everyone now and then reflects on his or her future life and home place in the City. We recognize that any personal desire or professional stake in this future, by any citizen, has an immense value! To capitalize on this value, we would like to initiate a process that involves Gera's citizens in shaping their public domain. With the continuous help and effort of officials, professionals and volunteers "New Gera" will take shape, the city becoming your home!

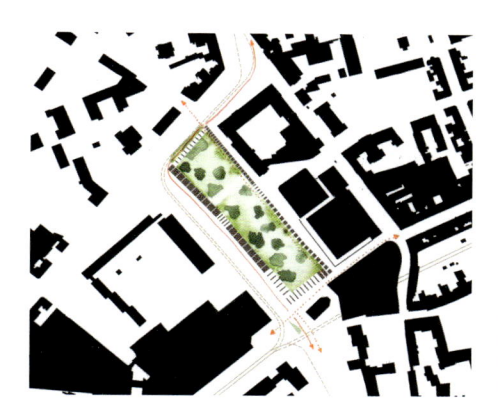

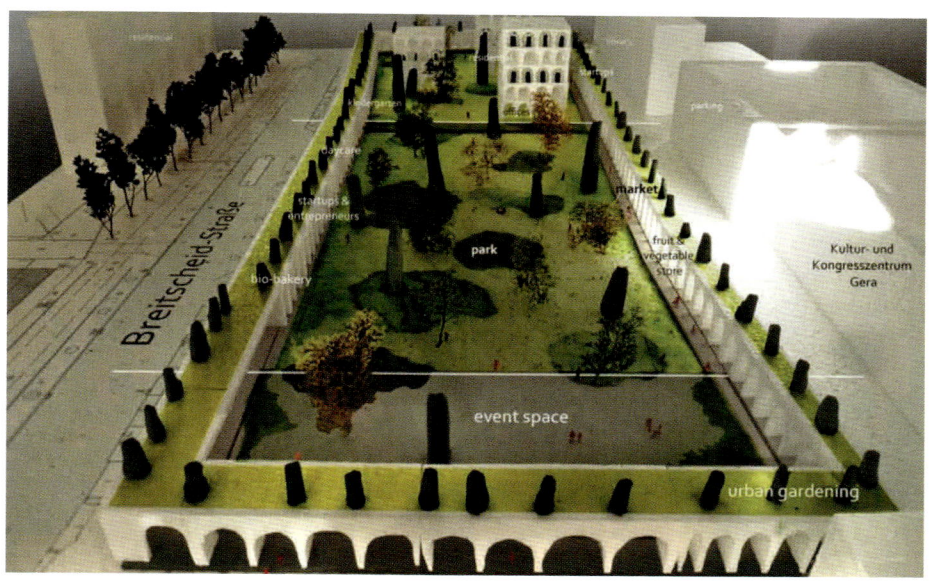

FRANZISKA SCHIEFERDECKER (DE)
FILIP STASKIEWICZ (DE)
WOLFGANG HILGERS (DE)
LANDSCAPE ARCHITECTS
FRIEDEMANN RENTSCH (DE)
ARCHITECT

OLEG GOI (UKR)
STUDENT IN ARCHITECTURE

LABOR4+/ RENTSCH ARCHITEKTUR
MARIENSTRASSE 20
01067 DRESDEN, DE
T. +49 1774741764

SPECIAL MENTION - GERA (DE)
Gera's Golden Centre

TEAM POINT OF VIEW Gera's biggest potential is its citizens, who are actively involved in the co-creation of their city. This potential will be activated by the first stage of the "72 Hours Gold Action". The emptiness in the middle of the city of Gera will be transformed into "Gera's Golden Centre". After this activation phase, participatory processes will be initiated in the second stage – "Let's Use And Rebuild Together!". The results and ideas are then, in a future third phase, to consolidate, leading to "Gera's Strong Centre", with valuable open spaces and sustainable development.

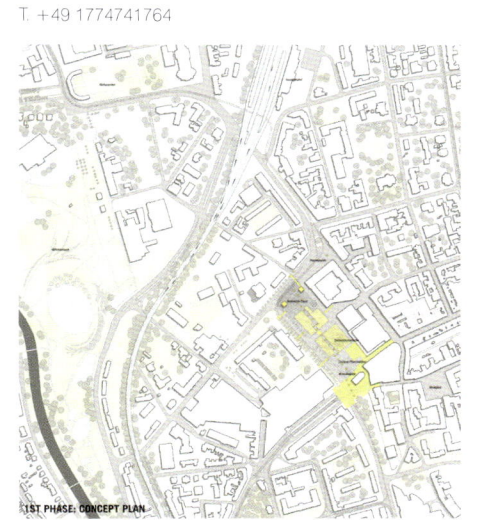

1ST PHASE: CONCEPT PLAN

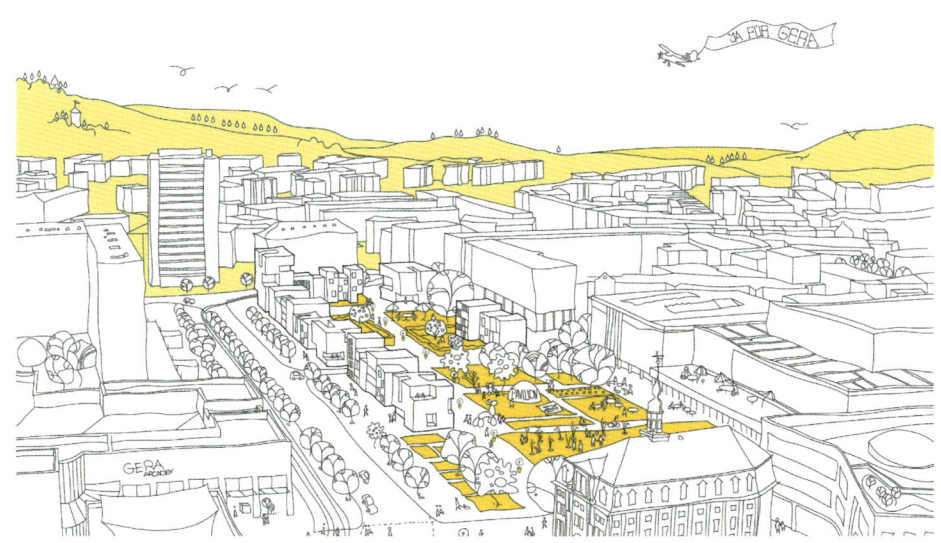

GOUSSAINVILLE
FRANCE (FR)

CATEGORY: **URBAN - ARCHITECTURAL**
LOCATION: **COMMUNAUTÉ AGGLOMÉRATION ROISSY PORTE DE FRANCE, GOUSSAINVILLE**
POPULATION: **31,390 INHAB.**
STRATEGIC SITE: **922 HA**
PROJECT SITE: **52 HA**

SITE PROPOSED BY: **CA ROISSY PORTE DE FRANCE, TOWN OF GOUSSAINVILLE**
OWNER(S) OF THE SITE: **TOWN OF GOUSSAINVILLE, PRIVATE**
COMMISION AFTER COMPETITION: **MANAGEMENT OF THE ARCHITECTURAL AND/OR URBAN PROJECT WITH PARTNERS**

Interview of the site's representative

PRESENTATION OF THE SITE WITH REGARDS TO STRATEGY

The site corresponds to the historical village of Goussainville. Nestled in the Croult Valley –a small indirect tributary of the Seine– the village forms an island in the heart of a highly dynamic territory. To the West, an extension of the historical village, now a town centre, has developed on the plateau along the Paris-Lille railway line. To the East, the Paris-Charles de Gaulle airport –the world's third biggest (passenger flows) and number one platform (airfreight)– is an interregional employment hub. To the North, the territory is connected to the Paris "orbital expressway" –also called "la Francilienne". However, these infrastructures cause a number of problems: spatial segmentation, urban isolation, noise exposure and atmospheric pollution.

HOW IS THE SITE CONNECTED TO THE SESSION TOPIC - THE ADAPTABLE CITY?

Affected by the presence of the Charles de Gaulle Airport, the built fabric of the old village of Goussainville has been frozen for more than 40 years. Because of the Noise Exposure Plan, no new populations are allowed to settle there; and because of the protected perimeter around the church, none of the buildings can be demolished. As a result, numerous buildings are currently walled up, or in an advanced stage of dilapidation. Nonetheless, approximately 300 people still live in the village. Can the old village –as a symbol of the adaptable city, subject to some of the toughest constraints found in the vicinity of a big city– regenerate and restrictions turned into advantages?

CAMILLE LE BIVIC (FR)
FLORENT VIDALING (FR)
ARCHITECTS

RAPHAËL HOYET (FR)
URBANIST
JULIETTE TOUCHAIS (FR)
ARCHITECT

15 AVENUE SIMON BOLIVAR
75020 PARIS, FR
T. +33 646296134 / FLORENT.VIDALING@GMAIL.COM
T. +33 635412117 / CAMILLELEBIVIC@GMAIL.COM

213

WINNER - GOUSSAINVILLE (FR)
Base Vie

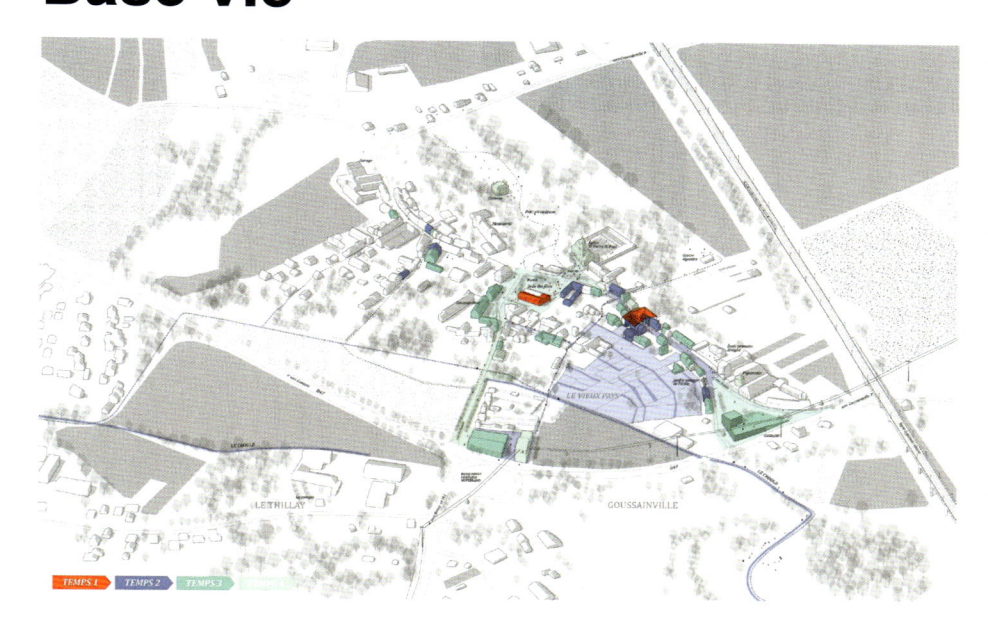

TEAM POINT OF VIEW A support that reinvents and reveals

While the territory adapts to metropolitan changes, the Vieux Pays of Goussainville remains frozen, unable to use or emancipate the global logics to generate desirable urban conditions. The village suffers from airlines noise, the church thanks to its classification as a historical monument saved it, but most inhabitants left. Today, the new metropolitan and local issues bring the village in a privileged position; the Vieux Pays must reinvent itself.

The project is a shelter, the shelter is a worksite, the worksite is collaboration, collaboration is the project.

The project is a shelter protecting from weather and pollution, as supporting local ambitions and initiatives. The shelter is a worksite, connecting the rehabilitation of a historic heritage to the emergence of a sustainable activity within the Vieux Pays. The worksite is collaboration, where actors arrive beforehand and take part to the everyday life of the village, renovating as well as reactivating. Collaboration is the project: it gathers and reveals spatial, social and economic qualities, it adapts the project to events and time, from then it participates in metropolis metamorphosis.

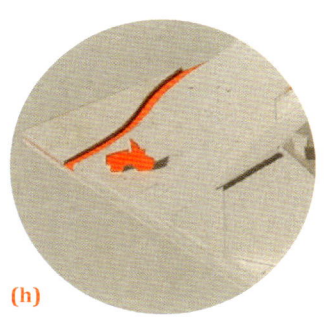

JURY POINT OF VIEW The quality of the project lies in its humanism and the proposal it makes to revitalise the old village: Bringing together people and know how to regenerate and restructure the entire village; Establishing the conditions for intervention on the site with a collaborative and integrated approach. The project is the site works process and the site work is a process of activating a territory; A large, integrative collective construction with a social, community and circular economic perspective.

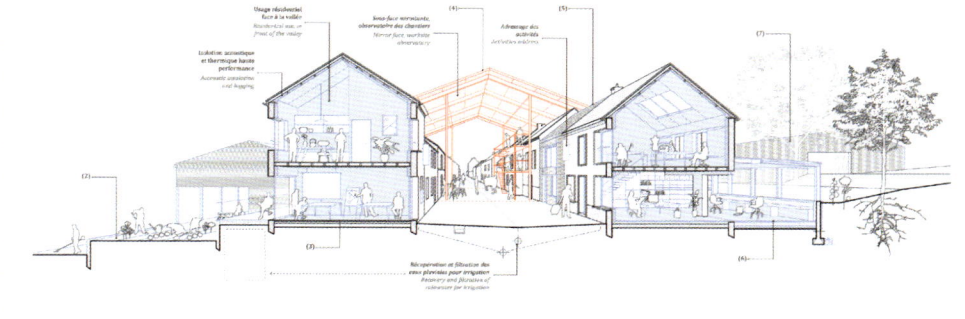

DIANA LEVIN (AT)
SIDONIE BOUILLEROT (FR)
ELODIE BRU (FR)
FRANCOIS RICROS (FR)
ARCHITECTS

LEVIN.D.ARCH@GMAIL.COM

RUNNER-UP - GOUSSAINVILLE (FR)

Des racines et des ailes

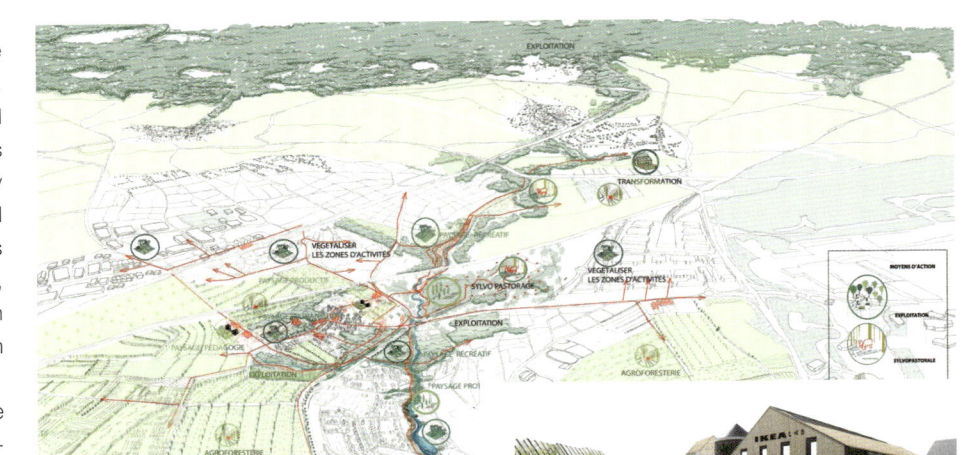

TEAM POINT OF VIEW Goussainville challenges us in the way of a modern Pompeii. We propose to reverse the situation and consider it as a windfall for the inhabitants to reconnect with their territory, particularly affected by disconnections. Economical pressure induced by the airport shows its limits in form of a race of space-consuming projects, resulting in increasing farmland consumption as industrial and commercial follow land push forward.

The village does not strictly belong to the metropolitan corridor, but the noise-pollution-plan moderates land speculation. Emissions produced by the airport contribute to pollution level peaks. To support the securing of land property and the reduction of atmospheric pollution, we propose to develop forestry on a local scale and to let the village shine as a wood-laboratory display.

Goussainville's future implies the foundation of agricultural activities, of the social landscape and natural spaces within the area. Forestry under a much larger angle, our proposal develops within decades and implies a diversified pool of key players. Between city and village, it articulates around 3 objectives: ecology, landscape and production.

As a unifying resource, it persists in time with principles of circular economy and shared governance. While public funding are expected as project instigator, private funding are hoped for to create sustainable connections with all significant players of forest-based activities.

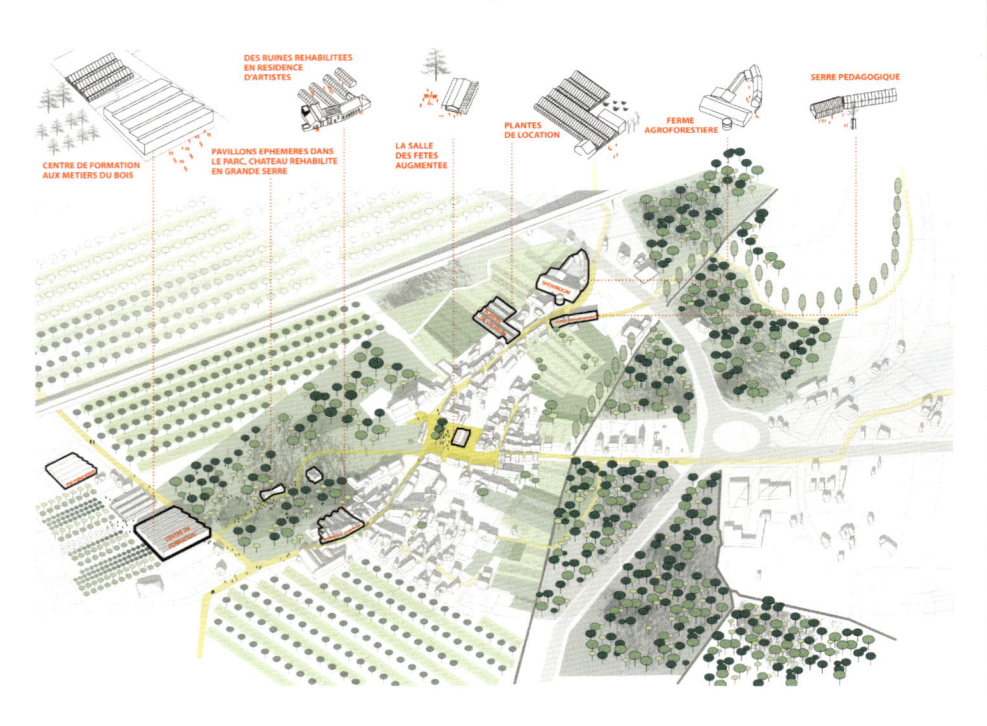

JURY POINT OF VIEW The project is focused on highlighting the landscape as an "active substance". In this way, the wider region of Val d'Oise becomes the locus of the development of the wood industry in Ile de France and Goussainville is its nerve centre, its laboratory. By introducing a set of activities associated with the industry, Goussainville gains not just national impact, but also and above all impact at a regional and local scale, fostering a system of circular economy, opening up areas that are currently mono-functional. The idea is to reconstruct the territory over the long term, to recreate a genuine ecosystem in which the landscape is simultaneously recreational, protective and productive.

GUILLAUME DURANEL (FR)
FRÉDÉRIC BLAISE (FR)
JULIA LENOIR (FR)
ARCHITECTS

GUILLAUME DURANEL
BOITE N°15
14 RUE BOTZARIS
75019 PARIS, FR
T. +33 627117619
GUILLAUMEDURANEL@YAHOO.FR

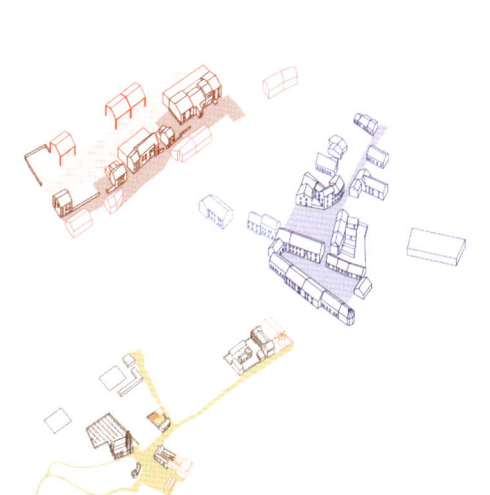

SPECIAL MENTION - GOUSSAINVILLE (FR)
Vieux Pays – Stepping Forward

TEAM POINT OF VIEW The proposal considers Goussainville's traditional features as its beast asset – we therefore take advantage of the existing metropolitan dynamics and turn them into opportunities. We propose a multi-programmatic strategy at different scales. The airport proximity is an opportunity to develop a new type of hotel and apartment-hotel in abandoned houses. The old town can then welcome a craftwork nursery space that could be a way to restore existing buildings. Finally Goussainville's inhabitants are very attached to this part of their town and we propose to develop public equipment that will benefit everyone.

JYVÄSKYLÄ
SUOMI-FINLAND (FI)

CATEGORY: **URBAN - ARCHITECTURAL**
LOCATION: **KORTEPOHJA, JYVÄSKYLÄ**
POPULATION: **135,000 INHAB.**
STRATEGIC SITE: **37 HA**
PROJECT SITE: **3.7 HA**
SITE PROPOSED BY: **CITY OF JYVÄSKYLÄ, THE STUDENT UNION OF THE UNIVERSITY OF JYVÄSKYLÄ JYY, NCC RAKENNUS OY JYVÄSKYLÄ**

OWNER(S) OF THE SITE: **CITY OF JYVÄSKYLÄ, THE STUDENT UNION OF THE UNIVERSITY OF JYVÄSKYLÄ JYY, NCC RAKENNUS OY JYVÄSKYLÄ**
COMMISION AFTER COMPETITION: **COMMISSION AT THE LEVEL OF URBAN PLANNING AND / OR ARCHITECTURAL DESIGN**

Interview of the site's representative

PRESENTATION OF THE SITE WITH REGARDS TO STRATEGY

The city of Jyväskylä is located in the lake district of Central Finland. Jyväskylä´s population growth rate is one of the highest in Finland. With the population of 135,000 the city is the seventh largest in Finland. Jyväskylä is a school and university city –with 47,000 students during the academic year–, providing a diversity of educational offers for people of all ages. The multidisciplinary University of Jyväskylä and the JAMK University of Applied Sciences are among Finland's leading research and educational institutions with an increasing number of international students. The strategy of Jyväskylä is to be a versatile and liveable city with a wide array of housing types and strong neighbourhood centres. Jyväskylä wants to emphasise on a rich and lively city life. The site is in Kortepohja, a 10,000-inhabitants district only 2 km. away from the city centre. There are several student housing buildings located there and over 2,000 students living onsite. The goal is to find creative and innovative solutions to densify and strengthen the vitality of the area without losing its original characteristics and values.

HOW IS THE SITE CONNECTED TO THE SESSION TOPIC - THE ADAPTABLE CITY?

The Northern part of Kortepohja has been listed by DOCOMOMO as one of the nationally significant modern architectural environments in Finland. Bengt Lundsten designed the city plan in 1966 and the area has maintained its original characters until today. The project area to the South is not as coherent as the North, though it follows the same principles: white geometric buildings, large courtyards and green areas between the buildings, car free connections and long internal axis. The objective of the competition is to study how to densify Kortepohja's Southern part reducing the oversized parking areas without losing the original characteristics and values of the area; and how to develop Kortepohja as a vital city district with a more diverse mix of uses.

FREYKE HARTEMINK (NL) - FREYH STUDIO
JARRIK OUBURG (NL) - OFFICE JARRIK OUBURG
MACIEJ ABRAMCZYK (PO)
ARCHITECTS

FREYH STUDIO
DR.JAN VAN BREEMENSTRAAT 1
1056 AB AMSTERDAM, NL
T. +31 618994859
FREYKE@FREYH.NL
WWW.FREYH.NL

WINNER - JYVÄSKYLÄ (FI)
The Nolli Gardens

TEAM POINT OF VIEW Today, with the Internet, individuals become more attached to a virtual collective and less to their physical surroundings. The challenge is to create an attractive local centre where the physical buildings themselves form the catalyst for social integration. Korthepohja's original plan could be described as a series of well-defined objects in an open field, the spatial qualities of which do not always meet the social ones. Our proposal inverts the modernistic scheme. It is the social ambition and public space shaping the buildings.
In 1784 Giambattista Nolli drew a revealing map of Rome. He represented enclosed public spaces, such as the interior of the Pantheon, as open civic spaces. For a community open and shared spaces offer inhabitants a mutable appropriation. The new 4/5-story student building encloses a communal square. On the upper levels the apartments face either the garden or the street. The communal corridor is interrupted by the shared 'Nolli Gardens', breaking the long vista, and adding collective program and social interaction to the common space. The building for the elderly is 3-story high and encloses a garden. The apartments face both street and the communal space that doubles as the access to the apartments. This communal space is a winter garden and is programmed with communal activities. A supermarket and a restaurant are located on the ground floor and a 1-story underground parking garage completes the building.

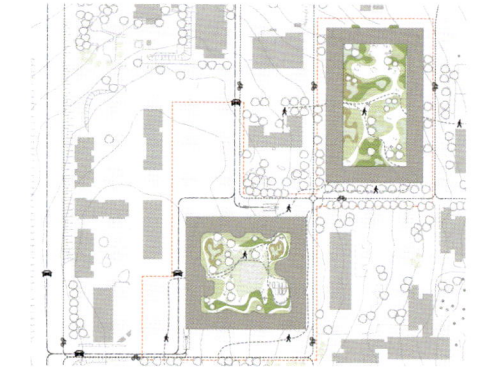

JURY POINT OF VIEW The blocks of the competition area are demarcated by a strong gesture in the form of entities that respect the old street network and leave it unaltered. The design is based on a distinct student block and a corresponding central block. A particular attention was given to the courtyard as a place for social encounter. By analysing the life between the buildings within the overall structure and architecture of the site, the proposal offers a strong new concept for a communal environment.

RIIKKA KUITTINEN (FI)
MIIA MÄKINEN (FI)
VIRVE VÄISÄNEN (FI)
ARCHITECTS

LUO ARKKITEHDIT
PAKKAHUONEENKATU 12
90100 OULU, FI
T. +358 503596113
INFO@LUOARKKITEHDIT.FI
WWW.LUOARKKITEHDIT.FI

RUNNER-UP - JYVÄSKYLÄ (FI)
New Kids on the Blocks

JURY POINT OF VIEW The project proposes infill building with multi-storey blocks. The approach is sensitive and subtle, consciously avoiding grand gestures. Rhythm, condensation and densification changes mainly work well within the totality. The structure is smaller in scale than at present and would in places be able to cope with even taller buildings. The pedestrian landscape and its surroundings are pleasant due to the alternating dot-like building masses, low yard buildings and openings between the buildings.

TEAM POINT OF VIEW Kortepohja is a mix of rigid straight-lined buildings and lush greenery with wild topography. Buildings are situated in a rectangular way and greenery runs wild, connecting the Kypärämäki and Tuomijärvi green areas through the competition area. New urban focus points are created while the relaxed openess and flow of space is maintained. Inspiration and principles are also found from the DOCOMOMO listed blocks in Kortepohja.

The new square emphasises on Kortepohja's position as a regional centre by creating a clear urban focal point for the area. New types of active urban places are introduced. A supermarket is situated on an illuminated hybrid building containing commercial space and parking. Half of the parking is situated under a deck bordering Kortepohja Square.

Old student buildings are replaced with medium scale housing and student apartments are organized in resilient units. Building volumes lower down and the social intensity rises towards the middle of the block. A long housing block, 'Carved Block', is placed directly on the square. The rich variety of outdoor and common spaces and proximity of services makes the block very suitable for senior citizens and also families. Adaptable 'Flexi Houses' are situated on the decks connecting Kortepohja Square and Sloping Park. Spatial changes can be made very easily by closing and opening doors and building or turning down only one wall.

ASKE HAGENBØL HANSEN (DK)
CHRISTOPHER GALLIANO (DK)
MORTEN VESTBERG HANSEN (DK)

HARALDSGADE 27, 1.TH
2200 COPENHAGEN, DK
T. +45 26466964
FOLKARKITEKTER@GMAIL.COM
WWW.FOLKARKITEKTER.DK

ALBERT PALAZON (ES)
ARCHITECT

LEA VILLALBA (UY)
RAUL ÁLVAREZ (ES)
ARCHITECTS

CARRER ROSSELLÓ 157-159, 6E 2A
08036 BARCELONA, ES
ALBERTPALAZON@GMAIL.COM

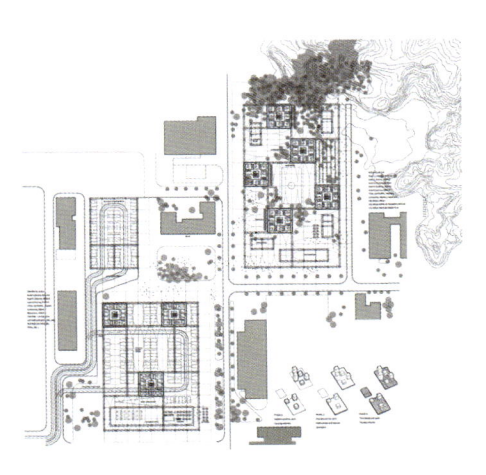

SPECIAL MENTION - JYVÄSKYLÄ (FI)
Exchange City

TEAM POINT OF VIEW The masterplan is a high-dense urban structure. We propose a scale decomposition that creates outdoor spaces with various spatial possibilities. The buildings are constructed in locally sourced timber with a flexible and protective white steel facade. As an overall social strategy for Kortepohja we suggest to transform all parking lots into active parking garages –hubs– each with a public function. These hubs are programmed and used by people from all over Jyväskylä. All the hubs are designed to be as flexible as possible to ensure new programs can be implemented over time.

SPECIAL MENTION - JYVÄSKYLÄ (FI)
Fog

TEAM POINT OF VIEW A vertical structure: a 3-dimensional grid that can host a wide variety of situations while proposing a new growth system. A white concrete frame and a clean vertical core generate free floor plans to fill with any program. These vertical structures can grow in height, according to their context, surroundings, views and orientation: a new rich and complex skyline. An etfe semi-transparent foil covers the base of the towers creating a greenhouse effect over the green public areas, right around the new intervention. A warmer microclimate with an open attitude to the city.

MATTEO BIASIOLO (IT)
MARKUS VON DELLINGSHAUSEN (DE)
ARCHITECTS

TIM BACHELLER (US)
ARCHITECT

MAT.BIASIO@GMAIL.COM
WWW.OCD.WORKS

SPECIAL MENTION - JYVÄSKYLÄ (FI)

Tree Village

TEAM POINT OF VIEW We propose a group of "trees" as a new landmark and gathering point for the area of Kortepohja. As a hybrid of urbanism and Finnish landscape, our project is a link between the natural and the constructed. Our strategy is a loose and flexible repetition of modules that can easily integrate with existing urban fabrics as balanced infill housing providing living, communal and outdoor spaces. An on-going process of additions into the interstitial spaces of the neighbourhood, the densification and development of plots can easily be subdivided into different phases in strict relation with the use of existing buildings.

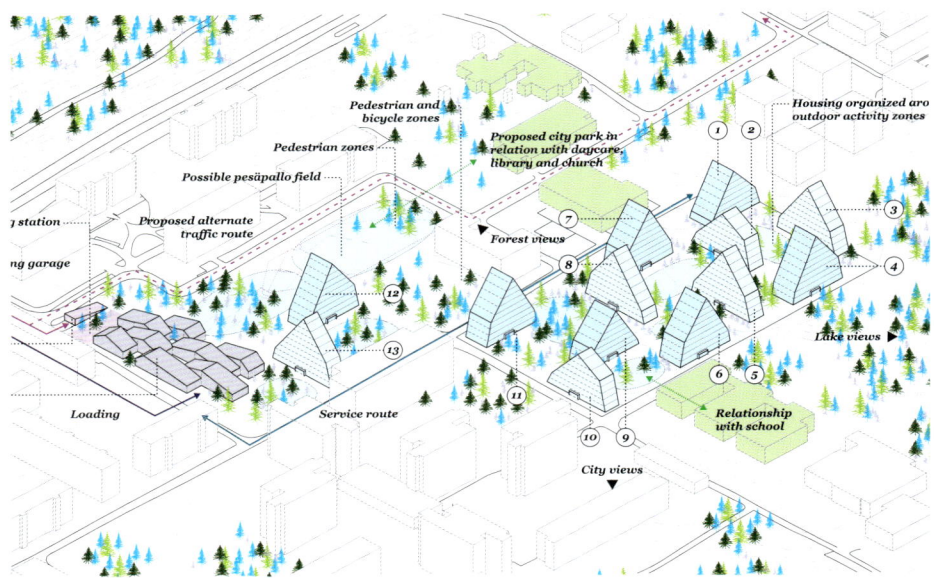

LA CORRÈZE
FRANCE (FR)

CATEGORY: **URBAN - ARCHITECTURAL**
LOCATION: **TURENNE - ARGENTAT - USSEL**
POPULATION: **TURENNE 822 INHAB. - ARGENTAT 3,016 INHAB. - USSEL 9,948 INHAB.**
STRATEGIC SITE: **TURENNE 28 SQKM - ARGENTAT 22 SQKM - USSEL 50 SQKM**
PROJECT SITE: **TURENNE 14 HA - ARGENTAT 0.8 HA - USSEL 2 HA**

SITE PROPOSED BY: **MUNICIPALITIES OF TURENNE, ARGENTAT AND USSEL WITH SUPPORT OF CORRÈZE DEPARTMENTAL STATE SERVICES (DIRECTION DÉPARTEMENTALE DES TERRITOIRES 19)**
OWNER(S) OF THE SITE: **DIFFERENT OWNERS**
COMMISION AFTER COMPETITION: **DÉPARTEMENT SCALE WORKSHOPS, CONSULTANCY ROLES, PREOPERATIONAL URBAN STUDIES, DESIGN AND PROJECT MANAGEMENT WITH PARTNERS**

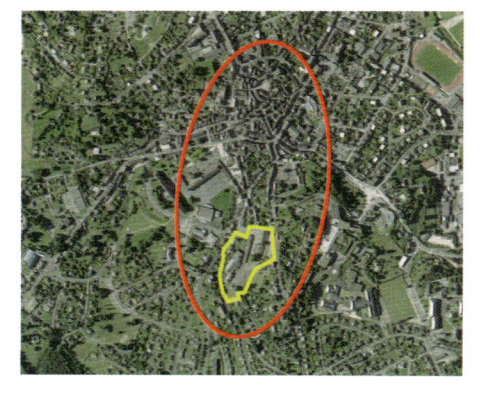

Interview of the site's representative

PRESENTATION OF THE SITE WITH REGARDS TO STRATEGY

Three sites are proposed in Corrèze: Ussel, Argentat and Turenne. The Municipality wishes to rethink their approaches to development and is looking for urban and architectural innovation with shared objectives: to consolidate their historical centres and nuclei; to maintain amenities and services; to offer new housing conditions suited to new ways of living and working in rural areas; to reintroduce contemporary forms of housing into the existing fabric; to optimise their landscape and tourist potential; and to establish a better dialogue between traditional and contemporary architecture.

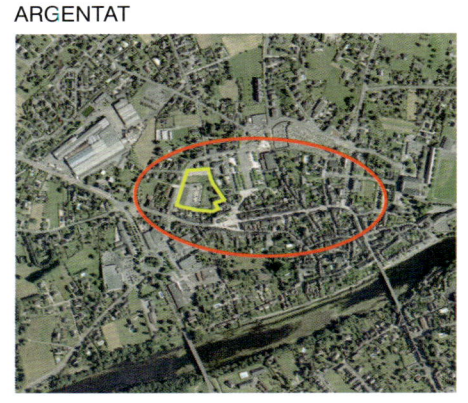

HOW IS THE SITE CONNECTED TO THE SESSION TOPIC - THE ADAPTABLE CITY?

The continuous polarization into big cities, where investment and innovation are concentrated, raises questions about the future of rural spaces situated outside areas of metropolitan influence. It masks the difficulties of huge areas made up of shrinking communities, villages and towns in rural sectors. How can we reintroduce the question of the future of the countryside into the debates on urban transformations and changing ways of life? How can these territories adapt and resist the effects of demographic shrinkage, population ageing and economic decline?
Apart from raising the question of adaptation, the three sites in Corrèze more broadly call for a contemporary conception of rurality in terms of habitat and lifestyles, activities and services, project production and alternative modes of development.

ALEXANDRE DUBURE (FR)
THOMAS NOUAILLER (FR)
JENNY REUILLARD (FR)
ARCHITECTS

2 RUE DU CHAROLAIS
75012 PARIS, FR
ALEXANDRE.DUBURE@GMAIL.COM

WINNER - LA CORRÈZE (FR)
Clubhouses

TEAM POINT OF VIEW The Clubhouses project proposes to develop a network across the territory of La Corrèze. These built places, "Corrèze-houses" are activators to establish a project culture on each site. As the figure of a spiral that can extend keeping the same shape every time, this project culture is based on the search on each site for simple urban and completely adaptable structures, which regulates the scale, the programs and their operational modes resolutions over time. Their definition is different in each site: a cultural house in Ussel; a welcoming place for future residents of cooperative housing in Turenne; and ownership and existing management (the constructions, public spaces , soils) by residents in Argentat. The houses must also allow returning, disseminating and expanding approaches.

They allow new associations, born of clubs that gather different skills around a common goal. These clubs are evolving and new practices emerge in turn enrich this project culture. The response of the project simply proposes a framework: the establishment of responses to both pragmatic and innovative in these territories accepting the paradoxes and diverting them. The role of designers is for us to leverage the adhesion surfaces between places and people.

JURY POINT OF VIEW The basis of the project is the installation of a network of "Maisons Corrèze", that can be reproduced in other villages appropriately to each context: cultural cooperative in Ussel, co-working craft centre artisanal in Argentat, village hall in Turenne. The image of the clubhouse is reinterpreted and adapted to the small village context. The project proposes several housing scenarios for small cooperative housing programs carefully embedded in the existing fabric. The section drawings express relations of proximity and interactions with public space.

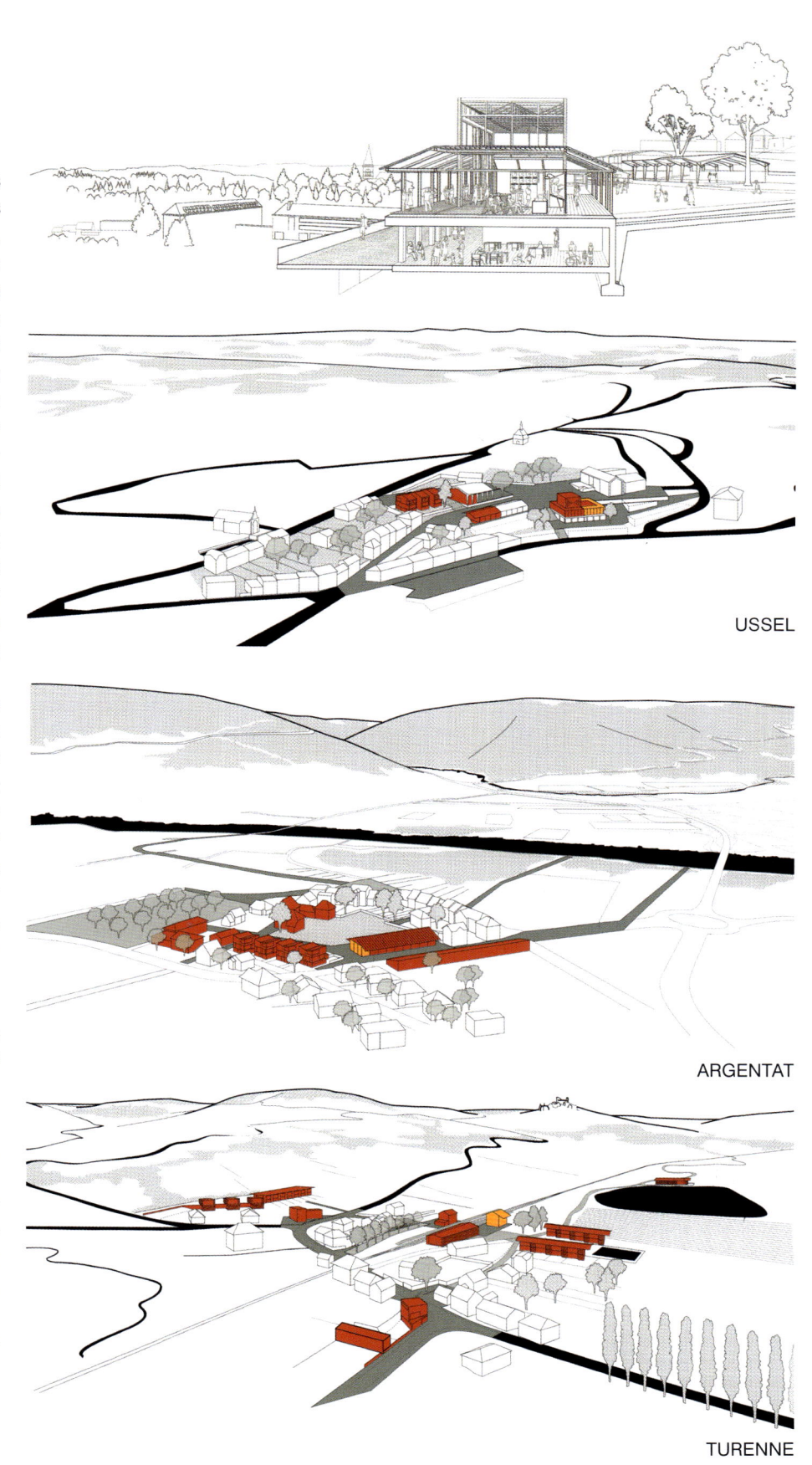

USSEL

ARGENTAT

TURENNE

YASMINE GAIZI (FR)
VICTOR MIOT (FR)
JEANNE MOULLET (FR)
ARCHITECTS

ARCHIPEL - ARCHITECTS ASSOCIATION
T. YG: +33 611260785
T. VM: +33 612540487
T. JM: +33 680559506
CONTACT@ARCHIPEL-AA.COM
WWW.ARCHIPEL-AA.COM

WINNER - LA CORRÈZE (FR)
Sharing Islands

TEAM POINT OF VIEW How to wake up the inhabitant as "citizens" instead of addressing them as "consumers" in rural areas? The quality of "community life" depends as much on reinventing of rural urbanity as on the inhabitants' re-appropriation of the rural space in the long term. Starting from a reflection on "sharing scale" we outline an altruist approach to rural urbanity as an alternative to individualistic centrality. The "sharing scales" intensify social interactions and re-locate the citizen's actions and behaviours in the midst of its territory. Catalysts create a frame for sharing based on citizens' initiatives and programmatic dialogue. In so, we re-define living conditions in abandoned downtown areas and prepare for the emergence of a new urban tissue. The hatching of scattered islands on a case-by-case basis creates urban development possibilities reflective of the picturesque aspect of each village. The ambition of establishing a "sharing" archipelago purports to re-invent "community life" in rural cities; in the old town, the original housing estate and the more recent suburban houses, which currently do not co-exist, will meet again.

JURY POINT OF VIEW The project draws on the trope of the archipelago as its structural principle, applied at small scales. Project sites/islands are identified in each village's territory beyond the Europan sites alone. Each site is made up of several islands connected together. Four types of island are distinguished: Residential island, mixed island, amenities island, village centre island. The imaginative concept of the island governs of the architectural form, in which shared spaces are everywhere, conceived as catalysts of uses and sociability.

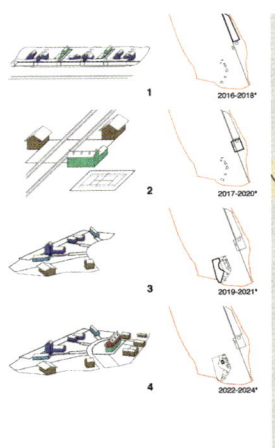

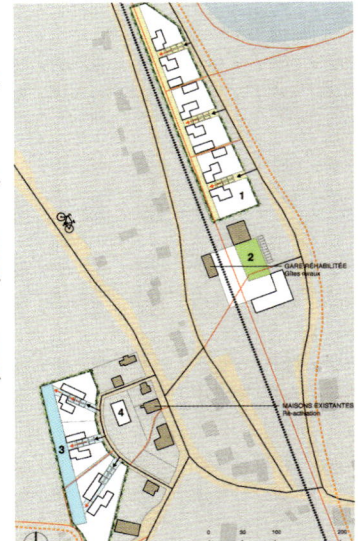

VALLEY ISLANDS - TURENNE

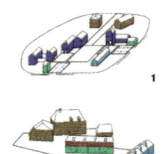

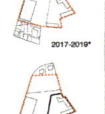

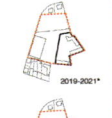

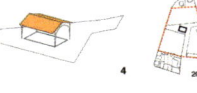

VILLAGE CENTRE ISLANDS - ARGENTAT

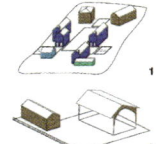

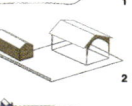

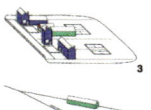

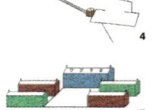

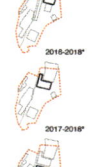

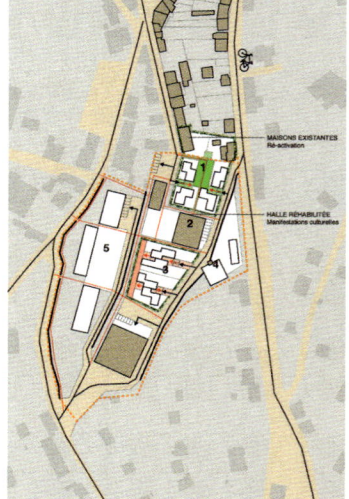

POINT OF VIEW ISLANDS - USSEL

PAULINE MARCOMBE (FR)
MAJED KATIR (FR)
ARCHITECTS

PMMK ARCHITECTES
T. +33 750493650
PMMKARCHITECTES@GMAIL.COM
HTTP://CARGOCOLLECTIVE.COM/PMMK

SPECIAL MENTION - LA CORRÈZE (FR)

New Nomads

TEAM POINT OF VIEW "New Nomads" sees an opportunity in combining the desires of a generation constrained by the limitations of urban living and an ageing "rural" population suffering from the effects of urban migration to create a new solution. Turenne, Argentat and Ussel would provide residencies to progress personal projects. In turn, this would help create new industry, educational and agricultural developments whilst advancing existing structures that help restore the village centres as desirable. Instead of a "disconnected tourism", "New Nomads" injects an optimistic population to reboot an unrealised potential.

LINZ
ÖSTERREICH (AT)

CATEGORY: **URBAN - ARCHITECTURAL**
LOCATION: **LINZ**
POPULATION: **198,500 INHAB.**
STRATEGIC SITE: **19 HA**
PROJECT SITE: **1: 2.4 HA / 2: 0.3 HA / 3: 6.7 HA / 4: 1.2 HA**
SITE PROPOSED BY: **WAG & CITY OF LINZ**

OWNER(S) OF THE SITE: **WAG WOHNUNGSANLAGEN GES.M.B.H.**
COMMISION AFTER COMPETITION: **URBAN PROJECT MANAGEMENT ROLE, DESIGN OF PUBLIC AND LANDSCAPE AREAS, FURTHER INVOLVEMENT IN ARCHITECTURAL FOLLOW-UP PROCEDURES**

Interview of the site's representative

Wolfgang Schön, Director of WAG Wohnungsanlagen GesmbH.
Gunter Kolouch, Department of Urban Planning, City of Linz

PRESENTATION OF THE SITE WITH REGARDS TO STRATEGY

Housing archaeology of the post-war modernist era in Linz-Oed calls for a re-appropriation of public space. It is an opportunity to rediscover the history of housing, to jointly re-appropriate characteristic in-between spaces by acupuncture interventions, to combine housing and working in a new centre-typology and to reflect on new articulations of the future road space and its network.

HOW IS THE SITE CONNECTED TO THE SESSION TOPIC - THE ADAPTABLE CITY?

The result of the Europan 13 competition shall provide a strategic urban masterplan to transform the adjacent in-between spaces of the residential area (Ps3) through punctual interventions, improving the existing qualities in the central public area of Europastraße (Ps4), therefore connecting the two poles on which we focus: the new mixed-use centre-building complex with attractive public space (Ps1) and the entrée-building typology to attract attention and urbanize the corner (Ps2).

DID YOU DEFINE A SPECIFIC PROCESS FOR THE URBAN DEVELOPMENT OF THE SITE AFTER EUROPAN COMPETITION?

WAG Wohnungsanlagen GmbH will implement important urban planning measures to improve living quality in Linz-Oed over the next few years. Plans have been made to commission the winning Europan team with the mixed-use centre-building complex by rebuilding the outdated shopping centre. The scope of commission has yet to be defined. Implementation starts in 2017 with the demolition of the shopping centre. The building of the mixed-use centre-building complex (Ps1) will start in 2018. The building of the entrée-building typology (Ps2) will start at the end of 2018. The renovation of the Albert-Schöpf residential area will take place between 2017 and 2021.

BENNI EDER (AT)
THERESA KRENN (AT)
ARCHITECTS

STUDIO UEK
PERNERSTORFERGASSE 5/B4
1100 VIENNA, AT
T. +43 16003843
OFFICE@STUDIO-UEK.COM
WWW.STUDIO-UEK.COM

WINNER - LINZ (AT)
All Tomorrow's Parties

TEAM POINT OF VIEW Öd presents a well-preserved picture of the development of subsidized housing of the last 50 years. The spatial macrostructure of the area appears as an assemblage of islands: large residential areas of the 70s, 80s and 10s, enclosed school campus and open area of social infrastructures. The idea is to understand the district as a network of manifold collectives, overlapping and interfering on both their territories and characteristics. The project aims at identifying, strengthening and connecting the collectives through participative processes on the islands inner areas, and projective spatial interventions on the borders.
The interventions –from the size of one parking lot to the size of a square– carry in themselves the scenario of sharing and belonging as well as the one of change. In order to install these interventions, the project follows a certain storyline: identifying and exposing existing and resilient structural elements both built and landscaped, making use of their spatial qualities, re-interpreting and enriching the elements programmatically.

JURY POINT OF VIEW The project proposes a simple concept and detailed answers of all tasks in the competition brief. Both urban integration (layout of individual buildings and height development) and architectonic formulations (arrangement of functions, innovative adaptable housing floor plans and addressing of underrepresented user groups) clearly answer the task. The project also proposes positive approaches just like the creation of a central place, connections to Albert Schöpf Siedlung development, porosity of the dam and the parking space with an integrated skatepark playground.

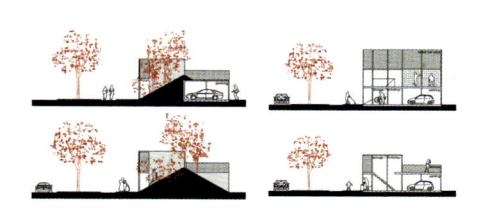

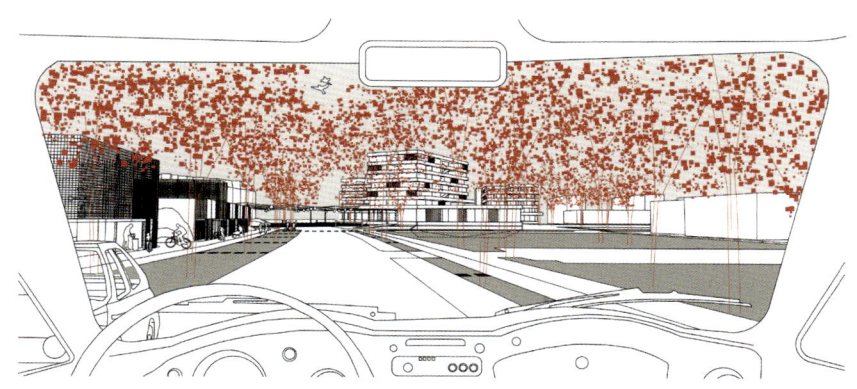

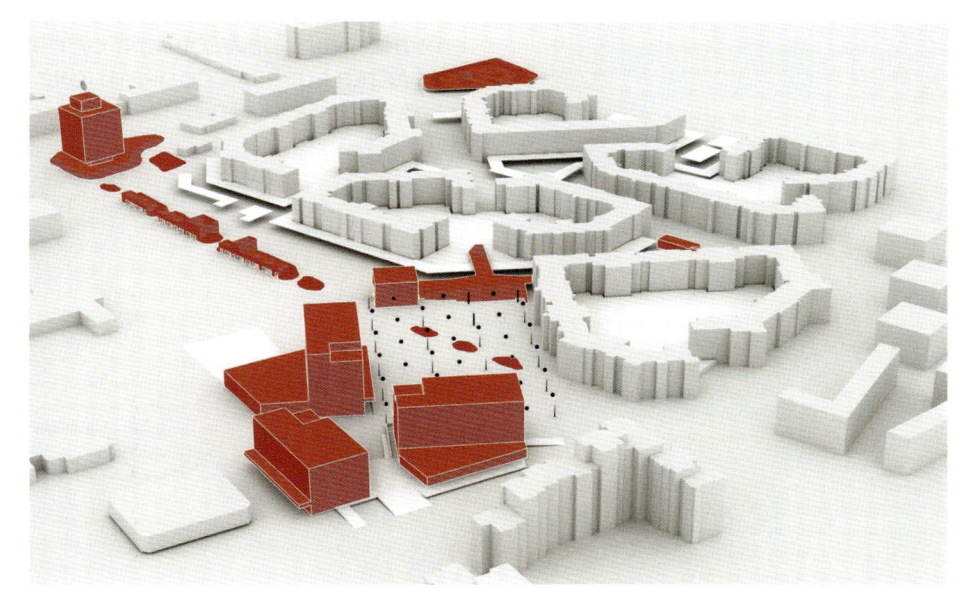

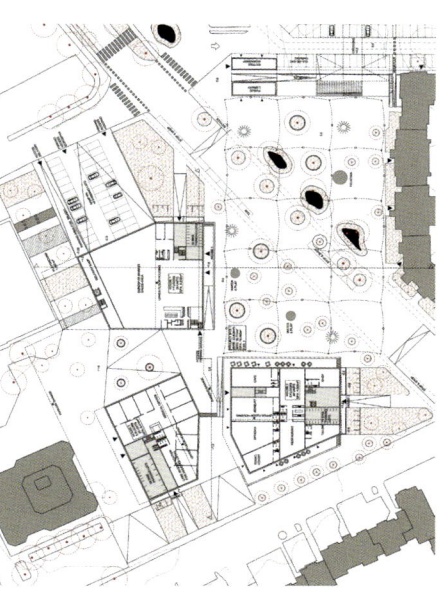

SOFÍA SOLÁNS (ES)
MARÍA VASALLO (ES)
ISABEL SÁNCHEZ (ES)
ARCHITECTS

SARA SOLÁNS (ES)
PSYCHOLOGIST

1 CALLE SANTA CRUZ DE MARCENADO
28015 MADRID, ES
T. +34 658766204
WWW.MADTEAMARCHSTUDIO.WIX.COM

SPECIAL MENTION - LINZ (AT)

LinkingLinz

TEAM POINT OF VIEW The project proposes a change in the perception of planning linked to new value systems and communication tools in our society.

In Linz, there is a great need to give the inhabitants a leading role in the development of the city. To achieve this goal, the urban strategy will be developed in stages: it is first proposed to create a mobile app (LinkingLinz) for citizenship involvement. Then, once the communication between inhabitants is established, the urban strategy can take place in the neighbourhood.

MARL
DEUTSCHLAND (DE)

CATEGORY: **URBAN - LANDSCAPE - ARCHITECTURAL**
LOCATION: **AUGUSTE VICTORIA COLLIERY SHAFT 3/7**
POPULATION: **86,000 INHAB.**
STRATEGIC SITE: **AUGUSTE VICTORIA 3/7 AND SURROUNDINGS**

PROJECT SITE: **90 HA**
SITE PROPOSED BY: **RAG MONTAN IMMOBILIEN GMBH**
OWNER(S) OF THE SITE: **RAG AG**
COMMISION AFTER COMPETITION:
WHEN INDICATED, OUTLINE URBAN AND LANDSCAPE PLAN

Interview of the site's representative
Dr. Manfred Gehrke, Head of the department for business development, City of Marl

PRESENTATION OF THE SITE WITH REGARDS TO STRATEGY
Since the closing of the Bergwerk Auguste Victoria (AV), the city has been planning along with RAG Montan Immobilien GmbH to develop the grounds of the AV 3/7 mining pit for the settlement of commercial and industrial enterprises. New businesses with a total of one thousand new workplaces are supposed to be created on the site. The site is particularly suitable for companies from the logistics sector as a result of the direct proximity to the autobahn, the existing rail connection and the port on the Wesel-Datteln Canal.

HOW IS THE SITE CONNECTED TO THE SESSION TOPIC - THE ADAPTABLE CITY?
One primary goal is to create as many workplaces as possible onsite. For this, a functional urban planning concept is in development in order to be able to react to inquiries from potential users with a great deal of flexibility.

DID YOU DEFINE A SPECIFIC PROCESS FOR THE URBAN DEVELOPMENT OF THE SITE AFTER EUROPAN COMPETITION?
The concrete possible uses are currently being determined within the framework of an in-depth feasibility study. The development of the site should take place directly after the completion of the feasibility study at the end of 2017.

ELENA FUERTES GONZÁLEZ (ES)
RAMÓN MARTÍNEZ PÉREZ (ES)
JORGE SOBEJANO NIETO (ES)
ARCHITECTS

ÁLVARO MOLINS JIMÉNEZ (ES)
LEDO PÉREZ VÁZQUEZ (ES)
STUDENTS IN ARCHITECTURE

TALLER DE CASQUERÍA
GLORIETA DE BILBAO 1, 4° IZQUIERDA
28004 MADRID, ES
T. +34 917958877
HOLA@CASQUERIA-CASQUERIA.COM
WWW.TALLERDECASQUERIA.COM

WINNER - MARL (DE)
WEEE Marl!

TEAM POINT OF VIEW Contemporary mining categorizes certain materials as "specially relevant" due to the relation between resource shortage and high demand. Nowadays most of them are Rare Earth materials, the worldwide demand of which has vastly increased from 1,000 to 150,000 tons a year between 1953 and 2012. China is currently the main producer with over 37% of the natural deposits and 97% of the global production. Most of the extraction companies are settled there. European countries are forced to import 100% of its Rare Earth needs, although part of the most important sectors in the current Occidental economy require high amounts of it for its production processes. Europe, the US and Japan are the biggest Electronic and Electronical Equipment (EEE) consumers worldwide. This process obviously generates an enormous amount of waste called WEEE - Waste Electrical and Electronic Equipment. WEEE will increase in the coming decades with an expected rate of a least 4% per year. We propose to develop a WEEE-Treatment station in Marl, willing to become the leading initiative in Europe.

JURY POINT OF VIEW The project introduces a consistent solution, particularly for a reprogramming of the site: Coal mining is supposed to be succeeded by urban mining: an economic concept of recycling electronic devices and components. It not only provides realistic work perspectives for former miners, but also perspectives to transform Marl into a new hub of a modern closed-loop economy. The project is positively assessed as an innovative approach to the subsequent use of a former industrial site even if the spatial manifestation remains open and requires further processing.

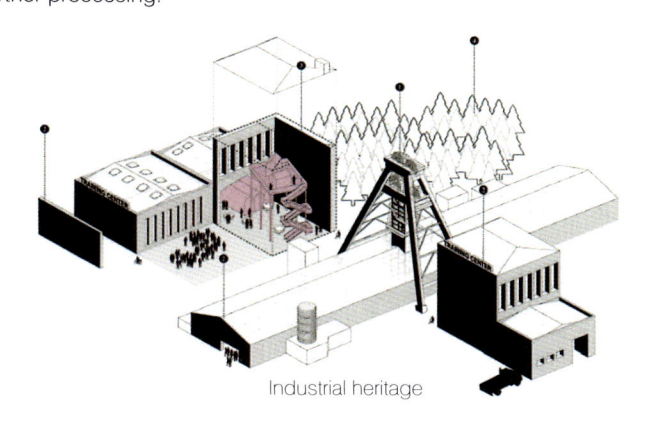

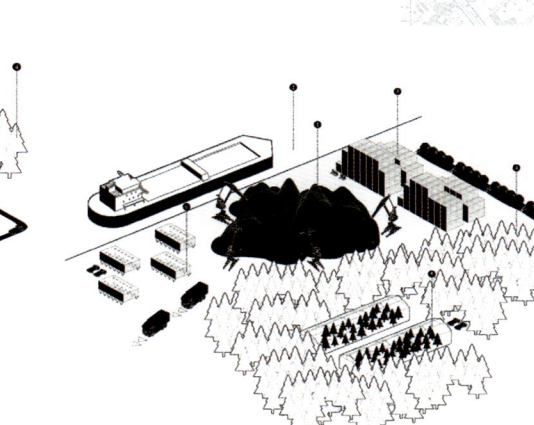

Industrial heritage

Mixed scale system

New landscapes

FRANCESCO CECCARELLI (IT)
DAVIDE AGOSTINI (IT)
MATTEO BATTISTINI (IT)
STEVE CAMAGNI (IT)
ALESSIO VALMORI (IT)
ARCHITECTS
SARA ANGELINI (IT)
ENGINEER-ARCHITECT

GIULIA DALL'AGATA (IT)
INTERIOR ARCHITECT

LAPRIMASTANZA
VIA GUALDARELLI 385
47025 MONTIANO, IT
T. +39 3405914080
LAPRIMASTANZA@GMAIL.COM
WWW.LAPRIMASTANZA.COM

RUNNER-UP - MARL (DE)

GReen-GRay Factor

TEAM POINT OF VIEW GReen-GRay factor is a process based on the "sensing the spirit of entrepreneurship" motto and defined in 4 steps:
-1- Cleaning_reducing ground contamination by planting species able to dismantle metals; these fast-growing plants can easily be cut and replanted in a very cheap but very profitable loop; a small initial investment for a long run profit!;
-2- Connecting_preserving and reinforcing the existing links by creating a solid and robust four-mode transport/traffic connection so that any project line offers supraregional accessibility;
-3- Flexible phasing_arranging a hardcore rectangular platform, a gray grid of axes and streets in which plots can be freely set along the X and Y axes to develop the new logistic district; this process could lead to very different final set-ups;
-4- Bonding_giving the opportunity to every company involved to take out of the grid elements that could interfere with the logistic process while maximizing the plot surface for specific productive purpose. The outside space is called the green filter; it acts as a pollution/noise barrier, a resilient and sustainable landscape and the main area for waste management and worker/administration parking areas. Sharing this space means minimizing costs and maximizing profits. Gray energy is produced inside the platform, and green energy outside. This is a chemical reaction between the "metallic" grid and the "oxygen" green.

JURY POINT OF VIEW The project proposes a stable frameset for process-oriented and long-term reactivation. The design therefore proposes a clearly delineated rectangular area for the development of different industries and dimensions surrounded by a green space. The design represents an intelligent solution even if the question of a new program for the site remains unanswered.

AMADO MARTÍN (ES)
SAMUEL LLOVET (ES)
LUIS BELLERA (ES)
DANIEL BURSTON (GB)
ARCHITECTS

JPAM ARCHITECTURE & URBAN DESIGN
C/PAMPLONA 9N, 2 5A
08018 BARCELONA, ES
T. +34 933208801
JPAM@JPAM.EU
WWW.JPAM.EU

SPECIAL MENTION - MARL (DE)

The Spine

TEAM POINT OF VIEW The Spine is based on the reinforcement and clarification of the existing structure and spatial organization of the Auguste Victoria Mine 3/7. Without depending on or compromising the existing buildings and open spaces, the recognition and development of the transversal streets as the main structural element will allow future uses to be positioned with great flexibility, maximizing opportunities and minimizing costs. The proposal aims to break the segregated condition of production areas towards an integrated model, blurring the perception and definition of borders.

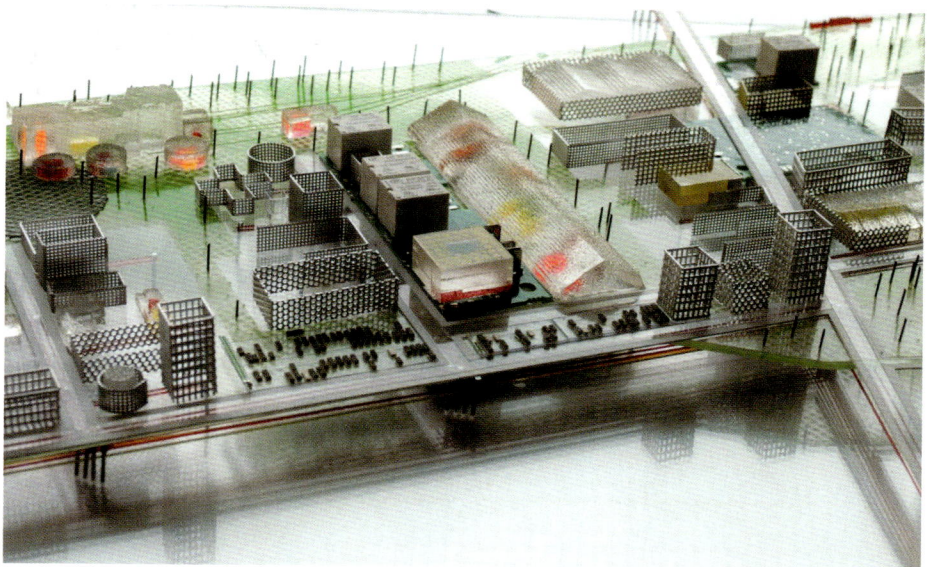

ØRSTA
NORGE (NO)

CATEGORY: **URBAN - ARCHITECTURAL**
LOCATION: **ØRSTA, MØRE OG ROMSDAL**
POPULATION: **10,500 INHAB.**
STRATEGIC SITE: **99 HA**
PROJECT SITE: **13.5 HA**

SITE PROPOSED BY: **ØRSTA MUNICIPALITY (IN COLLABORATION WITH MØRE AND ROMSDAL COUNTY)**
OWNER(S) OF THE SITE: **ØRSTA MUNICIPALITY AND PRIVATE SITE OWNERS**
COMMISION AFTER COMPETITION: **PLANNING COMMISSION**

Interview of the site's representative
Gunnar Wangen, Head of Planning and Environment Department
Europan Norway

PRESENTATION OF THE SITE WITH REGARDS TO STRATEGY
Though encompassed in beauty, Ørsta suffers from being in the hinterlands of the more prosperous Sunnmøre Coast to the west. Ørsta is facing a historical possibility to rethink its urban centre when the municipal plan from the 80's is being reassessed. The old plan suggested routing E39 along the coast of Ørsta, seizing valuable land and paralyzed development in the centre of the town for over 20 years. Through participating in Europan 13, the municipality of Ørsta and the county of Møre and Romsdal joined forces in the quest of rediscovering and revitalizing the centre of Ørsta and strengthening its position in the region of Søre Sunnmøre.

HOW IS THE SITE CONNECTED TO THE SESSION TOPIC - THE ADAPTABLE CITY?
Centrally located in the heart of the town centre the Europan site has the possibility to improve urban life and better connect the central areas in Ørsta and the site to the public functions within the study area. The Europan process has generated great local engagement and many inhabitants of Ørsta are already volunteering in the process of renovating and reactivating the town centre.

DID YOU DEFINE A SPECIFIC PROCESS FOR THE URBAN DEVELOPMENT OF THE SITE AFTER EUROPAN COMPETITION?
Europan 13 in Ørsta has so far been a success story. The municipality is determined to use the winning project as a point of departure for a new master plan for the town centre, starting in the fall of 2016. The municipality will engage the winning team in making the supporting documents for the plan based on their project Connecting Ørsta. The municipality is also interested in inviting the other awarded teams to a participatory workshop in Ørsta.

JENS NYBOE ANDERSEN (DK)
KARL JOHAN BAGGINS (DK)
LANDSCAPE ARCHITECTS
MARIA CRAMMOND (DK)
ARCHITECT

KRONPRINSESSEGADE 10, 3 TV
1306 KØBENHAVN K, DK
T. +45 40504948
JENSNYBOEANDERSEN@GMAIL.COM
KARLJOHANBAGGINS@GMAIL.COM
MARIACRAMMOND@GMAIL.COM

WINNER - ØRSTA (NO)
Connecting Ørsta

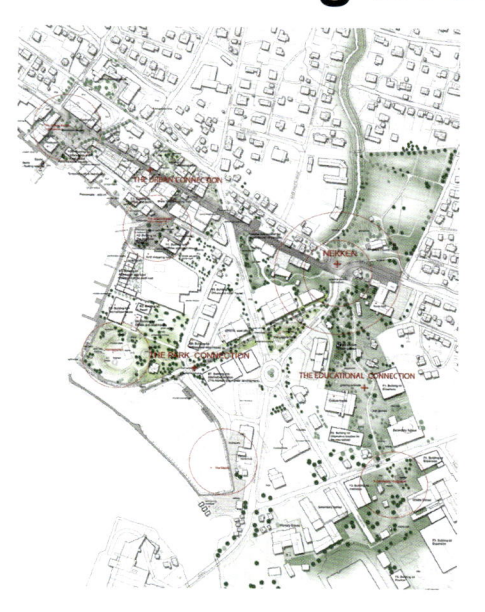

TEAM POINT OF VIEW The main concept of the project is to establish clear connections and identities in Ørsta. Today Ørsta consists in many small and unconnected 'islands', functioning internally, but not as a whole, inhibiting the city 's flow. In our proposal the city centre consists in 3 main connections:
- The Urban Connection links together the Culture Square, Vikegata, the Market Square, Nekken and the administrative centre at Ørsta City Hall. The connection with the squares, the dense city scale and commercial and cultural facilities gives it a clear urban character.
- The Park Connection runs from Hamneparken all the way to Nekken. The park typology is the structuring element – parking and infrastructure are designed with a green character.
- The Educational Connection runs from Nekken to Ørsta Stadium. Education is the structuring element with playgrounds, institutions, schools, stadiums and community houses. The connection ties the institutions together and provides with the opportunity to meet across ages. Besides, the Harbour Promenade binds the 3 main connections together and crosswise. We suggest a promenade as an Add-On to the existing quay. A cold and warm seawater swimming pool, inspired by a Japanese Sento, is placed by the Culture Square – a quiet, yet ambitious urban landmark of Ørsta. The Harbour Promenade is the physical link between Ørsta city centre and the sea.

JURY POINT OF VIEW The project shows a good understanding of the local challenges and the scale of the town. It proposes to create a new spatial hierarchy in Ørsta by establishing three new main connections across the central areas: the urban connection, the park connection and the educational connection. While the urban and the park connection propose structural interventions, the educational connection proposes a new programmatic rearrangement strengthening the relations between the schools, the cultural house and the town centre. The project can become an effective planning tool for the city, both in a short- and long-term perspective.

ANDERS LIISBERG LARSEN (DK)
ANNE-RAGNHILD LARSEN (NO)
ANNE-METTE HJØLLUND (DK)
CHRISTIAN STAHLFEST HOLCK SKOV (DK)
JAN LOERAKKER (NL)
LEA OLSSON (DK)
LOUISE DEDENROTH HØJ (DK)
RIE DAVIDSEN (DK)
ARCHITECTS

STUEN
ROSENBORGGADE 19
1302 KØBENHAVN K, DK
STUEN@STUENARCHITECTS.COM

RUNNER-UP - ØRSTA (NO)
Urban by Nature

TEAM POINT OF VIEW Ørsta has the potential to become an urban centre in the region of Søre Sunnmøre. The city has a strong retail position and a natural surrounding that is attractive to families. It is in the combination of these qualities that "Urban by Nature" envisions Ørsta in the future: an intensified natural setting that creates urbanity, enhances shopping conditions and attracts new inhabitants to the urban core.

The green-urban structure of Ørsta is optimized by 3 strategic interventions: a) a high-quality residential area along the water front; b) a variety of green urban spaces and shopping experiences; c) connected public spaces adapted to the climate and making the natural surroundings accessible in all seasons.

The project envisions this new physical connection on 2 levels. First, a series of green corridors are designed, flowing into the urban core of Ørsta, connecting city and periphery and allowing for nature and urban life to merge. At this level the project introduces a new landscape path "landskapsstien" binding the city centre and the surrounding nature together. Second, in the core of Ørsta, an urban surface is shaped as a place of densification, strengthened by a series of intense green public spaces and a waterfront promenade.

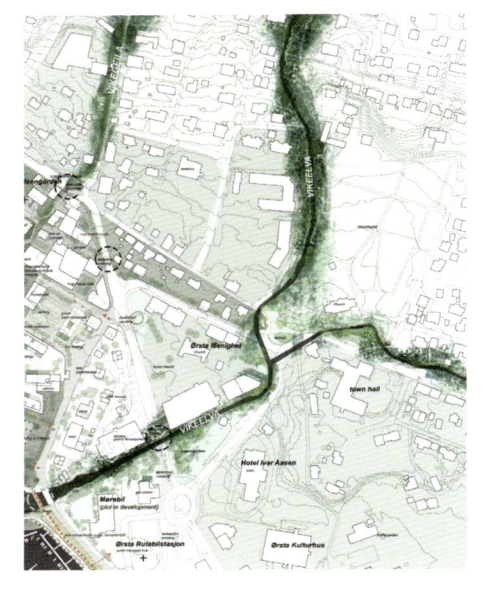

JURY POINT OF VIEW The landscaping strategy, visualized in a beautiful and poetic yet site-specific atmosphere, would strengthen Ørsta's identity both on a local and regional level as well as beyond. The three main places of town centre intensification is a believable strategy, but the scattered spatial interventions between the corridors, especially along the waterfront is less enthusiastic. The highly detailed landscape appears to be mainly motivated by aesthetics and the project would benefit from including further considerations on possible operative qualities of the green corridors.

LEONARD MA (CA/FI)
ARCHITECT

CARMEN LEE (CA)
ARCHITECT

WWW.PUBLICOFFICE.CO

SPECIAL MENTION - ØRSTA (NO)

Utmark

TEAM POINT OF VIEW In Norway the term Utmark describes a natural environment where the freedom to roam can be exercised. Typically uninhabited or uncultivated areas, Utmark can be accessed by anyone, and does not bear any obligation to be productive as the "public" spaces of urban life. Utmark once applied to the shorelines and beaches and stipulated that no building could occur within 100m of the shore to allow free access to the sea. This project proposes to establish a 100m long pier as the reference point for the future development of Ørsta's waterfront as an explicit strategy to re-establish the shoreline as a space to roam freely.

SELB
DEUTSCHLAND (DE)

CATEGORY: **URBAN - ARCHITECTURAL**
LOCATION: **INNER CITY**
POPULATION: **15,000 INHAB.**
STRATEGIC SITE: **5.14 HA**
PROJECT SITE: **2.88 HA**

SITE PROPOSED BY: **SELB TOWN COUNCIL**
OWNER(S) OF THE SITE: **MOSTLY PRIVATE OWNERSHIP, SEVERAL PLOTS OWNED BY SELB TOWN COUNCIL**
COMMISION AFTER COMPETITION: **URBAN MASTER PLAN**

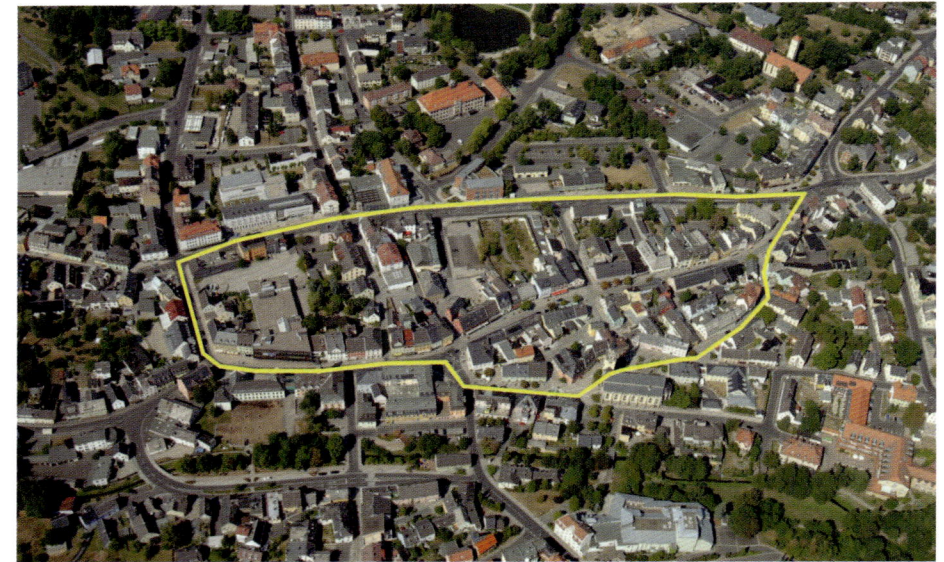

Interview of the site's representative
Helmut Resch, Municipal Planning Authority

PRESENTATION OF THE SITE WITH REGARDS TO STRATEGY

The site is located at the heart of the town and is of outstanding strategic importance not only for the area to be dealt with, but also for the development of the town as a whole. The town is equally concerned by a revitalization of the district and the strengthening of the functioning of business, service, and housing. Ultimately, however, it is also about sending an important signal of awakening in the town of Selb and generating a positive internal image.

HOW IS THE SITE CONNECTED TO THE SESSION TOPIC - THE ADAPTABLE CITY?

For a city undergoing change, which has to overcome big challenges with respect to a rearrangement of the town centre, the topic of the "Adaptable City" is naturally of central importance. The solutions found have to be robust enough to guarantee a large degree of flexibility.

DID YOU DEFINE A SPECIFIC PROCESS FOR THE URBAN DEVELOPMENT OF THE SITE AFTER EUROPAN COMPETITION?

Based on the competition results, a workshop is supposed to be held with the goal of harmonizing the ideas of the prize winners with wishes and suggestions from the population. Practice-oriented building blocks that can possibly lead to the realization of measures are supposed to be developed step-by-step. The award-winning results serve as a basis for a wide-ranging discourse with the citizenry and particularly with owners in the planning area. The intention is to create a masterplan for the centre of the town that takes interdisciplinary aspects into account and should contribute to a sustainable development of the important area.

IRENE CLIMENT SILVAR (ES)
IÑIGO CORNAGO BONAL (ES)
LARA FREIRE ROMERO (ES)
ANTONIO GARCÍA MARTOS (ES)
CLAUDIA SÁNCHEZ FERNÁNDEZ (ES)
MARIO VILA QUELLE (ES)
ARCHITECTS

CALLE PEZ 27, OFICINA 316
28004 MADRID, ES
T. +34 635839017
URBANTOOLKIT@GMAIL.COM

WINNER - SELB (DE)
Urban Toolkit

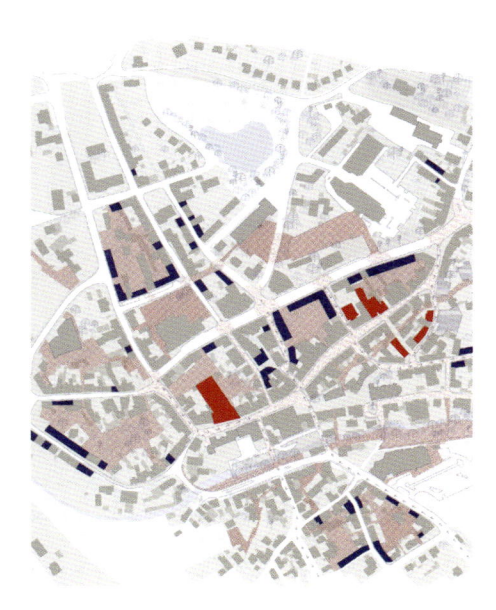

TEAM POINT OF VIEW "Urban Toolkit" proposes an open regeneration process to develop in a framework where diverse agents work together to transform Selb into a more resilient city. The process can develop in a fragmented way through time and space thanks to the urban toolkit. The urban tools allow different agents to exchange spaces, goods, services, rights or money to transform urban conditions into more sustainable ones from a systematic and integral point of view.

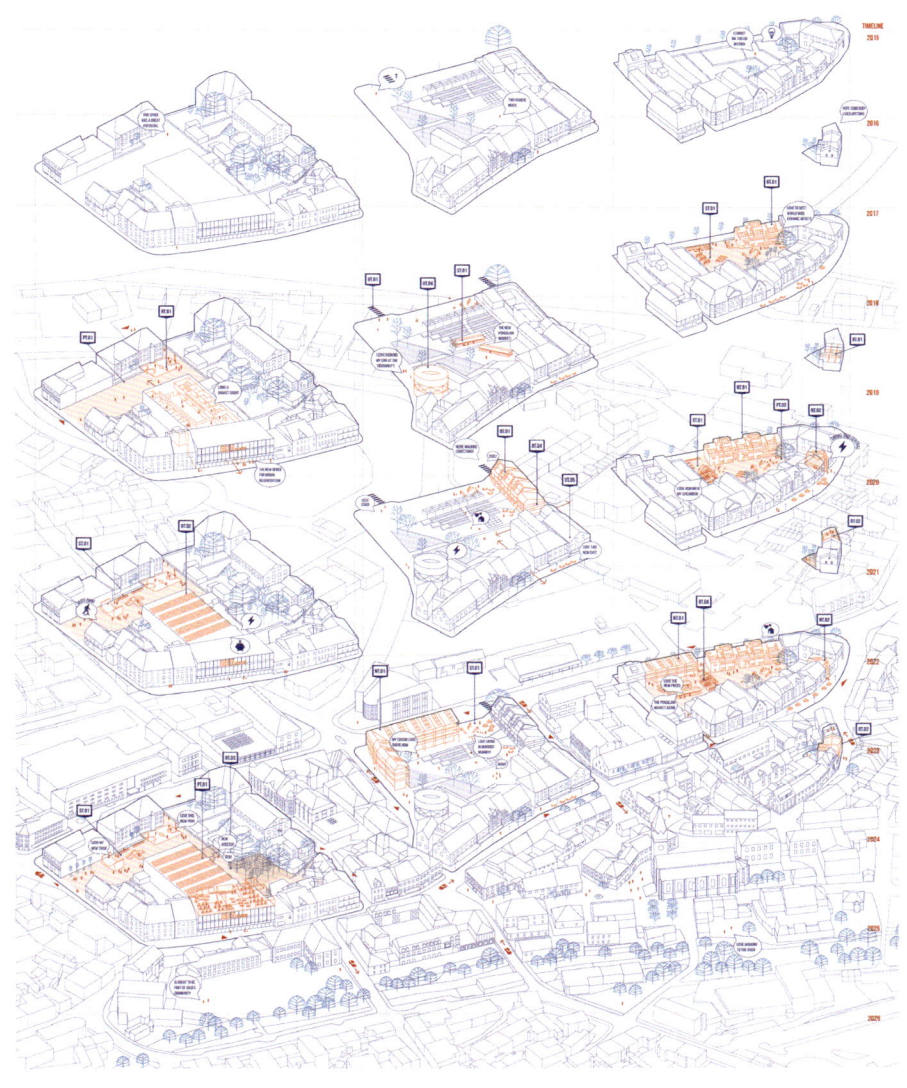

To develop and manage this player-based process our proposal is to create the Office for Urban Regeneration (OUR). Their role is to connect and mediate the 3 sectors of agents (municipality, private economy and civil society), promoting the implementation of transformation projects as well as to communicate, monitor and further develop the tools and the whole regeneration process.
A decentralised, networked and context guided urban transformation process needs specific temporalities for each partial intervention. The urban toolkit allows performing different interventions in many opportunity areas and constantly adapt urban conditions to unplanned scenarios. The result is a city as a constant work-in-progress. Although the process is open in many ways, the main guiding strategies and objectives are clear: constantly built a more resilient city; compact, complex, sustainable, inclusive and cohesive, sustainable and open to serendipity.

JURY POINT OF VIEW The project is principally a very well-designed description of a strategy for how to deal with the town. Further than theory, it succeeds in formulating concrete approaches to solutions in small, nearly unnoticeable options for interventions, of which all are conceivable. There is no final solution here –Selb is not yet finished– and the most diverse methods are nevertheless revealed to the viewer; what is promised is an overall activation of the town.

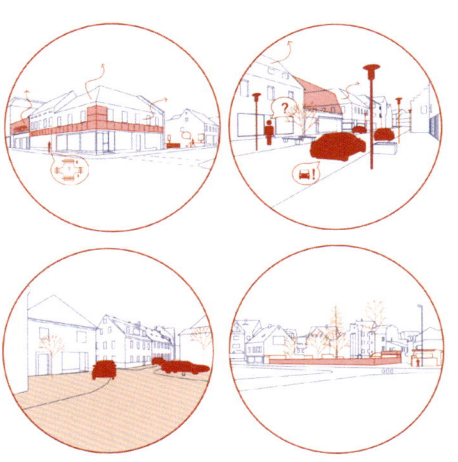

KATARZYNA FURGALINSKA (PL)
MICHAL LISINSKI (PL)
ARCHITECTS

UL.MISJONARZY OBLATOW 15/3
40-129 KATOWICE, PL
T. +48 501619883
K.FURGALINSKA@GMAIL.COM

RUNNER-UP - SELB (DE)

Round The Corner

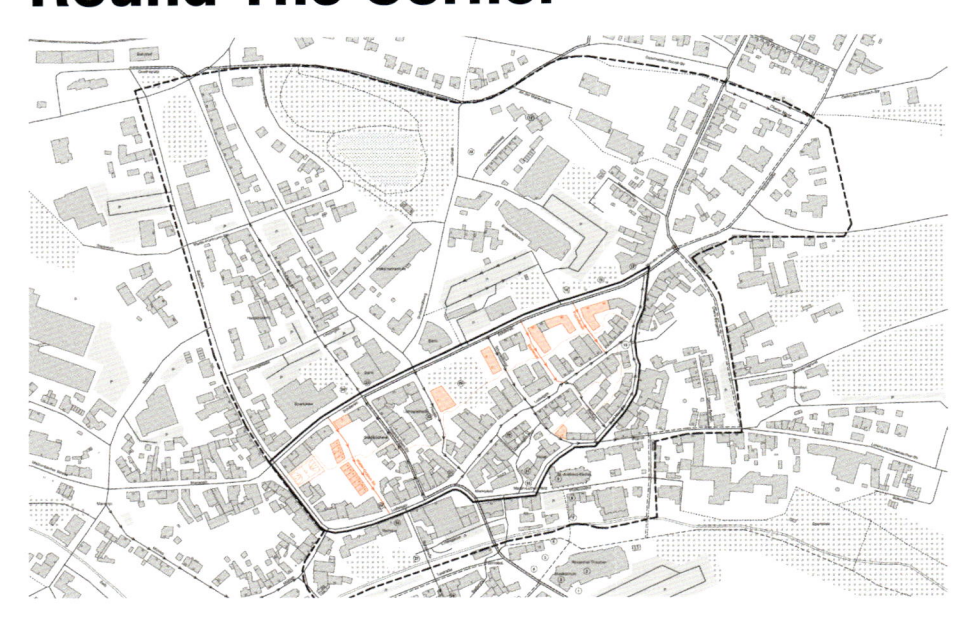

TEAM POINT OF VIEW A need of human interaction was what once brought people together to form towns and seems to be the only thing that can come to rescue it. Proximity, human scale, familiar environment are things that start to be appreciated again and to decide about the quality of live.

As a shrinking town Selb faces persistent decline in urban density. The town tissue loses its resilience and ability to heal its tears, which make it especially vulnerable and prone to further decomposition. Bringing density and continuity back into the urban tissue is a key objective of the project. The 4 main principles of the proposed long-term redevelopment strategy are: urban consolidation, eliminating infrastructural barriers, flexible phasing and focus on place making. A wide range of supporting ad hoc tactics aim at making the project site more animated, connected and inclusive.

Ludwigstraße, as a backbone of the project area, is enhanced as a square rather than a traffic route, while existing and proposed perpendicular plug-in streets play a role of a communication and parking supply base for both designed and existing buildings. The new volumes are also designed to outline the site block structure. The proposed new communicational and compositional principle clarifies the site organisation and strengthens the street corners as the points of the highest potential of urban interaction.

JURY POINT OF VIEW The project proposes to create 6 North-South connections by means of three new small cross-connections through formerly private unused inner courtyards. This approach is not initially innovative, since space is here created using classical urban planning means. At the same time, opening up the inner courtyards not only creates space for new construction. It also gives rise to a scaled town centre with diverse new visual and pathway connections. A completely new perception of the centre may arise if the community manages to realize this catalysing effort.

BRUNO OLIVEIRA (PT)
MARLENE DOS SANTOS (PT)
ARCHITECTS

CATARINA BOTA LEAL (PT)
ARCHITECT
ELEONORA RE (IT)
FRANCESCA TRENTA (IT)
STUDENTS IN URBAN PLANNING

ESTUDIO ODS
GOLDRA 295F
8100-223 LOULÉ, PT
T. +351 965648998
ESTUDIODS@ESTUDIODS.COM
WWW.ESTUDIODS.COM

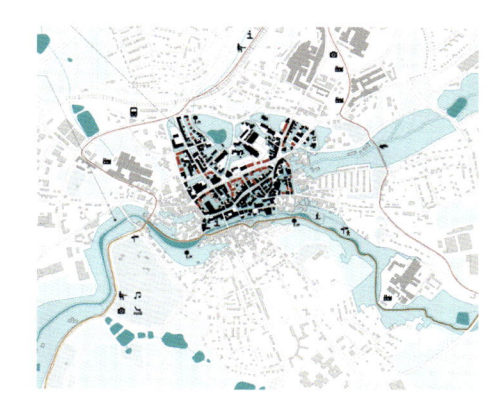

SPECIAL MENTION - SELB (DE)

Identity + Intensity

TEAM POINT OF VIEW Identity in contemporary societies can be distorted over the influence of the globalization process. In a diluted context like Selb the notion of locus loses intensity and trends to be transformed, driving citizens to cultural detachment from the city. The proposal defines a dual storyline of 15 characteristic vectors, whereby each intervention concept is processed. We set the rules to ensure a suitable functioning and the coordinates for later management. The introduction of new uses and links anchored to the site physical or cultural heritage enhances adaptability that can be gradually introduced combining existing elements with new wider meanings.

STREEFKERK
NEDERLAND (NL)

CATEGORY: **URBAN - ARCHITECTURAL**
LOCATION: **STREEFKERK**
POPULATION: **2,500 INHAB.**
PROJECT SITE: **1,678 HA**
SITE PROPOSED BY: **WATERSCHAP RIVIERENLAND**
OWNER(S) OF THE SITE: **WATERSCHAP RIVIERENLAND**

COMMISION AFTER COMPETITION:
POSSIBLY PARTICIPATION IN A PROJECT TEAM WORKING ON FUTURE DIKE REINFORCEMENT OR SUPERVISION FROM THE LANDSCAPE/ ARCHITECTONIC PERSPECTIVE CONCERNING THE DEVELOPMENT OF THE SITE

Interview of the site's representative

PRESENTATION OF THE SITE WITH REGARDS TO STRATEGY

The site is situated on the dike bordering the Lek River and to the West of the centre of Streefkerk. Requested are small-scale, conceptual proposals for reconstruction on, in, or along the dike, while respecting the urban and surrounding rural landscape. The technical design of the new dike and the existing architecture elsewhere along the dike should be taken into account. The challenge is to reconstruct a plot of land –limited in space, between river and hinterland, with a considerable difference in height while at the same time anticipating a higher water level in the future due to a rising sea level– that blends in well with the surroundings.

HOW IS THE SITE CONNECTED TO THE SESSION TOPIC - THE ADAPTABLE CITY?

Located in a delta region, almost 60% of the Netherlands is potentially flood-prone, either from sea or river water. The country is renowned for its experience in the field of flood defense and technical know-how about water management. Waterschap Rivierenland manages more than a thousand kilometers of dikes in the vicinity of large rivers. Owing to the rising sea level and the increase in heavy downpours, the dikes along the rivers will require reinforcing if the hinterland and towns and cities are to avoid flooding. In the Deltaprogramma 2015 the national strategy for rivers is laid out. The competition site forms part of a dike reinforcement that will be carried out between 2014 and 2017. Demolition and construction on condition that the foundations can be levered up (raised on their supporting piles) in connection with future reinforcement. Proposals can serve as examples for tackling the realization of the developments in the national Deltaprogramma 2015. Streefkerk requires a lively landscape along the dike that connects the river and the village.

MARIE SALADIN (FR)
MARION VASSENT-GARAUD (FR)
ARCHITECTS

STUDIO SAVA
105A SCHIEDAMSEWEG
3026AE ROTTERDAM, NL
T. +33 668895087
CONTACT@STUDIO-SAVA.COM
WWW.STUDIO-SAVA.COM

WINNER - STREEFKERK (NL)

In-Between

TEAM POINT OF VIEW The consequence of the dike rising imply an artificial divorce of the urban quality of the city created by the connection to the road and the rural quality of the polder territory. To adapt the project to this situation, we conceptually split the volume of the typical local Dutch house into two parts. The top part is lift and provides a new covered, open and shared space located in between the two original floor, which remain the traditional intimate and private space. This space is in-between the air and the ground, top and bottom, public and domestic life. It is an open field of possibilities for both the inhabitants and the development of the city. The use of pillars and jacking system is treated as an advantage. They are extended up until the level of the road, which turns them into a skeleton combine with a central axis that provides its structural and energy core. It is a spine that runs from the floor to the roof to capture natural power from the sun, wind and rainwater. The slab of the in-between is used to connect several houses and locally distribute and share harvested resources. The union of individual houses in a network is a way to be sustainably future-proof. The design of this case study house aims at accommodating various ways of living in synchronicity with the earth, the street, the water and the air. We stem the project from a typological proposal, with which we aim at creating a resonance on a larger, territorial scale.

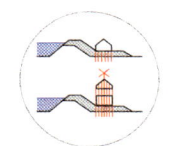

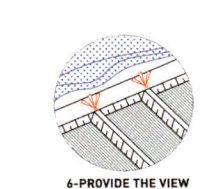

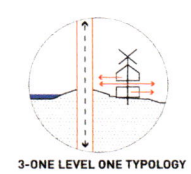

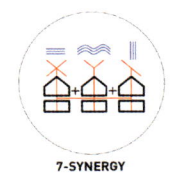

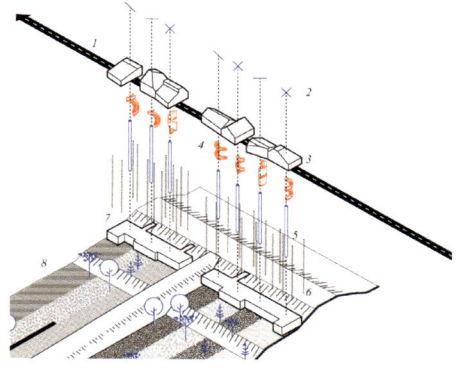

JURY POINT OF VIEW It is a typical Europan project in the sense that new housing typologies are used as a tool to address the assignment in Streefkerk. Furthermore, it is an innovative version of the socio-economic significance that dike housing has traditionally had. In addition to this pilot location, the strategy (with adaptations) can also be implemented on various other locations. The suggested architectural end result is attractive: a varied silhouette along the dike that almost looks as if it has always been there.

1-USE CONTRAINTS AS OPPORTUNITIES
2-SPLIT AND LIFT
3-ONE LEVEL ONE TYPOLOGY
4-RECYCLE OLD IDEAS
5-USE THE FORCES
6-PROVIDE THE VIEW
7-SYNERGY
8-CREATE INTER CONNECTION

250 **CARLOS ZARCO SANZ** (ES)
SARA PALOMAR PEREZ (ES)
ZUHAL KOL (TR)
JOSE LUIS HIDALGO (ES)
ARCHITECTS

JOAQUIN COSTA 4, 3B
28200 (S. L. DE EL ESCORIAL) MADRID, ES
T. +34 626197758
INFO@OPENACT.EU
WWW.OPENACT.EU

RUNNER-UP - STREEFKERK (NL)

Protodike

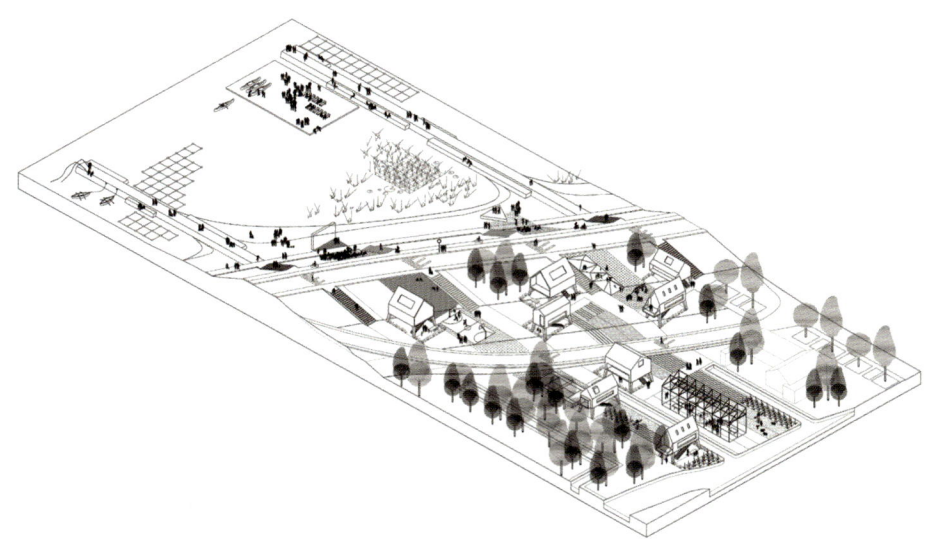

TEAM POINT OF VIEW Dikes generally draw a coastline as set by the boundary between water and land; on one side of the line, there is water; on the other, land. This at once expresses and reinforces an attitude about the way humans use and occupy the littoral terrain, which privileges certain programs –while excluding the possibility of other programs– such as an economy based on the biological productivity of the fluctuating gradient of water/s or social daily life activities that can occur on/around the water. In Streefkerk as well, the boundary created by the dike is predominant and eliminates potential mutuality. Therefore, the proposal focuses on the reciprocal programmatic, economic, ecologic, socio-cultural relationships between land and water by asking 'how can a blocking infrastructure be developed to connect', and aims at using the resulting conversation central to organizing a prototype -PROTODIKE- infrastructure of an alternate urbanism and land use that can be adapted and implemented in varying locations for dike reinforcements. To re-open the possibilities that a more complex understanding of the relationship between land and water would permit, the Protodike is established on two deceptively single moves of groynes and strips to have effect on generating new patterns of land use, new economies, new socialities and ultimately new urbanization based on a contradictory relationship to connect while blocking.

JURY POINT OF VIEW Reconnecting the dike, polder and river is strong and both programmatically and spatially interesting. Infrastructure, housing, agriculture, aquaculture and leisure activities merge and give the traditional polder dike new cultural significance in the landscape. To some extent a chaotic mix of high-tech and local culture is created and this, too, could be interesting. The open final result —a modern version of a loosely differentiated rural development— pleased the jury, but the architectural visual language is (consciously or not) somewhat clumsy.

LETICIA MARTÍNEZ VELASCO (ES)
CARLOS SORIA SÁNCHEZ (ES)
ANA ROSA SORIA SÁNCHEZ (ES)
ARCHITECTS

146 RUE DE CHARENTON, BP 42
75012 PARIS, FR
T. +33 781790846
OPINAANVAN@GMAIL.COM

SPECIAL MENTION - STREEFKERK (NL)

Opínaanvan

TEAM POINT OF VIEW The main aim of our proposal is to develop a system that complements the work of the Delta Programme in the protection against flooding now and in the future. In this sense, our exercise is more interesting if understood from its potential as a system or strategy rather than as the individual solution of a given area. A sort of architecture that allows reforming, rebuilding and changing its image. A non-form architecture than can spontaneously absorb additions, subtractions or technical modifications without disturbing its order.

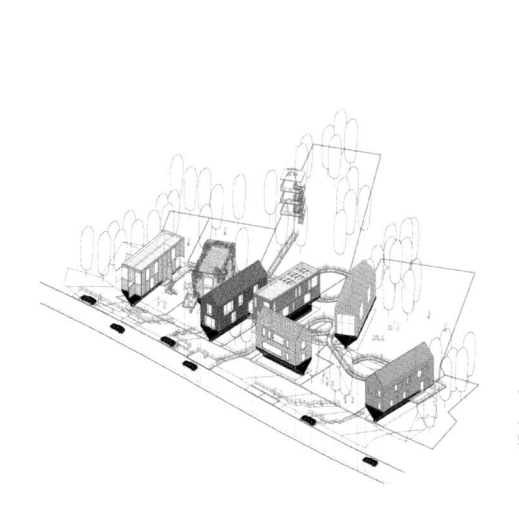

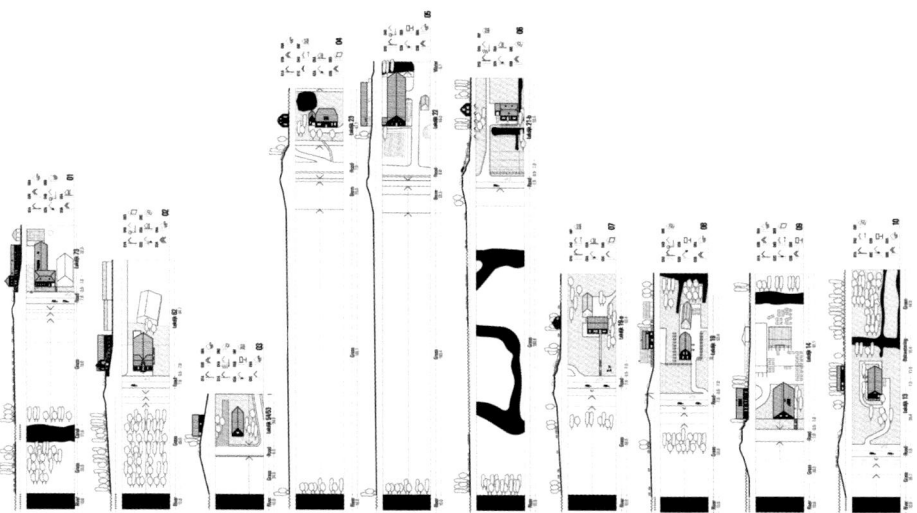

WARSZAWA
POLSKA (PL)

CATEGORY: **ARCHITECTURAL - LANDSCAPE**
LOCATION: **WARSZAWA POWIŚLE**
POPULATION: **1,720,000 INHAB.**
STRATEGIC SITE: **175.9 HA**
PROJECT SITE: **3.5 HA**
SITE PROPOSED BY: **CAPITAL CITY OF WARSAW**

OWNER(S) OF THE SITE: **CAPITAL CITY OF WARSAW, STATE TREASURE OF POLAND**
COMMISION AFTER COMPETITION: **DETAILED ARCHITECTURAL DESIGN OF THE EXHIBITION AND LANDSCAPE DESIGN OF THE SURROUNDING GARDEN. THE EXACT SCOPE OF THE COMMISSION WILL BE NEGOTIATED**

Interview of the site's representative

PRESENTATION OF THE SITE WITH REGARDS TO STRATEGY

The current Capt.Stanisław Skibniewski "Cubryna" Garden was formerly part of a 1,300-meter-long riverside park. In 1975 the park was reduced, separated from the river and changed into an island between the lanes of the new expressway called Wisłostrada. In 2003 the road was placed in a tunnel, restoring the connection between the park and the river. After years of demise, the riverbanks once again attract crowds of people in summer but its potential is still untapped. It is crucial to find a way to attract different activities to make this place lively all year round. One idea is the design of the exhibition of stone treasures recovered from the river in the Capt.Stanisław Skibniewski "Cubryna" Garden, situated between the Vistula and the Kazimierzowski Palace, where many of those valuable items were originally located. This exhibition shall be part of the revival scheme for the area and bring urban life closer to the riverbanks.

HOW IS THE SITE CONNECTED TO THE SESSION TOPIC - THE ADAPTABLE CITY?

Powiśle has a long tradition as an industrial district providing services to other areas in Warsaw and a dwelling place for the poor. Public and private projects from the first half of the 20th cent. aimed at connecting the city centre with the Vistula, raising the area's profile. However, it lasted until the beginning of the 21st cent. for the district to finally loose its peripheral character. The opening of the University Library in 1999 –with its garden and green areas on the roof– started a self-accelerating process of attracting the public, encouraging diverse activities and starting projects of different uses, scales and forms. Industry is pushed out and replaced by residential developments. The area adjoins the University Library, Copernicus Science Centre and riverside boulevards, which now under reconstruction. The implementation of the exhibition of stone treasures shall help overcome the monotony of scientific and cultural functions and provide multifaceted uses, vitality and diversity to the place.

FERNANDO EIROA LORENZO (ES)
JORGE GARCÍA ANTA (ES)
ALBERTO SEOANE SESAR (ES)
ARCHITECTS

ALCALDE SALORIO SUÁREZ P1 L4
15010 A CORUÑA, ES
T. +34 981256020
INFO@LCGARQUITECTURA.COM
WWW.LCGARQUITECTURA.COM

WINNER - WARSZAWA (PL)
River Gate

TEAM POINT OF VIEW Polish pavilion expo brussels 1958 (unbuilt) – The project tried to more directly convey the visitor information and environment. It rationally used all space-time media and communication channels, simultaneously storming all the senses of visitors, who would enjoy the content of the pavilion under a huge perforated cover. It would be built without pillars, without walls, without any woodwork or vertical glazing. The exhibits would act with the films while visitors cross the pavilion. Screens and projection devices would be placed below the cover. River gate cubryna garden 2015 (proposal) – Ensuring proper linkages with Vistula River is the main intention. On the other hand, keeping the place potential and its value must be compulsory. A huge Corten steel cover creates an open space pavilion that can work as an open museum with different activities. Moreover, it creates a place to sit down, read a book and rest under trees. This is a place without architectonic barriers, open 24/7, using new technologies. The exhibition is completed with multimedia events, even with films and performances. Exploring, exhibiting and learning are the principal goals in order to generate an original experience. The treasures can be seen without directly touching or approaching them, due to the sheet of water or their position floating over the ground. Finally, a hanging balcony connects all the pavilion with the treasures and the river.

JURY POINT OF VIEW The project positions itself along the Weichsel River with a strong gesture visible from afar. It proposes an open form as an exhibition building with suspended exhibits to be viewed from below as well as from a continuous gallery, which also offers a good view outside. It is an iconographic solution that is capable of dealing with the dimensions and orientations of the surroundings and visible as a landmark from a distance. The combination of the simplicity of the object, the harmonious positioning and the spatial quality resulting from it is impressive, although the exhibition concept should be questioned.

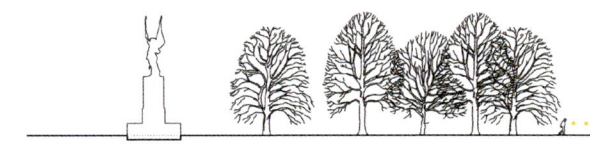

MATTIA BIAGI (IT)
ANNACHIARA BONORA (IT)
LORENZO CATENA (IT)
VALERIA LOLLOBATTISTA (IT)
VALERIO SOCCIARELLI (IT)
ARCHITECTS

T. +39 3282769569
GNOMONE.ARCHITETTURA@GMAIL.COM
HTTP://GNOMONE.BLOGSPOT.IT
HTTPS://
IT-IT.FACEBOOK.COM/GNOMONE.ARCHITETTURA

RUNNER-UP - WARSZAWA (PL)
Apport Plus Support

TEAM POINT OF VIEW With the larger scale ambition of reconnecting the district and the Vistula river through Cubryna Gardens, the project proposes the grafting of the park to the already developed system of public open spaces in the region.

The main actions are two. Juxtaposing a new grid of birches to the pre-existing trees, to thicken the wood limit of the area and join the wood system identifying the parks nearby. And creating a series of modular actives strips under the tree crowns, parallel to the main axes of the district to encourage the crossing to the river.

As a norm, the project guides present and future transformations of the park layout. This way an extreme flexibility of the system is granted, as several activities can fit the modular strips without deceiving the project original sense and functionality. Beyond open-air activities, the strips are thought to accommodate a flexible number of glass pavilions, the transparency of which will offer continuity with the surrounding landscape.

For the first phase, the project proposes 4 pavilions to host the exposition and a small cafeteria. Considering the project as a growing organism and according to the available resources, the number of pavilions could increase along the future. They could accommodate different kinds of activities linked to city life (seminaries, workshops, meetings…) The advantage would be for both the young and the elderly, stimulating a peaceful coexistence.

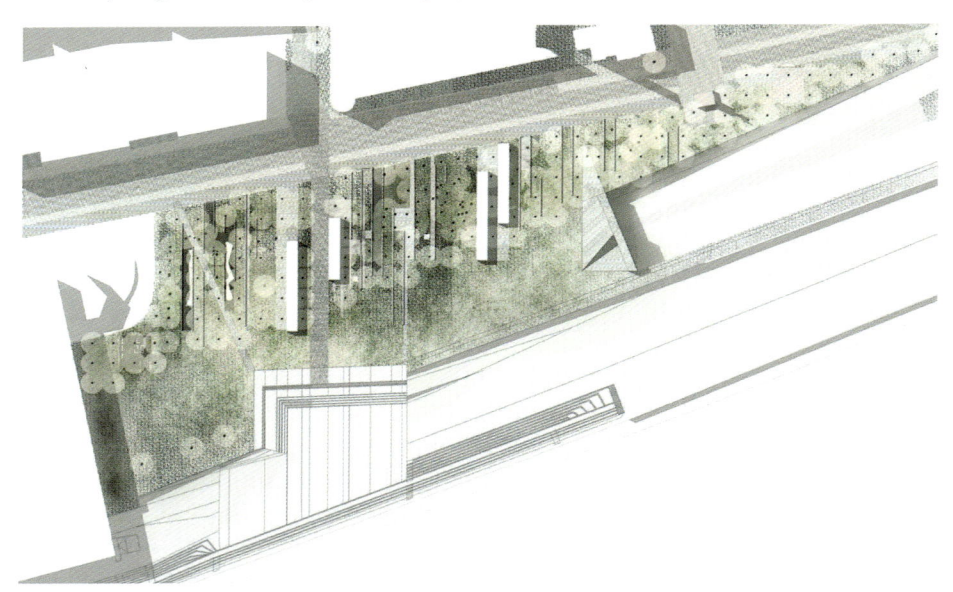

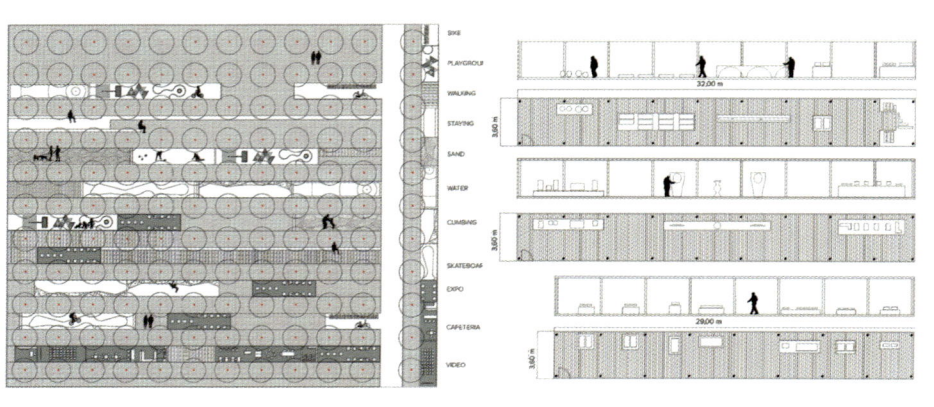

JURY POINT OF VIEW The project proposes a structure that endeavours to orthogonally strengthen the link between the city and the river, therefore crossways to this space. The closed volumes are slightly raised off the ground and transparent. They give rise to a subtle and very easy solution that allows the park and vegetation a great effect and a lot of space. The lightness of the design, which only selectively affects the existing situation, is however simultaneously also its problem. It is questionably whether the solution can hold its own within the surrounding scale and environment.

LAURA BONELL (ES)
DANIEL LÓPEZ-DÒRIGA (ES)
ARCHITECTS

ROGER DE LLÚRIA 116, 2-2
08008 BARCELONA, ES
T. +34 936676977
OFFICE@BONELLDORIGA.COM
WWW.BONELLDORIGA.COM

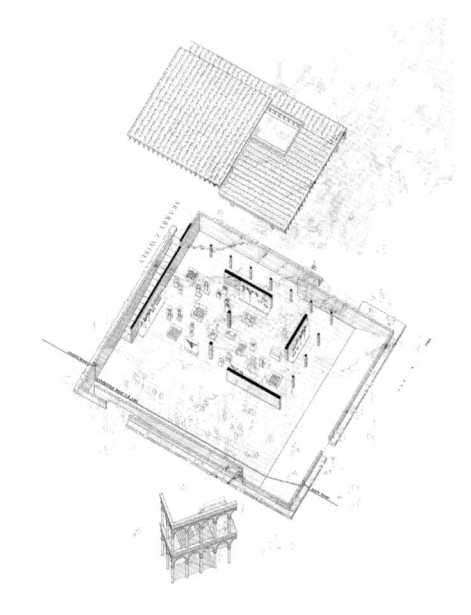

SPECIAL MENTION - WARSZAWA (PL)

I Am a Treasure

TEAM POINT OF VIEW The project aims to provide a new context for the "Treasures of the River Vistula", both physically and symbolically. The exhibition space is situated at the end of the Kazimierzowska Axis, keeping the street alignment and creating an urban relationship with the place where the stones once were. Visitors reproduce the act of "going down the river" to discover the treasure by descending to a semi-buried pavilion covered by concrete beams and layers of water, where the pieces are lit by thousands of reflections that create an atmosphere that has a character of its own.

ANNEXES

Europan 13, is:
49 sites
15 countries
12 national juries

154 prize-winning teams:
44 winners
49 runners-up
61 special mentions

JURIES

BELGIQUE / BELGIË / BELGIEN – SCHWEIZ / SUISSE / SVIZZERA / SVIZRA (ASSOCIATED)

URBAN/ARCHITECTURAL ORDER
MARTINE RIDIAUX (BE),
Architect, Direction of operational planning of Wallonia
EMMANUEL LAURENT (BE),
Head of Property Development Department / ArcelorMittal Belgium Real Estate (and Holland)

URBAN/ARCHITECTURAL DESIGN
ANNEMIE DEPUYDT (BE),
Architect, bureau uapS, Paris
LAURA FALCONE (IT),
Architect, Obiettivo160, winner Europan 11 Sambreville (BE)
Makan RAFATDJOU (FR),
Architect-Urbanist, Paris
BERNARD DEFFET (BE),
Architect-Urbanist, Liège

PUBLIC FIGURE
BERNARD REICHEN (FR),
Architect-Urbanist, Reichen et Robert & Associés, Paris

SUBSTITUTES
JEAN-MICHEL DEGRAEVE (BE),
Architect-Urbanist, Habitat-Concept,
V-P Europan Belgium
FABIENNE HENNEQUIN (BE),
Architect-Urbanist, Liège

REPRESENTATIVES EUROPAN SWITZERLAND
Two representatives of Europan Switzerland join the Belgian jury and replace **MRS RIDIAUX** and **MR LAURENT** to evaluate the projects submitted on the Swiss site
ROBERT PROST (FR),
ENSAM engineer, architect DESA, Paris
JÜRG CAPOL (CH),
Architect, Lausanne

DEUTSCHLAND - POLSKA (ASSOCIATED)

URBAN/ARCHITECTURAL ORDER
KARIN SANDECK (DE),
Architect, Bavarian State Ministry of Interior, Munich

URBAN/ARCHITECTURAL DESIGN
LOUIS BASABE MONTALVO (ES),
Architect, Teacher at ETSAM, Madrid
PROF. DR. LISA DIEDRICH (DE),
Landscape Architect, Professor at the Swedish University of Agricultural Sciences in Alnarp, Munich
DR. THORSTEN ERL (DE),
Architect, Heidelberg
RAINER HOFMANN (DE),
Architect, Bogevischs Buero, Munich
PROF. DR. MICHAEL KOCH (DE),
Architect, Professor at the Hafen City University, Hamburg

PUBLIC FIGURE
ULI HELLWEG (DE),
Architect, Urbanist, Director IBA Hamburg

SUBSTITUTES
PROF. CHRISTIAN KERN (DE),
Architect, Professor at the TU Wien, Munich
ULRICH TRAPPE (DE),
Architect, Dresden

REPRESENTATIVE EUROPAN POLSKA
JOANNA KUSIAK (PL),
Urban Sociologist, Warszawa

ESPAÑA

URBAN/ARCHITECTURAL ORDER
JAVIER MARTÍN RAMIRO (ES),
Directorate General of Architecture, Housing and Land, Ministry of Equipment

URBAN/ARCHITECTURAL DESIGN
JOSÉ JUAN BARBA (ES),
Architect, Publisher METALOCUS, Madrid
SABINE MÜLLER (DE),
Architect, SMAQ – architecture urbanism research, Berlin
FERNANDO DE PORRAS-ISLA (ES),
Architect, Urbanist, Teacher, Madrid
JOSÉ MIGUEL ROLDÁN (ES),
Architect, Roldán + Berengué, Teacher, Barcelona
JUANA SÁNCHEZ GÓMEZ (ES),
Architect, DJArquitectura, Teacher, Europan Prize E7, E8, E10, E11, Granada

PUBLIC FIGURE
MARCEL SMETS (BE),
Urbanist, Teacher, Louvain

FRANCE

URBAN/ARCHITECTURAL ORDER
NATHAN STARKMAN (FR),
Director of APUR (1989-95), and then of the Agence d'Urbanisme de Lille Métropole, France
BERNARD ROTH (FR),
Founder of AMO (Architecture et Maîtrise d'Ouvrage), France

URBAN/ARCHITECTURAL DESIGN
AGLAÉE DEGROS (BE),
Architect-urbanist, Rotterdam / Brussels
MARINA CERVERA ALONSO DE MEDINA (ES), Architect, Landscaper, Secretary General IFLA Europe (International Federation of Landscape Architects), Barcelona
MATTHIAS ARMENGAUD (FR),
Architect, AWP - PJU 2010 NAJA 2006, Paris
PASCAL ROLLET (FR),
Architect, Lipsky&Rollet Architects, Paris

PUBLIC FIGURE
PIERRE VELTZ (FR),
Engineer, sociologist and economist, specialist of the organisation of companies and territorial dynamics, President OIN Paris-Saclay

SUBSTITUTES
ALESSANDRO DELLI PONTI (FR),
Architect-urbanist, Winner E12 Mannheim (DE), and then of the international competition that followed the Europan competition
AGNÈS VINCE (FR),
Ministère de la Culture et de la Communication, Directrice de l'Architecture adjointe au Directeur des Patrimoines, associated public figure
ISABEL DIAZ (FR),
Chef du bureau des stratégies territoriales DGALN/DHUP/AD1, associated public figure

HRVATSKA

URBAN/ARCHITECTURAL ORDER
BOJAN BALÉTIC (HR),
Architect, Zagreb School of Architecture, member of Supervising Committee of Varaždin students centre
DAMIR HRVATIN (HR),
Architect, City of Poreč, Head of the Dpt. of Spatial Planning and the Environment, Poreč

URBAN/ARCHITECTURAL DESIGN
KREŠIMIR ROGINA (HR),
Architect, Peňezic&Rogina architects, Zagreb
JORDI QUEROL (ES),
Architect and city planner, Barcelona
SIMON HARTMANN (CH),
Architect, HHF Architects, Basel
NIKOLA RADELJKÓVIC (HR),
NUMEN, designer/urban designer, Zagreb

PUBLIC FIGURE
SONJA LEBOŠ (HR),
Urban anthropologist, Zagreb

SUBSTITUTES
VANJA RISTER (HR),
Architect, Zagreb School of Architecture, Zagreb
KRISTINA CAREVA (HR),
Architect, Zagreb School of Architecture, Zagreb

ITALIA

URBAN/ARCHITECTURAL ORDER
TOMMASO DAL BOSCO (IT),
Head of Department for Urban and Territorial Development, Institute for Finance and Local Economy (IFEL) - ANCI Foundation (National Association of Italian Cities), Italy

URBAN/ARCHITECTURAL DESIGN
ROBERT HOLTON (NC),
Architect, Professor at the Louisiana College of Art & Design, North Carolina
HANS JÖRG DUVIGNEAU (DE),
Architect Engineer, Germany
MAURO SAITO (IT),
Architect and urbanist, Italy
SABRINA CANTALINI (IT),
Architect, winner E7 Seregno, Italy
LUIGI COCCIA (IT),
Architect, Professor at School of Architecture and Design of Ascoli Piceno - University of Cameri-no, winner E7 Pescara, Italy
GUILLAUME CHATELAIN (FR),
Architect, winner E12 Milano, Italy – 2nd jury session

PUBLIC FIGURE
PAOLA PIEROTTI (IT),
Architect, Journalist, co-founder of PPan, a communication and networking platform for the built environment – 1st jury session

JURIES

NEDERLAND

URBAN/ARCHITECTURAL ORDER
ANNIUS HOORNSTRA (NL),
Vice-director city development and transformation at the municipality of Amsterdam
SJOUKJE VEENEMA (NL),
Project developer at housing corporation Lefier

URBAN/ARCHITECTURAL DESIGN
STEFAN BENDIKS (DE),
Architect and jointly-partner in Artgineering, Rotterdam/Brussels (runner-up Hoogvliet E6)
MARIANNE SKJULHAUG (NO),
Head of institute of urbanism and landscape at Oslo School of architecture and design
TJERK RUIMSCHOTEL (NL),
Urban designer and chairman of BNSP
PETER VEENSTRA (NL),
Partner and landscape architect at LOLA (winner Sintra E8)

PUBLIC FIGURE
KAYE GEIPEL (DE),
Deputy Editor-in-chief at Bauwelt

SUBSTITUTES
JUDITH KORPERSHOEK (NL),
Architect and partner at Architectenbureau-K2 (winner Amsterdam-Noord E6)
ESTHER STEVELINK (NL),
Architect and partner at GAAGA (runner-up Groningen E6, winner Maastricht E10)

NORGE

URBAN/ARCHITECTURAL ORDER
KRISTIAAN BORRET (BE),
Bouwmeester of Brussels Capital Region
SVERRE LANDMARK (NO),
Marketing Director at Asplin Ramm Eiendom AS

URBAN/ARCHITECTURAL DESIGN
ELLEN HELLSTEN (NO),
Architect and partner Ghilardi + Hellsten
UMBERTO NAPOLITANO (IT/FR),
Architect and partner of LAN
CRISTINA GOBERNA (ES/US),
Architect and partner of Fake Industries, Architectural Agonism
KATHRIN SUSANNA GIMMEL (DK),
Architect and partner of JAJA Architects

PUBLIC FIGURE
TATJANA SCHNEIDER (DE/UK),
Architect and researcher, writer and educator at the School of Architecture in Sheffield

SUBSTITUTES
MIIA-LIINA TOMMILA (FI),
Architect and winner of Europan 12 in Asker – 1st jury session in Bergen
CLARA MURADO (ES),
Architect and partner at Murado & Elvira Architects, Europan 9 Winner in Trondheim

ÖSTERREICH - KOSOVO (ASSOCIATED)

URBAN/ARCHITECTURAL ORDER
TINA SAABY (DK),
City Architect at København Municipality
PETER ULM (AT),
C.E.O. of 6B47 Real Estate Investors AG, Wien

URBAN/ARCHITECTURAL DESIGN
IRÈNE DJAO-RAKITINE (FR),
Landscape Architect, Director at DJAO-RAKITINE - London, Research Assistant at the ETH Zürich, Visiting Critic to the London Mayor's Project Review Panel
TINA GREGORIC (SI),
Architect, Partner at dekleva gregoric arhitekti, Ljubljana, Professor & Head of the Dpt. for Building Theory by Design, Institute of Architecture and Design TU Vienna
SASKIA HEBERT (DE),
Architect, Partner at subsolar* architektur und stadtforschung, Berlin Winner E9 Spremberg, University of the Arts, Berlin
MAX RIEDER (AT),
Architect, Urbanist and Lecturer, Director at maxRIEDER, Wien

PUBLIC FIGURE
CHRISTIAN KÜHN (AT),
Architect and Critic, Wien, Dean of Studies of Architecture & Professor at the Institute of Architecture and Design TU Wien, Board of the Austrian Architectural Foundation, Member of OECD-Working Group Evaluating Quality in Educational Facilities

SUBSTITUTES
THOMAS PROKSCH (AT),
Landscape Architect and Lecturer, Partner at LAND IN SICHT - Büro für Landschaftsplanung, Wien
FLORIAN SAMMER (AT),
Architect, Wien, Winner E7 Krems, Dpt. for Housing and Design, Institute of Architecture and Design TU Wien

REPRESENTATIVE EUROPAN KOSOVO
One representative of Europan Kosovo joins the Austrian jury to evaluate the projects submitted on the Kosovar site
LULZIM KABASHI (HR),
Architect and Partner at IVANIŠIN. KABASHI. ARHITEKTI, Zagreb

PORTUGAL

URBAN/ARCHITECTURAL ORDER
JOAN BUSQUETS (ES),
architect, urbanist, professor at ETSAB and Harvard University, Barcelona
LEONOR CHEIS (PT), landscape architect,
studio NPK, Lisbon

URBAN/ARCHITECTURAL DESIGN
MARIA MANUEL OLIVEIRA (PT),
Architect, professor of architecture
at the University of Minho
RICARDO BAK GORDON (PT),
Architect, professor of architecture at the IST Technical University of Lisbon
ELISA PEGORIN (IT),
Architect, PhD student, winner Europan 10
in Cascais (PT)
BRUNO RODRIGUES (PT),
Architect, Estudio ODS with Marlene dos Santos,
Winner Europan 12 Vila Viçosa (PT) and Europan 9 Poio (ES), Loulé

PUBLIC FIGURE
JOÃO CABRAL (PT),
Architect, professor Faculty of Architecture of Lisbon University, study on Urban Policy
in Portugal

SUBSTITUTES
JORDI HENRICH (ES),
Architect, practice on public space and urban design, teacher at the University of Barcelona
FILIPE JORGE SILVA (PT),
Architect, editor of architecture publications
(Argumentum), Lisbon

SUOMI-FINLAND

URBAN/ARCHITECTURAL ORDER
PIA SJÖROOS (FI),
Architect SAFA, E11 winner, Project Leader,
Regeneration Areas Project,
Helsinki City Planning Dpt.
BODIL V. HENNINGSEN (DK),
Architect MAA, City of Aalborg

URBAN/ARCHITECTURAL DESIGN
JUAN JOSÉ GALAN VIVAS (ES),
Associate Professor, Landscape Architecture,
Aalto university
HILLE KAUKONEN (FI),
Architect SAFA, Planning Development Manager,
Skanska
SANTERI LIPASTI (FI),
Architect SAFA, CEO Huttunen-Lipasti-Pakkanen Architects
SAMI VIKSTRÖM (FI),
Architect SAFA, E11 winner, Arkkitehdit Gylling-Vikström

PUBLIC FIGURE
ROOPE MOKKA (FI),
CEO, Co-Founder, Demos Effect

SUBSTITUTES
ANNE JARVA (FI),
Architect SAFA, Planning Director, City of Hyvinkää

SVERIGE

URBAN/ARCHITECTURAL ORDER
ROLO FÜTTERER (DE),
Professor, Städtebau und Freiraumplanung,
Hochschule Kaiserslauten
PEDER HALLKVIST (SE),
City Architect,
Municipality of Örebro

URBAN/ARCHITECTURAL DESIGN
EBBA HALLIN (DE),
Architect, former Europan 11 winner,
Arkitekturskolan KTH
SABINA JALLOW (SE),
Landscape architect, Malmö University
ANDERS OLAUSSON (SE),
Architect, former Europan 7 winner,
Wingårdhs architects
ELKE MIEDEMA (NL),
Architect, PhD Candidate, Chalmers University of technology, Dpt of Architecture

PUBLIC FIGURE
CARL MOSSFELDT (ES),
Senior advisor World Fellow Yale University

EUROPAN SECRETARIATS

EUROPAN EUROPE
Gip AIGP - Palais de Tokyo,
13 Av. du Président Wilson,
75116 Paris — FR
+33 1 40 70 08 54
contact@europan-europe.eu
www.europan-europe.eu

**EUROPAN BELGIQUE/
BELGIË/BELGIEN**
143, rue de Campine,
4000 Liège — BE
+32 4 226 17 17
secretariat@europan.be
www.europan.be

EUROPAN DEUTSCHLAND
Lützowstraße 102-104,
10785 Berlin — DE
+49 30 262 01 12
mail@europan.de
www.europan.de

EUROPAN ESPAÑA
Paseo de la Castellana 12,
28046 Madrid — ES
+34 91 575 74 01 /
+34 91 435 22 00
europan.esp@arquinex.es
www.europan-esp.es

EUROPAN FRANCE
GIP AIGP, Palais de Tokyo,
13 Av. du Président Wilson,
75116 Paris — FR
+33 1 76 21 04 82
contact@europanfrance.org
www.europanfrance.org

EUROPAN HRVATSKA
c/o Ministry of Construction,
Republike Austrije 20,
10000 Zagreb — HR
+385 1 6101852
europan-hrvatska@zg.t-com.hr
www.europan.hr

EUROPAN ITALIA
Piazza Manfredo Fanti 47,
00185 Roma — IT
+39 45 67 45 100
info@europan-italia.com
www.europan-italia.com

EUROPAN KOSOVO
UÇK 50/1,
10000 Prishtina — KO
+377 44 173 454
contact@europan-kosovo.org
www.europan-kosovo.org

EUROPAN NEDERLAND
info@europan-nl.eu

EUROPAN NORGE
Gøteborggata 27b,
0566 Oslo — NO
post@europan.no
www.europan.no

EUROPAN ÖSTERREICH
c/o Haus der Architektur,
Palais Thinnfeld, Mariahilferstrasse 2,
8020 Graz — AT
Dependance Vienna:
Mariahilferstrasse 93/1/14,
1060 Vienna — AT
+43 664 350 89 32 (Graz) /
+43 1 212 76 80 (Wien)
office@europan.at
www.europan.at

EUROPAN POLSKA
Biuro Architektury i Planowania
Przestrzennego, Urzędu m.st. Warszawy,
ul. Marszałkowska 77/79,
00-683 Warszawa — PL
+ 48 22 323 00 01
europan@europan.com.pl
www.europan.com.pl

EUROPAN PORTUGAL
Travessa do Carvalho 23,
1200–097 Lisboa — PT
+351 21 324 11 30
europan@europanportugal.pt
www.europanportugal.pt

**EUROPAN SCHWEIZ/SUISSE/
SVIZZERA/SVIZRA**
Chemin de Beau-Rivage 6,
1006 Lausanne — CH
+41 216166393
europan@bluewin.ch
www.europan-suisse.ch

EUROPAN SUOMI-FINLAND
Runeberginkatu 5,
00100 Helsinki — FI
+358 45 139 3665
europan@europan.fi
www.europan.fi

EUROPAN SVERIGE
Första Långgatan 12 B,
413 03 Göteborg — SE
+46 31 604 161
info@europan.se
www.europan.se

CREDITS

Europan 13 results

This book is published in the context
of the thirteenth session of Europan

Head of publication

DIDIER REBOIS, Secretary General
of Europan

Editorial secretary

FRANÇOISE BONNAT, Europan Europe
responsible of Europan publications

Authors

CARLOS ARROYO, linguist, architect, urbanist,
Carlos Arroyo Arquitecto, teacher, Madrid (ES)
AGLAÉE DEGROS, architect,
Artgineering in Rotterdam/Brussels (NL/BE),
teacher Brussels (BE)
JULIO DE LA FUENTE, architect, urbanist,
Gutiérrez-delaFuente Arquitectos,
teacher, Madrid (ES)
JENS METZ, architect, urbanist,
Plattformberlin, teacher, Berlin (DE)
DIDIER REBOIS, architect, teacher,
General Secretary of Europan, Paris (FR)
MATHIAS ROLLOT, Dr. in Architecture,
teacher, Paris (FR)
SOCRATES STRATIS, Dr. in Architecture,
urbanist, 'AA & U For Architecture,
Art and Urbanism', teacher, Nicosia (CY)
CHRIS YOUNÈS, philosopher, anthropologist,
teacher at the ESA school of architecture,
Founder and member of the Gerphau research
laboratory, Paris (FR)

English translation

FREDERIC BOURGEOIS
JOHN CRISP

Graphic design and layout

LÉA ROLLAND

Printing

UAB BALTO PRINT (Vilnius, Lithuania)

Edited by

EUROPAN EUROPE
Palais de Tokyo
13 av. du Président Wilson
75116 Paris
France
www.europan-europe.eu

ISBN N° 978-2-914296-30-4
LEGALLY REGISTERED
SECOND QUARTER 2016